REDIRECTING PHILOSOPHY: REFLECTIONS ON THE NATURE OF KNOWLEDGE FROM PLATO TO LONERGAN

In a contemporary climate that tends to dismiss philosophy as an outmoded and increasingly useless discipline, philosophers have been forced to reconsider much of what they have formerly taken for granted. *Redirecting Philosophy*, Hugo Meynell's reassessment of the foundations and nature of knowledge, is a compelling response to this trend.

This illuminating study surveys and analyses the views of the most influential contemporary thinkers in the English-speaking world (Wittgenstein, Strawson, Searle, Popper, Feyerabend, Kuhn, Rorty, Lonergan) and in continental philosophy (Husserl, Heidegger, Derrida, Foucault, Habermas). In setting those views against the background of classical philosophy, Meynell offers fresh perspectives on the basic problems that occupy philosophers today – problems such as scepticism, truth, experience, metaphysics, method, power, humane values, and the role of science.

An insightful, up-to-date guide to philosophy and the theory of science, Meynell's book will be stimulating and valuable reading both in and out of the classroom.

HUGO MEYNELL is a Professor of Religious Studies at the University of Calgary.

HUGO A. MEYNELL

Redirecting Philosophy: Reflections on the Nature of Knowledge from Plato to Lonergan

UNIVERSITY OF TORONTO PRESS
Toronto Buffalo London

© University of Toronto Press Incorporated 1998
Toronto Buffalo London
Printed in Canada

ISBN 0-8020-4314-3 (cloth)
ISBN 0-8020-8140-1 (paper)

Printed on acid-free paper

Canadian Cataloguing in Publication Data

Meynell, Hugo A.
Redirecting philosophy : reflections on the nature of knowledge from Plato to
Lonergan

Includes bibliographical references and index.
ISBN 0-8020-4314-3 (bound)
ISBN 0-8020-8140-1 (pbk.)

1. Knowledge, theory of.   2. Knowledge, theory of – History –
20th century.   I. Title.

BD161.M49 1998   121   C98-931120-1

Publication has been made possible, in part, by a grant from the Endowment
Fund of The University of Calgary.

University of Toronto Press acknowledges the financial assistance to
its publishing program of the Canada Council for the Arts and the Ontario Arts
Council.

For Julian and Letty

Contents

PREFACE   ix
ACKNOWLEDGMENTS   xiii

Part I: Prelude
1 Scepticism 3
2 Truth 20
3 Data 43
4 Reality 60

Part II: Anglo-Saxon Attitudes
5 Limits of Sociology: Wittgenstein, Bloor, and Barnes 87
6 Primitives and Paradigms: Winch and Kuhn 107
7 Anarchy and Falsification: Feyerabend and Popper 130
8 The Self-Immolation of Scientism: Sellars and Rorty 152

Part III: Continental Drift
9 Consciousness and Existence: Husserl and Heidegger 179
10 Deconstruction and the Ubiquity of Power: Derrida and Foucault 197
11 An Unstable Compromise: Habermas 222

Part IV: Recovering the Tradition
12 How Right Plato Was 241
13 On Being an Aristotelian 252
14 Two Methods: Descartes and Lonergan 266
15 Conclusion 279

NOTES 283
INDEX 323

Preface

The basic problems of philosophy are often dismissed as pseudo-problems; though often given notice to quit, they show no sign of doing so. Among the most important of them is the problem of knowledge. What is knowledge, and what are its conditions? Can we really know anything, and if so, how and why? What are the limits of knowledge? In English-speaking countries, the dominance of the 'linguistic philosophy' typified by what was taught and practised at Oxford in the 1950s seems to be nearly at an end. Perhaps it is time to look at this and other basic problems of philosophy from a fresh perspective.

A theory of knowledge is bound to have repercussions on one's conception of the nature of the world in general; an 'epistemology' will have implications for 'metaphysics.' Briefly, I would claim that the world or reality is nothing other than what conscious subjects or persons tend to come to know by the asking and answering of questions about their experience. The whole of what follows is an attempt to justify this claim, and to infer from it what appear to be its most important consequences.

I do not think the question of the possibility, nature, and conditions of knowledge to be the preserve of professional philosophers. For reasons which will appear in the chapters to follow, I believe the subject to be of great cultural importance, and to be such that most educated persons can grasp the main issues involved, and would benefit from doing so.

It seems to be rather widely held that the extension and application of the kind of 'objective' knowledge typified by the natural sciences is somehow at odds with the 'subjective' development and authenticity of human personalities. This leads to an effective contempt for humane values in some quarters, and a hatred of science and of systematic reasoning in general in others. I hope to show that this whole conflict is based on a mistake.

A few words about the overall structure and argument of the book are in order. The object of Part I is to clear some philosophical ground in the neighbourhood of the problem of knowledge. Chapter 1 investigates the sceptical claim that we can have no knowledge, or at least that we cannot know that we have any knowledge. It concludes that the supposition that we cannot have knowledge, in the sense of true belief that is justified, is self-defeating. The consequences of this conclusion for the nature of truth are considered in chapter 2, which argues for a version of the 'correspondence' view. For a statement p (say, 'The planet Saturn is larger than the planet Mars') to be true is, in typical instances at least, for a fact p to be the case, where no human individual or society makes the fact to be the case by uttering or assenting to the statement. The problem of the foundations of knowledge is raised in chapter 3, where it is argued that there is some 'given,' both in experience and in basic mental capacities whose operations are themselves (in a broad sense) objects of experience, on the basis of which we may come to state the truth about things, or at least make progress towards doing so. A theory of knowledge is likely to have repercussions on one's conception of the overall nature and structure of reality, or what is to be known; the metaphysical consequences of the epistemology developed so far are set out in chapter 4.

Parts II and III consolidate the results of Part I by examining positions of representative twentieth-century philosophers of the analytical and continental traditions. After a consideration in chapter 5 of what has been called 'the strong program' of the sociology of knowledge (which strives to explain what is called 'knowledge' exhaustively in sociological terms), and some reflections owed to Wittgenstein which seem to support it, I discuss the claim that people with different world-views do not so much envisage the same world in different ways, but may more properly be said to live in different worlds. I also examine Thomas Kuhn's critical assessment of the common assumption that successive scientific 'paradigms' really tend to approach ever more closely to the truth about the world. Chapter 7 criticizes Paul Feyerabend's epistemological anarchism, which he defends by implicitly presupposing in historical inquiries a method that he wrongly denies is applicable to science, and gives qualified support to Sir Karl Popper's thesis that a theory is properly scientific so far as, while it could conceivably be falsified in experience, it survives stringent attempts to do so. There is an incompatibility, as I argue in chapter 8, between Wilfred Sellars's aspersions on 'the myth of the given,' on the one hand, and his insistence, on the other, that 'science is the measure of all things.' Richard Rorty is more consistent in claiming that, if the human mind were to be in any sense 'the mirror of nature' – which he himself denies that it is – there would have to be a basis in experience in virtue of which some beliefs may properly be judged to be better founded, and thus more liable to be true or closer to the truth, than others. Rorty's own opinions, however, lead ineluctably to the astounding conclusion, outrageously paradoxical both to common sense and to science as generally understood, that we cannot, by appropriate exercise of our minds, come to hold true and justified beliefs about a world which exists and largely is as it is prior to and independently of our minds.

The attempt by Edmund Husserl to found knowledge in consciousness is commonly thought to have failed, for reasons that I give in chapter 9. But the inference drawn by Martin Heidegger and many others, that the foundations of knowledge are the objects of a fool's errand, is unwarranted, so long as the carrying through of Husserl's program remains a possibility; that this can be done is shown in the 'generalized empirical method' set out by Bernard Lonergan. Yet Heidegger is right to point out and deplore the tendency in those influenced by science to regard the world as simply consisting of objects to be dominated and manipulated; though the notion which some have derived from his writings, that this motive is the very essence of the scientific enterprise or of traditional metaphysics, is not only mistaken but dangerous. In chapter 10, I criticize the aspersions that Jacques Derrida casts on the metaphysical assumptions which he rightly claims have dominated European thinking from Plato to Husserl, and I argue that, however much is to be learned from Michel Foucault's association of knowledge with the acquisition and maintenance of power, he himself applies his thesis with a generality which renders it self-refuting. Jürgen Habermas's account of knowledge, as I try to show in chapter 11, is on the right path, as is his defense of basic principles of the Enlightenment; but these commit him, when properly followed through, to something much closer to 'first philosophy,' and as a consequence to some pre-Enlightenment accounts of the world, than he himself would care to admit.

I contend in Part IV that a thorough working-out of the views of the nature and grounds of knowledge, and of the world that is to be known, which have been advanced in the earlier part of the book, will issue in a return to some central elements of classical philosophy. As I try to show in chapter 12, Plato made the enormously important discovery, of which modern science is a massive vindication, that reality is an intelligible order which we discover by asking and answering questions about the things and events of our experience. Aristotle brought back together the sensible and intelligible aspects of things, which Plato had separated to an excessive degree, and in doing so, he set up a sound overall conception of mind, extramental reality, value, and their relations with one another. Such a conception of things has proved elusive since the rise of modern physical science, which in dismissing Aristotle's incidental errors overlooked the permanent worth of his central insights. I contend in chapter 15 that these may be confirmed and extended in virtue of the 'turn to the subject' inaugurated by Descartes and brought to fruition by Lonergan. However widespread the view that philosophy is at its end or near it, it is still as indispensable an enterprise as ever.

Acknowledgments

Earlier versions of chapters and parts of chapters have already been published, as follows: in *The Heythrop Journal*, chapter 13, and parts of chapter 2, 6, and 10; in *Lonergan Workshop*, chapter 12; in *Method*, parts of chapters 3, 8, and 9; in *Mind*, part of chapter 6; in *New Blackfriars*, parts of chapters 3, 7, and 10; in *The New Scholastic*, chapter 11; in *The Philosophical Quarterly*, part of chapter 7; in *Philosophy*, parts of chapter 1 and chapter 5; in *The Thomist*, parts of chapter 4 and chapter 8. They are reproduced here by kind permission of the editors of these journals.

The book owes a great deal to people with whom I have held philosophical conversations over the last twenty-five years or so – though most of them would strongly disagree with its conclusions. I should like to mention in particular John Baker, Andrew Beards, Alec Dolby, Shadia Drury, Damon Gitelman, Timothy Gorringe, Cathy King, Fred Lawrence, Harry Lewis, Ivor and Joan Leclerc, John Leslie, Jack MacIntosh, Bill Mathews, Jenifer, Julian, and Letitia Meynell, Elizabeth and Mark Morelli, Kai Nielsen, Terry Penelhum, Ullin Place, Jerry Ravetz, George Ross, Stanley Stein, Terry Teskey, Graham Watson, and Roger White. Leslie Armour and Peter Preuss, as well as two anonymous reviewers, made many valuable suggestions as to how the book might be improved.

I am very grateful also to Avril Dyson and Perlea Ashton for their hard and efficient work in typing the manuscript.

PART I: PRELUDE

1

Scepticism

Any investigation of the nature and possibility of human knowledge has to take account of some ancient arguments which have surfaced over and over again in the history of philosophy, arguments to the effect that such knowledge is impossible. By looking at some of these arguments, I hope to be able to give both a preliminary sketch of the nature of human knowledge and an account of how it is to be grounded and justified.

There are two typical reactions to arguments for scepticism in philosophy. One is to attempt to refute them; the other, to maintain that their irrefutability does not matter. My own view is that the irrefutability of sceptical arguments would matter a great deal, and that they can be refuted. I shall try in this chapter briefly to justify both contentions, and in later chapters to do so at length in the course of criticism of particular philosophers.

There are several kinds of scepticism, some at least of which have to be distinguished from one another before we can engage in useful discussion of the topic.

(i) Knowledge in the ordinary sense is impossible.
(ii) Knowledge, in the sense of 'true belief which is beyond the possibility of doubt,' is impossible.
(iii) There are no reliable means of attaining knowledge in the ordinary sense.
(iv) There are no absolutely reliable means of attaining knowledge in the ordinary sense.
(v) There are no means which can be justified of attaining knowledge in the ordinary sense.
(vi) There are no means which can be absolutely justified of attaining knowledge in the ordinary sense.

(vii) There is no way of finding out whether any of our beliefs represent the truth about a real external world.

(viii) A few facts – for example, our own existence, our own present sense-experiences, or the truth of propositions true by definition (analytic propositions) – can be known by us; nothing else can.

I shall call the thesis that scepticism is irrefutable, and that this does not matter, 'cosy scepticism.' A strategy much favoured by cosy sceptics is to assert that 'knowledge,' in the sense of 'true belief which is beyond the possibility of doubt,' is impossible (ii), and that there are no means which can be justified of attaining knowledge in the ordinary sense (v), while denying that knowledge in the ordinary sense is impossible (i), or that there are no reliable means of attaining such knowledge (iii). Two famous cosy sceptics, Nagarjuna and Hume, provide illustrations of the strategy. Both argue at length that an examination of our actual or purported methods of getting to know about things, of finding out the truth about the world or about human destiny, shows that they cannot be justified. But that such justification is impossible, they allege, by no means impugns a kind of common or garden knowledge which makes no pretension that it can be thus justified. So we may without qualms assent to the 'knowledge'-claims characteristic of eighteenth-century common sense, or of Mahayana Buddhism, if we are so inclined (as was Hume, in the former instance, and Nagarjuna, in the latter). It is only a highfalutin sort of knowledge which is really destroyed by sceptical arguments; knowledge claims of a more humble kind (that the sun is brighter than the moon, that it is a dagger that I see before me, that the Lord Buddha is merciful to his votaries) are left intact.[1]

It might fairly be asked of someone who defends cosy scepticism what he means by 'knowledge in the ordinary sense.' This is clearly a controversial matter, but it does not seem too far from the mark to propose, in accordance with a claim which is quite commonly made, that 'knowledge in the ordinary sense' is to be understood as 'true belief backed up by evidence.' Ordinary usage seems to support this. If you claim to know that Jones had arrived at the department by half-past eight this morning, I may properly contest your claim, either if he had not arrived by that time or if you had merely guessed that he had without any evidence for his having done so. At this rate, justifiability would be of the essence of knowledge, even if it is allowed, as I think it ought to be, that certainty is not.

Why does anyone maintain that belief must be certain if it is to count as knowledge? The reason seems to be this: it is true that, if Smith has a firm belief, supported by reasons, that p, but p turns out to be false, we properly deny that Smith knew that p. It is from this that it is apt to be inferred that Smith has to be absolutely sure of p to know it, since any risk to the truth of p is a risk to the truth of Smith's claim to know p. But Smith's belief that p must be certain does not follow from his knowledge; all that does follow, granting that he has some grounds for his reasonably firm belief that p, is that p happens to be so. If Smith's grounded and reasonably firm belief is to count as knowledge, p must be so, but there need be no other sort of 'must' about it, whether acknowledged by Smith or not. If I am officially informed that a meeting will be held in a certain room at a certain time, and I have no reason to think that it will not be, and ultimately it does take place there and then, then I can properly be said to have known that it would. If a fire which I could not reasonably have foreseen burns the building down in the meantime, so that the meeting does not after all take place, then I cannot properly be said to have known that it would. The difference between knowing and not knowing in this pair of cases is entirely in the event, and not in the least in my state of mind or in the strength of the evidence available to me.

Still, even if true belief lacks certainty and yet counts as knowledge in the ordinary sense, it has to have some measure of justification to do so. If this is accepted, it puts us in a position to relate to one another some of the types of scepticism which were distinguished at the beginning of this chapter. If there are no reliable means of attaining knowledge in the ordinary sense (iii), it seems to follow inevitably that knowledge in this sense is impossible (i), since 'knowledge' which is not justified, not obtained by means which are in principle reliable, is simply not knowledge in the ordinary sense. And the distinction between the views that there are no reliable means of attaining knowledge in the ordinary sense (iii) and that there are no means which can be justified of attaining knowledge in this sense (v), seems on examination to be a distinction without a difference. What would it be to have reliable means of coming to know, if it were impossible even in principle to justify them as such? It is difficult to see how we could just happen to be in possession of reliable means of coming to know, without being in any position to show why they were thus reliable. If we could not, there seem to be conclusions to be drawn which are of some importance. That sort of cosy scepticism would appear to be untenable, which insists that 'knowledge,' in the sense of 'true belief which is beyond the possibility of doubt,' is impossible (ii), and that there are no means which can be justified of attaining knowledge in the ordinary sense (v), while repudiating the views that knowledge in the ordinary sense is impossible (i) and that there are no reliable means of attaining such knowledge (iii). If we have no justifiable means of coming by knowledge in the ordinary sense, then knowledge in the ordinary sense would not appear to be possible.

It is worth noting that cosy scepticism is in substance identical with that anti-foundationalist position which is often claimed to be opposed to scepticism, or at least to be a viable alternative to it.[2] Anti-foundationalism is very popular in philosophy now, largely because the actual or alleged failure of empiricists to articulate satisfactory foundations for knowledge is supposed to indicate that it is fruitless to look for foundations of any kind. Anti-foundationalism is often thought to provide a way out of scepticism for the following reason. If the thorough justification or grounding of knowledge were necessary for there to be knowledge at all, scepticism would be inevitable, since such justification or grounding is not available; therefore knowledge can only be had if such justification or grounding is unessential to it.[3]

If knowledge is possible, it must be able to be thoroughly grounded.
But knowledge is not able to be thoroughly grounded.
Therefore knowledge is impossible.

The radical sceptic accepts both premises and conclusion of this obviously valid argument. The anti-foundationalist agrees with the cosy sceptic in accepting the second premise, and denies the conclusion at the cost of denying the first premise. However, as I have already tried briefly to show, there are rather good reasons for asserting the first premise and, as a consequence, for denying that any middle way is really available between foundationalism, which asserts that knowledge must be grounded, and that kind of radical scepticism which denies that knowledge is possible at all.

If there are no justifiable means of coming to know, there are similarly no justifiable means of distinguishing proper claims to knowledge from claims to knowledge falsely so called. This kind of scepticism is by no means cosy, since, if its implications are followed through, there will be no attempt to deal with differences of opinion about what is soundly claimed to be knowledge and what is not (say, that some women who own black cats have carnal intercourse with the devil, or that the moon is made of green cheese), by appealing to and applying such means. If we have justifiable means of arriving at knowledge, we have justifiable means of discriminating claimants to knowledge, according to whether they have been arrived at by these means or not. If we do not have the former, it is difficult to see how we could have the latter. Either we will be left in a chaos of conflicting and arbitrary opinion, since on this account all opinions are equally well or ill founded, or we will have to resort to propaganda, coercion, or whatever to secure agreement.[4]

One kind of scepticism maintains that there are no means which can be justified of attaining knowledge in the ordinary sense (v), and that as a consequence there are no reliable means of attaining knowledge in this sense (iii), so knowledge as ordinarily understood is impossible. Let us call this 'radical scepticism.' I have tried to establish somewhat briefly (I will have more to say on the subject later) that a self-consistent scepticism must be radical rather than cosy.

It is one thing to point out the appalling consequences of not being able to articulate the standards required for our statements if they are to count as knowledge; it is quite another to show how such standards might be articulated. And even supposing that such standards could be articulated, how on earth could they be justified?[5] To appeal to the standards themselves is to beg the question; to appeal to other standards is to be ensnared into a vicious regress, since these standards would require support by appeal to other standards still, and so on *ad infinitum*.[6]

Some would admit that if the question of standards of justification is permitted to arise, scepticism is the inevitable consequence; so they try to rule out the question as improper.[7] Taking science as providing paradigms of justified statement, one might urge that science itself sets the standard for the justification of statements, and so cannot itself reasonably or even intelligibly be required to submit to any other such standard. But it may properly be asked what is meant by 'science' in this context. One would presumably not mean by it the totality of judgments made by recognized scientists on matters within their technical competence. For hardly anyone would deny that at least a few of these judgments may be erroneous, or maintained as a result of inertia, prejudice of party spirit rather than through the application of methods which meet appropriately 'scientific' standards of justification. But if one means by 'science' what is known or reasonably believed as a result of application of methods which meet such standards, one has to go on to set out what these standards are and to show why they are appropriate. Short of this last stipulation, one might just as well appeal to public opinion or to some kind of religious faith.

It is not enough for the opponent of radical scepticism to establish that scepticism must be false for it to be appropriate for us to think and speak in anything approaching the way we actually do. For it is perfectly open to the sceptic to deny that these ways of thinking and speaking are really appropriate.[8]

If the usual ways of avoiding scepticism and its consequences are unsound, and if these consequences are so devastating, what is to be done? J. Kekes has suggested that the problems of life are independent of the theoretical frameworks which human beings set up for coping with them; and he infers that a standard of rationality based on the coping with these problems is so as well.[9] But Corbin Fowler has objected to this view, arguing that the notion of problem-solving is not sufficiently independent of the notion of rationality to be able to provide an external standard for it.[10] I believe this objection to be correct. Fowler himself well exemplifies one of the classical positions which I mentioned at the beginning of this chapter: there are no sound arguments against scepticism, but a moderate scepticism is harmless. 'It is high time we gave up the battle with radical scepticism when it is modest enough to argue only that we cannot show that rationality is warranted ... The sceptic can show that we do *not know that we have knowledge*, but he cannot show that we have no knowledge.'[11] But for reasons which I have already given, I cannot see how we can have knowledge, without being able to know that we have knowledge, since ungrounded 'knowledge' does not really count as knowledge, and if we can clearly apprehend the grounds for our knowledge, we can know that we have it. I conclude on this matter that Kekes is right against Fowler, that the problem of scepticism needs solving and that many of the proposed solutions will not do, but also that Fowler is right against Kekes, that Kekes's own proposed solution is inadequate as well.

I have just used the deliberately vague term 'apprehend' in order to forestall an objection. It is commonly and rightly urged that if knowledge of a proposition necessarily involves knowledge of the grounds for it, one is faced with an infinite regress.[12] But while to know something is necessarily to apprehend it in the sense intended here, to apprehend something is not necessarily to know it. My grounds for knowing that you are in Madrid, while I am in Barcelona, are characteristically something else that I know – for example, that your wife has mentioned to me that you would be in Madrid at this time. But my knowledge that you are here and now in the room with me is based on data in my visual field, and my aural and perhaps olfactory sensations, which are apprehended without (perhaps) being known. Whether one says, with Bertrand Russell and others, that what one knows *par excellence* are these data of direct experience (as is implicit in Russell's terminology of 'knowledge by acquaintance' as opposed to 'knowledge by description'),[13] or whether one maintains, with Ludwig Wittgenstein and his followers, that one does not know them at all,[14] does not affect the issue. If you prefer the former way of speaking, you can say that all other knowledge is grounded in a knowledge *par excellence* which requires no grounds, if the latter, that knowledge is ultimately grounded in an apprehension which is not itself knowledge. Nor need one take sides on the complicated issue of whether it is sensations as such, or physical objects in space, which are thus basically apprehended; granted the fact of basic apprehension, whichever way it is construed, infinite regress is avoided.[15]

It is one thing to show that there is nothing incoherent in the conception of knowledge-claims as having grounds; it is another to show that they do have grounds at times, and so amount to knowledge properly speaking, in the manner denied by the sceptic. What is the answer to the radical sceptic? The opening of the path towards this answer, I believe, is advertence to certain statements which are self-destructive, in a sense which I will now try to bring out.[16] A famous example is the verification principle. What is wrong with the principle that every meaningful non-analytic proposition is such that it can be verified or falsified in sense-experience? It is that there is no course of sense experience in which one can verify or falsify the putatively meaningful and non-analytic proposition, that every meaningful non-analytic proposition can be verified or falsified in sense experience. Another famous example is 'I never speak the truth'; since it follows from its truth that it must be false, it cannot be true. A slightly less obvious example is 'I never have good reason for the statements I make.' If there is good reason for making that statement, this is inconsistent with what is entailed by it; if there is not, there is no reason to take it seriously as a possible candidate for truth.

The existence of such self-destructive statements is well known, and does not by itself take us very far. But a fact about them which is not often noticed, but which I believe to be of fundamental importance, is that their contradictories have a kind of certainty about them. The contradictory of what, in one sense, *cannot* be so *must* be so in a complementary sense. It should be noted that this is not exactly the kind of certainty which is possessed by analytic propositions, of which the contradictories are self-contradictory. (I deliberately have referred to statements rather than propositions in this context, since who states them is often at issue. 'Smith never speaks the truth' is a proposition which is not in the least self-destructive; it only becomes so when uttered by Smith.) On the other hand, they have in common with analytic propositions that in a way they *cannot but* be true; they are not mere 'matters of fact,' at least if one takes as constitutive of matters of fact Hume's principle that 'the contrary of every matter of fact is still possible.'[17] They have a good deal in common with Kant's synthetic *a priori* judgments, in that they have a non-analytic sort of necessity, and are not to be verified or falsified by sense-experience.[18]

The next step is to advert to the basic mental operations by which these propositions are justified. One attends to the relevant evidence (as summarized in the last two paragraphs); one thinks out a range of possible ways of accounting for it (in this case, that each of these contradictories of self-destructive statements is true, or that it is false); and one judges to be the case that way of accounting for it which is actually corroborated rather than falsified by the evidence.[19] The evidence in the case of these statements is that their contradictories are self-destructive in the manner outlined; in the case of ordinary empirical propositions, it is some course of sense-experience. Now all of these three basic mental operations which I have mentioned seem necessarily involved in coming to know, or arriving at justified true belief; and none of them can apparently be reduced to the others. As has been well known since Hume,[20] one cannot validly come by a generalization simply by piling up observations of particulars; a 'leap' has to be made between the collection of observable instances, on the one hand, and the making of a generalization or the framing of a hypothesis, on the other. Furthermore, as has become clear from recent studies in the philosophy of science,[21] a further 'leap' is involved, at least in the case of the mature sciences, in matching observed instances to deductions from such a hypothesis. (There is no Leibnizian identity between any kind of streak on a photograph and an alpha particle as it is defined to be in terms of contemporary physics.) Logic, in the strict sense at least, makes the whole procedure of coming to know much more efficient and precise; but it is no replacement for it, and cannot be so, because the two 'leaps' which I have just alluded to, of envisaging possible hypotheses and explanations and making generalizations on the one hand, and of matching deductions from the hypotheses or explanations with observations, on the other, can never be dispensed with. Thus the threefold business of attending to evidence, of envisaging possibilities which might account for it, and of judging to be probably or certainly true that possibility which is best corroborated by the evidence cannot possibly be reduced to logic, unless one means by 'logic' the whole business of getting to know about things in its most general terms.[22]

According to Barry Stroud, what would establish the case against the radical sceptic would be the existence of 'a ... class of propositions each member of which must be true for there to be any language, and which consequently cannot be denied truly by anyone, and whose negations cannot be asserted truly by anyone.' He labels this class of propositions 'the privileged class.' He remarks that some propositions are impossible for one person, others for a class of persons, to utter truly. For example, Descartes cannot truly deny his own existence, and Cretans cannot truly declare that every statement made by a Cretan is false. However, he thinks that the self-guaranteeing character constitutive of the privileged class cannot be of this restricted kind. 'There is no one, whoever he might be, whatever language he might speak, or whatever class of people he might belong to, who could truly deny any of the privileged class of propositions.' What has to be done if scepticism is to be defeated, he concludes, is to show that there is such a privileged class, and that the propositions which the sceptic questions belong to it.

It appears to me that the existence of Stroud's 'privileged class,' and that the propositions which the radical sceptic denies belong to it, can be inferred from what I have already shown. It is perhaps not language as such with which scepticism is incompatible, but rather that aspect of language – there is no need to decide for present purposes whether it is constitutive of language as such – which consists in the propounding of justified true propositions. Stroud says that 'it is obviously extremely difficult to prove' that the propositions questioned by the sceptic belong to the privileged class, partly 'because talk about "language in general" or "the possibility of anything's making sense" is so vague that there seems to be no convincing way of deciding what it covers and what it excludes.'[23] I think if Stroud had attended to that aspect of language which consists in the making of justified true judgments, rather than language as such, he would have found no such difficulty. If justified true judgments are impossible, the sceptic can neither justify her sceptical position nor claim that it is true; if they are possible, 'knowledge,' as consisting of propositions which are true and justified, is obtainable.

The generality demanded by Stroud for propositions of the privileged class, if one grants the legitimacy of the demand, is easily obtained. Consider the proposition 'No one ever propounds justified or true judgments' and the statement 'I never propound justified or true judgments.' The former is wrong because it entails the latter; and the latter is wrong because it is self-destructive. The contradictory of the former is consequently in Stroud's privileged class. And the way to find out whether a proposition belongs to the privileged class is to find out whether its contradictory entails what is self-destructive in the manner that I have sketched. One member of the privileged class will be the contradictory of that brand of materialism which entails that people never really say or write what they do for good reasons, on the ground that 'good reasons' are occult entities and hence inadmissible as part of a sound explanation of anything. It follows, of course, that this kind of materialist cannot be expounding his materialism for good reasons, and therefore is not to be taken seriously.[24]

We are now in a position to go further than before in relating to one another the types of scepticism distinguished at the beginning of this chapter. The world, or reality, is nothing more or less than the sum total of what we tend to affirm to exist or to occur, so far as we stringently apply the threefold process, of attending to evidence, of envisaging possibilities to explain it, and of judging in each case as probably or certainly true the possibilities best corroborated by the evidence. For the notion of 'unreality,' and of what is merely 'apparent,' and so the notion of a 'real world' as contrasted with this, only gets any purchase on our thought so far as the threefold process does or could reveal judgments we have made or might make as false. So if there are means which can be justified of attaining knowledge in the ordinary sense – the contradictory of (v) – there are means of finding out whether at least some of our beliefs represent the truth about a real external world – the contradictory of (vii). Furthermore, if we know at all that we can come by knowledge of the real world in the manner described, we must know it with certainty. That we can do so could be merely probable, only if we could conceive of some further evidence, as is the case typically with empirical propositions, which would be such as to subvert the supposition; and no empirical evidence could possibly subvert the view that we tend to come to know the real world by attending to empirical evidence and concocting and testing hypotheses to explain that evidence. So if there are reliable and justifiable means of obtaining knowledge in the ordinary sense – (iii) and (v) – there must be absolutely reliable and justifiable means of obtaining such knowledge – (iv) and (vi). I do not mean by the absolute reliability of the method that its application could never incidentally lead one into error. However stringently one exercises one's capacity to observe and to envisage possibilities, there may always be some phenomenon one has failed to observe, or some possibility one has not envisaged. But the occurrence of such failures could only be known by a further exercise of the same capacities. It is only by further attention to evidence, further envisagement of possibilities, and further testing of possibilities against evidence that one could reasonably conclude that some judgments previously arrived at by exercise of these capacities were mistaken.

There remains the view that a few facts, like one's own existence, one's own immediate experience, and the truth of analytic propositions, can be known by us; and that nothing else can (viii). This can be seen to amount to little more than a misleading form of words, backed up by the assumption, which evaporates as soon as it is fairly examined, that judgment is identical with sensation or perception. What, apart from such an assumption, could make anyone confuse a past historical event with the pattern of marks on paper from which she got to know about it, or her friend's preoccupation with his grandmother's last words with noises the friend emitted and gestures he made? Such scepticism seems to be a matter of insisting that the only genuine case of knowledge is to be that kind of apprehension which, as I mentioned above, some philosophers have maintained was knowledge *par excellence*, while others have denied that it was knowledge at all. But why restrict the ordinary use of a term in this kind of way? What gain is there in legislating that in future tree sparrows shall be the only true sparrows and house sparrows not sparrows at all? If belief happens to be true, and there are sufficiently strong grounds for it, why deny it the usual title of knowledge?

It is one corollary of what I have argued, that there is a peculiar incoherence about the attempt to defend anti-foundationalism, to support the view that we can and ought to be content with 'groundless belief.' For either belief that belief is groundless can be soundly defended (by the inevitable threefold process of attending to the relevant evidence, thinking up ways in which it might be accounted for, and affirming provisionally or definitely the account which is best corroborated by the evidence) or it cannot. If it is not grounded and hence not able to be soundly defended, there can be no reason for affirming it, and consequently there is no point in taking it seriously. But if belief that belief is groundless can be grounded in this matter, why should not other beliefs be grounded in a similar manner – especially if the claim that the attempt to ground beliefs must founder on the shoals of infinite regress can be countered in the manner which I sketched above?

In the course of a well-argued and (in my opinion) quite justified attack on what I have called cosy scepticism, John Kekes makes the concession that, even if it were established that there was no non-arbitrary method of grounding our beliefs, our ordinary beliefs themselves would remain much as they are; what would have to be abandoned would only be the pretence of using rational methods to vindicate them, change them, or convince others of them.[25] But I think there are good reasons to doubt this. Would the entertaining of a proposition, or the disposition to entertain a proposition, even amount to belief, except perhaps in extreme and limiting cases, if some vestige of rationality were not presupposed in the establishment of it? In what normal sense of 'believe' could I believe that anything was the case, and maintain at the same time that there was just as good reason for believing the contradictory? Surely belief in the ordinary sense is tied up with the apprehension of there being evidence for what one believes, if only the evidence constituted by authority. For instance, if an individual believes some bizarre kind of entity to exist, like a hippogriff or a neutrino, he is likely at least to be able to confirm his belief by reference to the say-so of some privileged caste within his culture which he believes, again on some ground or other, to be in a position to know. Even Leontes had some observed fondling and affectionate glances to go on when he came to believe so absurdly, and with such tragic consequences, that his wife was unfaithful to him. It appears to me that a Hume-like notion of belief, as a feeling attached to an idea,[26] which in its explicit form would now be more or less universally rejected, is presupposed in any account of belief which makes it conceptually independent of any actual or supposed justification.

In fine, there is a standard of rationality which justifies belief in itself, as well as in all other rationally justifiable beliefs. How, in brief, is scepticism to be defeated? It is (i) by adverting to propositions whose contradictories entail statements which are self-destructive; (ii) by attending to the general form of justification implicit in the vindication of such propositions; and (iii) by noting that the real world, so far as we can form any coherent conception of it, is nothing more or less than the totality of what we tend to assert to exist or to be the case by thus justifying what we think and say.

Some readers may feel that I have not given sufficient attention to the sort of cosy scepticism known as Pyrrhonist, represented notably by the writings of Sextus Empiricus. Sextus tells his readers that the goal of scepticism, in the sense that he espouses it, is tranquillity.[27] The greatest enemy of tranquillity is the holding of opinions; so sceptics hold no opinions. They have no objection to stating how things appear to them,[28] or to conforming with the customs and usages of the societies in which they live. What is wrong with opinions may be brought out by showing that, whatever one is advanced, there are as good reasons against it as for it. Suppose we do come across an argument for an opinion which seems to us to be very strong; how can we ever be sure that there is not some argument on the other side which is just as powerful but which we have overlooked?[29]

This is confirmed by the fact that a vast range of mutually contradictory opinions prevail among humankind. Some people think that there are no gods, though most people would disagree with them; but those who do believe that there are gods differ from one another about whether these gods have thoughts and feelings, or are interested in human affairs. Just the same applies to matters of value.[30] Most people consider the consumption of beans quite harmless, but members of the Pythagorean sect would sooner eat the heads of their own fathers. Greeks admire manliness in the human male, but the Amazons went so far as to lame the boy children they bore in order to prevent it. Adultery is condemned as a rule, but some philosophers have approved of the practice; and the same goes for masturbation. In philosophy, of course, differences of opinion are notorious. There are the systems of Aristotle and the Stoics, while philosophers of the Academic school profess a kind of scepticism. But the dogmatic way in which they do so is anathema to Pyrrhonists, who regard themselves as still investigating everything.[31]

Crucial to Sextus's philosophy is the doctrine of 'equipollence'; that is to say, that for any opinion there are as good arguments against it as for it. There is no good reason that I can think of for believing this doctrine, which has the most absurd consequences, and is in any case self-refuting. There is better reason to believe that twice two is four than five hundred and six, that 'Sextus Empiricus' is the name of a philosopher of late antiquity than that of a breed of hamster. And what price the opinion, that the reasons for any opinion are never really stronger than the reasons for its contradictory? That there are two sides to many questions, and that it is best to hold at least some of one's opinions with due circumspection, is true, but a different matter entirely. What is more, it is evident that Sextus's work is itself full of opinions[32] – for example, about what the views of other philosophers are, why they ought to be rejected, what different moral and religious opinions prevail among the various sorts and conditions of humankind, and so on. And the view that, while the majority of people have opinions, they would be better off if they had no opinions at all is of course itself an opinion, and a singularly ill-founded one at that. Having opinions, however tentatively and conditionally held, seems to be essential to the human condition, and is certainly necessary for our survival.

That one ought to be in the habit of suspending judgment, in cases where the available evidence does not warrant a conclusion, is true and important; but it is just as important that one should be prepared to make a firm judgment of fact or value when it does so warrant, if tranquillity is really one's aim. Against Sextus's dogma about equipollence, one might reply with the cliché that he who hesitates is lost – though I suppose some might argue that death is the ultimate in tranquillity. The claim that reason often deceives is in some senses true, but at best it is very misleading. Bad reasoning, or the pretence of reasoning, is certainly very apt to lead to false conclusions, and even good reasoning may do so, if there is more evidence bearing on our judgment to which we might have attended, or more possibilities to be envisaged. The most conscientious deliberations of a law court occasionally lead to the conviction and punishment of an innocent person; a snap judgment taken on the spur of the moment about such a matter may yet turn out to be right. But the fact remains that the more rational (attentive, intelligent, and reasonable) a person is about any matter, the less likely she is to end up in error, with its frequently far from 'tranquil' consequences.

It is downright false that the abandonment of all opinion, or the sustained effort to get rid of reason and argument in the formation of one's opinions, is apt to lead to tranquillity. I once worked for a time as a garbage collector, and tended to go at the tasks incident to my trade without thinking much about them first, with the natural result that I made mistakes. 'Il faut réfléchir un peu' (one ought to reflect a little), said one of my more experienced colleagues, and he was surely right. The result of such reasoning would have been, presumably, that I would have come to better-founded opinions about what was in fact the case and what ought in consequence to be done about it. A near-relation of mine had carpentry lessons at school, and the statement of the carpentry master that his motto was 'Hit hard and hope' was scarcely meant as a compliment; and the implication surely was that he would be better off taking time to reason about what he was doing.[33] Sometimes people can be neurotically concerned about coming to the correct opinion on a theoretical or practical matter; and certainly that does not conduce to tranquillity. But it by no means follows that the opposite course of action, that of failing to form any opinions at all, is so conducive. A person who does not exercise her reason to find out whether she is, or is not, being threatened by a man-eating tiger, and so come to a sensible opinion on the matter, is in danger of being badly mauled or worse. Suppose a heroic resistance worker has used the cover of an waitress in a bar frequented by the occupying forces; to go by what is 'clear' – by what seems obvious at first sight and without the benefit of reasonable reflection – would probably result in the punishment of such a person as a traitor and collaborator when the day of reckoning arrives.[34] In such cases a little reasoning would appear to be desirable, so that one can come closer to a correct opinion in the interests of self-preservation or elementary justice. It may be conceded, of course, that to hold opinions on everything under the sun, whether one has grounds for doing so or not, is by no means a recipe for a quiet life.

Sextus might well say that the questions about the man-eating tiger and the alleged collaborator were 'clear,' in a way that the kind of opinion represented by philosophical, moral, scientific, or theological theories is not. I am not at all clear what Sextus means by 'clear,' but it appears to amount roughly to two things: (1) a statement is clear so far as it does not involve the postulation of unobservable entities, though these are acceptable if treated merely as useful fictions; (2) a statement of what merely seems to be the case is clear, as opposed to one which takes the risk of stating what is actually the case. To deal here and now with the Berkeleyan view of science, incidentally anticipated by Sextus, would take us too far afield. Briefly and summarily, in terms of the basic argument of this book, it is a matter of confusing the direct objects of experience (which exclude other minds and the events of the remote past, as well as the entities postulated by scientific theorists) with what can be affirmed intelligently and reasonably on the basis of experience (which includes all of these things).

As to the second of these conceptions of clarity attributable to Sextus, confining oneself to assertion of what seems to be so is supposed by him to enable one to take appropriate action in the affairs of everyday life. But on the way between mere experience and action, there inevitably intervenes what everyone else calls 'opinion.' The view that a gangster with a grudge against you merely seems to be in the offing does not justify evasive action; it is the opinion that there is (probably) a real gangster which does so. The berries which are just apparently poisonous may as well be eaten; it is only the really poisonous ones that are apt to cause prostration or death. For all practical purposes, Pyrrhonist sceptics do hold opinions, just as everyone else does. One is obscurely reminded of the story of the youthful pharmacist's assistant who was asked by a surprised customer whether he had a diploma. 'No, ma'am,' he said; 'but we have a preparation of our own which does just as well.' In this case, however, the assistant is older than he looks, and his qualifications, though he pretends they are fake, are in fact genuine after all. The fact is that 'seemings' are unintelligible except against the implied background of realities which are at least in principle available. To say that something seems to be so ultimately makes no sense unless some covert reference is being made to what *is* so, and might conceivably be *found out to be* so.[35] The patches of water which seem to lie on the road on a sunny day turn out actually to be due to a trick of the light when one comes up close to them; the seemingly honest employee might some day be found to have his hand in the till. Sextus maintains that Pyrrhonist sceptics do not dogmatically assert that nothing can be known, rather that they are still inquiring. But all real inquiry, as opposed to 'inquiry' that is predestined to get nowhere, presupposes underlying assumptions – for example, that evidence has to be followed wherever it leads, that one does not assume that one knows what is so already, that inquiry is quite likely to lead from ignorance or false opinion to truth, and so on. But such assumptions, once spelled out, amount to opinions.

The Pyrrhonist sceptic is apparently content to conform with the customs and usages of the society in which she lives. But one of the main uses of reason is to consider how far established customs and laws are bad, and how far they ought to be changed for the better. And any conclusion on such questions is, as they say, a matter of opinion. Some socially accepted customs – clitoridectomy, foot-binding, ethnic cleansing, sending little boys to work in mines for eighteen hours a day – are not good, and one ought not to put up with them. The omnivorous sort of 'criticism,' which would make the claim that these customs should be abolished just as ill founded as the claim that they should be retained or even adopted, is in effect no criticism at all. Hence the justice of Jürgen Habermas's comment on the 'postmodern' disciples of Sextus: that for all their radical posturing they are really conservatives.

The holding of opinions is more conducive to tranquillity than dying of thirst or getting entangled in powerful machinery, and it is frequently a necessary means of avoiding such undesirable states and situations. Of course, anyone is free to get into the habit of making little internal notes to himself, 'But of course this is not really an opinion,' when he decides not to go hiking in Death Valley on the basis of the opinion that he will probably die of thirst if he does so. But if he acts on his quasi-opinions just as he would on actual opinions, the note amounts to nothing more than what Paul Feyerabend would call a 'verbal ornament,' the role of which is to make the Pyrrhonist feel smug and superior to other folk.[36] That a degree of scepticism is suitable in the holding of most opinions, I wholeheartedly agree; it is this important principle of which scepticism is so gross an exaggeration. But I would emphasize the point, obvious to everyone but the Pyrrhonist, that this applies to some opinions more than to others; whatever one's view about the Loch Ness monster, doubts about its existence are more reasonable than doubts about the existence of Loch Ness.

What is the proper way, on the view that I have been expounding, to react to the existence of contradictory opinions? A good example lies to hand in the development of European medieval thought. Peter Abelard wrote a book, appropriately entitled *Sic et Non* (Yes and No), where he assembled sets of contradictory opinions from Scripture and the Fathers. Fortunately for the development of thought, and indeed for that of civilization in general, neither Abelard himself nor his successors inferred that arguments for and against every opinion were 'equipollent.' The ultimate result of his pioneering work was the 'method of the *quaestio*' made famous in the late medieval *Summae*. In following this method you begin by setting out, on every point that is raised, the arguments against your own position, so far as possible in the language that your opponent herself would use. Next you set out your view, and finally in a calm and respectful manner, you refute the arguments first given for the contradictory one. This method is seen at its best, of course, in Thomas Aquinas's work. In asking the question whether God exists,[37] Aquinas's arguments against the thesis that he is about to defend are so good that they were to be commended over seven centuries later by one of the most intellectually accomplished of twentieth-century atheists.[38] There are two sides to everything but Cambridge station, but, in the vast majority of instances at least, the case for one element in a contradiction turns out in the long run to be much better than that for the other.

In our own postmodernist times, it has become fashionable to be as sceptical of the dogmas of the Enlightenment as the Enlightenment was of the dogmas of religion, and so Sextus has found a number of admirers. But I fear that I myself cannot be counted among them. Certainly there are remarkable anticipations in his writings of the work of Foucault and Derrida,[39] but I must confess that I find this at best an ambiguous recommendation.

2

Truth

In the last chapter I tried to show that scepticism is refutable and that knowledge is possible, and furthermore, that there are foundations of knowledge which can be articulated and justified. One gains knowledge, or justified true belief, so far as one applies to an indefinite extent the threefold process of attending to data,[1] of envisaging possibilities, and of judging on sufficient ground that some rather than others of these possibilities are probably or certainly so. The real world, I briefly argued, is nothing other than what *is* thus *to be* known. In opposition to some extreme forms of idealism, relativism, and sociologism, there is good reason to suppose that there is an actual world prior to and independent of any human being's actually coming to know about it. Individuals and social groups, owing to their positions in the world and their preoccupations, will have carried the threefold process only so far; reality is always more than they know and to some extent other than they think they know, since there are always more data to which they may attend and more possibilities which they may envisage and judge as being probably or certainly so or not so. However, it may be acknowledged that if to conceive the real in terms of actual or potential knowledge is *ipso facto* to be an idealist, then this position is idealist.[2]

What bearing do these conclusions have on truth? Let us define a 'minimal correspondence theory of truth' as follows: (a) that '*p*' is true if and only if *p*; (b) that in typical instances at least one does not make *p* to be the case by affirming '*p*' – in other words, that *p* is the case prior to and independently of anyone's statement to that effect. For example, according to the minimal correspondence theory of truth, the statement 'the star Sirius is between five and ten light-years distant from earth' is true if and only if the star Sirius is between five and ten light-years distant from the earth, and this is the case prior to and independently of any person or community making a statement or having a thought to that effect. The version of the correspondence theory of truth which I shall try to defend adds the following to the minimal correspondence theory: (c) that one tends to know what is the case on any matter, and hence to make true judgments about it, to the degree that one follows through the threefold process of attending to relevant evidence, envisaging possibilities to account for that evidence, and judging to be so those possibilities which account best for it.

As Michael Dummett sees it, we have nowadays abandoned the correspondence theory of truth, since we are baffled by the attempt to describe in general the relation between language and reality.[3] But I believe that there is a sense in which we can characterize the relation between language and reality, sufficiently for the purposes of the minimal correspondence theory of truth at least. The difficulty is, as it were, that the moment we have articulated linguistically the relation between language and reality, reality is already within language. The solution to the difficulty is that we have implicitly, and can make explicit by reflection, a second-order conception of reality as that which we *would* come to speak about truly in a first-order way *if,* and *do* come to speak the truth about *insofar as,* we follow the threefold process described above.[4] Professor Dummett also raises the question of whether 'our notions of truth and falsity in some manner transcend our capacity for recognising a statement as true or false.'[5] In a sense they do, and in a sense they do not, as again can be brought out by our distinction between first- and second-order conceptions of reality. We can recognize statements as true and as false, and we thus have an implicit conception, which we can make explicit to ourselves, of what it is to recognize a statement as apt to be true or false, or as nearer to the truth or more liable to be true than another. We can thus apprehend in a very general way how it would be if the three-fold process had been followed through much further than we ourselves or other members of our culture have followed it through. In one sense, we absolutely do not know what is really the truth about the world, what we would say if the threefold process had been carried through to an indefinite extent, but at least *that* the truth about the world is what we would say if it had is something that we can know here and now. This seems to be the solution of the paradox alluded to by Plato, that we could not possibly come to know what we do not already implicitly know.[6] We at least have to have an inkling of the *method* by means of which we might arrive at the truth about the world, and thus indirectly of the truth about the world as what we might ultimately arrive at by application of the method.

Donald Davidson has given his support to what may be called the traditional view, that truth consists in 'correspondence to the way things are,' but he goes on to say that 'there is no straightforward and non-misleading way to state this.'[7] It seems that it is largely the difficulty of setting out exactly in what this 'correspondence' consists, whether straightforwardly or otherwise, which has made so many philosophers abandon the correspondence theory of truth altogether. But I believe that the nature of the relationship can be set out with at least relative straightforwardness if, as I have suggested, one attends to the manner in which we come to know. A true statement is one which states how the facts really are; it is accordingly one which would survive an indefinitely thorough application of the mental processes by a limited application of which we arrived at what we know and what we think we know (some of our knowledge-claims will almost certainly turn out to be false) so far. If Davidson means this when he says that the correspondence in which truth consists has to be seen in the light of 'the satisfaction in terms of which truth is characterised,'[8] then I am in agreement with him.

A number of difficulties in the correspondence theory of truth have been listed by George Pitcher.[9] Correspondence-as-correlation may be said to obtain between two sets of numbers, when, for example, in the case of each member of the first set, the corresponding member of the second set is to be found as a result of multiplying it by two. 'But without any indicated grouping, or without some rule being either explicitly mentioned or tacitly understood, it hardly makes sense to speak of correspondence; what, for example, could be meant by claiming, out of the blue, that 1 corresponds to 2, or that 12 corresponds to 6?'[10] Such an indicated grouping, and such a rule, according to Pitcher, are not to be found in the case of truth. But it seems to me that they are. To each of the statements '*p*,' '*q*,' and '*r*,' there is the fact *p*, *q*, and *r* respectively to correspond, just as in the case of the two sets of numbers mentioned above, 1 corresponds to 2, 3 to 6, and so on. The equivalent of the rule that one should multiply by two is, in the case of truth, the indefinite application of the threefold process, by which one discovers – or rather *the more* one applies the process, *the more* one *tends* to discover – whether there is a fact or state of affairs *p* corresponding to '*p*,' and so on. This is always in some sense 'tacitly understood,' by virtue of the very way in which the term 'true' functions in our language; the difficulty is to spell out what is thus understood. (The gap here is similar to that between the grasp of what is called 'generative grammar' that we all have just as speakers and that which is aspired to by such writers as Noam Chomsky.)[11]

Another kind of correspondence discussed by Pitcher is that exemplified by the jagged edges of a sheet of paper which has been roughly torn in two; this he calls 'correspondence as congruity.' He points out that in the case of this kind of correspondence, as opposed to that previously described, correspondence is a matter of degree, and can be more or less perfect or exact:[12] 2 times 3 is not 'about' 6 or 6 'to a reasonable degree of approximation,' but just 6.[13] Two pieces of paper might fit together pretty well when seen with the naked eye or with a child's magnifying glass, but when seen through a more powerful lens, might not do so at all. The relation of correspondence in which truth consists seems to have a lot in common too with correspondence as congruity, with a more and more intense or extensive application of the threefold process as equivalent to the use of a succession of more and more powerful lenses in the case of the edges of the torn piece of paper. Aristotelian physics seems well supported by observation, and hence liable to be true, at one fairly early stage of application of the threefold process to the relevant phenomena, poorly at another when Newtonian physics seems thus supported; Newtonian physics seems a mere approximation when one is in a position to compare its virtues in this respect with those of Einstein's physics, and so on. Pitcher maintains that to envisage the correspondence relation supposedly involved in truth as either correspondence as correlation or correspondence as congruity is subject to more or less insuperable difficulty; I have argued, to the contrary, that it has something in common with both.

Correspondence theories of truth are often impugned by the suggestion that we are in no position to compare or contrast what is asserted by us in our language, on the one hand, with any 'reality' supposed to exist independently of our language, on the other. But we may indeed make a contrast between what is asserted in our language here and now and what would be asserted in a language which presupposed an indefinitely thorough and prolonged application of the threefold process. 'If someone wants to know whether a given thought or assertion agrees with reality then he would have to know for this purpose not only the thought itself but reality as well. How can he do this?'[14] He can use the threefold process to find out progressively more and more of what is so, as opposed to what at any time merely seems to him to be so. Reflecting on this process, he can then get, as it were, a second-order grasp of the truth as that to which his statements and beliefs approach, so far as he uses his mental faculties appropriately, and falsity as that to which they are prone so far as he fails to do so, and of the actual world as what would tend to be known through the medium of the statements and beliefs which are approached by means of such appropriate use. G.E. Moore apparently held at one time that 'true' was a simple and unanalysable property.[15] This looks as though we ought to be able to determine which propositions or statements are true by something like simple inspection, which of course we cannot. And yet we do have a means of finding out whether statements are liable to be true by determining whether they survive further investigation. And investigation reduces to what we have described as the threefold process.

The view that I am commending seems close in some ways to that advocated by Hilary Putnam, that 'truth is to be identified with justification in the sense of idealised justification, as opposed to justification-on-present-evidence.'[16] But I do not care for the name 'internal realism' with which he has labelled his account, since the epithet 'internal,' which alludes to belief-systems, so strongly suggests that there were no facts, things, or states of affairs prior to human beings having beliefs about them. On the contrary, we have excellent reason, due to the application of the three-fold process to our belief-systems over many generations, to believe that the world of things and states of affairs, which to be sure we tend to get to know through our justified beliefs, existed and had the properties we find it to have long before humankind came into existence to have beliefs about it – that there were white dwarfs at least roughly as described by astronomers, dinosaurs as described by palaeontologists. Yet Putnam can write: '"Truth," in an internalist view, is some sort of (idealised) rational acceptability – some sort of ideal coherence of our beliefs with each other and with our experiences *as those experiences are themselves represented within our belief system* – and not correspondence with mind-independent or dis-course-independent states of affairs.'[17] But many of the states of affairs, to which our minds and our discourse aspire truthfully to correspond, *are* independent of human minds and discourse, in the crucial sense that they might have obtained and been as they were even if there had come into being no human persons to think or to speak about them. Who, other than a subjective idealist, would seriously maintain that it might not have been the case that the history of the cosmos and of the earth developed just as it has done up to the appearance of the human species, but that a marauding asteroid at that time collided with the planet, obliterating all life? Admittedly (and this is the truth in 'internal realism' as expounded by Putnam), such states of affairs are nothing other that what would be said or thought to obtain in the ideal state which presupposed the indefinitely extended application of the threefold process.

As to the Putnam passage in italics, I wish to insist that our belief-system itself tends to approximate to knowledge of real states of affairs, which in the relevant sense are prior to and independent of our belief-system, so far as it is subjected to the threefold process. Certainly there are 'various points of view of actual persons reflecting various interests and purposes that their descriptions and theories subserve,'[18] but these points of view may be made to include what approximates to justified true belief, to knowledge of how things really are, by just the same means. One may, after all, have an interest in getting to know the truth, whether it subserves one's other interests and purposes or not, and stringently test one's descriptions and theories accordingly. Contrariwise, a conscientious individual may be impelled by the force of evidence to adopt beliefs which conflict with what are her interests and purposes in any ordinary sense. Research sponsored by tobacco companies may seldom turn up data which support the contention that smoking is dangerous to health, but it is not in principle impossible that it might do so.

With regard to subjective idealism, I believe it can be shown that, granted an assumption which few would dispute, the notion (espoused, for example, by Richard Rorty)[19] that truth is internal to systems of discourse, at least when shorn of the major qualifications which I have just mentioned, leads to the extreme idealist position that we bring what is generally thought of as 'the real world' into existence in the process of coming to think and speak 'truly' about it. The assumption, to which Alfred Tarski in particular has drawn attention,[20] is that some belief 'p' (say, 'grass is green') is true if and only if p (in this case, grass is green). But in the case of any belief 'p,' according to the account in question, its truth depends only on the system of discourse within which it occurs, and not on anything external to that system. So it follows that the truth of such a belief as 'the star called Sirius is between five and ten light-years from the earth' depends only on the system of belief and discourse within which it is embedded; and therefore, given the generally accepted assumption mentioned above, the fact that the star called Sirius is between five and ten light-years from the earth depends on human belief and discourse. To generalize the point: so far from it being the case that there is a real world within which human opinion is a small and not very significant part, at this rate it is human opinion which creates the world.[21] Of course, one can if one chooses define 'truth' in such a way that it follows that fire and water are chemical elements, and that some people cast spells which cause illness and death in others, so long as a sufficiently large number of people say that it does, and this is coherent with their other opinions and perhaps with their ways of acting as well. But if one defines it in this way, one seems to be leaving out a crucial aspect of what is generally meant by 'truth,' which involves correspondence with what may exist prior to and independently of any beliefs of ours in the manner that I have described.

If truth is a matter of correspondence in the manner I have suggested – if the truth of any statement 'p' depends on the obtaining of state of affairs p and only on this – then it looks as though truth must be in some sense a timeless property. For let us suppose that p is a state of affairs which obtains only for a very limited time – say, that the oldest surviving first cousin of the prime minister of Canada at that time was within seven miles of Calgary Tower throughout the first day of November 1986. Then a statement to that effect will be true, at whatever time or place it is made, and whether or not the person who makes it is in a position to do so with good reason. It must be admitted that there is a trivial sense in which truth changes as states of affairs change; thus, supposing the person mentioned in the example leaves the neighbourhood of Calgary on the second of November 1986, the statement that she is within seven miles of Calgary Tower may be true on the first but false on the third. But this is due to the fact that the relevant state of affairs is not specified enough in such cases; it was not clear what time was in question. Also, states of affairs may be the case whether any human being makes a true statement to that effect or not, or whether or not she is in a position to make a well-founded statement about them. This supports the common-sense view that water consisted of hydrogen and oxygen long before anyone came to claim that it did, and that it was the case that dinosaurs existed millions of years before the rather recent times that human beings came to make statements about them. Yet the truth of the statements 'Water consists of hydrogen and oxygen' and 'There were dinosaurs millions of years before the twentieth century roaming the face of the earth,' supposing they are made at all, depend on whether the states of affairs in question are the case, and on nothing else. That they have to be coherent with other statements that we make for us to have good reason to believe that they are true is quite correct, but by no means incompatible with what has just been said.

The points which I have just made seem to be overlooked in statements like the following: 'The scientific method is based on the assumption that truth is neither absolute nor unchanging. Rather, truth is a judgment that, by the agreement of an informed community, produces desirable results ... It is on this assumption that we argue that all judgments should be held as hypotheses to be tested, evaluated, and reconstructed.'[22] One is inclined to inquire: what about the judgment represented by the last thirteen words of this statement? How could that be subject to testing, evaluation, and reconstruction, assuming that it is held at all? In general, the quotation seems to express very well a rather common confusion between what is true and what is supposed at any time or in any place to be true. On the view I am defending here, suppositions as to what is true ought to be tentative, so far as relevant evidence is liable still to be obtained and relevant possibilities still to be envisaged. That judgments in many matters ought to be tentative does not imply that truth itself is not in an important sense absolute and unchanging, but merely that what is supposed to be true is often false, or is only an approximation of the truth. The implications of the second sentence of the quotation seem to be sinister as well as absurd; since it may well be that 'by the agreement of the informed community' it will be 'desirable' to suppose, for example, that someone has committed a crime when in fact she has not done so, and consequently when the statement 'She has committed the crime' is not true. To take a parallel case, may it not seem 'desirable' to the educational authorities in a country to put out a version of its past history which prompts unconditional patriotism in students, or unconditional adulation of the ruling political party? But would that make this version 'true'? It may well seem 'desirable' to suppress rather than to attend to some relevant evidence, and to ensure by hook or by crook that some possibilities are not envisaged; and in this case one heads away from truth, however august the authority which assures one that one is not doing so.

I believe that the problem of truth has been rendered more puzzling than it ought to be by the taking of mathematical truths as a paradigm for the understanding of truths of other kinds. P.F. Strawson has rightly insisted that this is a paradoxical procedure; but Michael Dummett has sought to remove the paradox by showing that the process of coming to know is much the same in mathematics as in other areas of inquiry.[23] But I wonder whether it is not all the same more profitable to clarify the notion by beginning from more straightforwardly factual examples, from common sense, history, or the sciences. For the paradox involved in maintaining, in effect, that we mentally construct the stars in their courses, or Henry VIII complete with his six wives and his court, does not seem to be so glaringly obvious in the case of mathematics. So I do not see why we should not defend the correspondence theory of truth in these other areas of inquiry, while remaining agnostic about the truths of mathematics, where the claim that they are dependent on human mental construction seems of less *prima facie* absurdity. It seems natural to say that it might still be a fact[24] that the star Sirius was between five and ten light-years from the planet Earth, even if there had evolved no human beings or other rational creatures to make statements or entertain thoughts to that effect. But I am not so sure that it would have been a fact that the fourth digit after the decimal point in the expansion of *pi* would have been 2, even if there had been no mathematicians to work out that it was.

Like the Beaver in *The Hunting of the Snark*, I am a remarkably poor mathematician,[25] and have little authority indeed to speak on the philosophy of mathematics. But what I think I can say is this: whatever basic stance one takes on this subject, whether one is a 'Platonist,' a 'formalist,' or an 'intuitionist,' my argument is not affected. I understand that 'Goldbach's conjecture' is to the effect that every even number is the sum of two prime numbers. There is as yet no proof for it, but it has turned out to be true of every even number examined up till now. Is Goldbach's conjecture, then, true or false, or neither true nor false? Platonists would say the former; it is here and now the case, and always has been, in the eternal realm of numbers, either that every even number is the sum of two primes or that not every even number is the sum of two primes. According to the intuitionist, there is no eternal world of numbers, so it is neither true nor false that every even number is the sum of two primes, until someone finds a proof one way or the other. I have no idea which party is right, but my main point is that I need not care about the matter for the purposes of my argument. (According to John Wisdom, Wittgenstein once said of God, 'Couldn't he half exist?,' and one might perhaps apply the moral to numbers.) Whether or not pure mathematics is 'objective,' and in whatever sense it is so or not so, the objectivity of the statements of common sense, science, history, interpretation, and so on, is in my view not impugned; or at least I see no good reason to think that it is so.

I have said that the account of truth advanced here is not relativistic; there is a sense in which what is true at all is true for ever and ever. But it is at least equally opposed to that overweening confidence in the truth of the beliefs which one happens to hold, or even those of one's own culture as opposed to others, which has been so often and so rightly deplored. For this account tends to emphasize the tentative and provisional nature of very many of our claims to truth and to knowledge; more evidence may turn up which bears on them, or other possibilities to account for presently available evidence may be envisaged. Such evidence may well have been attended to, or such possibilities considered, by cultures very different from our own. On the other hand, there is no substantial case for extending such a tentative attitude to most common-sense statements about observable events in our immediate environment. The theories of science, perhaps even the most impressive ones, may come and go, but that I am in a room in Calgary here and now, trying to think and write about the nature of truth, is a judgment confirmed by a large amount of supporting evidence, and impugned by none. That our statements of fact about the observable world about us are nearly always true, apart from those deliberately intended to be false, does not, on the account I am giving here, have simply to be dogmatically asserted; it can be supported by argument. That G.E. Moore and those around him have vivid sense-impressions as though of Moore having a right hand, when no other explanation of this (electrodes planted in the brains of all those concerned and appropriately stimulated, or whatever) is forthcoming, is the best possible evidence that Moore has a right hand.[26] If the truth is to be had in judgments selected from among possibilities to explain the data of experience, then these judgments have overwhelming support as true. The same applies to common-sense judgments made by persons of other cultures, or in the remote past. Unless Xenophon intended to deceive his readers, or was himself deceived, the ten-thousand Greeks truly believed that they saw the sea one day while they were marching back to their native country. On such a matter, the probability of their being mistaken is vanishingly small.

It must be granted that some judgments, of which the truth may appear to be a matter of common sense, have theoretical implications which turn out to be false. For example, to the ordinary person up to five hundred years or so ago, that the earth was stable (give or take an occasional earth tremor), and that the sun, moon, planets, and stars moved round it, would have seemed a matter of common sense. However, the threefold process applied over a long period by the scientific community has now made it overwhelmingly probable (what conceivable evidence might tend to subvert the view at this stage of history?) that this seeming judgment of common sense is false or at best, as one might put it, 'true in a limited sense.' (If all that is implied is that the earth *feels* stable, and that the sun *appears to* be moving round it if one notes its position at successive hours of the day, then no falsehood is involved.) Thus one of the effects of the threefold process is to refine common sense and to set out more clearly its scope and limits, to distinguish between those elements of it which yield stable and reliable truth-claims and those which do not, or (if one prefers a conception of common sense according to which common-sense judgments are true by definition) to distinguish truths which are really a matter of common sense from alleged truths which are a matter of common sense falsely so called. And it is merely common sense, one might say, that to make the kind of distinction just referred to is *not* just a matter of common sense; it similarly is only a matter of common sense that one trusts the expert, and *not* the person of common sense, on matters within the expert's speciality.

It follows from what I have said that this rather eschatological account of the ultimate criteria of truth – the set of judgments which would be arrived at by the threefold process if it were applied indefinitely – does not entail that we may not have confidence about the truth of a great many of the judgments which we make here and now, particularly when we exercise the threefold process to an adequate degree. In particle physics or in cosmology, the recent rapid turnover of theories gives ground for a considerable degree of scepticism as to how much of what is now believed to be true in these fields is in fact true. But this would hardly apply, say, to most verdicts arrived at by a properly conducted court of law. At the beginning of the proceedings of such a court, perhaps evidence seems ambiguous, some of it pointing towards the accused as guilty of the crime as charged, some of it pointing away from him. But as time goes on, let us suppose, more evidence is attended to, and more possibilities are envisaged, and so a reasonable judgment is progressively confirmed that he did not commit the crime. Such conclusions can in general be relied on. Every now and then, the most judicious verdict turns out to be mistaken; after the court is dissolved, and after the accused has undergone punishment, evidence may turn up, and possible ways of accounting for it may be envisaged, which will confirm the judgment that he was not guilty after all. But it is to be noted that the more thorough the exercise of the threefold process, the more rare such cases tend to be, and further, that when such verdicts are appropriately overturned, it is only due to further application of the threefold process.

I believe that many objections to the correspondence theory of truth derive from failure to distinguish between two ways in which statements may reasonably be said to correspond or to fail to correspond with the world. Let us call 'correspondence' the relations between the true statement 'p' and the real state of affairs p, assuming the minimal correspondence view of truth, and 'corroboration' the relation between the true statement 'p' and the evidence in experience which tends to confirm p.[27]

Except on some very curious epistemological and metaphysical views, a fact and the evidence for a fact are often, perhaps virtually always,[28] distinct from one another. I may have evidence, say in a letter which lies open before my eyes, that my aunt is arriving at my house on a visit next week, but what makes my expectation true, the actual arrival of my aunt next week, can hardly be maintained to be identical with the visible marks on paper which constitute the evidence for my expectation. Similarly, my evidence for the truth of a statement about the remote past can only be some sense-experience in the present or remembered from the comparatively recent past. And even where the immediate present is concerned, short of behaviourism, it seems evident that what you think and feel is one thing and the evidence by which I arrive at true judgments about your thoughts and feelings is another. All these cases bring out the distinction between correspondence and corroboration, the relationship, on the one hand, between a true statement and the actual fact which makes it true and, on the other, between the same statement and the evidence which makes it worthy of being believed.

I think that the correspondence view of truth is rejected as often as it is largely because one fails to distinguish between these two types of correspondence, and assumes that all correspondence must be of the nature of corroboration. Furthermore, the human mental creativity exercised in getting at the facts through statements that 'correspond' to them is apt to cozen the inquirer into supposing that such 'facts' are themselves due to mental creativity, in contradiction to the minimal correspondence view of truth. And the coherence view of truth, which is often supposed to be an alternative which excludes the correspondence view, seems plausible, on the grounds that the question whether any statement 'corresponds' with what is the case is indeed to be settled largely by its coherence with other statements supposed to be true (partly due to their coherence with one another, partly due to the corroboration of each by evidence in experience).

The supposed difficulties in the correspondence view of truth have caused some philosophers to cast around for alternatives. The 'coherence' theory of truth was the favourite among idealist philosophers, attracted a few logical positivists, and has been revived by some contemporary epistemologists.[29] Idealists often maintained that there are degrees of truth, since truth properly speaking can inhere only in the propositions constitutive of the system which correctly describes the universe as a whole; under the present dispensation propositions could aspire only to be somewhat truer than others. The logical positivists in question, who were attracted to the theory due to their fascination with the systems of pure mathematics and theoretical physics, thought of truth as coherence in terms of the scientific theories which prevailed at the time.[30] They also dismissed as metaphysical, and therefore nonsensical, the view that language somehow represents a world of facts existing or obtaining outside language.

Now there is no doubt that, in the case both of our ordinary beliefs and of the beliefs constitutive of science, one very important indication of whether a belief is true is whether it is consistent with other beliefs which we already hold. In a recent issue of *Time*, two distinguished scientists were reported as saying that, rather than expanding like the rest of the cosmos, a collection of many thousands of galaxies, including our own, may be speeding all together towards a point in the direction of the constellation Virgo. 'Rather than try to assimilate the new finding, most of their colleagues are proclaiming that it must be a mistake. No one can explain what Lauer and Postman have done wrong, despite strenuous efforts to do so. The analysis is incorrect, they say, simply because it doesn't fit in with any existing theory of how the cosmos works.'[31] One obvious objection to coherence theories is that we demand of our judgments not only mutual consistency, but support by experience. But a sophisticated coherence theorist will retort that experiences as experiences are not literally consistent or inconsistent with anything, and that to be made so, they have to be reflected by statements or judgments. A satisfactory coherence theory will include such statements or judgments among those coherence between which coherence is to be sought if truth is to be attained.

Granting for the moment the impressiveness of the case of the sophisticated coherentist as I have represented it, the fact remains that experiences, or the judgments that reflect them, do have and apparently ought to have a place of special significance in supporting judgments both of common sense and of science.[32] If I want to know whether it has just been raining, whether the garbage collector has come, or whether pulsars really exist, I had better attend to the empirical evidence on the matter (Does the grass seem wet? Do I appear to see or smell the garbage still outside awaiting collection? Do the recording pencils apparently make a pattern which can scarcely be accounted for in any other way than as the effect of pulsars?), and only on special occasions does the question of coherence with other beliefs or judgments arise. (Thus if I walked into a psychology laboratory which specialized in *trompe l'oeil* effects and was confronted by the spectacle of a sheep playing bridge, or was at a conjur-

ing show and seemed to see a beautiful person being consciously yet pain-
lessly sawn in half, I might properly, as they say, doubt the evidence of my
senses, on the grounds of lack of coherence between what I seemed at the
moment to perceive, on the one hand, and the remainder of my knowledge and experience, on the other.) Unless perceptions (or, if it is preferred, judgments reflecting perceptions or what appear to be perceived
events) are given pride of place in assessing beliefs (like those in devils,
positrons, phlogiston, or witch substance), most of our judgments could
never be non-arbitrarily impugned or corroborated.

It may be noted that, if coherence among our statements is the principal or sole means by which we know that our beliefs approximate to the
truth, this is not incompatible with the minimal correspondence view.
For it could still be the case that, even if coherence were the sign *par excellence* that we had reached the truth, or at least approximated to it, truth
was a matter of minimal correspondence, in the sense that 'p' was true
when p was the case and that, in standard instances at least, we did not
make p to be the case in stating that it was so. One might put it that a minimal correspondence theory of truth is quite compatible with a sophisticated coherence theory of verisimilitude, and that both are to be
affirmed. It appears, at least at first sight, to be one thing for there to be a
coherence between one's beliefs, including those which directly reflect
perceptions, on the one hand, and for the beliefs to be true of a world
that exists prior to and independently of our perceptions or beliefs, on
the other. And this, as I have argued, is that in which truth in the normal
sense consists. It does seem to be the case, however, that coherence
within one's system of beliefs, particularly when these beliefs include
ones which directly reflect experience, is an important criterion of
whether our beliefs actually are true of the world in the sense implicit in
the minimal correspondence view.

Ralph Walker has pointed out that the incompatibility between coherence and correspondence theories of truth is not obvious, that it is not
perfectly clear why assertion of the one should commit you to denial of
the other. As he puts it, 'the coherence theorist can accept that there are
facts, and that true beliefs correspond with them, provided he can give
his own account of what the facts and the correspondence ultimately consist in: they ultimately consist in coherence.'[33] But I think that what I have
called the minimal correspondence view is incompatible with the coherence theory in any but an extremely attenuated sense. The facts, on the
minimal correspondence view, obtain and are as they are prior to and
independently of any human beings or other rational creatures who may

come to have beliefs about them; and it is correspondence to the facts, the relation in each case of belief '*p*' to fact *p*, which makes beliefs true. On the other hand, it is to be conceded that the facts are not distinct from what would be believed in some conceivable set of beliefs; and, certainly, the set of beliefs concerned would have to be coherent. In fact, the set of beliefs in which the facts were believed would simply be the coherent set of beliefs which would be arrived at if the threefold process were carried through indefinitely. If this is all that is implied by some version of the coherence theory of truth, then that version is not incompatible with the minimal correspondence view. On the other hand, the totality of facts are not, and presumably never will be, believed in any actual set of (human) beliefs.

It is evident that both 'coherentist' and 'foundationalist' theories of the justification of our claims to empirical knowledge are subject to considerable difficulty, as Laurence BonJour admirably brings out in his book *The Structure of Empirical Knowledge.* BonJour argues, however, that while the difficulties encountered by the foundationalist view are insuperable, a version of the coherentist position can be salvaged by considerations which render it proof against the usual objections. I maintain exactly the opposite view, and will try to show in what immediately follows how BonJour's objections to foundationalism may be countered and where his version of coherentism breaks down.[34]

If every empirical belief requires justification by another empirical belief, we seem to be faced with either a vicious circle or an infinite regress, and the sceptical conclusion appears to follow, that there is no reason to think that any empirical belief is true. The foundationalist tries to stop the regress by maintaining that some empirical beliefs are justified in a way that does not depend on inference from other such beliefs. One influential way of doing this (and the one which I shall try to defend) is to maintain that, while all empirical beliefs have to be justified, in the case of some of these beliefs, the justification consists of reference to mental states other than beliefs which do not themselves have to be justified; these are described in various ways by various authors, but are usually said to be 'given,' 'represented,' or something equivalent. To this there is, on BonJour's view, one basic and decisive objection. If these allegedly given states are themselves cognitive, then they will be able to supply justification for other cognitive states, but will be in need of such justification themselves. But if they are not cognitive, while they may not be in need of such justification, they will certainly be incapable of supplying it. 'It is clear on reflection that it is one and the same feature of a cognitive state, namely, its assertive or at least representative content, which both enables it to confer justification on other states and also creates the need for it to be itself justified – thus making it impossible to separate these two aspects.' The reply which some have made to this objection, that apprehension of the given is a kind of *quasi*-cognitive or *semi*-judgmental state, able to confer justification while not requiring it, seems 'hopelessly contrived and *ad hoc*.' Thus appeal to the given appears, in the last analysis, inevitably to collapse.[35]

The basic problem for the foundationalist 'amounts to a dilemma: if there is no justification, basic beliefs' (i.e., beliefs which are not justified by reference to other beliefs) 'are rendered epistemically arbitrary, thereby fatally impugning the very claim of foundationalism to constitute a theory of epistemic justification, while a justification which appeals to further premises of some sort threatens to begin anew the regress of justification which it is the whole point of foundationalism to avoid.'[36] The solution which I propose to the dilemma is as follows. The justification of empirical beliefs is of two kinds: that on the basis of other beliefs and that on the basis of experience. We have already distinguished these, respectively, as justification and corroboration. Experience characteristically causes belief, but it may also corroborate it. For example, my present belief that my grey overcoat is hanging now in a corner of the room in which I am working is caused by the fact that, about a minute before composing the first draft of this sentence, I raised my eyes and had a visual impression as though of my grey coat in that state and position. But the visual impression is not only a cause of the belief, but also a justification, in that in asking whether my belief about the present whereabouts of my grey overcoat is true, I can properly appeal to the sense-experience which I enjoyed at that time as tending to show that it is. Certainly, it is conceivable that there should be some other explanation of why I had the experience that I did; my visual cortex might have been electrically stimulated accordingly, or I might have been under the influence of alcohol or drugs. But a rapid survey of the memories of my recent past confirms that these possibilities are far less likely. My coat's being where it appeared to me to be seems far the best available explanation of the visual appearance to me a few minutes ago of my coat being there, and it can be corroborated at any moment by another glance in the appropriate direction.

Are sense experiences themselves beliefs? If not, what cognitive status do they have, and how are they related to beliefs? I maintain that sense-experiences characteristically give rise to, and provide *prima facie* corroboration of, beliefs about material objects. (Here the view of C.I. Lewis and many others appears to me to be right, that sense-experiences as such form the ultimate basis, or more strictly a part of the ultimate basis,[37] for our empirical beliefs, against Anthony Quinton's opinion that it is perceptions of material objects and events in one's immediate environment which are in this way basic.) To raise experiences as such in one's present or (usually immediate) past to the level of explicit judgment or 'belief' requires a particular kind of attention. I have to concentrate in order to arrive at such a judgment as the following: 'My visual field at the moment has a thin cylinder of pure white near its centre. A rectangular patch of less pure white, covered with pale blue lines, provides the immediate background for this, and two rather knobbly lumps of greyish-pink are at the bottom left- and right-hand corners.' In fact, such registers of present experience, while it is not perhaps strange to call them 'judgments,' are at best limiting cases of 'belief.' One does not know whether this is the correct term to apply to them; perhaps 'quasi-beliefs' or 'semi-beliefs' is what they should be called. Yet it would be wrong to denigrate them in BonJour's manner as *ad hoc* inventions, as it is so obviously possible to produce instances of them at a moment's notice.

I conclude that BonJour's dilemma is a false one, due to the assimilation of corroboration to justification, and the corresponding assumption that sense-experiences must themselves either amount to fully-fledged beliefs or fail to provide any sort of justification at all for beliefs about immediately observable objects and other empirical beliefs. Why should philosophers be tempted to make this assimilation? One reason appears to be this: on occasions of ambiguity or doubt (Just what place have I arrived at? Which of two possible persons is this?), I may substitute justification for corroboration by replacing my experiences, present or remembered, with explicit 'beliefs,' or suggesting that someone else does so, by saying something like 'Now what, exactly, did you see or hear?' But, in the final analysis, such 'beliefs' are subject only to corroboration by reference to sense-experience ('Well, I do assure you, I had a clear impression for a couple of seconds of a bright green light shining in front of me; though I now agree with you, in the light of my later experience, that no such thing could have been where it appeared to me to be.')

As I have said, our beliefs about material objects seem to depend in this kind of way on sense-experiences, rather than vice versa. Admittedly, we could not talk about sense-experiences as such unless we could talk about perceivable material objects in the first place. At one time Lewis, as BonJour says, was inclined to say that sense-experiences were ineffable, at others, that they could be referred to by an *ad hoc* modification of ordinary language.[38] This change of mind might reasonably give rise to suspicion about sense-experiences and their role in the acquisition of knowledge, if it were not for the fact that this second account of the matter is perfectly satisfactory. I may well say, 'I have a visual experience as though there were grey wisps of hair moving about on the surface of the paper before me, though I know that there are not,' or 'There is a sound like an oboe perpetually playing A in my head, though I know perfectly well that no such sound is being made in my vicinity.'

Lewis's account, as BonJour sees it, is subject to the usual objections which have been made to phenomenalism. The claim (a) that sense-experiences are (a part of) the basis for our knowledge of the world is one thing; the doctrine (b) that all that exists in the last analysis is sense-experiences, and mind and bodies are just convenient ways of referring to clusters of these is another. The latter doctrine is certainly open to the standard objections, but I do not see why the former should be so. The alleged deficiencies in (a) seem due only to the mistaken belief that it leads to (b), and it is (b) which is phenomenalism in the strict sense. In accordance with (a), real physical objects are what we can come to know about by inquiry into our sense-experiences, and their being as they are is the best way of accounting for the sense-experiences which we have, but this by no means implies that the objects have no existence prior to or independently of our sense-experiences, as is implied by phenomenalism, properly speaking.

BonJour very usefully sets out what he calls 'the basic anti-foundationalist argument' in five propositions, one of which he says, in my opinion quite correctly, the foundationalist must contest. If my argument so far has been correct, the proposition which she can contest, or rather relevantly qualify, is number 4, which runs as follows: 'The only way to be in cognitive possession of such a reason (one which will epistemically justify an empirical belief) is to believe *with justification* the premises from which it follows that the belief is likely to be true.'[39] The trouble here is with the ambiguity of the term 'justification.' Empirical beliefs are characteristically corroborated by experiences, which are themselves not attended to in such a way as to be the object of explicit 'beliefs' such as would qualify, strictly speaking, as premises; when the experiences are not thus attended to, the beliefs to which they give rise are corroborated but not 'justified' in our special sense. All empirical beliefs require justification in a broad sense; but this can be either 'justification' in our special sense or corroboration. Ordinary empirical beliefs are subject to both types of justification; however, some 'beliefs' are subject only to corroboration, which is in terms of experiences such as cannot and need not receive justification of any kind in their turn. So the revised form of proposition 4 should run: 'The only way to be in cognitive possession of such a reason (one which will epistemically justify an empirical belief) is to believe with "justification" or corroboration the premises, or to enjoy or have enjoyed the experiences, from which it respectively follows by a process of "justification," or "follows"[40] by a process of corroboration, that the belief is likely to be true.' This is evidently perfectly consistent with foundationalism. The given is no myth.

Much the same applies to the pragmatic criterion of truth as to that of coherence. One important indication that a statement, whether of common sense or of science, is at least approximately true is that operations which are carried out on the assumption that it is so are on the whole more successful than those carried out on the assumption that it is not. If it were not true that diamonds are exceptionally hard, you would not be able to use a diamond cutter to cut glass. But the criterion is far from reliable. While telling nasty stories about a hostile group may be an excellent means of increasing solidarity within my own group, this is no indication that the stories are true. It is one thing for something to be the case about the world and another for us to be able to carry out any set of operations whatever. However, this does not prevent it from being the case that the success of our operations on the assumption that a judgment is at least approximately[41] true is often an excellent indication of its being so.

Confusion between correspondence and corroboration seems also to underlie some extreme pragmatist views of truth. These imply that the significance of 'p is true' is exhaustively determinable in terms of the success of the practices one is able to carry out on the assumption of the truth of 'p.' Now it may be agreed that the success of such practices is a large part of the evidence that p is the case and 'p' true, and consequently that experience of this success is an element at least of what corroborates 'p.' If this is all that is implied by the pragmatic theory of truth – if it is merely a matter, as one might put it, of 'soft pragmatism' – then there is no objection to it. But the extreme pragmatist views already alluded to – which might be labelled 'hard pragmatism' – give rise to many intolerable paradoxes, since it can hardly be the case that the truth of a statement about the past can be entirely a matter of the success of practices carried out in the present or future or, *pace* behaviourists, that the truth of the statement that you have toothache is dependent on nothing but the operations that people are capable of successfully carrying out on an assumption that you have it.

One important question connected with truth is: exactly what kind of entity it is that is supposed to be true, or rather 'true' in the primary sense of the term. (A person, or a straight line drawn in sand, can be 'true,' but such senses are surely derivative and marginal.) Is it a sentence, a statement, a proposition, a belief, a judgment, or all or some of these, or none of them?[42] It has been said that, while Kant was concerned with the relation of thought to the world, Wittgenstein, in common with twentieth-century philosophers in general, saw the matter in terms of the relation between language and the world. This change in the way of envisaging the question is often taken to constitute a philosophical advance. The reason for this is, I suppose, that it is thought that one can be 'objective' about language in a way that one cannot be about something so paradigmatically 'subjective' as thought; and so, if one is looking for an 'objective' account of the capacity of human beings to think or talk about a world which largely exists prior to and independently of themselves, their speech, or their thoughts, the attempt had better be made in relation to two 'objective,' that is, publicly observable, sets of entities, spoken or written language, on the one hand, and the world at large, on the other. However, I believe that to suppose that the alteration in viewpoint amounts to philosophical progress is an illusion, for the following reason. Language can be envisaged in (at least) two ways: first, as a mere ordered succession of sounds or visible marks; second, as expressive of meaning, and so among other things, as stating what is so and what is not so.[43] To think of language merely in the former way is only marginally helpful when one is studying problems of meaning and reference; it is only as expressive of thought that language's relation to extra-linguistic reality can be usefully envisaged.[44] Thus the relation of thought to reality turns out to be necessarily at issue after all. On the question of what is the primary vehicle of truth, the answer would seem to be beliefs or judgments (as items of thought), and sentences and statements (as items of language) only as expressive of them.[45]

In order to shed light on the problem of how one physical structure or structured series can mean another, without getting mired in the embarrassing and distasteful topic of subjectivity, philosophers of our time have often appealed to the analogy of a map[46] or a computer.[47] A map, it is claimed, can mean the city of Prague; a computer can mean by its output the state of one's pension contributions; so, at least in principle, the problem of meaning can be solved on a strictly physicalist, materialist, or behaviourist basis. But just the same applies to computers and maps as to language. It is conceivable that a bit of paper scrawled over at random by a four-year-old child could be used quite effectively as a street-map of Burlington, Ontario. But it would not be such a map until some conscious subject or person had taken it into her head to use it for this purpose.[48] It may be concluded that the way maps and computers mean things cannot be used exhaustively to explain, as it presupposes, if only indirectly, the way human beings mean things.

I conclude that it is beliefs or judgments which are, or fail to be, truth-bearing in the primary sense, and that statements and sentences are truth-bearing in a secondary or derivative sense, as expressive of such beliefs or judgments. It has been found convenient by many philosophers to talk of 'propositions' in this context. Now the term 'proposition' has a somewhat pompous or musty professional air about it; it was put into currency largely by Cambridge philosophers of the early twentieth century. One may well wonder whether it is really worth complicating the world with such entities, when we are already furnished with sentences, statements, beliefs, judgments, and facts.[49] And propositions themselves have a rather ambiguous nature, floating as they are apt to do between actual statements in their role of stating putative facts, possible statements in their role of stating putative facts, and putative facts themselves.[50] The point of these distinctions, which would seem at first blush to be merely pedantic, comes out when one asks the following question. Suppose no beings capable of doing astronomy had ever come into existence on Earth, due to the fact, let us say, that an asteroid had collided with our planet and destroyed all life there during the era of *australopithecus*. Would the proposition 'There are two giant planets in the solar system outside the orbit of Saturn' still have been true? One hesitates between saying, 'Of course, it would, because the relevant fact would have been the case' and 'of course it would not, because for a proposition to be true there must be someone who believes or states it.' To take a leaf out of Bertrand Russell's book: for the present king of France to be bald, there both has to be a present king of France and that individual has to be bald. Similarly, it may be felt that, for the above-mentioned proposition to be true, there both has to be such a proposition and it has to be the case that there are two giant planets in the solar system outside the orbit of Saturn. But, on the present hypothesis, there are no propositions unless there are statements or beliefs which express them, and this in turn presupposes the existence of conscious subjects or persons who make the statements or have the beliefs.

In what I have just said, I have assumed that there would at least have been facts if there had been no human persons to state or believe in them.[51] I take it that one would have to be a subjective idealist not to believe this, and an insane person if one lived accordingly. However, it has to be mentioned that one of the finest living philosophers, P.F. Strawson, has maintained the contradictory (while by no means being a subjective idealist). It is true that facts do not exist in quite the same manner that things do,[52] and are not instantiated in quite the same way as properties or relations are; it seems more appropriate to say that they 'obtain,' or 'are the case,' than that they 'exist' or 'occur.' But the crucial issue here is whether facts might in many cases have obtained – like the fact that the European swallow is a migrant or thorium is a radioactive element – even if no conscious beings had evolved to believe or state them.[53] And it seems to me that facts often obtain prior to anyone's believing or stating them, with just as much right as that with which things may exist and properties and types of relation occur or be instantiated.

On the question of what are the primary bearers of truth: the upshot of my argument is that judgments or beliefs are so, and that statements or sentences may be true only in a secondary sense as expressing judgments or beliefs. To reverse the priority is to insinuate the bogus view that an advance is made towards the solution to the problems of meaning and truth when they are conceived in terms of public and observable language rather than private and interior thought.[54] J.L. Mackie identifies two main problems that are faced by correspondence theories of truth; that is, 'to identify the items which are supposed to correspond where there is truth but to fail to correspond where there is falsehood, and to say in what the correspondence or non-correspondence consists.'[55] The items on the one side are primarily beliefs or judgments, which are a matter of thought.[56] On the other side there are real facts or states of affairs, which are a matter of things existing or not existing, or having or not having properties or relations. Mackie goes on to say: 'Characteristic failings of such theories are that one of the two items becomes a mere shadow of the other, and that the relation called correspondence remains hopelessly obscure.' Correspondence consists in the relation between what is judged to be so more or less reasonably here and now and the states of affairs which would be judged to obtain if the threefold process (of attending to evidence, of hypothesizing, and of judging those hypotheses to be true which are best supported by the evidence) were carried through to an indefinite extent. We have already remarked that it does not follow, as some idealists thought, that truth can only be a matter of degree at present; while scientific theory only approximates to the truth, common-sense judgments are in most cases very likely to survive intact an indefinite amount of scrutiny. It is exceedingly unlikely that the most stringent powers of ratiocination applied with the utmost rigour would ever converge on the contradictory of the proposition which I believe is confirmed by the whole of my present experience – that the sun is now shining in that part of the province of Alberta where I am writing the first draft of this sentence.

A word seems in order here about what are called the 'semantic paradoxes,' since these are sometimes supposed to make difficulties for a satisfactory conception of truth. The most famous, and probably the clearest, example of such a paradox is that of the liar. This may briefly be set out as follows. Suppose I say, 'I am lying.' Then if I am lying in the act of making that statement, I am telling the truth; but if I am telling the truth, I am lying. And this 'state of affairs' is surely self-contradictory.[57] It has been said that it does not really help matters to deny that the offending proposition is really a proposition at all, since to all intents and purposes it obviously is one. If 'Smith is lying' is or expresses a perfectly good proposition when uttered by someone else, why should it be any less of a proposition when uttered by Smith herself?[58] But it seems to me that if we approach the problem in terms of beliefs, statements, or judgments about putative states of affairs, it may quite easily be resolved. The statement 'I am lying,' when applied to itself, does not correspond to a putative state of affairs; as applied to a range of other propositions (when uttered, say, *sotto voce* to a friend at a political meeting), it does so correspond.[59] In his famous essay on truth in formalized languages, Alfred Tarski says that 'it is true that *p*' cannot be said in the same 'language' as '*p*,' but only in a 'metalanguage,' if paradox is to be avoided.[60] Thus 'I am lying' would make perfect sense as part of a 'metalanguage,' applying to items within the 'language,' and not to itself.[61] Tarski, as I have said, deliberately confines his attention to formalized languages. But it seems that ordinary language contains within itself the resources to creating *ad hoc*, for special purposes, devices analogous to Tarski's metalanguages. Ordinary language, one might say, includes, as well as many regions analogous to Tarski's languages, the capacity to produce as many analogues to his metalanguages as may be required.[62]

I have tried to argue in this chapter that, on the assumption about the nature of knowledge which I outlined in the last chapter, a version of the correspondence view of truth may be defended against recent objections to it. Truth turns out after all to be, in Aquinas's lapidary phrase, 'the conformity of thing and intellect.'[63]

3

Data

I have argued that knowledge needs and has foundations; it is now necessary to describe at greater length what these foundations are.

Contemporary philosophers often dispute whether there are any data or, if there are, whether they are perceived material objects or sense-data. Short of some data, it looks as though there are no foundations for knowledge; and short of foundations for knowledge, it looks as though 'anything goes,' as though any knowledge-claim was as good as any other. Both the contentions embodied in that last sentence, I maintain, are correct. But I shall argue that there are sense-data, and that these are in some sense the foundations of knowledge, or at least among its foundations. The most important argument against their existence, and their status as foundations in consequence, is that they cannot be referred to. This I deny. I shall argue that, while admittedly the primary reference of our expressions is to things within the public world, there is a secondary and derivative use of them to refer to sensation and feeling.

The empiricist account of foundations seems to be correct as far as it goes, but it requires supplementing. This account is of course well known among philosophers, as are the objections to it which have been brought forward in the last few decades. However, it is necessary in what follows briefly to rehearse it,[1] along with the objections to it.[2] The ultimate given, on the basis of which all human knowledge of matters of fact was supposed to be possible, was 'sense-data' or 'sense-contents.' Examples of such data would be the contents of my visual field at any moment, the sounds in my ears, the sensations in the parts of my body, and so on. It might be asked why these philosophers did not say roundly that we perceive physical objects, and that it is such perceptions which are at the basis of our knowledge. The answer is that much more is implied by

'There is a physical object of such-and-such a description over there' than by 'I am enjoying such-and-such a sensation or cluster of sensations.' For example, for me to be aware of a purple and approximately oval sensation at the centre of my visual field is one thing; for there to be a plum a short distance in front of me is another. If a plum is there, this sensation will be liable to be succeeded by other similar ones, given that I keep my eyes turned in roughly the same direction, and the light remains fairly good; other people will seem to report or react to the plum when they appear close to it, and I myself will enjoy certain sorts of tactile sensation if I reach out in that direction and certain sorts of gustatory sensation if I grasp the apparent object, and go through kinaesthetic sensations of bringing it to and putting it into my mouth, and so on. On the other hand, I may momentarily have a purple visual datum as though of a plum, or a smell or taste or tactile sensation of this sort, but not occurring as a member of the complex, in the usual relations to other members of that complex, that would be to be expected if there were actually a plum before me. The apparently seen, felt, smelled, or tasted plum might disappear, or not seem to be confirmed as present by other persons. In such cases, I am liable to conclude that my experiences are illusory or hallucinatory. In the long run, on the classical empiricist account, all of our knowledge is founded on such sense-experiences.

But how is our knowledge of physical objects supposed to be founded on such a basis? A once commonly held view is that talk about physical objects in space is simply an enormously simplified way of talking about actual and possible sense-experiences, that every statement about a physical object logically implies a very complicated disjunction of statements about sense-experiences, and nothing more. The great advances in logic achieved at the end of the nineteenth century and the beginning of the twentieth century, notably by Gottlob Frege and Bertrand Russell, seemed to make the actual execution of the task, of analysing any statement about a physical object in terms of statements about sense-contents, one which was feasible at least in principle.

A true empirical statement is one for which the implied disjunction of statements about sense-experiences turns out to be true; a false empirical statement is one for which it turns out to be false. Empiricists have traditionally been inclined to pride themselves on their way of thinking as both vindicating and exemplifying the scientific attitude. What are the grounds for this? It seems to be characteristic of the sciences that their practitioners conscientiously test their hypotheses against the available evidence in observation or experiment. It is easy to infer that a genuinely scientific statement is one in the case of which the implied disjunction of statements about sense-contents has been investigated with special care, and has turned out to be (probably) true.[3] A theory constitutive of a mature science, for all that its terms are likely not to correspond directly with anything observable, enables a range of anticipations of possible sense-experiences to be made which is far beyond that licensed by ordinary statements made about material objects. For instance, 'There is a yellowish heavenly body over there,' stated at night and accompanied by a pointing gesture, might imply merely that, if there were no apparent clouds in the way, a small disc or point of light would enter the visual field of any normally sighted person who looked as directed. On the other hand, 'There is a giant planet, of such-and-such a size and mass, at such-and-such a distance from the sun, travelling at such-and-such a velocity' would be capable, in conjunction with other assumptions, of licensing a true prediction that, given once again an apparently clear sky, experiences of a similar kind would be enjoyed by an observer who looked in the same direction in the sky six years or six-hundred years hence. A scientific statement, then, on the standard empiricist view, differs from a statement of ordinary language, in that its foundations in sense-experience will have been more thoroughly scrutinized and tested, and its support by sense-experiences in consequence more confirmed.

The difficulties in the empiricist account of foundations may be distinguished as being of two basic types: those arising from attempts to articulate those foundations themselves, and those which appear in attempts to show just how knowledge is supposed to be based on such foundations.

Sense-impressions, as generally conceived at least, seem ineluctably private to the individual who enjoys them. The fact that I have a pattern of blue markings on white at the centre of my visual field has no strictly logical implications for what other people in my environment may be enjoying in their experience. But language is a public affair, and there are solid grounds for the belief that it is only possible for individuals who share a public world to which their language has primary reference.[4] We could not learn from our parents and peers to use terms like 'red' or 'hot' in the way we do, except in relation to publicly perceivable objects which are really red or hot. If it were really private sensations of redness or hotness which were primarily at issue, how could I ever know that the sensation which I called 'red' or 'hot' was anything remotely resembling the sensation so called by anyone else? Even if it were proper, as indeed might be doubted, to refer to sensations as opposed to objects as 'red' or 'hot' at all, at least the very facts about how we learn language strongly militate against the view that it is awareness of the private entities which provides the basis for our knowledge of the public. On the contrary, it is only by virtue of a language learned primarily in interaction with publicly observable physical objects that we can talk, even granted that we can properly thus talk, of any private sense-experiences which we may enjoy in relation to them.

One fairly obvious solution to this difficulty[5] is to replace statements about sense-contents with statements about physical objects at the basis of the whole edifice of empirical knowledge. The trouble with this is that talk about physical objects, as has already been pointed out, seems laden with expectations and assumptions which prevent its being basic in quite the required sense. If the object of the exercise is to ground knowledge in experience, then it has to be admitted that talk of physical objects involves a great deal more than a mere record of what is given in experience.

In any case, whether we regard the given in terms of observed physical objects, or of sense-experiences, we have need of an apparatus of concepts to describe and to articulate it. But the whole point of empiricism is that our experience is sufficiently independent of our concepts and judgments to be a means of testing whether the concepts are liable to be instantiated, the judgments to be true. However, since we apparently cannot get at this 'given' apart from this apparatus of concepts on which it is supposed to provide a check, it begins to look as if the notion of any 'given' independent of that apparatus were a mere chimera.[6]

Not only have difficulties arisen about the nature of the supposed 'given,' but the manner in which knowledge of whatever is not 'given' is supposed to be based on it has also proved puzzling. How, for example, do we come to know about physical objects in the external world, when we have only sense-experiences to go on? Apparently not by deductive argument, since however profuse or detailed a description I and others provide of our actual or potential sense-experiences, we can make no sound deduction to the effect that any physical object exists or is present. Just the same thing, at a further remove from experience, applies to the theoretical entities postulated by scientists in relation to their observable effects, and to the thoughts and feelings of other persons in relation to their visible and audible behaviour. And even if one sets aside gnawing doubts about the propriety of inductive inference in general, there seems no properly inductive inference from any set of statements about actual or possible experiences to one about physical objects. Thus I might make such an inference from the fact that a certain complex of sense-experiences *A* had previously always occurred together with sense-experience *B*, that it would do so on some future occasion; but it would be quite a different matter arguing from such a complex of experiences to the existence or presence of a physical object. If the inferences cannot be justified deductively or inductively, it may well be concluded, they cannot be justified at all.[7]

One way out of the problem is to deny that we have only sense-experiences to go on, and to maintain that we have direct acquaintance through our senses with material objects in our immediate environment. Another is to insist that talk of physical objects is, in the last analysis, nothing but talk of sense-experiences that we do enjoy, or would or might enjoy in certain circumstances.[8] The first way out seems to fall foul, as I have already said, of the fact that much more seems to be claimed by the statement 'There is an object of such-and-such a nature in my vicinity' than what is directly entailed by any report on my experience here and now. As to the second, no one ever produced a satisfactory logical analysis of even the most simple statement about physical objects, let alone the more recondite declarations of the practitioners of the sciences, in terms of sense-experiences.

Even if it were conceded, in face of the difficulties, that we have direct experience of physical objects in space, as opposed to sense-experiences, it may be doubted whether we would be much further ahead on the road towards the solution of the problem of knowledge. For just the same difficulties arise about the relation of knowledge of other kinds to knowledge of, or acquaintance with, objects in our immediate environment, as about the relation between our knowledge of physical objects and our knowledge of or acquaintance with sense-experiences. In the ordinary sense of 'know' at least, where the use of the word is not more or less arbitrarily restricted by philosophical dogma, assumption, or fashion, I can 'know' facts about the remote historical past, about what other persons are thinking and feeling, and about electrons and neutrons. But it is apparently one thing to set out the evidence publicly available on these matters – for example, in documents and on monuments, in gestures and noises made by human organisms, and in tracks in cloud chambers and streaks on photographic plates – and another to claim that the facts for which such things are claimed to be evidence actually are so. Once again, the difficulties in showing that the logical path from the evidence to the allegedly known facts is deductive or 'inductive' (if indeed the latter demonstration, whatever is amounted to, would provide any consolation) seem insurmountable. And those who cleave to the faith that talk about thoughts and feelings is really after all merely talk about actual or possible vocalizations and gestures (behaviourism), or that talk about nuclear particles is nothing but a convenient way of speaking about actual or possible observations or practices (operationism), are apt to overlook the generality of the problem. To say that talk about your agonizing pain is really nothing but a compendious way of talking about your actual or hypothetical screams and contortions may merely shock or seem rather odd, but to say that talk about George Washington or Edmontosaurus is abbreviated talk about marks on paper or noises liable to be emitted in certain contingencies by historians or palaeontologists is to stretch credulity indeed.

Another possibility is to acknowledge that, while physical objects (or whatever) are not directly knowable, they are indirectly knowable as causes of our sense-experiences.[9] But, it may reasonably be asked, what is the path from the direct to the indirect kind of knowledge? How, if at all, are we justified in traversing it? If we say that the existence of physical objects is the simplest explanation for our experiences, as Russell suggested at one stage of his career,[10] what justification do we have, if any, for claiming that what is postulated in such explanations, however successful these are in practice, really exists or is as we say it is? It has been suggested that it is enough merely to describe the procedures which we actually follow in attributing feelings to others, in validating or invalidating a historical claim, and so on, on the basis of our experience and that such description ought to satisfy the sceptic.[11] But the sceptic may quite reasonably retort that merely to describe such a procedure is a very different thing from justifying it. Someone who believed in goblins and leprechauns rather than in fundamental particles, and in what we would call myth and legend rather than what we would call history, could do as much. Admittedly we have procedures by which we purport to test in experience the claim that such-and-such an alleged historical event actually occurred, or that someone other than oneself has these feelings or thoughts rather than those, but it is another thing to justify the claim that the procedures in question actually do tend to establish the real occurrence of the historical fact, or the real existence of the thoughts or feelings.

As A.J. Ayer sees it, 'it does not greatly matter whether we regard the need for analysis as superseding the demand for justification, or whether we make the justification consist in the analysis.'[12] But it is one thing to analyse in detail the grounds for making a statement; it is another thing to show how they do ground the statement, at least in those cases where there is good reason to suppose that the fact stated by the statement is one thing, the ground on which one has the right to state it, another. Suppose I ask a haruspex how he knows that a certain state of the entrails of the birds he disembowels indicates that his gods are angry, another that they are in beneficent mood. I cannot see how an accumulation of information, however detailed, as to how he relates the one actual state of affairs to the other putative state of affairs, will give me an adequate answer to my question. It would only do so if he admitted that all that was meant by 'the gods are angry' was that the entrails of the birds were in one observable state rather than another.[13]

It is due to these and other similar difficulties that some philosophers have concluded that knowledge has and needs no foundations, no 'given' element, whatever. I have already said a good deal about this matter, and have some further comments in this paragraph and the two following. Empiricists have of course supposed that there is some such element in knowledge, on the basis of which we can arrive at it or test it as such. But why, it may be asked, should such an assumption be made? Wilfred Sellars has put into currency the phrase 'the myth of the given.'[14] Certainly, our society is not normally given to question reports made by individuals in certain circumstances. But that such reports are not questioned is no more than a matter of social convention. It is not that the statements treated as 'basic' – those which we accept as reasons for modifying, abandoning, or confirming other statements, but which we do not regard as themselves liable to such modification, abandonment, or confirmation – are somehow of themselves 'certain' or 'incorrigible.' Rather, it is only that we do not bother, since we have no inclination to question them. And some reports which might be felt to be incorrigible are thus questioned, when they run counter to assumptions which are socially acceptable. A dentist may well conclude, when he has taken all the usual steps to anaesthetize a patient's tooth, that the patient's statement that his tooth is still hurting is to be rejected. And that famous respect for the evidence of one's senses, on which the more sentimental chroniclers of the scientific movement have laid such emphasis, looks dubious indeed when one takes a more objective look at the history of science.[15] Theorists have shamelessly brushed aside evidence which did not conform with the hypothesis which they were advocating; nor has posterity invariably rejected their views when they have done so.

The fact is that scientists can get on with their job, of investigating phenomena, theorizing, and carrying out experiments, each in the manner appropriate to her discipline, without being dictated to by philosophers.

Every now and then, sciences go through a fundamental and revolutionary change in theory. But it is mistaken in principle to look for some overall criterion in accordance with which the later cluster of theories in the science concerned is 'truer,' 'more in accordance with reality,' or whatever, than the earlier. Such changes in the activities and ways of speaking of scientists are just the same in principle as similar changes in other social groups; they are the proper concern of the sociologist rather than the epistemologist.

It is the actual consensus of the sciences which determines what is true about the world, what are the facts, and not their supposed deference to an overall method of investigation which vanishes into thin air the moment one takes serious steps to find out what it is. The ancient problem of epistemology, of how we can attain knowledge and understanding of the real world, is a pseudo-problem. The zoologist is our authority on elephants, and the chemist our authority on hydrochloric acid; there is no encyclopedic professional lady or gentleman who can be our authority on knowledge in general, in all its departments. How people acquire and pass on those thoughts, skills, and ways of speaking and writing, which society dignifies by the name of 'knowledge,' is a matter of empirical psychology, which is itself just another branch of natural science.[16]

The foundations once proposed for knowledge have thus proved, or at any rate have been alleged, to be inadequate. But the thesis often advanced as a consequence of this, that there are no foundations for knowledge, and in particular that there is no 'given,' no data, in relation to which we can test the truth of our claims, leads to conclusions which seem at least equally difficult to accept, as I have argued at length in earlier chapters. Is there any way, it may be asked, of revising or repairing the older account of foundations, or of substituting a new one, in such a way as to meet the difficulties?

Any proposal about the foundations of knowledge must have two components: (i) a description of whatever it is that is supposed to be 'given,' and (ii) an account of the procedures which are to be applied to this 'given' if knowledge is actually to be obtained.[17] To deal with the 'given' first: are perceptions of material objects 'basic,' or are sense-experiences? As I have already tried to show, both claims are subject to difficulties, which have led not a few to deny that there is any 'given' element in knowledge. However, it seems to me that the difficulties can be resolved if each is taken to be basic in a different manner, the latter in respect to experience, the former in respect to language. To put the matter roughly and succinctly, we could not speak of a real public world unless we had experiences which are in an important sense private to us; however, we could not speak of these experiences unless we could in the first place speak of material objects in a public world. *Qua* givenness to sensation, experiences are basic; *qua* language and the judgments expressed in it, material objects are so. We could not talk about material objects unless we had the requisite sense-experiences; on the other hand, we could not speak of sense-experiences unless we could speak of material objects.[18]

Empiricists have always stressed the role of experience in verifying or falsifying our claims to knowledge. It is often objected that there is no way in which experience can be described apart from theory, indeed, that it only occurs within a framework of theory. I will try to show that this claim is in one sense true and in another sense false; but when taken in the sense in which it is true, it does not constitute a valid objection. Since the later work of Wittgenstein became known, it has been widely held among philosophers that we could not, for example, talk about sensations of red unless there were physical objects that are red, since, short of the existence of such objects, there could be no way of showing that one person's sensation of 'red' was the same as another's, and so the word 'red' in its common sense could not form a part of language as a public instrument of communication. Thus the language in which we describe our sensations, it is concluded (rightly, in my opinion), is ineluctably parasitic upon the language with which we talk about physical objects, and thus, as Thomas Kuhn puts it, presupposes 'a world already perceptually and conceptually subdivided in a certain way.'[19] I admit that a language about sensations which is not subject to these conditions is impossible. However, we can easily describe our sensations as sensations by ad hoc modifications of the language we use about physical objects. I might characterize a certain sort of visual experience by saying, 'It is *as though* a collection of brightly coloured objects were moving about approximately six inches in front of my eyes.' The qualification 'as though' would indicate that I did not imply, for instance, that if I groped or lunged in their direction I would be able to feel them or brush them aside. It does not seem fair to say that such a remark would not so much be a description of my sensation as a mere exclamation accompanying it. The remark might be true or false, in a way that mere exclamations could not be. If I had the sensation, for example, while taking part in an experiment in which my brain was being stimulated by electrodes, I might lie to the effect that I was or was not having an experience of the kind described – perhaps to placate or confuse the experimenter.

The ordinary language in which we, and *mutatis mutandis* human beings of other cultures and environments, have been brought up enshrines and encapsulates a set of general expectations about how things will turn out, and about the general ordering of the world of our experience as extended in space and time. (Of course, the presuppositions of 'ordinary language' vary a great deal with place and time; all that is necessary for my purpose here is that 'ordinary languages' should have in common that they serve to describe sensible objects for immediate practical purposes.) But this by no means entails that it cannot be used, for example, with *ad hoc* modifications of the kind I suggested above, to describe our experiences themselves.

So much for the basis of empirical knowledge. By what means is knowledge to be erected on this basis? The first point to be made is that the procedures for arriving at knowledge on the basis of experience cannot be reduced to logic in the strict sense; and I think that the widespread contemporary despair of the possibility of finding foundations for knowledge is due largely to the assumption that, if there were such foundations, the means of building knowledge upon them could be thus reduced. I believe that empiricists were correct in their view that knowledge, or at any rate much knowledge, is founded in a certain sense on sense-experience, but they erred on the manner in which it is thus founded. Each human being, however primitive or sophisticated her cultural milieu, learns in the course of growing up an ordinary language which consists quite largely in judgments framed in terms of conceptions which have been tested through a wide range of experience; and our instinct is usually to move directly from enjoyment of the relevant complex of experience to the making of the apparently appropriate judgement – that is, to the effect that something really is as it seems to be in our experience. It does not usually prove worth our while, when there seems to be a dagger before us – when our visual and other experiences are appropriate to this – to delay our instinctive propensity to judge that there is a dagger before us. No single one of the vast array of ordinary languages can be mainly erroneous in the normal judgments of observable physical fact which it makes or presupposes; otherwise its users would not have survived. One needs to be able to talk about poison berries and tigers, and indeed to be able to make rather a large number of true statements about them, given that one is able to think and talk at all, if one is going to survive in a jungle full of poison berries and tigers.

Mentally to divide the experience which is at the basis of the judgment from the judgment itself requires some pains and some sophistication, but it can quite readily be done, as has been demonstrated *ad nauseam* by those philosophers who have written of 'impressions,' 'sense-data,' 'sense-contents,' and so on. Any occasion in which we recognize a difference between what is so and what seems to be so involves some kind of exercise of this capacity. Suppose I am in a psychology laboratory, and all the visual cues have been arranged in such a way that, when I walk through the door of the laboratory, I believe that I am entering a room of a certain shape which contains objects of certain kinds such as might have been expected. I am invited to alter my position a little, and I come to see that my earlier belief was in many respects false – for example, that the apparent far end of the room does not exist, but is due to the judicious placing of mirrors, and that the apparent music stand is the result of separate pieces of wood and metal of appropriate shapes, colours, and textures having been placed at various distances from my eyes. Suppose I now leave the room, and subsequently enter it again. Owing to my previous course of experience, I am now likely to interpret my visual cues in a different manner from before, and make a different judgment about the real state of affairs in the room. If asked to report both on my experience and on my belief about what is actually the case in my environment which is based on that experience, I can honestly say, 'It is with my visual field as though I were in a rectangular room with a music stand, though I have grounds for believing that this is not actually so.' In an extreme case, presumably, the whole room might be a visual hallucination to which I had been subjected by the electrical stimulation of my visual cortex, and I might know that this was so.

The fact is that a person may honestly report her experiences, without, however tentatively, making any judgment about states of affairs external to those experiences themselves.[20] (Admittedly, she could not do so, unless she could also make judgments about observable physical states of affairs; but that is another matter.) It is therefore misleading to assimilate all *prima facie* reports of sensation to more or less mistaken or tentative statements about objects in the reporter's immediate physical environment, as one may be tempted to do in an effort to show that there need be no such entities as 'sense-experiences' at all. One may quarrel with the terminology, but it does seem odd to deny what is at first sight the obvious fact that we may enjoy sense-experiences, but withhold judgment altogether about the public state of affairs which accounts for them. I think that what motivates some philosophers to engage in this curious manoeuvre is the fear that, if such entities as 'sense-experiences' are allowed to gain any footing in our ontology, we will find ourselves altogether cut off from the public world of physical objects and events. But this fear is groundless. The real world, including physical objects and whatever else there may be, consists in what is to be known by judgments for which our sense-experiences provide the basic evidence. One is in danger of losing the real world not as a result of admitting that there are sense-experiences, but as a result of confusing the real things which are the potential objects of adequately grounded judgments, with the experiences which ultimately provide the grounds for these.

What is the relation of sense-experience to the judgments in virtue of which we come to know the real world? It seems that, in order to know a world consisting of real things and events which exist largely prior to and independently of ourselves, we have not only (1) to enjoy sense-experiences, but also (2) to conceive possibilities, and (3) to judge that some of the possibilities are realized.[21] In other words, we have to be at least to some extent attentive, intelligent, and reasonable, in the senses described at the end of the first chapter. For example, to know that a horse and cart have just passed by my window, I characteristically have (1) to have had visual and aural sensations as though of a horse and cart passing my window, (2) to have conceived the possibility of its having done so, and (3) to have judged that this possibility is the one that best fits the evidence. It is worth noting, for later attention and discussion, that not only the conscious contents of experience (red sense-data and so on), but also the conscious acts of conceiving and judging, appear to be items of which I am directly aware, and can, by appropriate attention, make myself more aware; they seem in a sense to constitute, in fact, another aspect of 'the given,' apart from sensation and feeling. (Locke made this point when he argued that 'reflection' on the operation of our minds, as well as 'sensation,' is a source of the 'ideas' which are the basis of human knowledge.)[22] This is perhaps most obvious in cases where I am puzzled for a while as to what to make of my experience – say, when an impression is very fleeting or faint. In such a case, rather than moving directly from the impression as though of a horse and cart to the judgment that there is a horse and cart in my vicinity, I may wonder for some time, 'What was it?,' and only later hit on the possibility, let alone establish the fact, that it was a horse and cart. It is also worthy of remark here (the matter will be discussed at greater length in the next chapter) that the two kinds of questioning which are apt to underlie, respectively, the conceiving of possibilities and the making of judgments ('What might this be?' or 'Why might this be so?' and 'Does that exist?' or 'Is that so?') are also activities of which we are directly conscious, and to which we may attend. However, it is one thing to exercise these types of mental capacity, and to be in some sense aware of doing so; it is another to spell out this awareness to ourselves. Every human person does the former; to do the latter is very rare. David Hume was, of course, an enormously intelligent man (good at framing conceptions and concocting hypotheses, at asking and answering questions of the what and why kinds) and a highly reasonable one (good at affirming what he had conceived as so in accordance with the available evidence); but for all that he conceived and affirmed in effect that he was no conceiver and affirmer, but a mere bundle of sensations and memory-traces.[23]

It may be objected that these acts of conceiving and judging to which I have alluded, and the acts of questioning which characteristically underlie them, are subjective mental events which could only be referred to by the kind of 'private language' which was pilloried by Wittgenstein, and hence that to postulate them at all is inadmissible. The answer is that no such conclusions can be validly drawn from what Wittgenstein actually says on the subject of private languages, even if one accepts what he says as correct. A private language, on Wittgenstein's account, is one which refers to inner and private events for the occurrence of which there are no usually concomitant public criteria in the manner, for example, that writhing, groaning, and a constrained manner of speaking are characteristic of pain.[24] But there are plenty of public behavioural criteria by means of which we can recognize that someone is wondering or inquiring, or has conceived a possibility, or judges that it is so.

If this is the correct account of the manner in which our experience is related to our knowledge of the real world, none of the puzzles mentioned earlier remains to plague us. For at this rate, it is neither the case that to talk about material objects is in the last analysis just to talk about sense-experiences nor the case that material objects are what are directly given in our experience – with the difficulties that each position entails. Russell's one-time view, that the existence of a world of material objects commends itself as the best explanation of our sense-experience, is in a manner vindicated,[25] as is the thesis that material objects are rightly to be postulated as causes of our experience. For to conceive that a state of affairs in the physical world may be so, and to judge that it is so, on the basis of experience, is indeed to provide an explanation of that experience. And to say that such-and-such material objects are within our environment is often to explain why we have the experience we do, and thus to assign a cause for that experience.

The claim that there are two aspects of the given, each basic in its own way, has further to be elaborated and justified. The ultimate foundations of knowledge in experience do not, at least normally, consist of propositions which, in any useful sense, can be said to be known. I can articulate the foundations of my knowledge in my experience by the use of certain expressions, full of phrases like 'sense-data,' 'sense-contents,' and so on, in which analytical philosophers of the generation of Russell and Moore used to be very proficient, but I need not do so, and I do not characteristically do so, and only in so far as I did so would my apprehension of them at all plausibly be worth calling 'knowledge.' While a red patch at the corner of my visual field may be the grounds of my knowledge that my wife's dressing gown is in the living room of my house, it is an abuse of words to claim that I know that I have such a patch at the corner of my visual field, except perhaps in the case that I give my attention to the matter. Usually, for practical purposes, the justification of knowledge-claims by appeal to experience stops short with some reference to perceived physical objects and events. 'How do you know that your aunt is arriving here tomorrow?' 'Well, here is a letter in her handwriting informing me of her intentions to that effect, and she is usually a reliable person, who sticks to her plans.' Theoretically, the question could still be pressed, 'How do you know that there is a letter before you of the kind that you say?' The reply could be made, 'I have visual and tactile sense-impressions appropriate to this being so, and I have no reason to believe that I am habitually or temporarily subject to hallucinations regarding such matters.'

In principle, it seems that our statements about material objects in our immediate vicinity can characteristically be justified in this kind of way, for all that we very seldom find it worth while so to justify them. However, that the ultimate term of most 'How do you know that ... ?' questions is appeal to sense-impressions does not imply that it is doubtful whether we can really perceive or come to know about a publicly shared world of physical objects, or that we might in the last analysis have no knowledge of anything but sense-impressions; one could only reach such a conclusion by dint of confusing the content of a judgment (that such-and-such a state of affairs actually is the case) with the ultimate grounds in experience by which such a judgment may be supported. Still, we could not talk about such experiences if we could not talk about the physical objects and states of affairs which characteristically occasion them. This is the real lesson to be learned from Wittgenstein's disparaging remarks about private languages.

What is apt to go wrong in discussions of this matter is well illustrated by Wilfred Sellars. Sellars attacks the notion of 'foundations' of knowledge, and what he calls 'the myth of the given,' as 'misleading, in that it keeps us from seeing that if there is a logical dimension in which other empirical propositions rest on observational reports, there is another dimension in which the latter rest on the former.' This, of course, is precisely the position for which I have been arguing. Sellars himself protests that he by no means wishes to claim that human knowledge has no foundation at all, in a sense that would suggest that it was on the same level as rumours and hoaxes. He also remarks that 'empirical knowledge, like its sophisticated extension, science, is rational, not because it has a *foundation*, but because it is a self-correcting enterprise which can put *any* claim in jeopardy though not all at once.'[26] But either he can spell out what it is to have reasonable grounds for putting a claim in jeopardy, or he cannot. If he cannot, he is forced into that radically anti-foundationalist position (maintained, for example, by Feyerabend)[27] according to which one might as well change one's beliefs as a result of a threat or a bribe as because of adequate empirical evidence. If he can, then the spelling-out of what counts as such 'adequate empirical evidence' amounts to nothing less than an articulation of foundations. The latter, it seems clear, is closest to Sellars's actual position,[28] which would much less misleadingly have been expressed as a revised positive account of foundations and of what, and in what sense, is given, than as a rejection of foundations and of any given element in human knowledge. And as a matter of fact, his misleading terminology has encouraged some philosophers to adopt the view that there are no foundations of knowledge whatever, and no element in knowledge which is in any sense given. And at that rate, the only difference between knowledge, on the one hand, and rumours and hoaxes, on the other, is social acceptability.

To cite conscious mental activities as relevant to the theory of knowledge is to invite the charge, much feared by analytical philosophers, of 'psychologism.'[29] However, it is one thing for the forming of concepts and hypotheses and the propounding of judgments to be mental acts and thus presumably to be a matter of psychology in some sense; it is another thing for the qualities attributed to things and the distinctions drawn between them by the judgments to be merely a matter of psychology. It is by an act of understanding which may fairly be thought of as mental (how else would one think of it?) that I grasp that the square root of two cannot be the quotient of any two integers, however large; but it by no means follows that what is grasped through the act of understanding is a matter of psychology. And it is only this last view which can be called 'psychologism' in any sense which is very obviously vicious. The mental operations involved in coming to know are, in a broad sense at least, a proper topic for psychology, but one should not infer that what is to be known by means of them is so.

How empiricist is the account of foundations which I have outlined? It is certainly empiricist in that it attempts to articulate foundations of knowledge in experience – even finding some use for that notion of raw sense-experience, so characteristic of earlier twentieth-century empiricism, and now so widely believed to be discredited. It is not empiricist, however, in the sense that it by no means obviously follows from it that every object of knowledge is an actual or even a potential object of experience. For it is one thing for a judgment to be confirmed by experience, for it to have grounds in experience; it is another thing for what the judgment is about to be an actual or even a potential object of experience. The existence of 'mass' in Newton's sense may be verified in countless instances in a scientist's experience, but it does not correspond directly to anything which can become the direct object of his experience; and the same applies to the thoughts and feelings of other persons in relation to the observable evidence which you or I may have for them. There is another way in which the account is empiricist according to one criterion, not another – in a sense which applies to Locke, but not quite to Hume or to most subsequent empiricists. Like Locke's view, it does not entail that any of our 'ideas' are innate. But it does admit what Locke would call 'reflection,' as well as 'sensation,' as a source of 'ideas.' That is to say, it acknowledges that we not only undergo sense-experience, but also employ our minds with respect to it, asking questions, forming hypotheses, envisaging possible explanations, marshalling evidence for or against our hypotheses or possible explanations, making judgments as to what is so on the basis of our experience and our hypotheses, and so on. It further acknowledges that this conscious activity of our minds with respect to sensation may also come to our attention (for all that it has been excluded by and large from attention by modern empiricists, as well as by their successors in the analytical movement), and itself become the basis for further questions, hypotheses, and judgments. What do seem to be innate are predispositions to perform the mental acts which will enable us to acquire knowledge when applied to the contents of experience; we acquire concepts or 'ideas' in the course of such performances, but it is quite unnecessary to suppose that the concepts or 'ideas' are themselves innate.

But whatever the rights and wrongs of introspection as a method of investigating human mental phenomena, the matter most importantly at issue here, the articulation and defence of foundations for knowledge, does not depend on it. That human beings attend to experience, frame hypotheses, and judge, as means of getting at the truth about things, is certainly so, as I showed in the first chapter; the denial of this thesis is self-destructive.

In what sense, if any, is it useful to say that the given is the object of perception? The trouble with the term 'perceive' and its cognates, as with most terms referring to sense-experience, is that they are ambiguous. 'I perceive x' may only imply 'I have a sense-impression as of x.' On the other hand, 'I perceive x' tends to imply all of the following: (1) I have sense-impressions as of x; (2) I judge that x is where it appears to me to be; (3) x really is where it appears to me to be. Only in the first sense, and not in the second, is it proper to say that the given is the object of perception. And it seems more natural to understand the term in the second sense. Suppose Smith says that she has perceived a man running furtively across her lawn at dusk. If in fact there was no man there, does it not seem appropriate to say that Smith was mistaken in what she claimed to perceive?

What, briefly, is the relation of the real to the given? The real is what one tends to come to know, to form true judgments about, so far as one is as attentive, intelligent, and reasonable as possible. One aspect of what one can thus come to know is that there are data of sensation and feeling to which oneself and others are subject; another, that there are mental procedures that oneself and others may apply to them. But at all events, the real, the actual world, of which what is 'given' in experience is only an insignificant aspect, is what one can know as a result of applying the mental procedures to the data in an appropriate way.

4

Reality

So far, I have been attempting to give an account of knowledge, of what it is to know. I have tried to show how knowledge is possible at all, the nature of the truth which it entails and to which it aspires, and the kind of data upon which it is based. A 'metaphysics' should issue from this, in the sense of an account, in the most general terms, of what there is to be known. What I hope to do in this chapter is to sketch how one might go about constructing a rational, critical, and in a sense 'scientific' metaphysics.

It goes without saying that a great many current conceptions of metaphysics are abusive. On one account, metaphysics is whatever is not science or common sense, where science and common sense are assumed to be good things. On another, metaphysics consists of an abuse of language which is brought about by a wrenching of it out of its normal context. Again, metaphysics is supposed to substitute a bloodless dance of categories for the spontaneous outflow of religious feeling, or the idolatrous constructions of humanity for the Word of God. However, it seems in general much clearer that metaphysics is to be repudiated than exactly what metaphysics is.

A traditional definition of metaphysics is 'the study of being *qua* being.' It is perhaps understandable that many should complain, when confronted by such a sententious formula, that such an inquiry is a waste of time, and one had much better get on with the more fruitful business of pursuing one of the particular sciences. (Ezra Pound once remarked that, since the Renaissance, a philosopher had been someone who was too damned lazy to work in a laboratory; and the same may be felt to apply *a fortiori* to the metaphysician.) And yet there are problems that do not seem to go away, however often or confidently it is asserted that they have done so or are about to do so, problems that may be said to be concerned with 'being' or 'reality' at a very high level of generality. Those who brush the problems aside may perhaps sometimes be suspected of arbitrarily taking sides on them. For example, the psychological doctrine known as behaviourism is based on the assumption that all talk about thoughts, feelings, and emotions is in the final analysis reducible to talk about the behaviour of organisms. But it is one thing to allow such an assumption to dominate one's work, another, to set it out clearly, yet another, to examine and to justify it. If any examination of the account of the relation of mind to matter implied by behaviourism has to be of such generality as to enter the realm of the 'metaphysical,' it would seem to be still worth carrying out, unless indeed we are to accept behaviourism quite uncritically as a dogma. Just the same applies to writing which assumes the existence or non-existence of a deity. The fact is that every passage of speech or writing which makes claims as to matter of fact involves certain assumptions about the ultimate constituents of things, and about the nature and interrelations of appearance, reality, mind, matter, experience, causality, things, properties, events, space, time, God (if God exists), and so on. Let us call each such set of basic assumptions (including the ones mentioned earlier, that talk about minds is reducible to talk about the behaviour or organisms, that there is or is not a God) a 'metaphysic.' Let us say that metaphysics is an attempt to discuss, and to come to well-founded conclusions about, the question as to whether any such metaphysic is to be preferred, as more approximating to the truth about how things are in the world, than any other.

Empiricism, idealism, materialism, critical realism, and naive realism will at this rate each be a metaphysic; that is to say, each consists of theses about the existence, nature, and interrelations of actual or alleged basic constituents of reality (like those listed above). Any attempt to discuss the rival merits of any of them, or to defend any one as more appropriate than the others, will count as metaphysics. The arguments by which Plato, Leibniz, or Hegel established their conclusions about the ultimate nature of things evidently count as metaphysics according to our conception; and this does seem in conformity with ordinary usage. Perhaps it is obvious that one such metaphysic (say, materialism) is to be preferred to the rest, or at least that another such (say, idealism) should be repudiated; but it would be as well all the same to have the reasons for this spelled out, just in case they turned out to be prejudices. So many things which have seemed to go without saying, like the geocentric cosmology, have turned out to be wrong. And the notion of 'absolute rest' seemed obviously applicable and unproblematic to most people, until Einstein showed otherwise.

Metaphysics, as I have already mentioned, is often abusively contrasted with science. But what is it, it may reasonably be asked, except the acclaim of persons who are well placed socially that makes science science, as opposed to, say, opinion or speculation? What is the essence of science, and on what articulate basis is it to be distinguished from what is not science? Science, it would commonly be claimed, is constituted by a method which makes its statements liable to approach the truth about the world. What is this method, and why do those who use it tend to approximate to affirming the truth about things? I believe that attention to the ramifications of this question is a good way of finding the right method for metaphysics. As Thomas Kuhn asked, In what kind of a world is scientific inquiry possible?[1] This question is of too great a level of generality to be itself scientific, but it does not appear at least at first sight to be either senseless or unimportant.

I do not think that attention to the implications of the possibility of science in the world leads ineluctably to the crude metaphysic known as 'scientism.' But scientism is, I believe, a plausible parody of the truth, which is perhaps the reason why it is as dogmatically accepted by some as it is passionately rejected by others. 'Science is the measure of all things,' says Wilfred Sellars, 'of what is that it is, and what is not that it is not.'[2] Now if one means by 'science' the application of the methods of physics, chemistry, and biology exactly as they are to all phenomena, it seems to me that Sellars's remark is certainly false, for reasons which I will give presently. However, if one means by 'science' a generalized employment of methods exemplified by science at its best, with each type of case handled in the manner appropriate to it, it seems to me correct. I will also try to bring out that the application of such methods, so far from being destructive of anything worth calling a metaphysic, results in a metaphysic of a recognizably traditional kind.

The error of scientism is that it applies uncritically to the whole of reality a series of conclusions which have been arrived at by the investigation of one aspect of it, typically the physical and chemical. How can we know that it is an error? The pattern of argument by which we can know it will be found to be applicable, interestingly enough, to every erroneous type of metaphysic. Scientism can be shown to be self-destructive, by the kind of argument I employed in the first chapter. Why does anyone reasonably believe what the scientist says about her speciality? He can only do so on the assumption that the scientist says what she does because it is reasonable for her to do so. And what does the scientist's reasonableness consist in? It implies that she has, or at least that her authorities have, attended to the available evidence relevant to the subject; that she or they have envisaged a number of ways of accounting for that evidence; and that she or they present their conclusions as the ways in which that evidence may best be accounted for. Now it follows from scientism that human behaviour, including human expression of opinion, is never to be accounted for as due to such attentiveness, intelligence, and reasonableness (to revert to the jargon I introduced in the first chapter), since these are not and cannot be reduced to the laws of physics and chemistry. Therefore it is not really the case that the physicist or the chemist propounds her theories because there is good reason for her to do so, or that anyone else accepts her theories for good reason. The scientism which is often supposed to be a corollary of science, in fact, is destructive of science.[3]

Is the emphasis on these mental activities as constitutive of science then subversive of the results of science? Not at all. On the contrary, it encourages submission to the opinions of scientists within their specialty, as they will be more likely than anyone else to have attended to the relevant evidence and to have canvassed the widest range of possible explanations; and hence they will be best placed to make the correct judgments about the aspects of the world with which they are concerned. But it is one thing to have faith in scientists with respect to matters within their expertise, quite another, to put up with deliverances on the overall nature of things put out by themselves or others on the basis of their work.

Someone might perhaps say (though he would be less likely to say it now than he would have been a few decades ago) that logic and experience alone are enough for science.[4] But, as I have already argued at length, such a view is untenable, except on a misleadingly broad conception of what is meant by 'logic.' As has been clear since the work of Hume,[5] there is no valid logical inference from any series of particular observations to a generalization, and *a fortiori*, there is none to an explanatory hypothesis. A range of observations may well be adequate grounds for supposing that a white dwarf star may exist at a certain point in space, but the hypothesis cannot be strictly inferred from the observations. And what applies to the exercise of intelligence applies also to that of reasonableness. I cannot logically infer any observation statement from typical judgments of theoretical science. Presumably the relevant observations support the view that neutrinos exist against rival suppositions, but I cannot directly infer the relevant observations from the judgment that there are neutrinos, or vice versa. Logic enormously facilitates the exercise of intelligence and reasonableness, but it cannot replace them in the discovery of what is so.

In expounding the work of Willard Quine, Alex Orenstein says in effect that what commits us to a metaphysic (Quine would say an 'ontology') are 'our most literal referential uses of language, our sciences. Hence the question of which ontology we accept must be dealt with in terms of the role an ontology plays in a scientific world view.'[6] It will be seen from what I have said that a dangerous ambiguity lurks in this statement. What is presented as a 'scientific world-view' ought to make room not only for the objects actually described and explained at any time by scientists, but also for the activity and achievement of scientists themselves; however, it very often does not. In particular, a general account of things which dismisses, in the name of science, all talk of inquiry, framing of hypotheses, marshalling of evidence, and so on, as mere 'mentalism,' replaceable without remainder by a more 'scientific' way of talking, should be rejected out of hand.

One common objection to this kind of mentalism is that it must lead to Cartesian dualism, with minds cut off from each other and from extramental reality apart from the special grace of God. Now the implied metaphysic is Cartesian to the extent that it involves the possession by persons of properties, and their entering into relations, which cannot be analysed exhaustively in physical terms. But this by no means implies that persons are cut off from knowledge of the real world or of each other. For the real world is nothing other than what one tends to get to know by the exercise of attentiveness, intelligence, and reasonableness. The notion that 'reality' could be utterly outside the range of our knowledge, in the manner of Kant's 'things in themselves,' merely makes nonsense of our conception of reality. We learn the meaning of the term 'real' (here is a useful leaf to be taken from the book of the linguistic philosophers) by contrast with expressions like 'merely apparent' and 'unreal,' in the context of making judgments over-hastily or on insufficient evidence, and subsequently revising these judgments.

Husserl remarked that Descartes was on the track of discoveries still more important than those he actually made. If the sketch I have given of the foundations of knowledge is correct, then Descartes was largely right. He was by no means misguided, in spite of what has been claimed by so many recent philosophers, in searching for a reliable basis for our knowledge of the world; he was also right in finding this basis in propositions whose contradictories are self-destructive, like doubt that one is a doubter. However, he was wrong in thinking that the existence and veracity of God had to be proved, before we could be confident of our ability to know the world by use of our intellectual and rational powers. God, his argument runs, as a perfect being, will not be such a cad as to allow Descartes to be deceived, if Descartes exerts himself to the uttermost to achieve clear and distinct ideas on every matter about which he inquires. But the underlying supposition, that the real world might somehow be other than what we tend to get to know by intelligent and reasonable investigation of evidence, is not really a coherent one. (I think that Descartes is right in seeing some connection between our ability to know about a real external world and the reasonableness of belief in God, but that is another matter.)[7] The way to the correct view on the matter is to attend, first, to the self-destructiveness of the thesis that true judgments are impossible, and that one does not tend to make them by the envisagement and testing of hypotheses in relation to experience, and second, to the fact that the real world is and can be nothing other than what true judgments are about. Certainly, I can on the basis of evidence make true judgments about myself, but just as certainly, I can on the basis of evidence make true judgments about what is other than myself. There is, I suppose, a sense (emphasized by Locke with his talk about 'secondary qualities') in which my sensations are internal to myself, in my ears or eyes or skin or (perhaps more strictly) in the relevant parts of my brain. It seems to me that it is the assimilation of judgment to sensation which has given rise to the Cartesian bogey that one might be solitary in the universe. As the object of my own judgment and that of others, I am and am as I am as distinct from other persons and things.

The real world is not, at this rate, in spite of the claims or the assumptions of empiricists, merely what we perceive or might perceive; it is what we tend intelligently to conceive and reasonably to affirm on the basis of experience. The so-called problem of other minds, a typical artifact of empiricism, is simply dissolved once one has grasped this principle. I cannot see or hear what you are thinking and feeling. On the other hand, I can come up with various suppositions as to what you may be thinking or feeling, and confirm one or other as more likely to be so than the rest by attention to your noises and gestures. Operationism in physics may be seen to be based on just the same error as behaviourism in psychology. The fact that I cannot see or smell a neutron by no means implies that I may not form the hypothesis that such a particle exists, and propound the judgment that it does so as the best explanation of a range of phenomena connected with bubble-chambers and so forth. Similarly, the fact that I cannot perceive any person or event of the remote past does not imply that I cannot have knowledge of such persons or events, since that such a person acted in a certain way, or that such an event took place, may account better than any rival supposition for evidence available in the present.

Something should be said about the role of questioning in this account of knowledge. Though Plato and Aristotle were both very interested in the role of questioning in the acquisition of knowledge, the subject has been comparatively neglected in later philosophy. (Among the moderns, R.G. Collingwood is a conspicuous exception.) One comes by a hypothesis or hypotheses as a consequence of asking, with respect in typical cases to evidence available to one's senses, 'What may this be?' or 'Why may this be so?' The final step in coming to know consists in getting an answer to the next question which arises, with respect to any hypothesis one has excogitated, 'Is that so?' It will be seen that what I have called 'intelligence' is a matter of skill in asking and answering the first kind of question, and what I have called 'reasonableness,' the same with respect to the second. It is characteristic of the second type of question, as opposed to the first, that it can be answered yes or no. I cannot answer yes or no to the question 'What is the normal temperature of human beings on the Fahrenheit scale?', but I can to the question 'Is the normal temperature of human beings on the Fahrenheit scale 98.4?' I cannot answer yes or no to the question 'Why, when I pass an electric current through water, does the level of the water slowly go down, and colourless and odourless gases appear at the terminals?' But I can answer yes or no to the question 'Does water consist of hydrogen and oxygen?'

How are these epistemological principles to be applied to metaphysics, and how is a metaphysic to be derived from them? The main thing to be borne in mind is that the right metaphysic is the obverse of the right epistemology; if this is the way in which one comes to know, that cannot but be the fundamental nature and structure of what thus comes to be known, or is to be known. The varieties of defective metaphysic on the market are each due to a relative emphasis on one or two of the three mental faculties essentially involved in coming to know at the expense of the rest. The naive realist assumes, as Bernard Lonergan has expressed it, that 'what is obvious in knowing is what knowing obviously is':[8] before you have taken a look, you have to make do with fantasies, hunches, or theorizings, but once you have taken a look you can just brush these mental constructions aside. This may seem to do very well for some common-sense examples of knowledge: before I take a look, I may suppose that the cat is or is not in the furnace room, but once I have taken a look, I know that she is or is not. But this certainly will not do for knowledge in history or theoretical science, or indeed for knowledge of the thoughts and feelings of other persons, since I cannot take a look at Robert the Bruce, or a black hole, or your toothache or musings on the demerits of this chapter. The idealist notices what is wrong with naive realism, and is impressed by the amount of mental construction involved in our knowledge of things. But he infers from this that what naive and critical realists both think of as the real and objective world is nothing but a construction by the human mind. However, if the naive realist and the empiricist exaggerate the role of experience in knowing, the idealist exaggerates the role of constructive intelligence; both neglect the role of judgment and of the exercise of 'reasonableness.' The critical realist agrees with the naive realist so far as she is convinced that what we get at by our mental constructions exists and is as it is largely prior to and independently of our mental constructions, but she takes the idealist's point that mental constructions are involved in getting at it. You do not make advances in knowledge in the manner of Kepler, Darwin, or Einstein just by piling up observations. But that does not entail that such great men made up their (and our) world by their brilliant intellectual constructions.

To which traditional brands of metaphysic does what I have called 'critical realism' most closely correspond? The first Western philosopher to envisage ultimate reality as an intelligible somehow lying behind the sensible was Plato. Remarkably, he affirmed the importance of mathematics for apprehending that intelligible reality, a very long time before it became a cliché that mathematics is the language of science. The next important step was taken by Aristotle, who saw that one got to know this intelligible reality, 'things in their causes' as he put it, by dint of putting questions to experience.[9] He also distinguished, though only in passing, the two types of questions I mentioned. Now whatever was made of Aristotle and his influence at the time of the Renaissance – when he was the pretext, as Bacon complained, for the substitution of 'agitation of wit' for the detailed investigation of phenomena – science has remained, and must remain in order to be itself, a basically Aristotelian activity. After all, it can only yield an increase in knowledge of the real world so far as it asks the two types of questions we have distinguished in relation to an ever-widening range of phenomena. The next important step was taken by Thomas Aquinas. On his view, there are two aspects of reality, each one corresponding to one of the two types of question: 'whatness' and 'thatness,' essence and existence. 'One might suggest that scientists will find the philosophy they seek,' or perhaps rather ought to seek, 'by reflecting on their method and through its structure arriving at the corresponding, isomorphic epistemology and metaphysics.'[10] And this seems to turn out, in broad lines, to be Thomistic Aristotelianism. Observation is related to hypothesis as Thomist matter to form, hypothesis to verification as Thomist essence to existence.

It is time to look at common objections to the metaphysical enterprise, in the light of what has been said. Metaphysics, it is complained, does not investigate the nature and structure of reality, as it is often claimed to do, since this is done by science. If the metaphysician protests that her business is to investigate the whole of reality, while science only investigates a part, then she ought to do this by compiling an encyclopedia of the sciences, which in fact she does not do. If she maintains that she should not only assemble the results of scientific enquiry, but integrate them into a world-picture, it is by no means clear what such a thing would amount to. One possibility would be the reduction of all other sciences to physics. There might be difficulties of a philosophical nature in reducing the mental to the physical, or the organic to the inorganic, but from that point on the problems would be scientific, so once again the metaphysician's supposed special contribution would be superfluous. Another conception of metaphysics sets it in competition with the natural sciences, claiming that while they deal with mere appearances, it deals with the underlying reality. This may be attractive to those who associate science with a materialism they find unpleasant; however, it does not seem in the last resort intelligible. Certainly appearances may be deceptive, but their deceptiveness is a matter of their conflict with one another, rather than with something of another order. As A.J. Ayer says, 'What possible experience could authorize our making a distinction between appearances as a whole and a quite different reality?' Some have sought to cast mystical experience in this role. But there are no convincing arguments that such experiences, however impressive they are to those who enjoy them, yield information about anything more than their own psychological condition.[11]

On the account I have given, however, it is by no means the case that the metaphysician has the melancholy choice between being an encyclopedist of the sciences, or carrying out a physicalist reduction while prepared to deal with a few residual philosophical problems, or setting up a fruitless rival intellectual enterprise to science in the name of mysticism or whatever. The sciences, for all their differences, are at one in advancing as they do by attending to experience, propounding hypotheses, and judging provisionally as true those hypotheses best corroborated by experience. The metaphysician sets out, in general terms, of what nature and structure the world must be for this to be possible. It is on the basis of this that she may construct the world-picture (materialist, idealist, monist, critical realist, or whatever it may turn out to be) into which the particular sciences are to be fitted. As to 'appearance' and 'reality,' the wise metaphysician will admit that it is absurd to say that all appearances are deceptive. And yet, if the account I have sketched is at all on the right lines, she will have reason to say that appearances are clues to reality rather than reality itself; this is because our knowledge is achieved not merely by attending to appearances, but by investigating, hypothesizing, and judging on the basis of them. Consequently, the metaphysician does not claim that reality transcends appearances as a result of some mystical intuition; she affirms it on the basis of attention to the process of coming to know. As to the materialism apparently implicit in science, it is quite correct so far as it amounts to the view opposed to idealism, that there really is a world which we tend to get to know by scientific investigation, but it is incorrect so far as it either amounts to naive realism or self-destructively entails that the mental operations involved in knowledge are reducible to physical processes.

It may be held that the most general conceptions in terms of which we envisage the world do not belong to the world itself, but rather are imposed upon it by our understanding. This was in effect Kant's way of treating the traditional problems of metaphysics. In more recent times, what Kant explained in terms of human understanding has been seen in terms of human language, as was done by Rudolf Carnap. Carnap, as befits a logical positivist, regarded himself as a sworn enemy of metaphysics, and was understandably distressed and affronted when 'ontological' or metaphysical commitments were attributed to him. 'I should prefer not to use the word "ontology" of the recognition of entities by the admission of variables ... It might be understood as implying that the decision to use certain kinds of variables must be based on ... metaphysical convictions.' In order to cope with the difficulty, Carnap distinguished between 'internal' and 'external' questions about existence. For example, within the framework of talk about things, we can ask the internal question of whether cows exist. The external question about the existence of things would be either metaphysical and therefore meaningless or a question about whether we were to adopt a certain form of language. But Willard Quine, in opposition to Carnap, asks what the fundamental difference is between ordinary predicates like 'is a cow' or 'is odd' and ones like 'is a thing' or 'is a number.' He answers that the difference is only a matter of degree of generality. According to Carnap, 'cows' refers to cows in a straightforward way, while 'things' covertly refer to the language of things. But Quine finds this arbitrary. Why could one not just as well say that 'cows' makes covert reference to the language of cows?[12]

It will be clear from what I have said that I agree with Quine against Carnap on this matter. As is by now notorious, a thoroughgoing empiricism, such as that underlying Carnap's position, cannot be made self-consistent (how could you conceivably test in experience the non-analytic proposition that all non-analytic propositions must be capable of being tested in experience?). But clearly Carnap is right to the extent that there is some difference of kind here, in that the existence of cows is a straightforwardly empirical matter in a way that the existence of things as such is not. One might put the distinction summarily, from my point of view, by saying that questions are metaphysical when they relate to the world as it is by virtue of the very fact that it is knowable, rather than to how it just happens to be and may be found to be by investigation of experience. One can in a sense test propositions about metaphysical matters, but by appeal to the nature of knowledge as such rather than to particular items of experience.

The manner in which one might establish the existence of things – rather than saying, for example, that they were logical constructions out of sense data – is perhaps a good way of illustrating the application of the method of metaphysics I have sketched. The real world, I claimed, is what is to be known in judgments arrived at by putting questions to experience. Among such judgments, I find that a certain man called Jean Chrétien is one and the same as the prime minister of Canada in 1995. The more data I investigate which bear on the subject, the more possibilities I envisage and test, the more strongly this judgment tends to be confirmed. On the other hand, one's supposition that Bill Clinton is one and the same as the constitutional monarch of Great Britain tends not to survive such investigation. What applies to persons applies also to ordinary physical objects, 'things' in the narrower sense.[13] A sustained course of inquiry would culminate in the judgment that the block of wood lying on the table beside the front door of my house is the same as one removed from an ancient English oak a few years ago, and that the open yellow pen lying beside me on this desk is the same as the one my daughter took to school last week. So it is that judgment divides up the world into different things each characterized by its own properties and relations. Just because they (and we) are causally interrelated, it does not follow that there is only one real Thing or 'substance' (as in Spinoza's system);

just because things can be shattered and cut asunder, it does not follow that I and this pen cannot be genuine things after all (as on Leibniz's view). True, for a thing to be a thing it has to have a degree of independence of other things, and of indivisibility, but such requirements do not need to be carried to extremes to help to found the reasonable judgment that *A* is one and the same thing as *B* (as the morning star is one and the same thing as the evening star), or another thing than *C* (as the morning star is another thing than the planet Mars). And if reasonable judgment is the criterion of reality, and not experience as such, there is no ground for the radical empiricist view that things and persons are subjective constructions out of sense-data.

Aristotle has often been blamed for reading the structure of language, and in particular of the subject-predicate proposition, onto the world. Yet if the real is known in judgments, and judgments are typically expressed in subject-predicate propositions, one might say that it is a large part of Aristotle's genius that he saw that this was precisely what one had to do.

Many philosophers have contrasted metaphysics with analysis. But it seems a consequence of what I have said that every analysis presupposes a metaphysic. Suppose, for example, that, following David Hume,[14] one 'analyses' the relation of cause and effect in terms of constant conjunction between sense-data. The whole activity seems to presuppose that sense-data are real, whereas relations of cause and effect are unreal, or at least less real. No wonder that, as W.H. Walsh remarks, 'few self-styled analysts have contrived to stick to pure analysis without the open or covert advocacy of a metaphysical point of view.'[15]

Karl Popper has shown himself as more in sympathy with metaphysics than have the logical positivists, or indeed most modern philosophers. As he sees it, the role of metaphysics is to propose somewhat nebulous theories which may later be cast in a testable, falsifiable form, and so become scientific.[16] I agree with Popper that it is very important that persons should speculate in the way that he mentions, and indeed that much metaphysics has been thus useful. However, I maintain that the sort of aims which I have described have been more central to metaphysics as it has traditionally been understood. And, in fact, it may well be argued that the right metaphysic as I have sketched it amounts virtually to a making explicit of the overall view of the nature of things implicit in Popper's own thought. Popper is well known for his insistence that investigators should be very fertile in hypotheses, and stringently attempt to falsify each hypothesis in confrontation with the empirical evidence.[17] What is this but the demand for the utmost attentiveness, intelligence, and reasonableness, together with the conviction that only thus can the truth about things come to be known? And I have already argued that these principles issue in a metaphysic of a very traditional stamp.

I have tried to show that metaphysics is not only a possible but also a very important activity, that the arguments against it can be refuted, and that the prejudices against it ought to be dispelled.

While I dealt with scepticism at some length in the first chapter, this seems the context for a comment on a position often associated with scepticism, and closely allied to it – relativism.[18] Relativism is indeed not seldom asserted, or assumed, to be a necessary consequence of developments in contemporary thought. But so far from its being a necessary consequence of such developments, or indeed of anything else, I believe that it is not even a coherent doctrine, and that this can easily be shown. What is basically wrong with it is a misapprehension about the nature and implications of human judgment. It is of the essence of judgment to stake out a claim about what is the case.– not what is the case (whatever this would mean) merely for myself, the reader, the average member of the British Israelite persuasion, or the majority of the aboriginal inhabitants of Australia. It is either the case that the last dinosaurs perished from the face of the earth between sixty and seventy million years before the moment when I append a full stop to the first draft of this sentence, or it is not. It merely confuses the issue to maintain that it is so for the vast majority of professional palaeontologists, but not so for most fundamentalist Christians, when what is really meant is that members of the former group rightly or wrongly believe that the putative fact in question is the case, those of the latter, not. (And 'merely for' whom, one may ask, is the proposition true which is expressed by the concluding twenty-three words of the last sentence?) There is an instructive and amusing tale about the nonsensical tangles a university instructor in anthropology got herself into when she informed her class, which included at least one native American, that the ancestors of these people had almost certainly come over the Bering Strait between ten and twenty thousand years ago.[19] The native American protested that, on the account given by his own people and believed by himself, they had sprung directly from the soil of South Dakota. The lecturer replied that what the student had said was true in the world of his own culture, but not in the world of Western anthropologists. This story is surely a *reductio ad absurdum* of any thoroughgoing relativism, and the 'moderate' or less thoroughgoing kinds lack the merit of consistency. Certainly, the situation in the anthropology class required rather careful handling; the student should not have been told more or less curtly or contemptuously that the belief so dear to him and his people was stupid or just plain wrong. The lecturer might have been at pains to acknowledge, either at the time or in private after the class, the merits of the culture which set store by such beliefs, and even the fact that the belief itself expressed a feeling of attachment to and affection for one's environment from which people of Western culture had a great deal to learn. But she should have insisted firmly, all the same, that the student's belief was, taken literally, almost certainly false. And false, period; not false for some group or other.

It must be acknowledged that many statements are couched very much in terms of the preoccupations and immediate situation and environment of the person who makes them. But the state of affairs which makes them true or false is not often relative in the same way. A sportsman may say that there is a cock pheasant within twenty yards to the left of him; plainly the truth of this as it stands is relative not only to the time and place in which he says it, but also to the direction he is facing at the time. But let us say that he is facing north in a particular wood in England at 11:16 a.m. on the twenty-fifth of January 1996. In that case it will either be true or false, to the end of time and wherever one is in space, that within this particular area there is or was a cock pheasant. That is true or false absolutely, and not in relation to anyone whatever.

It might be asked with what right, when there are so many well-known objections in the field against me, I presume to believe in a form of scientific realism (which implies, for example, that it is vastly probable that oxygen and alpha-particles exist prior to and independently of human thought and discourse about them). And how is this to be inferred from the basic theory of knowledge, and the metaphysics derivative from it, which I have been putting forward? The answer to these questions may be deduced from what I have already said, and will be expounded in more detail in later chapters, but it seems worth while to set it out now in summary form. One tends to get to know, to believe truly and with good reasons, by attending to evidence, by envisaging possible explanations for it, and by judging to be so the explanation which best fits the evidence. The contradictory of this thesis is self-destructive; either it is itself based on evidence, and so on, in which case it is self-refuting, or it is not, in which case it is pointless to take it seriously. The task of metaphysics is to articulate the overall nature and structure of the reality which is thus to be known; that of science, to describe and explain its detailed aspects (to state *that* and *why* they are as they are). The essentials of metaphysics can in principle be spelled out here and now, as we have in the last analysis no coherent account of the real except what is thus to be known. But the conclusions of science at any one time are apt to be merely provisional, since more evidence may always turn up, more possible explanations be envisaged. This is not the case with metaphysics, however, since further evidence could not conceivably be attended to, or further hypotheses be envisaged, which would corroborate or impugn the claim that in general reality is what is to be known by judgment based upon attention to evidence and envisagement of hypotheses.

It is a great mistake, though a common one, to suppose that the limits of experience are the limits of knowledge. On the contrary, by asking questions, and coming up with hypotheses and judgments in answer to them, we can get to know, on the basis of our experience, a world (containing stars and planets, cabbages and anthropoid apes, greenfinches and hawthorn blossom, quarks and leptons) which exists largely prior to and independently of our experiences. (Are we really to say that none of these things exist, or are as they are, except 'relative' to ourselves, or depending on our experience?) When description and explanation reach a high level of sophistication, as they have done notoriously in the case of the natural sciences, they are expressed in terms of entities and properties (mass, force, electron, valency, and so on) which are not direct objects of experience, but are invoked to explain experience. While every scientific theory is in principle liable to modification – since, as I have said, there are always more experiences to be undergone, more possibilities to be envisaged – some are established as so beyond reasonable doubt. Galileo's law of free fall has been confirmed by experience in millions of instances since his time; it remains accepted, for all that it has been set in a far wider framework of explanation, as an application in special circumstances of far more general laws, than he himself could have envisaged. And however much our conceptions of hydrogen and oxygen may be modified in detail by new discoveries about the nature and behaviour of fundamental particles or whatever, it is difficult to conceive of circumstances in which it would be appropriate for scientists to deny that hydrogen and oxygen are real substances and that water is a compound of both. Rather similarly, most statements of observable fact made by those who are in a position to observe them do not have to be overturned as a result of subsequent inquiry; that the written letters on the page here and now before my eyes are black, given that it is true now (as it is if I am neither dreaming nor hallucinating), and allowing for the different ways of expressing this important proposition which would be appropriate to different places and times, will never at any time or in any place be truly denied.

It is supposed to be one of the great puzzles of philosophy how, by means of our experiences and our concepts, we get to know about a world which, except on some very bizarre assumptions indeed, exists and largely is as it is prior to and independently of our concepts and experiences. The short answer is that the world which exists prior to and independently of our experiences and concepts is nothing other than what we tend to get to know by critical assessment of our concepts in the light of our experience. But of what overall nature is this world? There is excellent reason, as Galileo and Locke saw, to suppose that the sensible qualities as such of the things and events of which it consists do not really belong to them, but are strictly speaking a matter of the impinging of light, sound, and whatever upon our sense-organs. So what really does belong to them, other than the intelligible and theoretical properties that persistent and methodical inquiry converges on attributing to them? But to suppose this is the essence of scientific realism.

Unfortunately, the metaphysics which ensues from these reflections turns out to be closely approximate to that developed by Plato, Aristotle, and Aquinas. Plato's 'forms,' like the things and properties postulated in mature physical sciences, are after all intelligible realities to be known by inquiry into the sensible.[20] For Plato, at least in some phases of his thought, the intelligible and real world of 'forms' tends to be too separated from the merely apparent world of our experience, and it seems impossible to account for the reality of change. The two worlds were brought together more firmly by Aristotle, who clearly maintained that it is one world that the ordinary person knows by experience, and that the scientist knows in a more complete and sophisticated way 'in its causes'; and he deals brilliantly with the phenomenon of change. Aquinas was to show more distinctly that the world has a 'thatness' as well as a 'whatness,' a consequence of being able to be affirmed by judgment as well as conceived by theory. Certainly it is not enough, in the light of modern thought, simply to reaffirm the metaphysical conclusions of these philosophers; to bring their achievement up to date, one has to show in detail how their metaphysics is to be epistemologically grounded. And this is exactly what I have tried to do.

But why, it might be asked, should one not be content with a merely pragmatic interpretation of the relation between scientific theory and reality?[21] This question, however, seems to presuppose an answer to another question: what is this reality to which scientific theory is alleged either to have some relation or to lack any relation? (Nothing but obfuscation is to be gained, by the way, through the use of quotation marks –

'reality' – to which some authorities see fit to resort in this context.) I have been arguing at length that reality is nothing other than what our judgments tend to affirm so far as they are as much due to attentiveness, intelligence, and reasonableness as possible. But science, when indeed it is worthy of the name, is a matter of applying this threefold process in a sustained and systematic way to certain ranges of data; it fails to tell us the truth about things, only in so far as a further application of the process would ultimately lead us to discard its assertions and the theories in terms of which they are cast. But, as I have already said, many scientific judgments are so strongly confirmed that their falsification is exceedingly unlikely. While it is sometimes said that scientific disagreements fail to be resolved in the course of time, this seems to be merely false. However odd the quantum theory may be, and however rebarbative to many people's common sense or cherished assumptions, the sheer weight of the evidence, and the impossibility of alternative ways of explaining it, has led to its general acceptance among physicists, and among the informed public due to their authority.

One reason why people seem disposed to interpret scientific theory in a purely pragmatic way is that the entities and properties with which it deals are not direct objects of experience. But on this assumption, one wonders how they deal with the things and events of the remote past and with the thoughts and feelings of other persons. What is sauce for the goose is sauce for the gander. We know about other minds and the things and events of the past not as objects of experience, but, as in the case of the theoretical entities and properties postulated by natural scientists, as objects of judgments selected from hypothesized possibilities and verified in experience. If we are to say that the latter type of entity is just a practical fiction, should we not by parity of reasoning say the same of entities of the former types? And is it even remotely plausible, even sane, to say that other people's thoughts and feelings are simply practical fictions that we use to cope with their behaviour, or that Charles I of England is merely a useful device for anticipating marks made on documents, noises emitted by professors of seventeenth-century history, and the like?

It has been pointed out that the concerns of many philosophers, especially those in the continental tradition, arise from the well-founded conviction that scientific method is inapplicable to questions of human science and to morality. But it is necessary to distinguish, in my view, between rationality itself and its special application within the natural sciences. Certainly, scientific method in the narrower sense is not applicable to ethics or the human sciences; the difference between good and bad, and the meaning of meaning, cannot be accounted for, even in principle, in terms of physics and chemistry. But it does not immediately follow that the rational method proper to these questions has no analogy or likeness to the methods of natural science. And in fact, if one attends to the basic form of inquiries in the social or human sciences, one finds that it is, in very general outline, just like that in the natural sciences. In finding out the point of a tribal ritual, or what was meant by Sallust in his history of the Jugurthine War or your grandmother in her correspondence, one attends to the data available, one hypothesizes that the author concerned may have meant a number of things by what he is recorded as writing, and one states on this basis what he probably did mean. The crucial difference between the natural and human sciences is that, in the case of the latter, conscious human subjects – whose actions are to be reckoned as more or less attentive, intelligent, and reasonable – are the objects as well as the subjects of inquiry. In finding out what Frederick the Great was up to in waging such-and-such a war, or invading such-and-such a country, we exert our own attentiveness, intelligence, and reasonableness to determine the mixture of attention and lack of attention, of understanding and limitation of understanding, of reasonableness and deficiency in reasonableness, as these would express themselves in a person of his culture and circumstances, that would sufficiently explain his actions.

'But,' it will be asked, 'are not attentiveness, intelligence and reasonableness so conditioned by the contingencies of different cultures, as to make it impossible to erect on them the general conclusions argued for in this work?'[22] For all the vast range and variety of human culture and human development, this seems to me not to be so, for two main sets of reasons. The first may be called the argument from survival, the second the argument from anthropology. Unless 'primitive' human communities and their members used their minds in the same basic ways as we do ourselves, they would not have survived. In fact, inhabitants of the primeval jungle or desert would have to be much more rational than the ordinary contemporary European or North American in noticing certain types of sensory clue, and in hypothesizing and judging accordingly about the presence of dangerous animals and hidden water supplies. Of course, it is one thing to exert these powers, another to spell out to ourselves that we exert them, and to draw the full epistemological and metaphysical consequences from the fact that we do so. In anthropology, it seems to be of the essence of the discipline that, by using our intelligence and reason on the available data, we can in principle discover what the members of other cultures are up to in doing what they do. And what could to 'be up to' something amount to, except to be acting on the basis of having certain judgments of value and fact arrived at through certain understandings or misunderstandings of a certain range of data? Any explanation of human action which did not have this general form would hardly count as an explanation of human action at all.

In the first part of this book, I have tried above all to establish the following two propositions.

1. It is self-stultifying to deny that one can speak the truth, or to deny that one tends to speak the truth so far as one makes sure that one has good reasons for what one says. Reasonable *judgments* are made on the basis of possibilities envisaged by *understanding* supposed to account for evidence in *experience.*

2. The actual world, or reality, is nothing other than what true judgments are about and properly justified judgments (those based on the widest range of experience and the widest range of possibilities envisaged to account for that experience) tend to be about.

Certain consequences appear to follow for our knowledge of what is good and bad, right and wrong. It seems evident on the face of it that we can come to properly grounded judgments on these matters, just as we can on matters of fact in the more restricted sense. On what basic criteria are such judgments properly made, and how can these criteria be established as such? Suppose someone comes up to a stranger in a public place and gives him a heavy blow in the stomach. Most of us would regard such an action as bad or wrong. Why would we do so? In what would we take the wrongness or badness of that action to consist?

It has been said that the starting point of the philosophy of Jürgen Habermas is 'the dilemma of the inadequacy of scientific methodology as a foundation for ethics, and yet the imperative need to provide some such foundations.' I agree both that there is an imperative need to provide foundations for ethics and that 'scientific methodology' in the narrower sense that I distinguished earlier is quite inadequate for the purpose; but I can see no reason why a general rational method of the kind that I have outlined should not do so. The goodness or badness of a person, action, situation, or artwork cannot be ascertained by plunging it in hydrochloric acid or applying litmus paper. But one may very well establish – as people do every day – by intelligent and reasonable inquiry into one's own needs and feelings, and by one's observation of other people's expression of their needs and feelings, that an action or policy will tend to increase the sum of human happiness or fulfilment, without fairness being impugned, or rather that it will augment the vast mass of human misery or injustice. And this is what it is a for an action or policy to be good or bad. Good people, curiously enough, tend to try to perform good actions and commit themselves to good policies, while bad people have the opposite tendency. Similarly, one may apply the threefold process to the making of aesthetic judgments, which are concerned with the extent to which works of art, or artists through their works, are liable to contribute, through satisfying by the extension and clarification of consciousness, to the overall fulfilment available in human life.[23]

It might be said that the action was wrong or bad because such conduct is against the law or is forbidden by some sacred book. But it makes sense to press the question, to ask why one should obey the law, or take account of the prescriptions of that particular sacred book or any other. It might also be said, however, that the action is bad or wrong because actions of that kind tend to contribute much more to the sum of human unhappiness than they do to the sum of human happiness, or because the perpetrator of the action cannot possibly wish that the same thing should be permitted in similar circumstances to be done to him as he has done to his victim. In these cases, to press the question would scarcely make sense. If someone asked, 'But what's good about increasing the sum of happiness?' or 'What's bad about doing to others things you would not at all care for others to do to you?,' we would hardly know how to answer. Such characteristics of good and bad actions are, as one might put it, of the essence of such actions; someone who does not know that they have such characteristics is ignorant to that extent of the very meanings of the terms 'good' and 'bad' in moral contexts. ('But what's wrong with torturing young children for the fun of it?') It is in acknowledgment of this that utilitarians have sought to analyse 'good' in terms of the greatest happiness of the greatest number, and Kantians, in terms of the universalizability of the maxim in accordance with which an agent performs an action.[24]

Let us say that an action is 'fair' so far as it measures up to the criterion of universalizability. In that case, one may say that fairness and contribution to happiness are *of the essence* of moral goodness. But herein lies a pitfall for the unwary. It may be that in some, or even most, cases 'X is Z, in that it is Y,' without its being the case that in all instances where X is Z, X is Y. Many actions may be morally good, in that they tend to promote the general happiness, without it being the case that whenever an action is morally good, it tends to promote the general happiness.[25] On the whole, an action will at this rate be morally good so far as it is fair and so far as it contributes to the general happiness. But it does not follow from this that occasionally, by way of exception, an action may not be good even if it contributes to the general happiness – for example, if it is very unfair. The well-worn example of the innocent person 'punished' in order to placate a raging mob would fall into that category. Similarly, one might perhaps conceive of examples where an action's contribution to the general happiness was so great that a minor transgression against the principle of fairness would not count decisively against its goodness. Fairness and contribution to happiness may be of the essence of moral goodness, in the manner that I have outlined, without its being the case that, by way of exception, an action might be good although it is unfair, or an action might be bad although it tends to bring about the greater happiness of the greater number. Neglect of this fact leads to views in ethics which are both bizarre and dangerous, for all that they were quite recently very widely established, according to which to call an action 'good' had essentially nothing to do with any quality or result of the action itself, but was merely a matter of evincing a positive emotional attitude towards it, or bringing it about that more actions of that kind should be performed in the future.[26] It may be protested that one should hesitate to describe such respected opinions in such a disrespectful way. But it seems to me that an account, according to which the goodness of an action has nothing essentially to do with whether it promotes happiness or diminishes misery or whether it is fair, is bizarre and dangerous if anything is so.[27]

However that may be, for the remainder of this book I shall take it for granted that, other things being equal, fairness and contribution to overall happiness are indices par excellence of whether an action is good. It is not difficult to extend the application of the principle from the assessment of actions to that of persons and states of affairs.

The questions of metaphysics are commonly, and surely quite correctly, believed to have an important bearing on those of religion. Although I have written *ad nauseam* on this subject elsewhere,[28] it seems inappropriate to omit the topic altogether.

As is well known, Kant said that there were three central questions of metaphysics, those of God, freedom, and immortality. To cut a very long story very short, he thought that theoretical reason could neither prove nor disprove the reality of any of the three. Such alleged proof or disproof would involve applying the categories of cause and effect, thing and property, necessity and contingency, and so on, which were proper for the understanding of experience and so to the realm of appearances, to the realm of things in themselves, which is beyond the range of our experience. Such a proposition as 'Every event has a cause' is not true by definition, nor is it gathered *a posteriori* from experience (or we would be in no position to assert it); it is imposed *a priori* upon experience by the operations of our minds, and we have no good reason to suppose that it is applicable to things in themselves. While we must acknowlege that a rigid determinism applies to us as appearances, and so as subject to scientific law, this is not incompatible with our being free in ourselves. Against the opinion of David Hume,[29] Kant held that a person could not submit herself properly to the moral law, unless she believed herself to be free in a sense which was incompatible with physical determinism. (His point is that one cannot really deserve praise or blame for an action which one could not, given all the circumstances, do other than perform.)[30] As rational beings we are directly aware of a moral law to which we are subject – a law which demands that we should always treat other people as ends in themselves and not merely as means, and act towards them in such a way that we could will the principle underlying our action to become universal law. (The reason why it is wrong to rob a blind person is that I can hardly wish that if she were sighted and I were blind she would be entitled to rob me.)[31]

Now we ought, according to Kant, to act dutifully for duty's sake, and not on condition that we will in the long run be the happier for it. However, we should hope it to be the case that the highest good might ultimately be realized, of our achieving perfect purity of will and of happiness being apportioned to desert. Yet, surely few facts are more certain than that these desirable states of affairs do not obtain, if only the present life is taken into account. For it to obtain there must be a life after death awaiting human beings and an omnipotent God to ensure that justice is ultimately done.[32] I feel that there is a certain ambiguity in Kant's position on this matter. On the whole he seems to be saying that because these states of affairs are morally desirable and theoretical reason when properly understood can tell neither for nor against them, one ought to believe them, but sometimes he seems rather to be maintaining simply that we should act *as though* they were the case.

My own view is that Kant's argument does establish what one might call the existential relevance of religious belief, as entailing a state of affairs that persons of good will ought to wish was so. (The doctrine of karma has much the same function in some Eastern religions as belief in God and an afterlife in another world has in Western religions; it is to the effect that there is a kind of impersonal law in the nature of things which ensures that in the long run, over a series of reincarnations, every agent is punished for blameworthy, and rewarded for praiseworthy, actions.) But, in spite of Kant's authority (on one possible interpretation), I do not believe that the existential relevance of religious doctrine does anything whatever to establish its truth. On the contrary, one might say that the reason why religious belief is so widespread a phenomenon in human culture, even though it is false, is that, in those societies which have lacked it, not enough people were motivated to act for the general good when to do so went against their own individual interest, and so those societies perished. (I understand that the late Leo Strauss maintained that the fact that such beliefs as those in providence and the afterlife are false is something that can be endured with sufficient equanimity only by the wise, and should be kept by them as a closely guarded secret, otherwise society will inevitably fall to pieces.)[33]

I agree with Kant, and with other respectable people, that one ought to strive to act rightly not only if there is no short- or long-term reward, but even if there is a short- or long-term penalty to be incurred. But I do not think that there really follows the conclusion which is frequently drawn from this, that the eschatological prospects offered by the religions are completely irrelevant to morality. In this life, people are often punished not only *although* they are good, but *because* they are so. It was undoubtedly virtuous, but far from prudent, to harbour Jews in Nazi Germany, or to campaign for civil rights under the Soviet regime. Those of good will, even if they are themselves so virtuous as not even to wish that their own good conduct should be rewarded with happiness or at least that it should not be punished, can hardly wish a like fate to others, especially those whom they love. The present life is not notably kind to those who 'hunger and thirst after righteousness.'[34] An unquiet conscience may be uncomfortable, but it is scarcely more so than the misery that can be inflicted on a person, and on her family, by the full resources of a modern totalitarian state.

So one might say that there is reason to hold that it would be a good thing if one of the great religions, or something with equivalent eschatological implications, were true. What kind of evidence or argument, if any, would be such as to support or impugn the truth of a religion? It is a necessary condition of the truth of many religions that there should be a God. But does it even make sense for there to be a God? Positivists have denied this, more or less on the ground that nothing could count as seeing, hearing, or smelling God.[35] But it is difficult to see what would count as seeing, hearing, or smelling a theoretical entity postulated by physicists, or another person's thoughts and feelings, or a thing or event of the remote past; and it would be odd for that reason to rule out as meaningless discourse about such things. By 'God,' we mean something like a beneficent intelligent will which conceives all possibilities and wills those which actually obtain, rather as we human beings conceive and will our own immeasurably more restricted actions and products. This notion seems to make obvious sense at first sight, as is suggested by the fact that it is in such common use, but there may be some underlying logical flaws. We can see and hear human agents themselves, but we cannot apprehend the alleged divine agent by our senses. Is there perhaps some latent contradiction in the notion of a conscious agent who cannot in any circumstances be perceived? Suppose it is after all conceivable that such a being should exist.[36] Is there any further reason to suppose that it actually does so?[37] The existence and quantity of evil in the world would seem strongly to suggest the latter; on the other hand, the intelligibility of the world, its amenability to the kind of explanation which is exemplified by the sciences, might best be accounted for as due to an intelligent creative agent. Such a being could even at a pinch be regarded as in a sense benevolent, if the merciful ultimately obtained mercy, the mourners were comforted, and the meek inherited the earth.[38]

What of 'immortality' or life after death? (The thoughtful reader will note that one could have the latter without the former, if one continued for a limited time reincarnated or as a disembodied soul.) Some have suggested that the thinking, inquiring, judging, and deciding aspect of human consciousness must up to a point be independent of the sensible manifold into which it inquires, and that this degree of transcendence of the sensible and bodily indicates that it is liable to continue in existence after the dissolution of the body.[39] Others would argue that such accounts as this rely on a faulty account of our mental faculties, and furthermore, that every advance in brain physiology and related sciences tends to confirm the view that our thoughts and feelings are ineluctably dependent on our bodies, and so there is no survival of bodily death.[40] On the other hand, it is sometimes claimed that there are certain experiences undergone by the living which are scarcely explicable except on the hypothesis that at least some of the dead are self aware and occasionally willing and able to communicate with us.[41] Others would argue that the greater part of the alleged phenomena can be most economically accounted for as due to delusion or fraud, and the remainder are susceptible to more mundane explanation.[42]

There remains freedom. Most theists who are not Calvinists would agree that, if anyone goes to hell, it is by their own fault, and that the possibility of such fault depends on the radical notion of freedom which is incompatible with determinism. Some have argued that the very idea that human beings might be 'free' in this sense is radically confused. A 'free' action in this sense, they say, is one that is not determined, so presumably it must be arbitrary. But that an action is arbitrary consorts no better with the agent's freedom in performing it than its being completely determined by its preconditions. If, to the consternation of my students, I suddenly stand on my head during one of my classes and sing the Marseillaise in Hungarian, the students will not suppose that I am merely expressing the freedom of will which is my birthright; rather, they will think, and probably quite correctly, that the degeneration of my brain, which they have suspected for some time, has now reached an advanced stage. Appeal to the indeterminacy which is now so notorious a feature of physics, even supposing that it applies at the level of human action, can be similarly contested. On the other side, it might be insisted that indeterminacy of this kind is only a necessary, not a sufficient, condition of human freedom. Furthermore, could not explanation of free human action be of a kind which does not exclude the possibility of there having been alternative outcomes, even when all the preconditions are taken into account? To explain why I went to lunch how and when I did is not the same as to explain why I could not but have thus gone to lunch. A determinist might object that such explanations are incomplete. But the indeterminist might retort to that objection that it presupposes determinism to maintain that explanations of human actions which are complete in this sense are always in principle available, and so cannot be used as an argument for it. One might consider a typical case of moral conflict to illustrate the point. A man has a passion for cream buns, but not the wherewithal to buy any. However, he sees a tray loaded up with the objects of his obsession, and the vendor is temporarily out of sight. Shall he help himself, or shall he refrain from doing so? The precepts of his revered but long-dead grandmother incline him to abstain; the intensity of his cravings urges him to fall to. Whichever course of action he takes, it will be explicable, and hence not arbitrary. To say that whichever is the strongest impulse must ultimately win out is, again, to presuppose determinism rather than to furnish an argument for it; perhaps, in the case of true moral conflict, there simply does not happen to be an impulse which is 'stronger' in this sense.[43]

So arguments for and against God, freedom, and immortality may go back and forth. My object here is not to establish any religious or irreligious conclusion, but to indicate how metaphysical and other considerations might help to establish a case for or against some forms of religious belief.

PART II: ANGLO-SAXON ATTITUDES

5

Limits of Sociology: Wittgenstein, Bloor, and Barnes

What I have argued so far is in fundamental conflict with the statements and assumptions of many recent philosophers and sociologists. Thus one might well infer, from a number of passages in Ludwig Wittgenstein's *On Certainty*, that that philosopher held (i) that all justification is within a system; (ii) that the system ultimately depends not on what we see or perceive, but on how we act; (iii) that how we act, and the system of presuppositions which depends on this and within which all argument makes sense, differs radically from place to place and from time to time; yet (iv) that we feel inclined to say that the possibility of such a system and of the way of acting which underlies it depends on certain facts.[1]

The moral may be, and has been, drawn as follows. As human beings living in the place and at the time that we do, we have certain assumptions about how things are which are not questioned, and which are inextricably bound up with our whole way of living and acting. It is useless to ask how these can be justified, since all attempts at justification themselves presuppose them. Other human beings at other places and times have presuppositions which are utterly different from ours; to say that these are not justifiable, or to say that they fail to represent the truth about the world, is simply to emphasize their difference from our own.

According to this view, what is to count as evidence on any matter and why it is to do so are simply up to human groups to determine; and there is no criterion, apart from disagreement with other groups, by which such a decision could conceivably be wrong. According to the usual understanding of what is meant by 'rational' and what is meant by 'evidence,' at least some members of some societies can, by rational consideration of evidence, come to know what would have been the case even if they had never considered that evidence, or indeed even if they and the societies of which they are members had never come into existence at all. Such, it would usually be supposed, is our knowledge of white dwarf stars and of plesiosaur. If this is so, then the nature of rationality and evidence is dependent on what is the case prior to and independently of social convention, and not merely on social convention. If they did depend entirely on social convention, we would not be able to employ them to determine what is the case prior to and independently of social convention. It would follow that natural science as generally understood is impossible, and that the universe which we are supposed progressively to come to know by its means would be a social product, rather than society being a product of the processes of the universe, as science would unite with common sense in maintaining that it is.

As examples of writers who have interpreted Wittgenstein to this effect, I take the sociologists Derek Phillips and David Bloor. To be sure, Phillips states that Wittgenstein's later work provides a middle ground between the absolutist and relativist extremes in the theory of knowledge. But the alleged middle ground soon subsides into an extreme form of relativism. 'I am rejecting the conception of objectivity as correspondence with some mind-independent, and therefore mind-inaccessible reality in itself. Rather, I conceive of objectivity as that which meets public, intersubjective standards for warranting objectivity in particular scientific communities.'[2] But it may be asked in virtue of what, apart from mere *fiat*, the methods and standards of communities dignified by the epithet 'scientific' are more 'objective' than those of groups of astrologers, Catholics, schizophrenics, Taoists, or confidence tricksters, unless one assumes that they are especially suitable for gaining knowledge of a reality which exists prior to and independently of their investigation of it.

Phillips maintains that Wittgenstein's later work is directed against the assumption that words in an utterance are somehow correlated with objects for which the words stand. 'This idea assumes that all language has a particular use or employment, and Wittgenstein insists that there is a "multiplicity of language-games."' But the mere existence of a multiplicity of language-games has no such implication as Phillips claims. It only implies that, if it is a function of language to make assertions about a reality which exists largely prior to and independently of human communities and their languages, this is only one of its functions.

At the end of his book, Phillips raises the question of how the views which he himself puts forward are to be justified; never did a writer more conspicuously saw off the branch on which he is sitting: 'What validates the view of reality and science set forward in this volume? After all, I cannot argue that my view corresponds to "true" or "authentic" reality, to the way things "really" are.' And what if his reader persists in holding views contradictory to his own? 'If I wish to avoid exempting myself from my own thesis, I cannot meaningfully speak of false consciousness or mistakes here – as if I had some privileged access to reality ... and could compare the way things "really" are with your false and mistaken ... views. No, I must in the final analysis rest content with my *commitment to* a conception which I find more comfortable, pleasing, and useful *for* me.'[3]

A very similar account of Wittgenstein is to be found in an article by David Bloor. The status of logic and mathematics, says Bloor, is one of the central problems in the sociology of knowledge. As he sees it, Wittgenstein's work on the foundations of mathematics 'shows how sociology can penetrate to the very basis of these topics.'[4] The error which Wittgenstein exposes, we are told, is that of seeing mathematics and logic 'as being about a body of truths which exist in their own right independently of whether anyone believes them or knows about them.' This error can be avoided, according to Bloor, if one characterizes properly the activities of counting, calculating, and so on which are at the basis of mathematics. It is often protested that, if these do not reflect absolute necessities, they must merely be subject to individual caprice. 'Wittgenstein avoids this dilemma by stressing social processes.' In one passage of his *Remarks on the Foundations of Mathematics*, he takes that process of using a formula which is basic to arithmetic and shows 'the necessity of embedding it in standardized social practice. The crucial terms are sociological; "the way we always use it," "the way we are taught to use it" ... from this perspective, every instance of the use of a formula is the culmination of a process of socialization.'[4]

If we are thus trapped in our own procedures, it might be asked, how can we attain a vantage point from which we can study with fairness procedures different from our own? Bloor's answer is that 'one set of taken-for-granted procedures can be utilized to study another set.' Bloor thinks that his conclusions on logic and mathematics apply *a fortiori* to other kinds of knowledge; there is no truth which is not simply 'truth for' some special group, no valid form of argument which is not merely a form of argument accepted by a social group. If it is not the case in logic or in mathematics that the investigator's behaviour 'is structured by the pre-existing logic of the connections that he is exploring,'[5] still less is it the case in the study of the fabric of the heavens, the structure of the atom, the campaigns of the Duke of Marlborough, or the evolution of the marsupial mammals.

I have already said something about the consequences of such extreme conventionalism and relativism, and will have more to say below. But now I shall try to show how a more plausible and useful account of the ultimate conditions of justification, and of the relation of language to the world, may be come to on the basis of the passages I alluded to at the beginning of this chapter and other similar remarks of Wittgenstein. On occasion he talks about *the* language-game as though there were in a sense only one such.[6] This invites a speculation which may perhaps prove fruitful. Is there by any chance a set of basic assumptions and procedures implicit in all use of language whatever, or at least in all use of language for stating what is the case, and not simply an indefinitely large range of assumptions and procedures which differ radically according to place and time? Are there any grounds for holding that there is such a set, or even – canvassing a possibility that Wittgenstein in his last work does seem definitely to reject[7] – of justifying the assumptions and procedures? Wittgenstein speaks of our knowledge as forming part of a system. Is it possible to give some account of this system and its presuppositions, to find out what we take for granted as committed to the system, and perhaps to consider also how far we are right to take it for granted?

I argued in the first chapter that it can be shown that it cannot but be the case that we tend to come to make true judgments, and thus to get to know what is the case about the real world, so far as we go about it in the right way; and that the right way to go about it is, first, to attend to evidence, second, to think up a range of possibilities that might account for it, and, third, to judge as (probably or certainly) the case that possibility which seems best supported by the evidence. Philosophers have rightly looked for the foundations of knowledge and for the place where, in Wittgenstein's phrase, 'language hooks onto the world,' in propositions that are certain, but they have wrongly tended to identify this certainty either with analyticity or with direct confrontation in experience. The reasons for supposing that such foundations will not support the fabric to be raised upon them are rather well known; I have already had something to say about them.[8] But there is a third kind of certainty that tends to be overlooked, which I think Wittgenstein at least adumbrates in *On Certainty*, that the foundations of knowledge and of *the* language-game so far as there is just one, consist in propositions whose contradictories, though not self-contradictory, are yet self-destructive in the manner which I sketched. The certainty of these propositions consists not in their immediately striking us as true, but rather in that we discover that they could not but be true once we have attended to their implications.

In interpreting what Wittgenstein has to say in the *Philosophical Investigations*, Roger White seems to come close to what I have been suggesting: 'In imagining certain features of our world not to have obtained, one may be imagining the world to be such that it would be impossible to formulate the propositions which men do in fact utter.'[9] Whatever it is that must be true about the world for people to talk about it at all may be said to constitute a kind of *a priori*. In the early *Notebooks* Wittgenstein wrote: 'The general question round which everything that I write turns is: is there an order in the world *a priori*, and if so what does it consist in?'[10] Roughly, one might put it that, if what I have been saying is on the right lines, the *a priori* order which is in the world is to be discerned from the method that we have of coming to make true judgments; given that the judgments that the world is what true judgments are about, and that we are able in general to come to make true judgments by a method which is in principle reliable, are such that their negation is self-destructive. However, Anthony Kenny has adduced a number of texts which indicate that for the rest of his life, from the *Tractatus* onwards, Wittgenstein upheld the doctrine that any proposition which can be true can be false, with a consequent rejection of any synthetic *a priori*.[11] And in the *Grammatik* Wittgenstein says that 'the rules of grammar cannot be justified by showing that their application makes a representation agree with reality.'[12] But, so far as this implies, as I think it does, that we cannot show that by using our thought and our language we may come to speak about a world which existed largely prior to and independently of us and our language, it seems to be false for the reasons which I have given. At this rate, it could remain that every non-analytic proposition which could be true could be false, in one sense of 'could' though not in another. Some assertions, that is, while not self-contradictory, are yet self-destructive.

I think that Wittgenstein comes quite close to such a position, and thus in a sense to vindicating the *a priori* after all, in what he has to say about doubt in *On Certainty*. He maintains that there is a difference between cases where doubt is unreasonable and where it is logically impossible, though he denies that there is a clear boundary between the two kinds of case. That Cartesian doubt is self-destructive, in that it seems to call in question the very meaning of the terms used to express it, is hinted many times in *On Certainty*. You can only doubt, as Wittgenstein rightly says, where you can test. He adds that tests presuppose what is not doubted or tested, and that 'our doubts depend on the fact that some propositions are exempt from doubt, are as it were like the hinges on which those turn.'[13] What is the nature of these hinges on which doubt turns? Do they differ with the doubt, or with the social milieu of the doubt, or are they the same always and for everyone? Of course, either the first or the second is right if one means what is taken for granted as a matter of fact in particular instances of doubt. But if one means those assumptions upon which all doubt depends, and on which it ought to depend, then it seems to follow from what I have argued that the third must be right. For what is not doubted, so long as doubt remains coherent, is that one can in principle get at the truth by the threefold mental process described in the first chapter. And if there are no 'hinges on which doubt turns' which are and ought to be always the same for everyone, one is inevitably plunged into conventionalism and relativism.

It is true that 'I did not get my picture of the world by satisfying myself of its correctness,' and very likely indeed that 'it is the inherited background against which I distinguish between true and false.'[14] But the fact that one's picture of the world does not come to one with a critical basis does not entail that it cannot be supplied with one. And once it is thus supplied, there are means for distinguishing in principle between those aspects of one's inherited view of the world which certainly or probably get it right and those which get it wrong.

Of the theses tentatively ascribed to Wittgenstein at the beginning of this chapter, it looks as though we were committed to acceptance of the first and fourth and to rejection or modification of the second and third. Thus (i) all justification is within a system; (ii) the system ultimately depends not on what we see or perceive, or even on how we happen to act, but rather on how we cannot but judge of things on pain of self-destructiveness in our judgments; (iii) consequently there are limits to the variation from place to place and from time to of the system of presuppositions within which all argument makes sense; and (iv) the possibility of such a system, and the way of acting which goes with it, depends on the fact that the world cannot but be of such a nature that it is possible for us to make true judgments about it which are based on good evidence.

If true, these conclusions are important, as I shall try to bring out in the following rather apocalyptic remarks, and in somewhat more sober fashion throughout the rest of this book.

Let us consider the following three propositions, of which the first two are incompatible, the third compatible, with what I have argued so far.

(1) That each world-view, ideology, or religious stance is true for the person, group, or society which holds it. The question of its 'truth' in any more absolute sense does not arise.

(2) That some actual or conceivable world-view, ideology, or religious stance is absolutely true, but cannot be shown to be true, or more likely to be true than its rivals, on general rational criteria available in principle to every intelligent person.

(3) That some world-view, ideology, or religious stance is absolutely true, and can be shown to be true, or at least more likely to be true than its contradictory, on such general rational criteria.

I shall have a good deal to say about the first proposition, in the course of which I hope to bring out a few of its many absurdities, later in this chapter. What about the second? Hume said, in a famous phrase, that while errors in religion were dangerous, those in philosophy were merely ridiculous. Here, I believe, is an exception; the second proposition is very dangerous indeed. Either basic differences about how the world is, and what one ought to do about it, are trivial or people will be concerned to resolve them. They are hardly trivial, since people's whole way of life and the ends they pursue and think worth pursuing depend on them. So people will certainly try to resolve them, or at least to secure sufficient basic agreement on them for society to go on functioning. General principles of rationality, *ex hypothesi*, do not exist to be invoked; coercion, with the guns and the thumb screws, is the only way left.

Someone might object that, even if the second proposition has consequences which are pretty frightful from a practical point of view, it might still be true. *Reductio ad horrendum*, to coin a phrase, is not the same as *reductio ad absurdum*, and the possibility of the former in any instance does not entail the possibility of the latter. But the second proposition can scarcely be true if, as I argued in the first chapter, there is a non-contingent connection between the truth about things and what we tend to get to believe by following the principles outlined there. What is wrong with it can be succinctly set out in the maxim, *quod gratis affirmatur gratis negatur* (what is gratuitously affirmed is gratuitously denied). As Marx put it in an early article, if you claim that your own position is not to be argued for, why should not the same be claimed for a quite different and incompatible one?[15]

The third proposition seems to be the only one which is acceptable. Radical empiricism and scientism, on the one hand, and the older forms of natural theology, on the other, are odd bedfellows, but both are committed to it. They agree that, unless there are good reasons, which do not assume what has to be established, for believing, for example, that there is a God, one ought not to believe that there is one; where they differ is in their account of what the good reasons amount to, and consequently in their actual theological conclusions. The *Tractatus* seems to help towards providing a way of supporting the third proposition; here, we appear to be told, is how we are to come to speak of a world which exists independently of and prior to our thought and speech about it. Wittgenstein's later position, which may so easily be interpreted as issuing in the first and second propositions, is partly due, according to Roger White,[16] to his conviction that the *Tractatus* position, while it could not be sustained, was the only alternative. The empiricism which culminated in the work of Bertrand Russell and the logical positivists was one way of supporting the third proposition. I believe that empiricists are right in insisting that a general criterion for getting at the truth, or at least for moving towards it, can and should be found, but wrong in their account of what that general criterion is; it is this, and not the third proposition itself, which is in my view really refuted by the arguments which have been used against them by Wittgenstein and others whom I shall discuss in the course of this chapter. Wittgenstein's influence, I believe, ought to be a powerful incentive to finding out a better articulation of the manner in which the truth about things can in general be found and should in general be sought, since he has brilliantly brought out so many of the difficulties in the way. If I am right, the upshot of his work is by no means to show that these central traditional problems of philosophy can now be set aside, but to demonstrate just how important and indeed urgent they continue to be.[17]

Relativist views of a more or less extreme kind are sometimes argued from the point of view of the sociology of knowledge, as has been done in a very striking way by David Bloor and by Barry Barnes. I shall summarize their views in the rest of this paragraph and in the following two. The sociology of knowledge, they say, is often taken in effect to be applicable only to the systems of belief which one happens to think are erroneous. But this restriction should be resisted; all systems of belief are the proper concern of the sociologist of knowledge, and not simply those which some people in some cultures, including the sociologist of knowledge herself and her colleagues, happen to hold to be inadequate or untrue. Whether modern physicists' beliefs about electrons, or Azande beliefs about witch substance, are at issue, it must be insisted that the acquisition, maintenance, and transmission of systems of belief are subject to social factors which are similar in all cases.[18]

Empiricists are liable to object that, while modern scientific beliefs on the whole correspond with the data of experience, those characteristic of 'primitive' people do not do so. It is interesting to note that, before the atomic theory was universally accepted by physicists and chemists, just the same kind of objection was made to it as to these 'primitive' beliefs; atoms were not observable, and so ought to form no part of a truly scientific theory. But atomism won out, and the empiricists shelved their objections; this was because acceptance of the theory facilitated the performances characteristic of the professional specialities concerned. Now Sir Karl Popper's criterion of scientific method, that statements should be falsifiable and accepted as provisionally true only if they survive attempts to falsify them, is supposed to constitute a cross-cultural criterion of approach to truth; but in fact it is merely a recommendation by a rather influential person in one culture. And in any case it has been shown[19] that a conscientious adherence to Popper's principles would in fact have ruled out from the start most of what are now agreed to be the significant discoveries of science, since these have been propounded and maintained in the teeth of conflicting evidence. In the long run, it must be concluded that all 'proof,' 'justification,' and 'validation' boil down to modes of behaviour and ways of speaking which are characteristic of the way of life of particular social groups, and which cannot be further justified; this was one of the outstanding discoveries of the later Wittgenstein. The moral of all this is that scientists, including social scientists, should simply get on with their job, whether or not they are preoccupied in their spare time by methodological problems which are in the nature of the case incapable of solution.[20]

People have often objected to this recognition that there are different societies which have totally different theories as to the nature of the world, between which an unprejudiced rational adjudication is impossible, on the grounds that it seems to entail that there are as many different 'worlds' as there are divergent views of the world. But this conclusion by no means follows from the premises. One may just as well hold that, for all the divergent and indeed incommensurable views that there are of the world, we all live together in the one physical world, a basic tenet of materialism.[21]

Thus far a summary of the views of Bloor and Barnes. I strongly agree with them that sociologists should use the same principles to investigate and explain all systems of belief, whether they themselves hold them or not. I further agree that 'rational' procedures are not the monopoly of any one society, culture, or profession. But I have already argued that true belief, which is about the one real world, is not merely relative to the social context of the believer, but tends to be arrived at so far as a certain set of mental procedures is stringently followed. I believe that social factors can more or less encourage or frustrate the following of these procedures, and that the investigation of the manner in which they do so is the proper business of the sociology of knowledge.

What is involved in the assumption that we can come to know anything at all? Let us take an example. Suppose I come to know, either by being told or by working it out myself from the evidence, that the planet Jupiter is larger than the earth. The belief that it is so is one that many human beings within many societies have not held, and which would have been regarded as ridiculous had it been suggested to them; only some persons in some societies have known that Jupiter is larger than the earth. Now I want to suggest – not immediately to insist or to argue – that, if we know this, if we believe it truly, then what we know and believe truly was the case before there were any human beings or human societies to know it, and indeed might well have been the case if no human beings or societies had ever come into existence, and almost certainly will be the case long after human beings and their societies have perished from off the face of the earth. (We will consider later on the implications of the thesis, actually held by few but implied by surprisingly many, that it is not really true, in the last analysis, that human beings or societies come to know, or to believe truly on the basis of sufficient evidence, that things are so which would have been so even if they had never come to know them.)[22] I propose to call this putative capacity of human beings, and of the societies of which they are members, who exist at particular places and times, to know what is so at quite different places and times, and would have been so even if they had not known it, 'cognitive self-transcendence.'[23]

I deliberately did not make my first example mathematical; had I done so, I would have fallen foul of certain theories about the nature of mathematics which can be made at least to sound plausible. I wanted to avoid the fate which Karl Mannheim suffered at the hands of David Bloor.[24] Mannheim was concerned, as I am, to attack the view that knowledge and truth were utterly relative to the social situation of the knower; he pointed to mathematical truths as examples of truths which were not thus relative. In the light of Mannheim's claim, Bloor was able to assume that, if the very paradigm of absolute knowledge, mathematics, could be shown to be subject to social relativity, the same could be shown *a fortiori* of other sorts of knowledge. Bloor argued, as we have seen, a conventionalist theory of mathematics, on the basis of some texts from Wittgenstein, and the job was done. But in my opinion Mannheim made a tactical error of which Bloor took brilliant advantage. After all, one might be prepared to swallow the view that numbers and the relations between them were social constructions, and yet jib at the proposition that the stars in their courses are so.

A few other examples of the self-transcendence apparently involved in knowledge will serve to push home the point I am making. Suppose I come to find out, by looking at a textbook or listening to a university lecturer in ancient history, that the Athenians defeated the Persian army at Marathon in 490 BCE. On the usual view of historical inquiry, where self-transcendence is involved, whether this happened or not has nothing to do with anything anyone can do in the twentieth century CE; neither I nor society as a whole nor even the community of professional ancient historians can bring it about that there was or was not a battle of Marathon or influence the course of that battle in any way. However, I and other persons can find out, by consideration of evidence and deference to reasonable authority available in the 1990s, that such a battle, with the issue I have already described, actually took place. In this instance as in the other, it is apparently the case that we can come to know, by dint of experience and inquiry, what would have been the case if we had never existed, let alone had the experience or made the inquiry.

Someone may object as follows: That the planet Jupiter is larger than the earth and that the battle of Marathon as you describe it really happened are true only in and for some societies; for others, Jupiter is not larger than the earth, and there was no such battle. The idea that there is a real world independent of conceptual frameworks ignores the fact that, if there were, we as social beings subject to these frameworks could have no access to it. The curious thing about this view is that, though it seems to deny that self-transcendence is possible, it does at the same time assume its possibility and reality. For it implies that we are able to make true assertions about persons of other societies, to the effect that their conceptions of and beliefs about history and the cosmos are different from our own. Suppose I am an anthropologist, and I conclude from the evidence available to me that the planet Jupiter is much smaller than the earth from the point of view of the society which I am investigating, though it is larger than the earth from the point of view of my own society. Consider this conclusion itself. Is it true simply *in* the world-view of my society; or is it true *of* the world-view of the society in question? If the former, the possibility of my making any judgment whatever which is really about the beliefs of other societies (that is, about those beliefs themselves as opposed to those as somehow constitutive of my own world-view) would seem to be removed. If the latter, it follows that self-transcendence is possible; by consideration of evidence available within my own world-view, the world-view of my society, I have come to a true conclusion about what is the case independently of me and my society – in this instance, about the beliefs and conceptions characteristic of the world-view of another society. I conclude that denials of the reality of cognitive self-transcendence, so far as they are argued on anthropological grounds, in fact necessarily presuppose it.

Is there anything in common among these examples of self-transcendence, and can we spell out clearly and distinctly what it is? It might be claimed that there is nothing in common between inquiries as to what is so in cosmology, history, and anthropology, perhaps even that the term 'inquiry' is itself equivocal as applied to these examples. It has in fact been suggested that the belief that there is any single set of mental qualities and dispositions exercised in all sorts of inquiry, in all kinds of attempt to come to know, is sheer superstition.[25] But I think it can be demonstrated that there are, all the same, such basic mental qualities and dispositions, as I argued in the first chapter. And in all the examples of coming to know which I have mentioned in the last few paragraphs, three things seemed to be at issue: attending to a range of evidence available to sensation or consciousness; envisaging a set of possible explanations which might account for that evidence; and accepting as probably or certainly so the member of the set which appeared best to account for the evidence.

It seems as well to clarify the point just made by more examples. When one is considering the grounds that there are for choosing between Rutherford's theory of the atom and the account earlier advanced by Thomson, one attends to the manner of particle scatter when the atoms are bombarded; this is highly unexpected on Thomson's account, but is easily explained on Rutherford's, there is nothing which similarly tells for Thomson against Rutherford; so Rutherford's theory is to be accepted as the more probably true account of the nature of the atom. Here there is sensory evidence to be attended to, on photographic plates and so on; two incompatible explanations are available, both of them dealing with a wide range of the evidence, but only one of them accounting for a crucial portion of it; and a judgment accordingly is to be made that that one is probably so. Just the same method is applicable in a law court. What is available to the senses of the jury are exhibits and the reports of witnesses. On the basis of these, the jury will have to judge which of two possibilities the evidence tends to support – that the defendant is guilty of the crime of which he is accused, or that he is not.

It is to be noted, as very characteristic of cases of cognitive self-transcendence, that while the evidence available to sensation or consciousness in such cases cannot but be present in time and space, that which is judged to be the case on the basis of the evidence needs by no means be so. The court, on the basis of evidence here and now, is attempting to judge here and now whether the defendant is guilty of a crime supposed to have been committed there and then. If Rutherford was right in supposing, on the basis of evidence available to him at the time, that the atom consisted of a comparatively tiny nucleus surrounded largely by empty space, then this has been true of atoms long before human societies, let alone the community of twentieth-century physicists, let alone Rutherford himself, let alone this particular course of inquiry of his, ever came into being.

There is, of course, a sense in which the truth or falsity of a statement may partly depend on the context within which it is uttered, rather than on the actuality of the state of affairs to which it refers. To take a trivial instance: the truth of 'Barry Barnes is in Edinburgh now' depends on the time at which it is spoken. To take a more interesting and contentious example: suppose one were asked, in a social milieu within which the phlogiston theory of combustion was generally accepted, whether a sample of pure metal contained phlogiston; I think it might be less misleading to say 'It is true that it contains phlogiston' rather than 'It is false that it contains phlogiston,' even granted the falsity of the phlogiston theory itself. So far as the scientific theories that we now hold are in future shown to be false, by further employment of the method through which we arrived at them in the first place, the same will be found to apply to statements made in terms of them.

I have tried to make it clear by the examples discussed what would be involved in cognitive self-transcendence; that is, the capacity to come to know, to make grounded true judgments about, what actually is so, and not just 'so for me' or 'so for the members of my society.' The next question is whether such self-transcendence is really possible. The notion that one can come to speak the truth, to say what actually is so, rather than 'true for' or 'so for' just oneself or one's community, seems to entail that there are valid criteria of truth and standards of validity (in the sense of methods appropriate for the arriving at and preservation of truth) which are trans-social in character. But, it will be answered, it is difficult or impossible to see how there could be such criteria or standards or, even if somehow there were, how we could have access to them. For we are members of societies, and affected not just peripherally, but through and through, by the fact that we are so. Our concepts of 'truth' and 'validity,' like all our other concepts, are socially determined; thus we cannot come to assert what absolutely is so, rather than what is so for ourselves or our society. Thus it seems that cognitive self-transcendence is impossible.

However, the consequences of denying the possibility and actuality of self-transcendence, as I shall now try to show, are far more awkward than those of asserting it. To deny self-transcendence, as a possibility at least, is to be forced to the most amazing conclusions. Let us take the judgment 'Some of the dinosaurs had secondary brains in the rear part of their bodies' and assume for the purposes of discussion that it is true. This judgment, made here and now, has reference to a state of affairs which was the case many million years ago. Has it been so only within our culture, since the experts on the field within our culture started saying that it was so? Or was it so there and then? If the former, it seems to follow that human experts living in the nineteenth and twentieth centuries made to be the case something which was the case millions of years before they came into existence – a remarkable feat of retrospective creation indeed. But if the latter, the experts came to believe truly what would have been the case even if they had never come to believe it, and thus provided an example of cognitive self-transcendence. Apply the moral to astronomy and you will find that, on the former supposition, not only dinosaurs, but the stars in their courses, are created by society, or rather by the experts within society. So far from its being the case, as one might have supposed, that the existence of human beings and their societies depends on a whole series of interlocking conditions within the cosmos, these conditions themselves, having no nature or existence over and above the conception and affirmation of them by members of societies, are created by these societies. Human society, or rather that part of it which supports scientists, so far from being a product of the cosmos, is its creator. I submit that this is a little hard to swallow, particularly when one adds the rider that, given that this portion of society has some conception of itself and affirms its own existence, it is self-creative. But the only alternative position to the one that leads to these apparent absurdities is that which entails the actuality and possibility of what we have called cognitive self-transcendence.

But not only does denial of the possibility of cognitive self-transcendence, and the consequent espousal of social relativism, lead to these astounding consequences, it is actually self-destructive, for the kind of reason that I mentioned at the end of the first chapter. Consider the judgment that social relativism is true, that is to say, that no judgment is true except in relation to the social milieu within which it is made. Is this supposed to be true of all judgments whatever, in whatever social milieu thy may be made? If so, it is itself a judgement supposed to be true universally and not merely in relation to some social milieu, which is incompatible with its own truth. If, however, it is not supposed to be true of all judgments in all contexts, but only true for a particular group, then it is no longer a judgment to the effect that social relativism is true in the sense under discussion. It would appear that this judgment, that social relativism is true, purchases its essential generality only at the cost of self-destruction.

I have just argued that cognitive self-transcendence must be possible and must really occur. The next questions which arise are when and how does it occur, and what follows from the fact that it does so? In what circumstances, and why, do human beings escape relativity to social milieu, to such a degree that their judgments are about what is so, and would have been so in many cases even if the social milieu within which the judgments are made had never existed?

I attempted earlier to sketch the three basic mental capacities involved in cognitive self-transcendence, in coming to know what is really so; these were attentiveness to data available to sensation or to consciousness, intelligence in thinking up possible explanations for the data, and reasonableness in accepting from among these the explanation which is best satisfied by the evidence. The limits of the sociology of knowledge derive from the fact that it cannot rule out cognitive selftranscendence as impossible on pain of self-destruction. Its scope – and in my view, in opposition to that of some philosophers, it is a very important subject indeed – is the description and explanation of those features of societies which foster the exercise of attentiveness, intelligence, and reasonableness, and so promote cognitive self-transcendence, and of those which on the contrary tend to act against them. That these basic faculties are trans-social, that what they are and that they are is not simply a matter of social *fiat*, seems to follow from the fact that the consequence of their not being so would be self-destructive. Truth in judgment and validity in argument are achieved so far as attentiveness, intelligence, and reasonableness are exercised as far as possible;[26] and it appears from what I have said that these too are trans-social.

The profound differences between the belief-systems of different societies, which are of course a commonplace of contemporary sociology and anthropology, are perfectly well accounted for on this view. Every society encapsulates in its language and institutions a stock of factual and moral judgments, each of which is due to a certain degree of attentiveness, a certain degree of intelligence, and a certain degree of reasonableness.

Short of the assumption of some such basic uniformity between human beings and social groups, it seems to me, the anthropologist and the historian are debarred *a priori* from understanding human groups radically different from their own. But the nature of this basic uniformity involves no more than what is involved in the possibility of cognitive self-transcendence; and self-transcendence is achieved whenever anyone comes to make a true judgment about what is so. Contemporary anthropologists are surely right, against many of their predecessors, that a satisfactory account of a society must indicate why it is to some extent positively attentive, intelligent, and reasonable in its members to hold the factual and moral beliefs, and engage in the activities, that they do. But it may also be the case that such a belief or activity prevails only because certain evidence has not been available or, if available, has not been attended to; or that certain possible explanations of the evidence have not been envisaged at all; or that some of the explanations which have been envisaged have not been fairly and squarely confronted with the evidence and accepted or rejected accordingly.[27] This applies, it must be insisted, just as much to the beliefs and activities which prevail in the anthropologist's own society as to those in the society that is the object of his study.

That our concepts of truth and validity are social products does not entail that truth and validity themselves are so, any more than the fact that the concept of the solar system is a social product entails that the solar system is so, short of principles which, as I have argued, are self-refuting. Our society, like every other society to a greater or lesser extent,[28] puts us in touch with a method of arriving at or at least approaching the truth about things which is trans-social. Our community with its language and institutions provides us with the fruits of attentiveness, intelligence, and reasonableness as exercised so far, mixed in with what is due to failure in attention, restriction in intelligence, and defect in reasonableness. Each of us contributes in his own way to the process, either in such a way as to tend to advance knowledge of the truth in himself and others or in such a way as to obstruct or reverse it. Thus, with respect to any judgment of fact or of value taken for granted by one's community or by oneself so far, one can ask on what evidence it is based, whether there is some more satisfactory way of accounting for the evidence, and so on. Contrariwise, one can suppress all such inquisitive tendencies in oneself, and employ ridicule and other punitive measures to prevent them in others.[29]

It may be objected that different individuals can apply the same degree of attentiveness, intelligence, and reasonableness, and still adopt radically distinct and conflicting beliefs. This is certainly true – particularly of those to whom different aspects of the relevant data have been readily available. If Smith has met the colonel only on the parade ground, and Jones has met him only in the kitchen directed by his wife, they are liable quite reasonably to form very different judgments of his overall character. However, it is by no means inconsistent with this, and I believe can be argued from what I have already said, that there must in such cases tend to be at least a convergence towards agreement so far as the parties concerned attempt attentively, intelligently, and reasonably to pool their resources. What another person who has experience relevant to X says about X itself constitutes data likely to be relevant to my own knowledge of X. If Smith or Jones want a rounded view of the colonel's character, they had better listen to one another. When I disagree with someone about something, I am likely to progress in my knowledge of it by asking how far the opposed party has been more attentive to the relevant data and so on than I myself have and how far less so on the matter about which we disagree, rather than, as so often happens, each engaging in a kind of gang warfare on behalf of her own opinions. What social conditions tend to support the former state of affairs, and what the latter, are among the most important questions to be asked by sociologists of knowledge.

I believe that some persons have been driven to embrace social relativism through a very proper revulsion against what is called 'cultural chauvinism.' Why, it has been quite rightly asked, should we assume that our 'civilized' Western view of things is any more correct than the views of people whom we see fit to dismiss as 'savages'? If my argument so far has been on the right lines, we need make no such assumption, but need not be relativists all the same. In considering the beliefs of members of other communities, when these are opposed to our own, we may well have good reason to wonder whether, on certain matters at least, they have not been more effectively attentive, intelligent, and reasonable than ourselves. Thus I may well, after studying some anthropologist on the Kachin belief about 'nats,' in conjunction with Robert Crookall's books on evidence for the existence of discarnate persons, come to the conclusion that the Kachins are likely to be correct in their belief that some such beings exist, the anthropologist wrong in her belief that they do not.[30] However, the very practice of anthropology is committed to at least as much 'cultural chauvinism' as is entailed by the belief that, to a degree which has not on the whole been possible before and elsewhere, we in our culture may come to understand the beliefs and the institutions characteristic of other cultures. In one respect it can hardly denied that the anthropologist of my example has the edge on the average Kachin, so far as she is in a position to study and evaluate Kachin beliefs, but they are in no such position in relation to her beliefs. Anthropological studies may well issue *de jure*, even if they have not yet generally done so *de facto*, in at least as much criticism of our own culture by comparison with alien cultures as vice versa. By attending to the results of their attentiveness, intelligence, and reasonableness, we are able to find hints about the deficiencies in our own. This account, of course, so far from tending to relativism, is not even compatible with it; it assumes that what is so is to be known by the maxims involved in self-transcendence, including listening seriously to the opinions of other people, both inside and outside our own cultural milieu.

Every person of every culture who ever said anything true is capable of self-transcendence; natural and human sciences, including anthropology and the sociology of knowledge, come into being when the operations involved in self-transcendence are applied with persistence and thoroughness. It is this which gives the physicist the edge over the ordinary human being in what he says about the constitution of the stars and atomic nuclei, the anthropologist the edge over the average person in his own culture in what he says about the beliefs and customs of persons of alien cultures. I do not deny, indeed I would emphatically assert, that a Kachin could be in the same kind of position in relation to our anthropologist's beliefs and customs as our anthropologist is in relation to the Kachin's, if she exercised her capacity for self-transcendence thoroughly and persistently .

I have heard it claimed that there should be no such study as the sociology of knowledge, only the sociology of belief.[31] However, on the assumption that knowledge is true belief backed up by appropriate reasons,[32] the sociology of knowledge will have important tasks distinct from those of mere sociology of belief. It will not simply investigate the question of what people hold what beliefs and why they do so; it will attend particularly to the question of how far their beliefs are due to the exercise of that attentiveness, intelligence, and reasonableness which is liable to make those beliefs true. It will draw attention to the well-documented tendency of some members of institutions, even of institutions bearing the proud title of scientific, to brush aside inconvenient evidence, and to exert pressure on those who impugn established theories for however good reason. It will be 'value-free' in one sense of that much-abused expression, but not at all so in another. It will be so in that it subjects to examination, without fear or favour, the beliefs characteristic of social groups, and attempts to determine, as attentively, intelligently, and reasonably as possible, how far these have been determined by attentiveness, intelligence, and reasonableness, and how far by an irresponsible[33] flight from these due to intellectual inertia, party spirit, or unwarranted deference to, or contempt for, authority. It will not be at all 'value free' so far as truth is a value, and since it is interested in ascertaining the truth in general, and in particular the degree to which social groups foster in their members and in others dispositions liable to be productive of judgments which are true, as opposed to expressions of ignorance or of positive error.

Sociologists of knowledge have a way of explicitly denying the possibility of cognitive self-transcendence, but all the same in effect assuming its possibility and reality, as indeed they must, in relation to their own work. Robert Bierstedt, having clearly and distinctly set out the difficulty, says that it is insoluble, and signs off with a quotation from Kant to the effect that human reason can raise more questions than it is capable of answering. Judith Willer distinguishes between four kinds of 'knowledge' (the empirical, the mystical, the magical, and the scientific) between which she says that we have and can have no principles for rational comparison or choice; however, she concludes her book with a passionate, and on her own showing irrelevant, plea for the scientific kind against the others.[34] Bloor and Barnes follow much the same pattern. They assume the possibility of cognitive self-transcendence in what they say about social groups and the manner in which they try to establish that what they say is so, and that what their opponents say is not so; for all that their insistence that every criterion of truth or validity reduces to social convention entails that cognitive self-transcendence is impossible. Their claims that their position is compatible with materialism, and that there is just one 'world' rather than as many 'worlds' as there are views of the world, provide a nice illustration of the point.[35] Let us consider two interpretations of 'materialism': that it is merely the basic conventional assumption of a certain cultural group, no more true or false, no more or less soundly based, than the basic conventional assumptions of any other cultural group about how things are; or that it claims to represent how things basically really are, in a way that its rivals (for example, idealism, theism, and phenomenalism) do not. In other words, one may mean by 'materialism' either something that is merely *true for* a certain group of people or something that is *true of* the world. I dare say that most of those who have called themselves 'materialists' would agree with me that the latter is the only 'materialism' worth the name, but the former is the only 'materialism' which is compatible with the basic assumptions and arguments of Barnes and Bloor. Just the same applies to their belief (which I share, but for different reasons) that there is only one 'world.'

6

Primitives and Paradigms:
Winch and Kuhn

Some writers, as I have said, defend the proposition that we all inhabit one world as compatible with a thoroughgoing relativism. Others infer from relativism, more consistently I think, that those with different world-views really inhabit different worlds. Thus D.Z. Phillips writes: 'The saint and the atheist ... see different worlds ... Religious language is not an interpretation of how things are, but determines how things are for the believer.'[1] I want first to show that there is one sense in which Phillips's claim is certainly true, another in which it is at least rather implausible. This will provide me with some distinctions which will be useful in approaching Peter Winch's important and influential paper, 'Understanding a Primitive Society.'[2]

According to the theist, things and events of which the world of our experience consists are to be envisaged as due to the activity of God. If by 'the world of A,' I mean the totality of things and events that A believes to exist or to be the case, and A acknowledges the existence of God while B does not, it is quite plain that 'the world of A' differs from 'the world of B' in that the one includes God and the other not. In this sense of 'world,' too, we can say that the world of those scientists who lived before J.J. Thomson's great discovery did not contain electrons, whereas the world of scientists since his time has contained them. Similarly, one can say that the world of the Europeans who antedated Columbus did not contain America, whereas that of those who have lived since his time certainly does so.

But we are also inclined to say that there were electrons, or that electrons existed, before Thomson discovered them. If we did not, indeed, we would be more inclined here to talk about 'invention' than 'discovery.' Few would wish to say, to take another example, that the planet Neptune

only began to exist when human beings first came to know about its existence – when it first became a part of their 'world' in the sense that I have
given – in the 1840s. A few decades ago, again, no one knew of the existence of quasars. And yet it would be rather odd to say on these grounds
that there were no quasars, that the world did not contain such things,
until scientists first suggested that it did. There is thus a sense of 'world,'
at least as closely corresponding to that in ordinary language as the one
that I have described, in which the world did contain quasars before a
couple of decades ago, electrons before the time of Thomson, oxygen
before the time of Lavoisier. Let us distinguish 'the world' in this second
sense, which has contained quasars and electrons for many millions of
years, as the 'objective' world, from the various 'subjective worlds' of persons of particular physical or cultural environments, which may or may
not contain America, quasars, oxygen, the planet Neptune, or electrons. I
should add that I do not wish to beg any questions by my use of the terms
'objective world' and 'subjective world,' which should be understood for
the purposes of my argument here in exactly the senses which I have outlined.[3] (Of course, quasars and electrons form part of the objective world
in my sense only if the future pursuit of scientific method, which is nothing more nor less than engagement in the mental activities involved in
cognitive self-transcendence, does not tend to reject these notions as mistaken; if it did so, we would have to say that quasars and electrons form
part of the subjective world of persons of our particular place and time,
just as 'phlogiston' and 'the ether' formed part of the subjective world of
persons of other times and places, but do not form part of the objective
world.)

The second half of my quotation from Phillips makes me wonder how
he would deal with some of the cases I have cited. On his view, would a
chemist who used the concept of phlogiston and not that of oxygen and a
chemist who used the concept of oxygen and not that of phlogiston both
be interpreting in their different and apparently conflicting ways how
things were? Or would their respective languages merely determine for
each of them how things were for her? The first way of putting the matter
is such as to suggest that one or indeed both ways of describing things
might be wrong, might fail to describe them rightly; to use my own terminology, it brings out the question of how far the subjective world
enshrined in these theories corresponds to the objective world (assuming
that there is such a thing). The second way seems either to fail to attend
to this question or to assume that there is no objective world over and
above the subjective world of different human individuals and communi-

ties. But this last assumption appears to lead to positions to which almost no one (except perhaps Protagoras) would wish to commit herself, such as that no belief, either of general theory or relating to particular matters of fact, is ever false, except by virtue of internal inconsistency or incompatibility with other beliefs of the same believer. What the flat earther believes is true only if it is consistent with his other beliefs.

I said at the beginning of this chapter that I wished to say that Phillips's claim is in a sense certainly true and in a sense rather implausible. It is certainly true so far as one's 'world' and 'how things are' for one means the sum of things which one believes to exist or to be the case, but rather implausible so far as it means the sum of things and events which a person or community would tend to believe to exist and to be the case so far as she or it had considered justly all the relevant evidence. Clearly God exists in the subjective world of the theist, but not in the subjective world of the atheist. Furthermore, the atheist would be perfectly willing to admit that God exists in the subjective world of the theist. But, however it stands with Phillips, I am sure that most theists would wish to say that God exists in the objective world, and most atheists that God does not so exist, in the plain sense that if the belief which characterizes theists is correct, that which characterizes atheists is incorrect, and vice versa. Atheists do not deny that theists construe events, which they and theists acknowledge to be part of the objective world, in terms of the activity of God; they merely claim that theists are wrong in doing so. This is as much as to say that the theist and the atheist have contradictory interpretations of how things are in the objective world, just as phlogiston and oxygen theorists do (given, as I think may quite easily be shown, that for there to be phlogiston is for there not to be oxygen, and for there to be oxygen is for there not to be phlogiston). So far as theists and atheists live in the same world (and they do live in the same objective world, though they do not share the same subjective world), they interpret it differently. Thus Phillips's statement must be wrong, except on the supposition, with which few theists or atheists would agree, that for the theist to be right is not for the atheist to be wrong, and for the atheist to be right is not for the theist to be wrong.

I think that Phillips would likely urge that, while the question of existence in the objective world arises in the case of alleged physical objects or chemical substances, it does not do so in the case of God.[4] I do not suppose that he would hold the very notion of an objective world, as I have outlined it, to be based on an erroneous assumption. This would seem to lead to the paradoxical conclusion that Neptune did not exist before the

1840s, since it certainly did not exist in any human being's subjective world, and that there was no oxygen, for similar reasons, before the time of Lavoisier. But Professor Winch's paper, 'Understanding a Primitive Society,' raises questions which appear to make it highly problematic how far what I have called the objective world is distinguishable from the subjective world of one's own place, time, and culture. As Winch sees it, to say that we are correct in believing that people cannot be bewitched, and that the Azande are incorrect in believing that they can, is simply to impose on the Azande a conception of the correctness of belief which happens to apply within our own culture. For him it seems, to use my terminology, that questions of truth and falsity arise only within particular subjective worlds; consequently, we cannot make coherent sense of, let alone presuppose, a conception of truth and falsity which puts in the right, as having a correct view of the objective world, the subjective world of one particular culture as against the subjective world of another.

I think that this reduction of the objective world to the subjective worlds of particular individuals or communities, which seems to be the consequence of the general trend of Winch's argument,[5] is wrong both in the milder form, where it applies to the notions of religion but not to those of science, and in the stronger form, where it applies to both. But in order to vindicate this view, it is necessary for me to give some account of the nature of the objective world, such as differentiates it from subjective worlds, including my own. Very summarily, I wish to argue that every subjective world consists of a mesh of assumptions about what is the case, and that subjective worlds approximate to the objective world so far as these assumptions would, if they were put to the test, turn out to be justified. Every subjective world is, in fact, a complex of more or less explicit hypotheses about the objective world, whatever other function it may have in regulating the lives and the feelings of those who share it, and the critical attitude consists in making these assumptions explicit, testing them, and rejecting those that turn out to be false.[6] It is above all a matter of exercising the mental capacities of attentiveness, intelligence, and reasonableness discussed in the first chapter.

This critical attitude, I would hold, though it is certainly thoroughly developed (if arguably in a rather one-sided way)[7] in the natural sciences, exists to some degree wherever there is language. Winch rightly claims that rationality is a concept necessary to any language,[8] and thinks it is not too difficult to show both *that* this is so, and *in what sense* it is so. It would seem that wherever a language has reached that degree of development at which a state of affairs can be stated to be the case or not to be the case – which is as much as to say wherever a collection of ordered noises or gestures amounts to a language at all – the possibility will arise that a statement will be made alleging a state of affairs to obtain, which in fact does not obtain. Let us suppose that a primitive language applies the term 'swooth' to those statements the states of affairs corresponding to which are not deemed to be the case, 'bikki' to those statements the states of affairs corresponding to which are deemed to be the case. Thus the sentence which means 'The lagoon has sharks in it' will be said to be 'bikki' by one who believes the lagoon to have sharks in it, 'swooth' by one who believes the lagoon not to have sharks in it. It is evidently easy in principle to see how a tribesman could go through a procedure of investigation which would establish the matter one way or the other by sensory evidence, at least to a high degree of probability. And it is important to notice that it is essential to the concept of 'bikki,' as I have outlined it, that while evidence might have accumulated in such a way as to render it highly probable that a statement is 'swooth,' it tends not to do so in the case of a statement that is 'bikki.'

It seems to me that the word 'bikki' in the hypothetical language which I have described may properly be said to mean the same as our word 'true,' and the word 'swooth,' the same as our word 'false.' I am not denying that 'true' has a wider sense than 'bikki,' given that the use of the term is confined to the kind of context which I have mentioned. For instance, we are inclined to say sometimes that a person is true to her word, or that a whale is not a true fish. Let us suppose that in the tribal language we do not have a usage of either of these kinds with 'bikki.' In this case, rather than saying that 'bikki' does not mean 'true' after all, I think it would be better to say that, while 'bikki' does have the same basic meaning as 'true,' one could not correctly use the word 'bikki' in its language in all the contexts in which one could in English correctly use the word 'true.' This is because the meanings of 'true' in 'true to his word' and 'true fish' can be elucidated by reference to the meaning of 'true' as applied to statements, in a way that 'true' as applied to statements cannot be elucidated, at least at all readily, in terms of the meanings of 'true' in 'true fish' or 'true to her word.' A 'true fish' is an animal to which the essential characteristics constitutive of being a fish can correctly be ascribed, an animal of which certain statements are true in a sense which corresponds to 'bikki,' as opposed to one which, like the whale, has a collection of properties only superficially resembling those of fish properly speaking. For similar reasons, a tree sparrow is a true sparrow, a hedge sparrow not. Again, a person who is true to his word is one of whom it turns out on the whole to be the case that, when he says he will do X and not do Y, he does X and does not do Y. In fact, what he says is true in the sense corresponding to 'bikki,' in that when he says he will do something, he does it. Thus I want to say that the sense of 'true' with which I have been particularly concerned is in some sense basic, in that other senses of the word may be explicated in terms of it, in a way that they cannot be explicated in terms of one another, and in which it cannot be explicated in terms of any of them.

Someone might ask: What about a society whose concept of truth has nothing to do with this turning out of a state of affairs to be the case when it might not have been the case? I think that the whole idea of such a 'concept of truth' is nonsensical, since such a concept would not seem to have the minimal characteristics that a concept must have in order to qualify as a concept of truth at all. It seems to me that truth as conceived by the ideal scientist, though not always by those who speak in the name of science, is a thorough working out of the implications of this minimal concept of truth, for reasons which I set out in the second chapter. I understand that it was implicit in the world-view of the Aztecs, and the conceptual scheme which enshrined it, that if they were to stop performing the sacrifices, to us horrifying, which had been traditional with them, there would be a catastrophic convulsion of the elements. They were forcibly prevented from performing them in the end, and no such disaster as their world-view had led them to expect actually took place. To bring to light, and where possible to test, the factual implications of conceptual schemes seems to be of the essence of the comprehensively critical attitude. As Winch expounds them, Azande beliefs about witchcraft are hedged about with prohibitions such that they cannot be tested in this kind of way.[9] But this by no means shows that they are not really dependent on factual assumptions, or that these factual assumptions might not conceivably be tested – for example, by suspending all practices which were supposed to counteract the influence of witches on people's fortunes, and seeing whether the persons concerned were on the whole worse off as a result. There seems to be a difference of degree rather than of kind between these examples and some of the most recondite theories of modern science. On theories accepted previous to Einstein's general theory of relativity, you would expect either that observations of successive positions of the planet Mercury would be slightly different from what they actually are or that there would be found to be a small planet between the orbit of Mercury and the sun. Einstein's theory accounts for the actual movements of Mercury, without the postulation of a planet which has never been observed, and which our instruments would certainly be sensitive enough for us to have observed by now had it existed. Thus the subjective world which includes Einstein's theory is closer to the objective world than that which contains Newton's, so far as expectations about what is the case implicit in the latter turn out to be false, and contrary expectations about what is the case implicit in the former turn out to be true.

If we have here a concept of truth which is not culture-relative, it does not seem too difficult to derive a similar concept of rationality from it. If we say that a human being is rational to the degree that, wherever possible, she investigates the grounds for her beliefs and the actions based upon them, then we seem to have a concept of rationality which is basic in the same sense as our concept of truth. It will be seen that rationality is a matter of being attentive, intelligent, and reasonable in the senses suggested above, and truth that which tends to characterize our judgments so far as they are rationally grounded.

'There is no way of getting outside the concepts in which we think of the world ... The world *is* for us what is presented through these concepts. That is not to say that our concepts may not change; but when they do that means our concept of the world has changed too.'[10] To contradict what Winch says here would seem to commit one to the paradox that we can have a concept of what lies beyond our concepts; but it is just my contention that, in the relevant sense, we can. Our subjective world is precisely what is immediately presupposed by our conceptual scheme, and so, to be sure, when our concepts change, it changes. Our concept of the objective world is, by contrast, indirect; it is our concept of what our successively corrected conceptual schemes will or would approximate to so far as the errors involved in it are brought to light and rejected. I want to insist, in opposition to Winch, that *that* concept of the world does not change. The assumption made by nineteenth-century physics, that there must exist an ether at absolute rest in relation to which all else moved, was one which could be tested once technology was sufficiently far advanced. The assumption was duly tested, by the Michelson-Morley experiment, and found to be groundless. Thus, we see quite clearly the manner in which the subjective world which included the ether failed to correspond with what I have called the objective world. We can also see in principle how the objective world may, and indeed certainly will, fail to fulfil some of the assumptions implicit in the subjective world of contemporary science. Not, of course, that we can altogether get outside the conceptual scheme in terms of which we immediately envisage the world here and now; but we can do so to the extent that we can conceive of a limit towards which ultimately tends that critical correction of conceptual schemes which has gone on up to our own time, which continues now, and presumably will not terminate at this day or hour.

It might well be objected that the manner in which a concept like 'witch,' which forms a component in the subjective worlds of some ages and cultures, represents or misrepresents a feature of the objective world (if it does so at all), differs totally from the manner in which concepts like oxygen and the ether, on the one hand, or statements like 'There are sharks in the lagoon,' on the other, represent or misrepresent it. But all these, statements and concepts alike, have in common that they appear to presuppose, so far as they do not actually state, certain states of affairs to be the case which could be shown by investigation to be probably true or probably false. It does seem to be of the essence of witches, as the Azande believe in them, that they exert evil influences on people which can be averted by suitable precautions. It appears to follow that, if the precautions were not taken, the evil results would ensue. If they did not ensue, no doubt there are a number of manoeuvres by which the applicability of the concept 'witch' could still be argued; but just the same applies to discredited scientific concepts like those of phlogiston and the ether. Winch devotes a good deal of ingenuity to showing that there are no empirical consequences of the applicability of the concept 'witch' which are such that, if they were found not to obtain, the concept would absolutely have to be jettisoned[11] – but this would appear to apply to scientific concepts as well. He also suggests that Azande accounts of causation, at any rate so far as the evil influences of witches are concerned, might be quite different from our own notions of causation.[12] But if they were so different that, in the Azande view, it made no difference to the 'effects' whether the 'causes' were operative or not, it is difficult to see in what useful sense they could be called accounts of causation at all. That there may be within the society concerned all kinds of prohibitions against the relevant tests being made is not to the point, as I have already argued.

E. Evans-Pritchard is taken to task by Winch for his assumption that his own views, as determined by scientific culture, are 'in accord with objective reality,' whereas Azande beliefs about witches are not. Such an assumption, according to Winch, implies that for Evans-Pritchard 'the concept of "reality" must be regarded as intelligible and applicable outside the context of scientific reasoning itself.'[13] If reality is identical with what I have called the objective world, which is the term to which subjective worlds approximate so far as they are exposed to rigorous criticism, I think it can be shown that the concept of reality does transcend 'the context of scientific reasoning,' at least in one sense of this phrase. It seems essential at this point to distinguish between two senses in which a belief may be 'scientific.' First, it may be scientific in that it is held, whether critically or not, by persons who belong to a culture which has been strongly influenced through science, and by scientists themselves. Second, a belief may be scientific in that it tends to be justified by that constant testing of one's assumptions, that ensuring that they are scrutinized with the greatest possible attentiveness, intelligence, and reasonableness, which may be held to be the essence of science. Let us distinguish these as scientific (a) and scientific (b) beliefs. If what I have said is on the right lines, scientific (b) beliefs are what tend to be arrived at by a consistent and thorough pursuit of truth, in a sense of 'truth' which, as I argued above, may reasonably be held to be universal among users of language. The condemnation of witches as incompatible with scientific (a) belief is liable to be, to be sure, a case of mere cultural tribalism, of uncritical denigration of the values of other cultures which, rightly condemned by Winch, has seemed characteristic of much anthropological writing. But assertion that belief in witches is incompatible with scientific (b) beliefs may be worth taking a good deal more seriously; it is then to the effect that factual assumptions integral to belief in witches could be shown to be false by a thorough search for 'truth' in a sense of truth held, if I am right, implicitly by the Azande as well as ourselves. This may be a matter by no means of cultural prejudice, in that it is quite consistent with the conviction that many of our own most cherished scientific (a) beliefs are themselves false. If I acknowledge that beliefs which are scientific (b) have a claim which is unique in degree with regard to truth, it is by no means inconsistent with this for me to stigmatize as stupid or insensitive the uncritical dismissal of any belief which is rarely if ever held by those who hold scientific (a) beliefs. Nor indeed is it incompatible with my admitting that such 'unscientific' beliefs may sometimes enshrine certain just conceptions of the objective world of things and persons which our own scientific (a) beliefs have misrepresented, possibly owing to a dogmatism which is too apt to confuse temporary doctrines of scientists with that genuinely scientific and critical attitude which gave rise to them in the first place and constitutes them as scientific.

I think it is useful at this point to distinguish between two conceptions which we may have of 'the truth.' First, we may mean by 'the truth' what we here and now believe to be true on our more or less formally or informally tested hypotheses about the world. Second, we may mean by it what we would believe if this critical attitude were given indefinite scope over an indefinite period of time. This accounts for the paradox that we believe that a great deal of what we now believe to be true will turn out to be almost certainly false in the light of later inquiry and reflection. This is not to say that there is any one proposition which we at once believe to be true and to be false; it is merely that, unless we have a very strange view of the relation of our own age to what precedes and will follow it, we are likely to admit that a fair proportion of the propositions and theories to which we now give assent will turn out to be false, though naturally we cannot specify which. This ambiguity in our conception of truth, and so of reality, and the manner in which we can, as it were, get a purchase on the first concept of truth from the point of view of the second, does not seem to me sufficiently adverted to by Winch. The truth transcends our belief about what it is, and the belief of all other individuals and communities as well. This is because the results of our understanding of, and reflection on, our experience up to now are not necessarily the same thing as what would result from a more sustained, disciplined, and enthusiastic exercise of attentiveness, intelligence, and reasonableness than we are now able to achieve.

Winch is surely quite right to insist that 'magical' beliefs are a great deal more than causal theories in our sense; but I think he is wrong to argue as though they did not have this element in them at all. R.G. Collingwood, whom Winch cites with approval, distinguishes between true magic, which is a means by which its practitioners may stimulate themselves and others to activity deemed to be useful, and the perversion of magic in false causal theories.[14] But there seems to me to be persuasive definition involved here; Collingwood has no reason that I can see for calling the first kind of activity true magic except that he approves of it, or for calling the second a perversion of magic except that he deplores it. So-called rain-making ceremonies, one would have thought, are paradigm cases of magic; and I cannot believe but that these are meant, by learned and vulgar alike within the societies that engage in them, to cause rain, and not merely to encourage assiduous husbandry in those who take part in them, or to express the importance of rain for their way of life and very survival. That they also have these values and functions, I do not deny; and it is proper and salutary for Collingwood and Winch to have emphasized this aspect, as a corrective to so many writings on 'magical' beliefs and others characteristic of primitive societies. 'Civilized' societies probably have a great deal to learn from societies which they see fit to denigrate as 'primitive,' both in respect to the manner in which actions and ceremonies may be expressive of one's way of life and attitude to things and people and with regard to more practical concerns – like the therapeutic influence on some forms of mental disorder attributed to tribal dances. But to deny that magical beliefs also characteristically enshrine this element of assumption as to matter of fact is to go too far.

On the view that I have advanced, it is quite easy to see in what way beliefs which are 'magical' or otherwise alien may be deemed to be rationally defective, without being absolutely irrational or unintelligible, by those who do not share them. One may understand the way of life of a group by seeing how it is quite rational to act as they do if one believes or assumes that certain facts are the case, without oneself believing that these facts are the case. This enables one to avoid the extreme hypotheses of relativism and dogmatism – that each culture has its own standard of rationality which is just as good as that of every other culture, and that our own assumptions and theories about how things are are the only 'rational' or even 'intelligible' ones. The truly critical person subjects the assumptions of her own culture to rational scrutiny, in the kind of way that I have described, and not just the assumptions of other cultures. Winch is quite right to point to the danger of our simply criticizing other assumptions on the basis of our own, as though these last constituted some transcendent standard. But he does not advert to the existence and applicability of a standard of truth and rationality which transcends the limits of particular cultures; and this is the only means by which one may find a safe path between his own relativism and the dogmatism of his opponents.

What I have said about magical beliefs applies equally to religious beliefs, at least as they have nearly always and nearly everywhere been understood. In attempting to understand these, too, one must try to grasp both how they are indicative and expressive of the whole attitude to life of those who subscribe to them (the question on which authors such as Phillips and Winch concentrate their attention) and on what assumptions about matters of fact they are based. It is basic to the belief of most Christians, for example, that certain remarkable events occurred at some time in the past, and that certain other remarkable events will happen in the future. (Anyone who does not know what these alleged events are can find a convenient summary in the so-called Apostles Creed.) Hope or fear of the future, based on promises corroborated by signs supposed to have been given in the past, make quite rational and intelligible for the Christian (or Moslem or Jew) behaviour which would not otherwise be so. Phillips would wish to hold, I think, that religious belief has no bearing on the actual run of events in nature and history,[15] but on any objective analysis, traditional religious beliefs do have such a bearing. Thus this element of dependence on putative matters of fact seems to be as characteristic of religion as of magic. The unbeliever in any system of religion or magic need not insist that the system in which she does not believe is wholly irrational or unintelligible – what has fascinated the minds and hearts of human beings and determined the course of their lives could hardly be that; but she may hold that it depends on postulates or assumptions which, although they could perhaps conceivably be true, will be shown by detached and thorough investigation to be probably or certainly false.

Someone will protest that I have underestimated the vast divergences in behaviour and world-view which divide human individuals and societies. But it may be wondered whether certain uniformities do not have to be assumed if we are to explain at all the beliefs and actions of human beings in societies which are very different from our own. Plato is presumably not quite right in maintaining that we could not get to know anything unless we really knew it already; but at least it is not useful to ask a question, or to pursue an inquiry, unless one has at least an inchoate notion of the kind of thing that would constitute a satisfactory answer to the question or termination of the inquiry. It is of no use coming across the solution to a problem unless one can recognize it as a solution. What is it, in the human sciences, that is equivalent to the assumption underlying the natural sciences, that every phenomenon is susceptible to theoretical explanation? If there were no such equivalent, psychology, sociology, and anthropology would be pointless activities. I suggest, following Lonergan, that the requirement in the case of the human sciences is that every properly human action, disposition, and production can be accounted for as due to some compound of attention and inattention to experience, of intelligence and lack of intelligence in envisaging possibilities, and of reasonableness and failure of reasonableness in arriving at judgments of fact and value. Surely an alleged explanation of human behaviour which made no appeal to our own most basic types of mental activity would not count as a real explanation at all. And there is another reason, as I have already said, for saying that a measure of attentiveness, intelligence, and reasonableness, of the same general kind as we enjoy ourselves, must be universal in human societies. So far as people are not at all capable of cultivating them, in relation to the fundamental needs of human life and the principal dangers that threaten it, they do not survive.

I have argued that the human mind is in principle capable of finding out what is so, and not merely so for a particular culture or professional group, by applying certain basic capacities. I have suggested that scientific method is merely, in the last resort, a matter of applying thoroughly these basic capacities. Now it is often disputed whether or not scientific method is the only means of finding out the truth about the world. But it would be generally agreed, I suppose, by educated and uneducated people, that it is the supreme and unique merit of scientific method that it is the means of discovering what is true at least about some aspects of reality. For example, up to a few centuries ago our ancestors believed almost universally what would appear at first sight to be the case – that the sun moves round a stationary earth. We now believe, with confidence approximating to absolute certainty, that on the contrary the earth moves round the sun. They believed, or at least many of them believed, that earth, air, fire, and water were the elements, or fundamental building materials, out of which the world was constructed. We now believe that each of the 'four elements' is compounded of some among a much larger set of elements. We are indeed confident that, on such matters as these, we know a great deal more than any of the human beings of earlier times, and we attribute our knowledge to the pursuit of scientific method.

But Thomas Kuhn has argued that this conception of science is more or less an illusion,[16] and has backed up his case with a large number of examples taken from the history of science. Each generation of past inquirers, he says, had a general conception of how things were, and each generation was faced with phenomena which raised difficulties for its view. In this respect, contemporary scientists are no different from their predecessors. It is liable to be maintained that the theories of contemporary science represent the actual world, or are confirmed by observation and experiment, better than those propounded at any earlier time. But this seems to presuppose that one can characterize 'the world' apart from the theories one holds about it, and that one could have a theory-free description of observations and experiments. But our world-view, as one might put it, is constitutive of our world; is it not indeed obvious, when we come to think about the matter, that we cannot have a conception of the world apart from our conception of the world? It may seem more promising, at first sight, to try to show that our own view and the particular scientific theories which constitute it are better justified by observations than any previous view. But this account of the matter is subject to just the same kind of objection as the other. For it presupposes that we have some way of characterizing observable data which is independent of our world-view. However, it is by no means clear that a language which described sensations or sense-data apart from any world-view could ever be produced; it is certain that no one has yet constructed such a language.[17]

Thus, since the conception of an 'actual world' or 'real facts' to which the scientific world-view gradually approximates, and by virtue of approximation to which it is more or less 'true,' dissolves into incoherence under analysis, it may be asked what account ought to be given of the many changes in the opinions of scientists over the centuries. While it seems an illusion to suppose that scientific progress is really 'towards' anything, at least it is 'from' beginnings which are comparatively primitive. And any branch of science is originally 'primitive' in the sense that inquiry is haphazard, that there is no overall scheme which directs individual researchers and which suggests the general framework into which nature is to be fitted. A field of inquiry reaches maturity only when some genius proposes what Kuhn calls a 'paradigm,' a coherent system of concepts which confers order on the field and rectifies the deficiencies just alluded to. The prevalence of some such 'paradigm' is constitutive of what Kuhn calls 'normal science.' The contention of some philosophers of science, that scientists are or ought to be incessantly attempting to test the validity of their paradigms, is completely wide of the mark, as may be demonstrated by any number of examples from the actual history of scientific thought. On the contrary, the attempt is constantly being made, during periods of normal science, to force nature to fit the paradigm; and if this were not so, much of the day-to-day activity of scientists would simply not be possible. The idea that conscientious scientists always abandon paradigms which give rise to difficulties is even more wrong-headed, as can easily be shown by the fact that, in the whole history of science, there has never been a paradigm which did not give rise to such difficulties. However, paradigms do not last for ever; occasionally, when the difficulties given rise to by a paradigm are sufficiently obvious and notorious, there comes about a revolutionary situation in which there is no prevailing paradigm, and a number of candidates compete for the allegiance of workers in the field. This situation ends with the adoption of a new paradigm.[18] It is commonly assumed that in such cases the later paradigm is closer to the truth, or represents reality or the facts more accurately, than the earlier, but reasons have already been given for thinking that this account is erroneous.

So much for the general drift of Kuhn's argument. I admit his point that many theories which have been advanced as to how human beings come to know the truth about the world are misconceived, or at least so far inadequate that they are falsified by actual instances of developing knowledge. But I think that a case can be made, against his arguments, for the conventional view that scientific method is indeed a way in which human beings come to know more and more of the truth about the world.

Central to Kuhn's argument is the contention that we cannot characterize 'the real world' in any way except in terms of the theories which we hold about it. But it seems to me that, as I argued earlier in this chapter, what one might call a 'second-order' characterization of the real world is possible, which is such as to be independent of 'first-order' theories and judgments. I may conceive 'the real world' as that which first-order theories tend to describe so far as they do not give rise to false expectations of observation, and their application does not result in mistakes in practice. On this account, scientific theories are justifiably rejected and replaced by rival theories so far as these latter are better able to cope with such anomalies than are their predecessors, and therefore represent more accurately the real world. That one theory may be better than another, may be 'closer to the facts,' in this respect, does not entail that the fact that this is so, and the reasons why it is so, should be clearly grasped either by those who first advance it or by its first opponents. Kuhn seems often to confuse the distinct questions of what it is for one paradigm to be more true, to represent the facts better, than another, and what it is for its proponents at any particular time to have adequate grounds for stating confidently that it is or does so. The first proponents may not, in fact certainly will not, be able immediately to work out its empirical or practical consequences to the extent that will be possible to their successors.[19] If for a theory to approximate to the truth more than its rivals is for there to be more empirical and practical consequences which tend to confirm it and falsify its rival than vice versa, there is no reason why a wide range of these consequences should occur to those who are first in a position to entertain each of the rival theories.

That experience is crucial in the verifying or falsifying of theories has always, of course, been emphasized by empiricists. Kuhn objects that there is no way in which experience can be described apart from theory, indeed, that it only occurs within a framework of theory. I answered that objection at length in chapter 3. The ordinary languages in which people describe the physical objects and persons in their environment may well be claimed each to be like a large-scale example of one of Kuhn's paradigms, in that it involves a set of general assumptions about what things are like and expectations about how they will turn out. But this by no means entails that they cannot be used, if necessary with *ad hoc* modifications such as I suggested, to provide descriptions of objects and situations which transcend particular 'paradigms' in Kuhn's usual more restricted sense.

This point is crucial, and needs fairly extensive amplification and illustration. The experiences which first alerted Röntgen to make the investigations which led to the discovery of X-rays is one that can perfectly easily be described in non-technical terms.[20] I can say simply, 'When Röntgen was about to leave his laboratory one evening, he noticed a faint glow from a metal screen which was not to be expected on the basis of the physics of that time.' Of course, why it was not to be expected, why it demanded rather a fundamental extension of existing theory, needs a certain amount of scientific knowledge to explain. What is important for my purposes here is that the state of affairs which Röntgen observed, and which proved of crucial significance, can be described in non-technical language which could be translated without much effort into any of the languages of the world, and which is quite independent of the scientific conceptual framework either that Röntgen was previously accustomed to or that was later developed as a result of his discoveries.

Kuhn aims to show that the view of science as a steady accumulation of knowledge, or as an ever-closer approximation to the truth about the world, 'is entangled with a dominant epistemology that takes knowledge to be a construction placed directly upon raw sense-data by the mind.'[21] But if what I have said is correct, there is no necessity for such an entanglement; all that appears necessary is that a description of 'what is observed,' and a preliminary description of 'the world,' or 'the facts,' should be capable of being given in a manner which is to a sufficient degree independent of particular scientific paradigms. And that such descriptions can be given I have just tried to show. (The well-worn example of the duck-rabbit weakens rather than strengthens Kuhn's case. The duck-rabbit is not only either a duck or a rabbit, but a pattern of black lines on white paper or, at worst, a laboriously yet accurately describable pattern in someone's visual field.) It is also worth noticing that in this case not only what was observed can be described in non-technical language, but the fact that it was inconsistent with physical theory as it then existed can similarly be stated. It is quite difficult for non-specialists to understand Einstein's general theory of relativity, or to grasp why it is that this theory accounts better than its predecessors for what were for them anomalies in the observed motions of the planet Mercury; but one need have no knowledge of mathematics or physics to apprehend that the motion of Mercury is better accounted for by Einstein's general theory than by its rivals. This is because, though few of us are theoretical scientists, we all know what it is to be puzzled or surprised by a phenomenon in the light of our previous assumptions and expectations, and then to revise these in such a way that what previously seemed surprising or unexpected no longer does so.

In another case discussed by Kuhn, the discovery of Uranus, it is again quite easy to give a description of the succession of observations which prompted the discovery in terms quite independent of what was believed as a result of scientific investigation either before or after the discovery. What seem to have been the crucial observations were, first, that the heavenly body later to be identified as the planet Uranus moved its position in relation to other heavenly bodies on the successive occasions on which it was observed and, second, that as seen through the telescope it had an appreciable size and did not remain, as other heavenly bodies not previously identified as planets did, a mere point of light. These observable states of affairs could have been confirmed as so by anyone who looked through the telescope; Herschel might well have asked a less well-educated acquaintance to check them. Of course, to have seen the significance of these observable states of affairs, the reason why they necessitated a modification of existing views about the number of the planets, one would have had to know something about the theories of astronomy. To take a more contemporary example: anyone of sufficiently clear sight can ascertain that there is a streak of a certain shape, and in a certain position in relation to other streaks, on a photographic plate; but it takes a theoretical physicist to judge whether or not this is evidence for the existence of a previously unknown type of fundamental particle. Just the same applies in the case of fossils. Any observant person may come across markings of certain kinds in rocks, and it does not need much education to know that such markings are generally referred to as 'fossils.' But a specialist training is required if one is to judge that some fossil is evidence that a previously unknown type of animal, perhaps one crucial for our conception of the actual course of human evolution, existed at some time in the past.

I have tried to show that there is an important sense in which one can specify, apart from a 'paradigm,' the observable facts that are to count for and against its intelligent and reasonable acceptance by the scientific community. Even if one admits that there is a sense in which advocates of different paradigms live in different 'worlds,' there is also a sense in which these 'worlds' do have points of contact, as I argued earlier in the chapter. The upholders of each paradigm are wont to claim that it accounts best for the available evidence; and I have already given reasons for doubting that terms like 'evidence' and 'explanation' are simply equivocal as between different paradigms. To understand a paradigm which is a rival to the one held by oneself is to apprehend how it accounts for a certain amount of observable evidence; not to accept a paradigm which one understands is to believe that there is other evidence which tells against it, that this evidence supports another paradigm, and that this other paradigm explains at least a high proportion of the evidence explained by the first. The fact is that there is an ideal of attentive, intelligent, and reasonable inquiry in relation to which any particular paradigm may, at least in the long run, be judged. If there is, as one might put it, a meta-paradigm of the kind I have just sketched, then there is something external to particular paradigms by which they are in the long run validated, partly validated or wholly invalidated; and one is not constrained to that relativism for which each paradigm is 'right' according to criteria laid down by itself and 'wrong' according to criteria laid down by its rivals.[22]

Kuhn's position gains plausibility from the fact that, as he shows very clearly, the manner in which scientists come to be convinced that a prospective paradigm describes a range of phenomena better than its predecessors has often been misrepresented by philosophers of science. For example, it appears that a great number of the scientific discoveries of the past would never have been made had those responsible acted strictly in the manner that Sir Karl Popper would have them do – by searching diligently for evidence which told against their theory, and rejecting their theory so soon as this was found. (A useful discussion of the difficulties raised by Kuhn's arguments against Popper's theories has been provided by I. Lakatos; his references to Proust's theory, and the history of its acceptance by the scientific community, are especially pertinent.[23]) Modifications of Popper's views to meet these difficulties seem to me often either to fail to meet them or to concede too much to Kuhn. But I do not think it is too difficult to sketch a manner in which one may at once preserve Popper's insistence that it is of the essence of science to approach nearer and nearer to a true account of the world,[24] and meet the historical difficulties raised by Kuhn. Wherever two rival theories A and B are offered to account for the same range of phenomena (for example, the phlogiston theory and the oxygen theory), the more evidence there is which appears to confirm A and to be inconsistent with B, and the less evidence there is which appears to confirm B and to be inconsistent with A, the less reasonable it is to assent to B, and the more reasonable it is to assent to *A*. (Lakatos believes that a version of Popper's theory can be maintained against Kuhn's objections if one takes criticism to be a gradual and cumulative affair, involving the suggestion of alternative theories, rather than a matter of knock-down falsification. I believe this suggestion to be on the right lines.)

Kuhn's account of these matters appears to me to underestimate the degree to which one can suspend judgment on the truth of an hypothesis, can weigh pros and cons; what applies to the ordinary affairs of life in this respect seems to apply *mutatis mutandis* to scientific theories. One would imagine, from what Kuhn says,[25] that every scientist within a field must either accept without qualification or reject without qualification any candidate for the status of paradigm within that field. But surely there are and ought to be degrees of assent in these matters. 'Every problem that normal science sees as a puzzle can be seen, from another viewpoint, as a counter-instance,' but someone might reasonably hesitate between the viewpoints, and seek for reasonable grounds for holding the one rather than the other. Kuhn's position on this matter is strangely reminiscent of that of the theologian Karl Barth, that belief cannot argue with unbelief, only preach to it, since there is no viewpoint from which an intelligent and reasonable decision between belief and unbelief can be made. (Kuhn admits that on his view there is a similarity between the mental procedures of scientists and those of theologians.)[26] And yet it is surely possible for a scientist to assert that on the whole he is disposed to cleave to paradigm *X*, although he acknowledges that it gives rise to certain difficulties; or that he believes that paradigm *Y* does not correspond to the truth, although it accounts for some of the observable facts better than does any of its rivals (a uniformitarian geologist might well take this line about catastrophism, when he considered the evidence on the disappearance of the dinosaurs or the extinction of the mammoth); or that he accords paradigm *Z* provisional and qualified acceptance, until either more of its anomalies can be dealt with or a more satisfactory alternative can be found.

Related to Kuhn's oversight of the phenomenon of suspense of judgment is his apparent neglect of the possibility that someone may try to see, and in a measure at least succeed in seeing, a problem or a range of phenomena from another point of view than her own. Neglect of this possibility makes the 'incommensurability'[27] of rival paradigms seem much more thoroughgoing than it really is. But the assumption of extreme incommensurability seems to me not only fallacious, but politically and socially dangerous, as I argued in the last chapter, whether applied to disagreements about scientific theory or to disagreements of other kinds. Surely, in regard to every serious disagreement, it is salutary for the holder of one of two opposed opinions to say, on the subject of the other, 'that is how I would see the matter if I gave more weight to x, didn't know y, or had been brought up in environment z. Should I perhaps give more weight to x? Is y really as indubitable as I have assumed up to now? Is z really a background which distorts one's apprehension of things more than my own?' As I have said before, unless people are disposed to approach one another's opinions in the kind of way that I have just described, they cannot argue with one another, but only preach or hurl abuse; and where the matter at issue is or seems to be of some practical significance, the final outcome is almost bound to be either repression or open violence.

It is quite true that, as Kuhn effectively shows, particular kinds of questions about the world are not even asked, and indeed cannot be asked, before the existence of appropriate paradigms. But the fact remains that, throughout the whole process of creation, development, and replacement of paradigms that constitutes the history of scientific investigation, there are certain stable features. The investigator is always trying to explain what is observable, and admits sensory evidence as relevant to the truth or falsity of her explanations. Whether expectations in general, and apart from isolated instances which constitute anomalies or difficulties, are verified or falsified in experience, in the long run determines not only the particular answers which scientists give to the questions they put to nature, but also the form of the questions themselves. Thus the fact that even the kind of questions which are asked about the world changes with change of paradigm[38] does not imply that the succession of paradigms may not be, in one sense, cumulative, in that more and more of what is observable is explained. (Bernard Lonergan has cited from the history of mathematics and science a number of examples of what he calls 'inverse insight,' whereby an investigator comes to realize that a whole range of assumptions which she has been in the habit of taking for granted about the world is misconceived. Something similar seems to be alluded to by Wittgenstein in *The Blue Book*.)[29] Kuhn objects to such accounts on the ground that they depend on the availability of a neutral language in which the observations may be described.[30] But, as I have tried to show, such an objection will not stand up to examination.

It may be objected that what I have to say fails to do justice to the authority necessarily exercised within the scientific community. One cannot take seriously just any purported contribution to knowledge, or waste the time of scientists by publishing it in the scientific journals. If every wild surmise whatever, whenever, and by whomsoever advanced were to be carefully scrutinized, research would simply come to a standstill. And how can new work be assessed other than by its conformity or failure to conform with the paradigms now accepted by the scientific community? That some such exercise of authority is necessary, I would concede, but that it may be exercised other than in uncritical deference to the prevailing paradigms seems a consequence of what I have already argued. Where a contribution to knowledge is proposed which defies accepted canons, it should be asked: does the contributor understand the reasons why the conventional account is accepted by most investigators? Does she build up a plausible case for their having overlooked some observable fact or other? Does her theory account as well as the usual one for facts acknowledged by herself as well as her orthodox colleagues?

Kuhn admits that it might well be inferred that, if his account is correct, in matters of science 'might makes right.'[31] But although he denies that this is so, he does little to allay one's fears that this unpalatable conclusion does in fact follow from what he says. He seems in effect to have disqualified every other criterion determining the limits of permissible novelty in science except the *ipse dixit* of the scientific community, or rather the most influential members of it. He asks disarmingly what greater authority there could be than that of the scientific community.[32] But this authority, at least on the usual view and on the one that I have been putting forward, derives from the fact that scientists have been specially trained to take into account the widest possible range of sensible data within their field, and to consider the widest possible range of theories to explain them – in other words, to be as attentive, intelligent, and reasonable as possible within the limits of their speciality. They will tend to approach the truth so far as they do this, rather than submitting to tradition, authority, or emotional prejudice when they oppose it. That the acknowledged experts in physics, chemistry, biology, and so on do not quite always behave according to these admirable maxims may often become clear to the educated layperson. There are a number of discreditable but well-documented episodes from the history of science, and some from that of rather recent science.[33]

Towards the end of his book, Kuhn remarks that biological evolution provides an instructive parallel to the progress of science as sketched by himself. In both cases, he suggests, there is an advance from primitive beginnings in the direction of greater and greater elaboration, but there seems no need to postulate any goal or end-point of the development.[34]

But it seems to me that reference by way of illustration to Darwin's theory of evolution is singularly unfortunate, since it is just when applied to this that the oddness of Kuhn's account of science in general is particularly apparent. For Darwin's theory is deemed to be an advance on its predecessors largely in virtue of the fact that it enables one to determine roughly how living things really were in the successive ages of the past, and which animal groups really were descended from which other animal groups, in a manner which was quite impossible with the preceding theories. Here, above all, it seems very implausible to deny that scientific theory advances so far as it enables one to describe and explain more fully and accurately the facts as they actually are or were, and would be or would have been even if no intelligent and reasonable beings had evolved on earth to ascertain them. And I think that consideration of the nature of our investigation into, and consequent knowledge of, the remote past provides an important clue about the nature of human knowledge in general. It seems absurd to deny that one may come closer to finding out what really happened in the past by concocting theories about it and by looking for such evidence available in the present as tends to verify or falsify these theories.

But if truth is available in this way in the case of inquiry into the past – if historical and palaeontological theories do not merely become more elaborate and sophisticated over the course of time, but actually tend to approximate ever more closely to the truth – it is difficult to see why it should not also be so in the case of investigation into the past and present structure of the world in physics and chemistry. The fact that highly sophisticated theorizing is necessary to get at the truth does not imply, in the case of physics and chemistry any more than in the case of history and palaeontology, that the world-as-described-by-theory is somehow merely the creation of the theorists responsible; after all, the theories do have to be verified, at least as more probably true than such rival theories as have been concocted in the course of the history of scientific investigation. The fact that there are no observable things or qualities corresponding directly to the theoretically defined things and qualities (proton, electron, mass, electrical charge) postulated by scientists does not imply that these do not exist or occur in the real world, unless the unwarranted assumption is made that what is real cannot be anything other than the direct or potential object of sensation. This assumption, when consistently applied, leads inevitably to the absurd doctrine that not only the theoretical entities postulated by physicists and chemists but the things and events of the past as well are merely the mental constructions of theorists, and do not exist independently of and prior to their theories. But if we assume that the real world is not so much the object of sensation as what we progressively come to know, that this 'coming to know' is not merely a matter of sense-perception, but is to be had by a sustained process of attending to what is observable, concocting theories, and provisionally retaining those theories which most satisfactorily account for what we have observed so far, then scientific and historical knowledge are both really possible and actually of the real world, and all the paradoxes arising from both Kuhn's position and that of his empiricist opponents disappear.[35]

Kuhn remarks that there are a number of questions raised by his work to which he is not in a position to give an answer. Central among these is the question of what nature the world must be for the work of scientists to be possible within it.[36] Given the overall validity of my criticism of Kuhn, the answer would seem to be that, for scientific method to be possible and effective, the world must be what can come to be known by concocting theories to account for observable phenomena, by testing these theories in relation to these phenomena, and by retaining in each case the theory which stands up best to these tests until a better is found. This seems to be obvious to a degree, yet its implications seem to be overlooked both by empiricists, who underestimate the part played by theorizing in the acquisition of knowledge, and by idealists and relativists, who either do not sufficiently attend to the fact that the theories have to be verified in relation to an experience which is independent of them in order to qualify as knowledge, or think like Kuhn that such verification of hypotheses by reference to what is external to themselves is in the last resort impossible.

7

Anarchy and Falsification: Feyerabend and Popper

Kuhn rejects the thesis that there are available permanent canons for the advancement of knowledge, which apply always and everywhere; he avoids the conclusion that science is anarchic by his conception of 'normal science' constituted by the acceptance of 'paradigms.' Paul Feyerabend, on the basis of similar arguments, draws the anarchic conclusions and enthusiastically commends them. I shall summarize Feyerabend's position without comment in the next six paragraphs and afterwards proceed to discuss it.

Historical investigation (writes Feyerabend) shows that the most successful human inquiries have by no means proceeded in accordance with a 'rational' method. The fact is that there is no idea, however ancient or absurd, which is not capable of improving our knowledge. It might be objected that it is rational to accept theories if they conform with the facts, to reject them if they do not do so, and that science progresses by application of the same principle. However, we should rid ourselves of the assumption that, when a theory conflicts with the facts, it is always the theory which is to blame. 'Facts' are not somehow pure and uncontaminated by theories; the 'facts' one acknowledges in the present are actually 'constituted by older ideologies.'[1] 'Science knows no "bare facts" at all ... the "facts" that enter our knowledge are already viewed in a certain way and ... therefore [are] essentially ideational.'[2] Empiricists are apt to appeal to observation at this point, but the idea of pure observations and a language reflecting them, without any reference to human interests, prejudices, and assumptions, is a delusion, as linguists would now generally agree.[3]

Falsificationist doctrines are now perhaps more in favour than empiricism in the philosophy of science, owing to the great authority of Sir Karl

Popper. However, they turn out on examination to be no more satisfactory. Naive falsificationism, the view that a scientific theory ought to be rejected the moment any evidence turns up which conflicts with it, has been now generally abandoned for the excellent reasons that no theories in science fail to give rise to some difficulties of this kind, and that great scientific discoveries have often if not usually been made in the teeth of persistently conflicting evidence. To meet this difficulty, Lakatos and others have propounded a more sophisticated version of falsificationism, whereby a theory is to be allowed a certain time to prove itself, to show any latent strength or power of recovery that it may have, in the face of conflicting observations or experimental results. The difficulty here is that this modified standard is of real practical use only if some time limit is assigned. However, any time limit that one may set can easily be shown to be arbitrary: 'if you are permitted to wait, why not wait a little longer?' Either the principle amounts to something definite, in which case it rules out a great deal of what has been significant in science and of what almost certainly will be so in future, or it degenerates into a mere 'verbal ornament.' And the same applies to all tests which have been proposed to guarantee the 'rationality' of science. The conclusion appears unavoidable that 'given science, reason cannot be universal and unreason cannot be excluded.'

Popper's characteristic insistence that we hold theories, and even principles, tentatively so that they may constantly be subjected to criticism has been pushed to a self-destructive extreme in some of his writings, such as when we read that we require 'no definite frame of reference for our criticism,' and that 'we may revise even the most fundamental rules and drop the most fundamental demands if the need for a different measure of excellence should arise.'[5] (I think Feyerabend's point is that, if that principle is to be retained at all costs, it is inconsistent with itself, but that if it too should be rejected 'if the need for a different measure of excellence should arise,' we appear to be left with no methodological guidance at all.)

What conclusions are to be drawn? What we need, says Feyerabend, is an 'anarchistic epistemology.' We ought to 'use a multiplicity of inconsistent theories at any one time of the development of our knowledge.' The most effective participant in such a process as science turns out to be, if one studies its history, is 'a ruthless opportunist who is not tied to any particular philosophy and who adopts whatever procedure seems to fit the occasion.' Talk about 'the search for truth' and other such ideals in science should not deflect our minds from 'the most important question of all ..., to what extent the happiness of individual human beings, and to what extent their freedom has been increased.' One may infer from this that such things as our choice of basic cosmology are a matter of taste; an important difference between science and the arts, perhaps the only important one, is thus eliminated. Proliferation of theories is beneficial for science, while theoretical uniformity is at once bad for science and bad for the free development of the individual. Should we welcome the fact, if indeed it is a fact, that human adults are stuck with stable conceptual systems impermeable to basic change? Should we not rather hope 'that fundamental changes are still possible, and that they should be encouraged lest we remain for ever excluded from what might be a higher stage of knowledge and of consciousness'?[6]

It will be seen from the foregoing that, as I mentioned at the beginning of this chapter, Feyerabend is at one with T.S. Kuhn in his polemic against general criteria of rationality, whether empiricist or Popperian, by which one general theory ought to be preferred to another as more in accordance with 'truth' or 'the facts.' But Kuhn's approval of 'paradigms,' of single overall theories dominating each main department of science for most of the time, is anathema to him. Feyerabend objects to Kuhn's theory, and still more to the ideology which he detects as underlying it, as such as 'could only give comfort to the most narrow-minded and the most conceited kind of specialism.' As a number of social scientists have apparently told Feyerabend, they have now learned, as a result of Kuhn's work, how they can make their field really 'scientific' at last – by restricting criticism, by reducing comprehensive theories to one, by stopping students from speculating, by getting their more restless colleagues to conform and 'do serious work.'[7]

We should often remind ourselves of the fact that 'the sciences ... are our own creation, including all the severe standards they seem to impose on us ... it seems to me that an enterprise whose human character can be seen by all is preferable one that looks "objective," and impervious to human interests and concerns.' Science is much closer to myth than philosophers of science are accustomed to admit; it is one of many forms of thought developed by human beings, and not necessarily the best. It is only inherently superior for those who have already decided in favour of a certain ideology. Standards which are themselves abstracted from science, like those proposed by Lakatos, cannot validly be used as neutral arbiters in the dispute between modern science, on the one hand, and Aristotelian science, myth, magic, and religion, on the other.[8]

Thus far Feyerabend. The most fundamental objection to his position seems to me to be this: that his attack on 'methods' supposed to be operative in science is based on historical arguments, which themselves involve the application of 'methods' very like those he is attacking. While his book is called *Against Method*, he does, at least intermittently, argue methodically against method, and one's taking him seriously depends on the assumption that he is doing so. This comes out with special vividness in his discussion of the case of Galileo.[9] That great scientist, he tells us, far from deferring to evidence in propounding and commending his theories, defied evidence, and used 'irrational' and rhetorical means of persuasion to bring others over to his point of view. Here is a case which is among the paradigm instances of scientific discovery, which flagrantly breaks those rules of procedure on such matters which have been advocated by methodologists. But it is instructive to switch our attention for a moment from Galileo's own procedures to the procedures of Feyerabend himself in dealing with Galileo's case. Does he prefer theories on the matter in proportion to their aesthetic appeal? Does he neglect evidence, and rely instead on rhetorical devices of persuasion? Not a bit of it. Being no expert on the locality or period in question, I am not qualified to judge whether he has been biased in his selection and presentation of the evidence; but at least the form of his argument is of a kind that would appeal to the most stringent of methodologists. The conventional view of Galileo's procedures is X; Feyerabend's own view of them is Y; X and Y are incompatible. Feyerabend tests the two possibilities about Galileo's procedures in relation to the documentary evidence, and prefers the possibility Y which most satisfactorily accounts for that evidence.

Let us suppose for a moment that the foregoing account of the method of historical investigation employed, though apparently not adverted to, by Feyerabend is false. Suppose he were to admit that his survey of the data was biased, and omitted matter which at first sight at least had an important bearing on the question at issue. Or suppose he were to say, as one might expect on the basis of the 'unmethodical' procedures he recommends to practitioners of the physical sciences: 'I am advancing the account of Galileo's procedures and motives which appears to me most intellectually stimulating and aesthetically pleasing. I brush aside any documentary evidence which seems to tell in any other direction, and use all my powers of rhetoric, if necessary backed up by physical duress, to get others to share my point of view.' In this case of course – if his way of dealing with historical issues were anything like that which he appears to be commending for dealing with scientific matters – no one would have any good reason for listening to his arguments. They might regard him as a purveyor of interesting historical fictions – it may be fun for an author and his readers to envisage Queen Victoria having a clandestine affair with Disraeli, or Sherlock Holmes being one and the same as Jack the Ripper, and to work out the consequences – but not as an historian, that is to say, as someone who uses methods appropriate to finding out what was actually going forward in the past. And the whole force of Feyerabend's argument based on the Galileo case depends on his proceeding as an historian, and not as a fabricator of historical romances.

Feyerabend's attitude to the question of truth is ambivalent. His argument turns on the fact that what is actually true of the history of science is not in accord with the theories of his opponents as to the nature of science. Yet when it comes to science itself, he seems to regard the ideal of truth itself as a possible enemy to delightful speculation and untrammelled intellectual development. It may be wondered whether science does not become a very different enterprise indeed from what it has traditionally appeared to be if it is not regarded as at all in the business of finding out the truth about what is so, and would have been so even if we had never tried to find out the truth about it, but rather as the free creation of the human spirit, to be valued for its aesthetic and liberating qualities. Would Feyerabend wish to say that it is impossible in general to find out what is so? This is plainly a self-destructive thesis (is it so that it is impossible to find out what is so?), and in any case it is inconsistent with his own historical inquiries and arguments. But if it is in general possible to find out what is so, or at least to come ever closer to doing so, by using the appropriate methods, why should it not be possible in the case of science? Feyerabend might reply that knowledge of the truth is indeed the object of scientific inquiry,[10] yet that one tends to get at the truth not by doing anything so boring as following a method, but by preferring theories according to their outrageousness or their attractiveness. That thesis, however, would certainly need a great deal of justification. Many have followed the pleasure-principle in constructing and maintaining their view of themselves and of the world, but it would be a little curious to suggest that the cause of truth or of science was served by this.

I argued earlier that there are three fundamental mental operations involved in coming to know the truth about what is so in general which apply to scientific inquiry as elsewhere – attending to observable data, envisaging possible explanations for the data, and preferring as probably or certainly so the explanations which best account for the data. I labelled the dispositions to perform these operations, respectively, attentiveness, intelligence, and reasonableness. It appears to me that the whole strength and weakness of Feyerabend's position is due to his emphasis and concentration on the importance of the second disposition, together with a misunderstanding of the first and third and an underestimation of their importance. It is one thing to envisage a hypothesis, to entertain a possible explanation as possible. It is another thing to assent to the explanation as probably or certainly correct. Feyerabend is surely quite right that it is bad for the development of freedom in the individual, as well as for the progress of science, if possible alternative explanations cannot be envisaged, and that any method which inhibits this ought to be condemned. But it is one thing to insist that a multiplicity of conflicting theories ought to be envisaged as possible, quite another to claim that they could or should be assented to as true. The requirements of truth do not imply that intelligence should be in any way limited or constricted in its activity, only that one must employ reasonableness as well. The arguments of Kuhn and Feyerabend do bring out a difficulty about the operation of reasonableness, as conceived by both empiricists and falsificationists; and the only alternative seems either an unrestricted exercise of the theoretical intelligence and imagination as commended by Feyerabend or the restriction of these by more or less draconian social measures within the limits of 'paradigms' as described by Kuhn. These arguments will have to be considered below; for the moment I am only trying to make the point that to stress the importance of intelligence is not necessarily to undervalue the role of attentiveness and reasonableness in coming to know the truth.

Feyerabend's comparison of his own position with that of Hilary Putnam is particularly instructive in this regard. Putnam says that one ought to try to reduce the number of competing theories to one or none and Feyerabend, that as many as possible incompatible theories ought to be encouraged.[11] But Putnam's recommendations need not be in the least in conflict with those of Feyerabend, if Feyerabend's are understood as applying to the activity of intelligence in concocting theories and explanations, and Putnam's, to that of reason in determining which of them is most likely to be correct on the basis of the evidence given in experience. Fertility in the construction of hypotheses and theories is a (virtually) necessary condition of discovery of the truth about things,[12] but it is by no means a sufficient condition.

Feyerabend alludes to Putnam's 'rule of tenacity,' which is to the effect that one should retain an accepted theory unless it be found incompatible with the relevant data, and contrasts his own and Kuhn's 'principle of tenacity,' whereby you retain your theory 'even if there are data which are inconsistent with it.'[13] I have already tried to show that Kuhn oddly neglects the difference between the mere entertainment of a theory and the assertion of it as definitely true and its rivals as definitely false, and all the shades of confidence with which a hypothesis may be toyed with, suggested, or maintained. It seems to me that the same criticism can justly be levelled at Feyerabend. The lack of finesse in Putnam's rule (at least as Feyerabend presents it) gives what plausibility it has to the alternative proposed by Feyerabend; exponents of extreme positions, here as elsewhere, play into one another's hands. One should rather put it that a theory should be retained in so far as it is compatible with the relevant data. *Prima facie* inconsistency with data is good reason, but not always in itself sufficient reason, for rejection of a theory; if one has an alternative theory which accounts better for the relevant data, this constitutes good reason for accepting it. The conscientious scientist should be on the look-out both for data which would go against the theory which she accepts and for alternative theories which would account for the available data as well or better. Attentiveness and intelligence, to revert to the terminology introduced earlier, are necessary conditions of being reasonable, since if you are to select as probably true the theoretical possibility which best accounts for the available data, you must be both sufficiently attentive to advert to significant data and sufficiently intelligent to envisage the alternative possibilities. The trouble with Kuhn's 'paradigms' is that they may prevent you from being either; their virtue is that they represent the sustained exercise of attentiveness, intelligence, and reasonableness by the scientific community up to now.

My suggested modification of Putnam's 'rule of tenacity' enables one to meet, I think, a number of notorious difficulties about the confirmation of scientific theories. Lakatos ingeniously cites the case of Proust's Law as an objection to the falsificationist criterion of scientific rationality.[14] According to Proust's Law, the atomic weights of all the elements are integral multiples of the atomic weight of the hydrogen atom. Though it seemed to work for the other known elements, it appeared for some time to be falsified by the case of chlorine, whose atomic weight came out at 36.7 times that of hydrogen. Proust's Law was accordingly rejected by scientists, in the proper falsificationist manner. However, it was later discovered that there were two isotopes of chlorine, each of which conformed perfectly well to Proust's Law, and that the apparently aberrant atomic weight was due to the mixture of these isotopes in normal samples of chlorine. Thus Proust's Law was vindicated after all. Surely this would have been a good locus for the application of 'perhaps ... but' and 'on the whole ... though' which both Feyerabend and his opponents appear to neglect. At the time when the anomaly was not yet explained, it would have been appropriate to say that *perhaps* Proust's Law was true, *but* the atomic weight of chlorine amounted to a *prima facie* difficulty for it, and that *on the whole* the evidence supported it. Where a law explains a wide range of phenomena, but an apparent exception to it stands out like a sore thumb, there is a pretty good chance that the aberrant phenomenon will ultimately be explained as after all in conformity with the law, but the more such phenomena there are, the less reason there is for supposing that they will.

Perhaps what is at issue comes out more vividly in relation to matters disputed by recent scientists. Two may be selected – Bode's Law and the nature of quasars. Bode's Law determines the mean distances from the sun of successive planets. The question is whether it is mere coincidence that the planetary orbits conform to Bode's Law, or at least come somewhere near doing so, or whether there are dynamic principles operating in nature according to which the planetary system has to be disposed in such a way. There are some phenomena which are not quite what one would expect from Bode's Law in any case, and thus weigh in favour of the former possibility, as does the fact that no explanation of why Bode's Law should apply has yet found general acceptance. On the other hand, the remarkable coincidence of the fact that it applies to the extent that it does, and the intermittent appearance of explanations for it which seem not entirely without promise, tell in the opposite direction. A rather similar situation is the conflicting accounts of the nature of quasars given by recent astronomers. The question is whether they are or are not among the most distant objects in the universe. Their red-shift would suggest the former, and the strength of the radio signals from them, the latter. On the latter hypothesis, the red-shift might perhaps be explained as an effect of exceptionally powerful gravitational forces. But as against that, a vast amount of contemporary astronomical theory, which is strongly confirmed by other data, would have to be given up if the accepted explanation of the red-shift, in terms of distant objects receding from us at speeds approaching that of light, were given up.[15]

All these examples go to show that Putnam's rule of tenacity, that one should retain a theory except when it is incompatible with the evidence, and Feyerabend's principle of tenacity, that one should retain theories whether they are compatible with the evidence or not, do not exhaust the available options. But they do seem to confirm my own modification of Putnam's rule, as suggested above, as indeed do the principles to which Feyerabend himself seems committed when arguing as a historian.

The positive lessons to be learned from Feyerabend are all a matter, so far as I can judge, of applying at the level of intelligence, or the thinking up of hypotheses, theories, or possible explanations, maxims which he appears to want to apply at the level of reasonableness, or determining which of the hypotheses or whatever which have been thought up are most likely to be so on the basis of the evidence. The conscientious scientist should be alive both to the anomalies confronting the theory in which she believes and to possible alternatives; she ought at least to be intrigued, rather than contemptuous and hostile, when genuine difficulties for, and alternatives to, her paradigm are suggested to her. The 'normal scientist,' as just the opposite sort of person, was well worth a tilt. However, if we are to spell out what is to count as 'genuine' in this context, and are not to be committed to the impossible demand that every scientist should take seriously every lunatic who passes a remark about her field of research, we shall have to defy Feyerabend to the extent of insisting on the importance of some principles of method, and to try to refute his arguments to the contrary.

Central to Feyerabend's position are his aspersions on the usual attempts to clarify the business of choosing rationally between opposing theories. It is owing to the alleged failure of method at this point that one seems to be confronted with the bleak alternatives of either Feyerabend's anarchical conflict of theories or Kuhn's dogma imposed, in a manner which is in the last resort arbitrary, by the community of specialists. Empiricism fails, says Feyerabend, because it depends on the availability of a pure observation language, which is in fact impossible; falsificationism, because on a strong interpretation it effectively renders all scientific advance impossible, and on a weak interpretation it is arbitrary, self-destructive, or wholly ineffectual.

I agree with Feyerabend that neither strict empiricism nor strong falsificationism are viable. But, as I have already argued,[16] one cardinal thesis of empiricism does seem to be defensible, true, and of the utmost importance; that is, that there are states of affairs which are in some sense directly to be perceived, by reference to which theories about the nature of things are to be tested for their truth or falsity. These states of affairs are the data which scientific theories have to account for, and may most reasonably be held to approximate to the truth so far as they do account for them. Thus it is a certain pattern wont to be made by recording pens in a radio telescope which is the empirical evidence for the existence of pulsars. Though to apprehend why such patterns are evidence for the existence of pulsars needs a great deal of highly technical knowledge, the patterns, just as patterns, could no doubt be described, more or less laboriously, by the average layperson. Short of the possibility of some such ultimate appeal to experience, it is difficult to see how one can locate the difference between knowledge of the real world and any consistently and elaborately constructed system of falsehoods. No wonder Feyerabend has little use for the notion of truth.

What I have said by no means implies, as some have supposed, that in experience as articulated in ordinary language we apprehend the world more directly than is ever possible through our theories; it only entails our having access to, and being somehow able to describe, states of affairs by intelligent and reasonable reflection on which we may come increasingly to know what is the case about the world. So-called ordinary language, varying as it does vastly from place to place and from time to time, has no directly privileged position in relation to the real facts themselves; but, for reasons which I have already touched on, it does provide one with 'tweezers'[17] for grasping perceivable states of affairs by which one may confirm or disconfirm rival theoretical judgments. It is to be acknowledged that all real ordinary languages involve vast amounts of assumption, whether fairly reasonable or almost wholly superstitious, which cannot be removed from them short of developments in philosophy and the sciences which themselves are well beyond the scope of such ordinary languages. But if human societies are to survive at all, their languages must suffice at least for making gross discrimination between objects, types of objects, and qualities within the observable world. It is this aspect of ordinary languages which enables them to be used to articulate data to be explained, in a manner which is sufficiently independent of the theories purporting to explain them. The ordinary languages of the Navajo Indian, the Kalahari bushman, and the Esher clubman do vary a good deal, but not, I suggest, in the relevant respects. Each language has at least the means of making the gross physical discriminations I have described.

It seems worth reiterating that I am not defending empiricism as such, except in so far as all concessions to the principle that there is a crucial place for appeal to experience in the acquisition of knowledge may be labelled 'empiricist.' Where strict empiricism errs, in my view, is in confusing apprehension of states of affairs relevant to knowledge of the real world with knowledge of the real world itself. For the apprehension of states of affairs which are perceivable, one has to be merely attentive; for knowledge of the real world, one has to be attentive, intelligent, and reasonable – the constructive efforts of intelligence and the critical procedures of reason have to be applied to the data of experience. Short of this realization, one is inevitably driven to the view that true knowledge of what is independent of us is only to be had in sensation, while intelligence and reason have the role of producing subjective constructions which are mere means to such knowledge.[18]

As well as this cardinal and defensible doctrine of empiricism, a form of falsificationism can be defended in a manner which I have already sketched, and will develop at greater length later in this chapter. Feyerabend in effect confronts the falsificationist with a dilemma. Either she must abandon her theory the moment a scrap of *prima facie* evidence turns up against it or she must allow her theory some time to vindicate itself. In the former case, her principles have the singular consequence of ruling out most if not all of what have generally been claimed to be scientific advances. In the latter case, either she assigns a time limit, but then there seems no adequate reason for not assigning it earlier or later, or she simply chooses the moment at which to drop her theory, which will show the principle to be a mere 'verbal ornament.' I have already argued that the appearance here of a strict alternative is misleading, and that we do not really have either to go on indefinitely maintaining a theory or to reject it out of hand; that theories may be asserted or rejected with different degrees of confidence, according to the degree of their corroboration or falsification by *prima facie* evidence.

Feyerabend exhorts his readers to remember that scientific theories are human theories, arrived at by applying human standards. But it is also worth remembering that scientific theories, at least as generally understood, are supposed to yield knowledge of, or justified true belief about, a universe which exists independently of the scientist and the human community which supports him. Feyerabend reproaches Kuhn for having no clear view of the aim of science, but one may wonder what the aim of science is on his own view. Judging by some of his remarks,[19] one would suppose that its aim is simply that human beings should enjoy the exercise of their intellectual and aesthetic faculties as much as possible, and that even the truth about things is not worth pursuing if it gets in the way of this. I have already pointed out the difficulties which attend this account.

I have suggested that it is the thorough application of the three mental dispositions of attentiveness, intelligence, and reasonableness, which are operative to some extent in all human affairs, which both is constitutive of science as such and serves to vindicate the scientific world-view against myth and against at least some religion. I think Feyerabend might raise the same objection to my account as he does to that of Lakatos – that it involves the abstraction of certain alleged principles from the alleged practices of science, and the arbitrary use of them as devices with which to condemn alternative and conflicting world-views and procedures. But this would be wrong. The basic mental dispositions which I have outlined have to be current to some degree in any human society if it is to survive.[20] The scientific world-view commends itself as being at least on the way to the truth about the world because, and in so far as, it cultivates these mental dispositions in a very thorough way, far beyond the immediate requirements of survival. One may vindicate the scientific world-view, in other words, not merely on the basis of principles culled from itself; consideration of the method which underlies it, and which is exemplified to some extent in all human activity, indicates that it is the best method of coming to know what is the case about the world.

Feyerabend's anarchism is the more plausible so far as one fails to attend to the difference between the reasons and motives which underlie the original propounding of a theory and the reasons and motives for later acceptance of it as probably true. For Feyerabend does more or less admit that some centuries later than the time of Galileo himself evidence had been amassed which was such as to vindicate his main contentions against those of his opponents.[21] Granted, for the sake of argument, that those who were opposed to Galileo in his own time had as good or better reasons for contradicting his account as he had for contradicting theirs; it may yet be the case that we, who are in a position to attend to a wider range of data and entertain more hypotheses than were either Galileo or his opponents, have good reason to think that he was right and they were wrong, when the hypotheses are confronted with the data in the unprejudiced manner which, as I have already argued in opposition to Feyerabend, is at least theoretically possible. If one's object in the long term is to advance towards greater knowledge of the truth, it might be inferred that in the short term a theory, which, however apparently absurd in many respects, had at least something to commend it, should be given a run for its money. This is by no means to support anarchism; it is rather to suggest that one aspect of an effective method will be insistence that it be reasonable in the long term to take with some seriousness a possibility which seems somewhat unreasonable in the short term. To insist, with Herbert Feigl, that it is one thing to trace the historical origins of a theory and to point out the socio-political conditions which promote or promoted its acceptance, and quite another to test or to justify it,[22] would consequently seem to be appropriate.

It may be concluded that fertility in hypotheses is in general a necessary, but not a sufficient, condition for the advance of knowledge in science and elsewhere; that the advice that incompatible hypotheses be considered together is admirable, that they be simultaneously asserted is absurd; that the ideal of truth is not dispensable in science, or in any kind of serious investigation whatever; and that if it were, Feyerabend's own investigations into the history and practice of science, which are of assistance in establishing the truth so far as they are of any value at all, would be pointless. This they certainly are not; the prevalent confusion in the theory of knowledge could hardly have found a more eloquent or convincing *reductio ad absurdum*.

If Feyerabend and Kuhn are in error about the relation of scientific investigation and theory to the truth about the world, Popper's view seems to be fundamentally correct, according to the view I have outlined, but to need supplementation and revision to meet the objections which have been made to it. Popper is the most renowned and articulate contemporary exponent of fallibilism. I myself believe that a thoroughgoing fallibilism, which is supposed to apply actually to the statements constitutive of fallibilism themselves, is self-destructive, and consequently absurd. I would propose a less radical, but I think perfectly self-consistent, kind of fallibilism, which I shall argue is not self-destructive. A first-order fallibilism – applying to the natural sciences, history, and hermeneutics – may issue in, and in my opinion ought to issue in, a second-order infallibilism – applying to epistemology and metaphysics. More concretely, fallibilism is in general an infallible way of getting at the truth about the real world, or rather, fallibilism is an absolutely infallible way of tending towards the truth. Fallibilism is in effect an attempt to set out foundations for knowledge[23] or, what amounts to the same thing, to provide a way of distinguishing between knowledge which is adequately grounded, and so amounts to knowledge properly so-called, and what merely makes some pretensions to be knowledge. For reasons I have already gone into, this issue is not merely a technical one within philosophy, but it seems to be of some general cultural significance.

It is important to realize that Popper never claimed that falsifiability was the criterion for distinguishing between sense and nonsense, in the manner of the logical positivists with their verification principle. For Popper, falsifiability merely provides the demarcation between what is science and what is not science.[24] What is not science, what might be called 'metaphysics,' may be estimable in his view in all kinds of ways; for example, in that it makes suggestions about the world which may be refined in such a way as to become testable in empirical terms and so scientific.[25]

But what still remains is the question of the status of the principle of falsifiability itself. Is it itself a piece of science? Apparently it cannot be, since there is no conjunction of observation statements by which it could conceivably be refuted. But if it is a piece of metaphysics, how is it justifiable as preferable to any other metaphysical statement? No doubt it is an excellent rule of thumb for scientists to follow in their attempts to find out the truth about the world, but how can it be justified as such?

In *Objective Knowledge*, Popper set out powerfully, and to my mind quite convincingly, the account he had defended for decades of what it is for science to approach ever nearer to the truth about the world. All our scientific theories, he insists, remain guesses or conjectures. For such theories to be in the running at all, they must in principle be capable of refutation, by conjunctions of true observation statements; otherwise, they are not to count as scientific. Can we say on what grounds we ought to adopt some scientific theories in preference to others, as 'better' than them? The answer is that, if a new theory is to be preferred to an old one, it must succeed not only where the old one succeeded, but also where it failed, where it was refuted in the manner which has just been described.[26] It is to be inferred from this that 'no theory has been shown to be true, or can be shown to be true'; the best to which we can aspire is theories which are corroborated as better approximations to the truth than other theories, in that they have passed tests which those others have failed.

So much for the setting-out of what it is, on Popper's view, for science to approach closer and closer to knowledge of the real world; this can remain brief in the present context, since it is not in dispute. But it remains to ask how far this account can be justified, or if 'justification' is not to be regarded as a proper demand,[27] 'corroborated' as more worthy of assent than rival views on the matter. It may be suggested that it may be so justified or corroborated in accordance with the general principles of rational discussion.[28] But unless these principles are spelled out in more detail than is implicit in a mere mention, this is clearly not sufficient; a flat-earther could say as much in defence of his own cosmological theories. What evidence is there that Popper's own assertions on this matter are any more in accordance with the truth than their contradictories? Is the principle of falsifiability somehow itself infallible? If so, why is it so? If it is not infallible, how in principle could one non-arbitrarily decide to stand by it, or for that matter to set it aside?

Popper's own attempts to meet this point do not seem to me very impressive. They amount in effect to the following. (1) Arguments against realism are merely philosophical, and philosophers are by and large a pretty contemptible class of persons. (2) It is as misguided, and indeed conceited, to say that the world is a figment of mind as it is to say that beauty is in the eye of the beholder. (3) Language as such is committed to realism. (4) Men of no less stature than Albert Einstein and Winston Churchill have been supporters of realism. (5) It is a fundamental mistake to look for certainty anyway on this or on any other issue; this is of course of the essence of fallibilism.[29]

As to this last suggestion, it looks as though Popper has adroitly used the application of fallibilism to itself as a pretext for accepting some very inadequate arguments in its defense; fallibilism does at this rate indeed sound very fallible. Popper's comments on the matter are great fun to read – it is hardly possible to doubt that the appearance of trifling and irony are quite deliberate – but it can scarcely be said that they meet the issue head on. With regard to the first point, it is to be insisted that arguments for realism, as opposed to the mere assumption that it is true, are just as 'philosophical' as arguments against it; to say, as Popper does, that the latter are 'philosophical in the worst sense' amounts to nothing more than a thinly disguised announcement of a prejudice in favour of realism. And it is a curious piece of philosophical bravado to fall back on the claim that judgments of aesthetic value are objective in order to support the thesis that our knowledge in general is so; the former view is notoriously at least as much in need of defence as the latter. As to the fourth argument, one can only comment that it is hardly less convincing than the first, the second, or the fifth.

In fact, I believe that realism can be defended in a manner adumbrated by the third argument, and which I tried to develop in the first part of this book. The defence may be summarized as follows. If any sense is to be made of a distinction between the real world, on the one hand, and any merely apparent world, world-for-an-individual, or world-for-a-society, on the other, it is presupposed that some 'corrected view'[30] is available, at least in principle, from which such a real world might be apprehended. In the same manner that dreams and illusions, as is so often pointed out in connection with the philosophy of Descartes,[31] presuppose by contrast reality and its knowability at least in principle, so do these merely apparent worlds or worlds for such-and-such an individual or community which may be distinguished from the real world. Idealism and solipsism, each in its own way, amount to denial that there is a real world to be known by the process of learning which starts from the world apparent to any person or group, and proceeds by the appropriate mental process. But the very statement of idealism and solipsism, which imply that our so-called knowledge is not of a real world existing prior to and independently of ourselves and our minds, presupposes the conceivability of such a world, and so the possibility at least in principle of the 'corrected view' from which it might be known. Short of such conceivability and consequent possibility, even the denial implicit in idealism and solipsism is senseless. It is Popper's great merit to have described so forcefully the nature of the mental process by which we may tend increasingly to know the real world, as opposed to being confined to the worlds merely 'of' or 'for' ourselves as individuals or groups. As I have already argued at length, the notions of 'real world' and 'reality' only have a hold in our language and thought as contrasted with what may turn out on investigation to be 'illusory,' or 'unreal,' or 'mere appearance,' or whatever. Popper's principle of falsification amounts to a very ruthless and thoroughgoing recommendation for detecting and progressively eliminating the mistaking of 'mere appearance' for 'reality' in this sense, by constantly subjecting such 'mere appearance' to criticism. But to bring out how we tend to get to know the real world by such means is one thing; to justify or corroborate the thesis that there is such a 'real world,' and that we tend to get to know it in such a way, is another.

In effect, I have just summarized an argument to the effect that the proposition that there is such a real world, and that it is to be known in such a way, is itself to be known *a priori*; but it is not an analytic proposition. It is not exactly a contradiction to deny either that there is a real world or that it is to be known by stringent attempts to falsify our beliefs and assumptions. There is no strictly logical connection between the propositions 'I have carried out investigations on rigorously Popperian principles, which issue in a judgment to the effect that *x*,' and 'The world external to and independent of me is probably[32] characterised by fact *x*.' But it is not the case either that one can know by experience, in any ordinary sense of the word at least,[33] that there is a real as opposed to apparent world or that one progressively gets to know it through trying to falsify one's beliefs and assumptions in experience. Still, there is, as I have argued, a sense in which this thesis may be corroborated and its contradictory refuted through criticism, even though Popper seems to have failed to explain just how this might be done. The more we consider the question of what we could mean by 'reality' or 'the real world' supposed to be in some sense independent of our inquiring minds and the data upon which they operate, the more we realize that it can be nothing other than what we come increasingly to know by subjecting the data to a thorough process of inquiry. If reality were not in some kind of relation to our potential knowledge, at least in principle, we could not even intelligibly declare that it was beyond our capacity to know.[34]

Popper has written that all objections to his account with which he is acquainted assume that he has tried to solve the traditional problem of induction. But he maintains that from his point of view questions like 'How can induction be justified?' are badly formulated.

'Traditional formulations of the principle of induction ... all assume not only that our quest for knowledge has been successful, but also that we should be able to explain why it is successful. However, even on the assumption (which I share) that our quest for knowledge has been very successful so far, and that we know something of our universe, this success becomes miraculously improbable, and therefore inexplicable; for an appeal to an endless series of improbable accidents is not an explanation.'[35]

I believe that any plausibility that can well be attributed to the argument of this passage depends on a confusion of two questions, both of which may be understood as expressed by the sentence 'How is knowledge possible?' The first, which is the one attended to by Popper, is a demand for the causal preconditions of creatures evolving in the universe such as were capable of getting to know something about it, and of their founding and maintaining civilizations which would make this knowledge actual. (I would have thought myself that the meeting of such a demand would count as explanation of a kind; however, this is not the main point at issue.) The second question looks for an overall account of the nature and structure of the world, and of the human mind, which would explain how the latter is capable of gaining knowledge of the former. In attending to the first question, and claiming that it is unanswerable, Popper has misled himself into neglecting the second.

Let us concede to Popper, for the purposes of the present argument, that Kant's fundamental problem, 'How can synthetic judgments be valid *a priori*?,' was an attempt to generalize the problem of induction.[36] If the problem of induction (How can one validly argue from a number of particular premises of the form 'This S is P,' typically arrived at on the basis of observation, to the generalization 'All Ss are P'?) is itself badly formulated, one may well conclude, as Popper appears to do, that Kant's is a pseudo-problem. But it does seem that Kant's problem, whatever its historical occasion, is one aspect of the question we have just been considering. The principle of falsifiability is not an analytic proposition – it cannot, as we have seen, be corroborated in experience; and the problem of its justification cannot merely be brushed aside. How is the process of framing hypotheses (understanding possibilities), and 'corroborating' some of these while falsifying others by reference to observation-statements, appropriate for getting to know the truth about a world which exists and existed prior to and independently of such a process? By virtue of what does this process culminate in statements which are about what is thus independent of themselves?

Kant is notoriously difficult to interpret; but on one very natural inter-pretation of what he says his solution is to deny that our knowledge is actually about what is thus independent of itself.[37] Just because knowl-edge is constituted so largely by these *a priori* elements, he maintains that what comes to be known must be a world-for-us, in effect largely consti-tuted by the process through which we come to know it. I do not think this conclusion is correct, but it is at least an attempt to cope with a real problem. By what right, to take an example which particularly impressed Kant, do we maintain that the world is really characterized by causal rela-tionships, was so prior to humankind's coming to know about it, and would have been so even if human beings had never come to know about it, when the very existence of causal relationships, as opposed to the mere conjunction of observable events adverted to by Hume,[38] can only be established through a judgment which is at once synthetic and *a priori*?

As a matter of fact, I believe that fallibilism, or something very like it, can be justified as a series of what amount to synthetic *a priori* judgments. As I have already argued at length, philosophers do not always sufficiently take into account that some judgments are self-destructive without actu-ally being self-contradictory. For example, the following two propositions, if their implications are properly followed through, can be shown to be self-destructive: (1) that knowledge or true belief is impossible; (2) that it is in general to be arrived at other than by subjecting our judgments to rigorous critical appraisal. It is also in the last resort incoherent, as I have tried to show, to suppose that (3) the real world is other than what is thus to be known. Therefore, the contradictories of these propositions are cor-respondingly certain. I believe that it is failure to spell out these princi-ples and to work out their consequences which has rendered Popper liable to attack by epistemological conventionalists and anarchists. The consequences of (1) and (2) constitute an epistemology; those of (3), a metaphysics. In epistemological and metaphysical inquiries, as in those of other kinds, to be thoroughly critical is to select (provisionally at least) as true those judgments which are best corroborated by the evidence; but in epistemological and metaphysical inquiries, the alternatives are to be rejected as self-destructive, while in other kinds of inquiry they are to be rejected, in Popperian fashion, as falsified by evidence available to observation.

Popper's claim that the term 'knowledge' is more or less equivocal as between scientific knowledge and that of other kinds seems to me unfortunate. Any honest person wants to have knowledge rather than ignorance on the matters with which she is concerned, and to apply her knowledge; in doing so she is liable conscientiously to examine her previous assumptions not just when it suits her to do so, but when the evidence warrants. The mature sciences impress us as they do, it seems to me, as at least on the way to truth about the world just because they apply these principles in a thoroughgoing manner. And principles at least closely akin to those set out by Popper apply both to our moral lives and to the business of interpreting the speech and writings of others. Moral badness is quite largely a matter of failure to attend to evidence which might falsify one's assumption that one is a worthy fellow, or that the position of one's group or class within society is in accordance with the principles of justice. Again, in interpreting an obscure ancient author whose opinions and circumstances are little known, I will be the more likely to get at the truth the wider the range of hypotheses I am aware of as to what she might mean, and the more conscientious I am about rejecting those falsified by the evidence in the document before me. It is in accordance both with common sense and with most philosophy to include the pursuit of truth among the constituents of the good or virtuous life; on the account given in this paragraph, it can readily be seen why this is so.

Popper attacked the empiricists as trying to found knowledge on certainty; Peirce, his fellow-fallibilist, attacked Descartes for the same reason. If my arguments in this chapter are sound, the search for certainty by Descartes and the empiricists was in principle correct; at least if the results so far of applying a method for getting to know the truth must be constantly open to correction, the very method of obtaining these results can hardly be so. Short of certainty at least at the level of method, complete scepticism must inevitably follow.[39] As Popper sees it, 'All theories are hypotheses; all may be overthrown.'[40] But what could be the point of such a claim, except on the assumption that it is by being prepared to overthrow one's hypotheses when they conflict with the evidence that one may approach ever closer to the truth? And in what sense can I be prepared to overthrow the theory or hypothesis that the overthrowing of theories or hypotheses is the best means of approaching the truth? Only in that I can work out whether its contradictory is self-destructive, a kind of 'falsification' to which Popper does not seem to have adverted. Peirce stigmatized Cartesian doubt as at once impractical and insincere.[41] Insincere doubt is pointless, to be sure, but this does not imply that we cannot investigate the presuppositions of our inquiries, and attend to the question of on what indubitable principles they are based, and why and in what sense they are indubitable. In rightly stigmatizing the former kind of doubt as illegitimate, it seems to me, Peirce was misled into overlooking the importance of doubt of the latter kind.

It has been claimed that 'to take fallibilism seriously is to create problems for the notion of truth.'[42] I think this applies only to a fallibilism supposed to operate at the level of epistemology and metaphysics as well as elsewhere. If one acknowledges limits to fallibilism of the kind which I have described, the problems no longer seem to arise. It is *a priori* true, in that the contradictory is self-destructive, that one tends to get at the truth about things by being thoroughly critical in the formation of one's judgments. Apropos of Hume and Kant, Popper remarks that 'induction is invalid because it leads either to an infinite regress or to apriorism.'[43] I am inclined to retort that any thorough investigation of the nature and conditions of knowledge is bound to lead to aporia, scepticism, conventionalism, anarchism, or some sort of *a priori* account.

The complaint has also been made that 'it is hard ... to combine objectivism and fallibilism.'[44] Here again, it seems that this is only so if fallibilism is not conceived within the limits and with the qualifications I have proposed. An inquiry is properly speaking 'objective' if it is comprehensively critical, the type of criticism which is appropriate differing according to whether the inquiry is epistemological or metaphysical, on the one hand, or of some other kind, on the other. By being 'objective' in this sense, as I have tried to show, it will tend to arrive at propositions which are 'objective' in the sense of being so independently of the 'subjective' feelings, opinions, or attitudes of any inquirer.

It has been said that Peirce was driven towards a coherence rather than a correspondence theory of truth, in spite of his inclinations and intentions.[45] It seems to me that such a tendency could only be due to a confusion of two distinct ways in which, as I have already pointed out, statements may 'correspond' to what is independent of them. A statement may be tested for truth or falsity in relation to evidence available to the senses; but this evidence is certainly by no means always, and is perhaps rather seldom, identical with the state of affairs whose being the case or not being the case is strictly speaking what makes the statement true or false. Thus the statement 'Julius Caesar was stabbed to death' is true if and only if the corresponding event happened at some time in the past; it can be tested here and now, however, only on the basis of evidence available in the present. In general, in order to find out what is true about the real world on the basis of evidence available to the senses, one has to attempt to make one's statements coherent with one another. But this is by no means inconsistent with the thesis, which I have already argued at some length to be true, that it is by means of such coherence within one's statements, and correspondence (in one sense) with data available to one's senses, that one comes increasingly to make statements which correspond (in another sense) with the facts and states of affairs which make up the real world.

It has been suggested that 'we shall never be able to know whether our thoughts agree with reality or not.' Suppose we have criteria by which we purport to validate our methods of investigation; we may still ask how we can be sure that these reveal 'undistorted reality.' This will involve us in the invocation of more criteria, and the justification of these in yet more again, and so on *ad infinitum*.[46] On the contrary, it might be asked, how in the long run could one even make sense of the notion that any conception of reality was distorted, except by implicit reference to some in principle available yardstick which would indicate the distortion to be a distortion? In a sense it is true that we can never compare our thoughts with reality, but there is another sense in which it is not. Plainly we cannot directly compare the world as it is in itself with the world as we conceive it to be. But we can advert to the manner in which we correct our successive conceptions of the world, and maintain that our later conceptions of it more closely represent it as it really is than did our earlier ones. We have, as I have already said, a second-order conception of the real world, or the world as it actually is, as that to which our first-order conceptions approximate more and more closely as we strive to correct them in the light of experience. We do indirectly have access to the real world, as that to which our views of the world approximate to the degree that we criticize them rigorously.

According to Stuart Hampshire, 'We cannot now separate the world as we now see it, as a result of the infinitely complicated evolution of our ways of thought and speech as civilised beings, from the world as it really is, somehow divided into its elements by a "natural" system of classification.'[47] But, if what I have argued is on the right lines, there is an important sense in which we can do just this. Short of a rough-and-ready ability to judge what is actually so, as opposed to what merely seemed to them as creatures who had evolved in certain ways, our ancestors simply would not have survived. With the growth of the comprehensively critical attitude which issues in the sciences, the process of disentangling the real from the merely seeming is pushed further; the right classification, which correctly describes things as they are, would be that which, however widely or stringently applied, did not conflict with observation or issue in errors of practice.

Popper will have it that 'the idea of truth is absolutist; but no claim can be made for absolute certainty; we are seekers for the truth but we are not its possessors.'[48] But if we are not absolutely certain even of that much, must we not despair of truth altogether, with the consequence that we fail even to seek it? I believe that the answer is that one can be absolutely certain of some statements about the world and our knowledge of it which are at a very high level of generality, on the grounds that their contradictories are self-destructive. In this way, as I argued in Part I, we can be quite sure that the world or reality is nothing other than what properly corroborated judgments tend to be about. And 'properly corroborated judgments,' at what I have called the first-order level, are those which are susceptible of, and have been subjected to, stringent empirical testing. At that rate (first-order) fallibilism is infallible (at a second-order level), and must be so, if it is not to be self-destructive and so yield to conventionalism and relativism.

8

The Self-Immolation of Scientism: Sellars and Rorty

Two salient features of Sellars's philosophy are, first, his conviction that, as he puts it, 'Science is the measure of all things, of what is that it is, and of what is not that it is not,' and second, his opposition to what he calls 'the myth of the given.' I shall argue that these features are in fundamental conflict with one another and, further, that the philosophical principles developed in this book provide resources for a resolution of the problems which give rise to the conflict. As I suggested in the fourth chapter, these principles issue in a metaphysic which approximates to that of Thomas Aquinas. Sellars has himself given an estimate of Thomism, which he treats with some respect, as making common cause with him in its repudiation of 'idealism,' but which he ultimately finds wanting. A treatment of Sellars from a rather Thomist point of view may thus be not without interest. Sellars by no means capitulates to modern anti-metaphysical fashions; in fact, his view of the role of philosophy has a refreshingly old-fashioned ring about it. 'The aim of philosophy, abstractly formulated,' he says, 'is to understand how things in the broadest sense of the term hang together in the broadest sense of the term.'[1] This could of course be heartily endorsed by any recalcitrant metaphysician, including the Thomist.

What case is there for saying that a high veneration of science, as liable to tell us the truth about things, is in basic conflict with the view that 'the given' is a myth? That there is some *prima facie* case is clear enough, when one considers the reasons for supposing that science is apt to tell us the truth about the matters with which it deals. Scientific method is a matter of propounding and testing hypotheses; and to test a hypothesis is to appeal to facts or to phenomena which are as they are whether one maintains the hypothesis or not. That is to say, they are in some sense 'given,' in that it is not up to the investigator whether they are so or not; she has to look and see whether they are so. Why do the oxygen theory of combustion and Rutherford's theory of the atom form a part of science, in a way that the phlogiston theory of combustion and Thomson's theory of the atom do not? The obvious answer is that there is a substantial range of data or (merely to replace Latin with English) 'givens' which go to confirm the former pair of theories as likely to be true, the latter pair as likely to be false. It is not unfashionable at present to regard 'science' as merely a conglomerate of propositions stated as true by those prestigious persons called 'scientists' in their professional capacity. If this is so, it appears arbitrary to maintain that these propositions are liable to be true, let alone that 'science is the measure of all things.' One may, however, regard the propositions constitutive of science as essentially the result of the application of a method, and liable to be true of the matters with which it deals because and in so far as the method has been followed. But it seems impossible to characterize the method without reference to what is in some sense given. The investigator, in so far as she is scientific, cannot merely invent pointer readings, or say that the marks left by recording pencils are just what she would choose; she has to take such things as they are 'given.'

The considerations which I have just advanced suggest that this topic is of some importance, a point which seems worth making since the topic of 'the given,' and of the 'sense-data' in which it is often supposed to consist, has a very musty air about it, having been so much frequented by philosophers of a couple of generations ago. But as I argued in chapter 3, short of some 'given,' whatever it is held to consist in, in relation to which knowledge claims in science and elsewhere may be tested, I do not see how one is non-arbitrarily to adjudicate between real knowledge and knowledge falsely so called, or between science and pseudo-science. 'Pragmatism' does not really provide a viable alternative here; that action *a* has result *b*, successful or otherwise, in circumstances *c*, is just one kind of 'given' of which those seeking knowledge have to take account.

Why then does Sellars object to 'the given,' and how does he propose to dispense with it? As to the former point, there seems to be no valid strictly logical process, as any number of recent philosophers have pointed out, by which one can infer from the occurrence of any aggregate of private data to the existence of any real object in the public world. Consequently, it is argued, knowledge of such data cannot be the basis for knowledge of that world; and one cannot 'analyze' any statement about the public world in terms of statements about such data. 'It just won't do to say that *x is red* is analyzable in terms of *x looks red to y*.' Also, if such irreducibly private experiences existed, it is impossible to see how we could use our essentially public language to refer to them. How could anything *look* red unless in the first place something really *was* red, to supply some basis for the implicit comparison? Furthermore, there is something offensive to the rational and scientific mind about the notion that certain statements, to the effect that one is enjoying particular sense-experiences, are indisputable and self-validating; such claims are much too redolent of mysticism.

But Sellars's attention is mainly devoted to the latter question, of how we can dispense with such data in accounting for knowledge and for science, as I have already argued that we cannot. His suggestion amounts to the following: (1) There is a hidden propositional claim involved in every report about sensation; (2) This propositional claim is about the public world; (3) Such a propositional claim never merely asserts the occurrence of a 'given' or datum; it is thus subject to public dispute like other propositional claims. One is inclined to say, Sellars concedes, that a remark like 'It looks green' reports 'a minimal fact, on which it is safer to report because one might be mistaken' than if one roundly asserts that it *is* green; for example, 'the fact that the necktie looks green to John on a particular occasion.' But he rejects this account as committing him to a 'given' in the form of sense-data. The heart of the matter, says Sellars, is that experiences always contain propositional claims, which one may or may not endorse. '"X looks green to Jones" differs from "Jones sees that x is green" in that, whereas the latter both ascribes a propositional claim to Jones *and endorses it*, the former ascribes the claim but does not endorse it ... To say that "x looks green to S at t" is, in effect, to say that S has that kind of experience which, if one were prepared to endorse the propositional claim it involves, one would characterize as seeing x to be green at t.'[2]

What is envisaged here is Jones having an experience and making a judgment about the world in accordance with it, and someone else, say Smith, endorsing that judgment or not endorsing it. Jones, let us say, sees the necktie for the first time in a poor light, and says it is green, whereas Smith, who has seen it in a good light and knows it to be blue, does not endorse his statement. However, there is a crucial possibility which Sellars neglects, that Jones himself may fail to endorse his experience, in the sense of committing himself on the basis of it to the statement about the public world which it would normally license. Suppose Jones has himself previously seen the tie in more favourable circumstances. He may then very well say something like, 'This tie looks green to me, though I know very well that it is blue.' What I believe has contributed to Sellars's misapprehension of the matter is that 'This tie looks green to me' very often implies, if only tentatively, that the thing concerned really is green, and so would look green in more favourable circumstances. But he neglects the other possible meaning of the sentence, where there is a mere report of sensation, and no such implication about the public world, where, for example, the sufferer from jaundice complains, 'That chest of drawers looks yellow to me, though I know perfectly well that it is white.'

Sellars does imagine someone in the sort of situation I have described, saying 'I don't know what to say. If I didn't know that the tie is blue ... I would swear that I was seeing a green tie and seeing that it is green.'3 If the subject of this example doesn't know what to say, then he ought to know; Sellars has an interest in his not knowing what to say, since admission that there could be a mere report of sensation which did not somehow include, even if tentatively, a claim about the public world would involve him in acknowledgment of some kind of a 'given.' The conventions of language in fact provide the subject with several ways of expressing himself – 'It looks green to me at the moment, though I know perfectly well that it's really blue,' or 'I have an experience *as though of* a green tie, though I have overwhelming reasons for thinking that the experience is deceptive,' and so on. In an extreme case, for example, when Jones's brain is being stimulated in the relevant areas by means of electrodes and he knows this, he might say, 'I have a visual impression *as though of* a green necktie two feet before my eyes, though I know very well that there is nothing really there but empty space.'4

Those who believe that experiences, or sense-data, provide foundations for knowledge, have to face the objection that, for example, if there were not green things, we would not be able to talk at all of (the expression is a somewhat bizarre one, for all its currency in philosophy a few decades ago) green sense-data. But as I argued in chapter 3, granted that we can talk of real green objects in the public world, we can also, by more or less *ad hoc* modifications of the language which we employ for this, talk of experience *as of* green objects, of experience such as would normally license talk of green objects but does not in this case owing to special circumstances, and so on. It is liable to be objected that, if talk about sense-data depends on talk about physical objects in the manner I have just sketched, sense-data could not in any useful sense be the foundations of knowledge. But this, I think, would be a mistake. The fact is, as I have already argued, that language about physical objects which one observes is foundational in one sense, and that sense-data are foundational in another. We could not speak truly and with good reason about real physical objects, in other words, gain knowledge of them, unless we enjoyed experience *as though of* physical objects. Such experience in general licenses talk about real physical objects, enables us to make justified true judgments about them; but in special circumstances, as we discover, it does not. When asked to say what I see in an ordinary room which I have just entered, I may confidently state that I see a table; but having just the same experience in a psychology laboratory, I may warily declare that I enjoy visual experiences *as of* a table, suspecting that later experience may confirm the possibility that, this place having the reputation that it does, there will turn out to be no table there.

As Sellars says, 'if there is a logical dimension in which other empirical propositions rest on observational reports, there is another logical dimension in which the latter rest upon the former.'[5] So far as the metaphor of 'foundations' leads us to overlook this, it is certainly misleading. However, altogether to reject it seems to have the far more dangerous and paradoxical result which I mentioned at the beginning of this chapter, that there remains no sufficient criterion for distinguishing between science and pseudo-science, or between legitimate claimants and mere pretenders to the title of knowledge.

It is a misleading way of expressing the manner in which sense-data may reasonably be said to be the foundations of knowledge to say that knowledge that there are observable physical objects in one's immediate environment is founded on *knowledge that* one is undergoing certain sense-experiences. If knowledge is a matter of justified or grounded true judgment, *that* we are undergoing this or that experience seldom rises to the level of knowledge. Having the relevant set of experiences, we usually make a spontaneous judgment that the public state of affairs which we are apparently so justified in asserting is the case. The judgment merely *that* we are having certain experiences, and so knowledge of the matter on the definition just given, is a comparatively sophisticated achievement, which we learn as a result of reflection on the phenomena of error and illusion, or through a certain kind of philosophical training.

It may be asked how sense-data could be in any sense the foundation of empirical knowledge, if there is no strictly logical route from any set of statements about sense-data to any set of statements about physical objects, or vice versa. The answer is, as I have already argued, that statements about physical objects and events can be related to sense-experiences as their ultimate grounds, without the connection being in any strict sense logical. This is most obvious in the case of historical events, where it seems quite evident that it is one thing, say, to claim that George Washington was the first president of the United States, another thing to set out the grounds available in experience to persons in the twentieth century for this claim. Thomists and idealists have always emphasized that the active role of the human intellect is coming to know the real world; this has tended to lead idealists, though not Thomists, to be doubtful or at least equivocal about the reality of that world prior to, or independently of, human thought about it. Thomists, in common with empiricists, emphasize that knowledge starts with experience, but they also maintain that, due to the functioning of what Aquinas called the *intellectus agens* (which amounts to the questioning and hypothesizing aspect of the mind), we can get to know of, or make justified true judgments about, affairs (like the existence of electrons, Julius Caesar, and God) which cannot, at least now in the case of the second, be direct objects of experience.[6]

Bernard Lonergan has pointed out 'the isomorphism of Thomist and scientific thought,'[7] with the scientist's observations related to his hypotheses as the 'matter' of the Thomist to his 'form,' and the hypotheses of the scientist related to his verifications as the Thomist's 'essence' to his 'existence.'[8] There is, furthermore, an 'intentional' relation for the Thomist between the contents of the mind and the real world which the mind comes to know; in other words, the world is just what the mind aims at knowing so far as it strenuously applies itself to questioning the phenomena of experience.[9] A Thomist might thus well agree, on his own terms, with Sellars's dictum that 'science is the measure of all things,' on the ground that, when the presuppositions of science are clarified and generalized, they will be found to issue in a Thomist metaphysics or overall account of reality. Just as the *intellectus agens* 'abstracts' the 'quiddities' or 'essences' of things from the world of common experience, so the scientist gets at the real nature of things, or at least moves towards doing so, by the active propounding and testing of hypotheses. Though logic in a strict sense is an important aspect of this process, the process, as Hume, Popper, and others have conclusively shown, cannot possibly be reduced to it. But once the nature of this process is clarified, it may easily be seen how our knowledge of the world might in an important sense be 'grounded' in the sense-data constitutive of experience, without being truth-conditionally related to statements regarding such experience. (The murder of Edward II of England in the fourteenth century could not conceivably be *a matter of* any experience which might be enjoyed by a historian in the twentieth century; but for all that, such experience may well be relevant to establishing that this event occurred, and of what nature it was.)

Sellars will have it that it is a false dilemma, that knowledge must either have 'foundations' which themselves need no support, or that it is just a set of mutually reinforcing propositions. 'Empirical knowledge, like its sophisticated extension, science, is rational, not because it has a *foundation* but because it is a self-correcting enterprise which can put *any* claim in jeopardy, though not all at once.'[10] However, it is hard to see what the view that knowledge is self-correcting, or indeed that it is empirical, amounts to, unless a particular kind of 'given' is assumed in deference to which the corrections are made. Moreover, unless some restrictions are put on the criteria according to which science is to be 'self-correcting,' the possibility is left open that the opinions of scientists will be just as scientific if they are 'corrected' due to bribery or career prospects. That no individual observation-claim ought to be sacrosanct must indeed be acknowledged; observations should not be taken seriously unless repeatable. But to acknowledge that individual fragments of 'the given' have very little weight in themselves by no means implies that appeal to 'the given' has no place in science or epistemology. To take a parallel case: that it may be rational to suspect the report of any one witness in deference to a consensus of other witnesses by no means entails that all appeal to witnesses is mistaken or a sham. In the long run, I believe, the dilemma which Sellars tries to stigmatize as false is a true one; short of a 'given' of some kind, no adequate justification of most knowledge-claims is possible.

It is a main task of philosophy, according to Sellars, to fuse the common-sense and the scientific conceptions of the world and humankind within it into a single coherent view.[11] The Thomist is perfectly capable of doing this; reality or 'being' consists of existing essences, to be grasped as to *how* they are and *that* they are by the 'agent intellect' acting upon appearances. If 'essence' is the aspect of reality to be grasped by hypotheses (understanding possibilities), and 'existence' is that which corresponds to their verification, and 'potency' is that which is equivalent to the experience which both suggests each hypothesis and provides the means of testing it, then Thomist metaphysics is at once presupposed and vindicated by a scientific method whose essence is progressively to discover reality by the *verification*[12] of *hypotheses* in *experience*.

How far do Sellars's own philosophical principles enable him to fulfil the task he sets for philosophy? He finds the Thomist tradition wanting, notably in its view that the intellect, in order to reflect reality, must be immaterial. He remarks on the temptation to maintain that speech reflects the world because the thought which it expresses does so; he will have it that the opposite is the case. This leaves him with the problem of how speech might be explained as reflecting the world, without any appeal being made to thought. Let us suppose, he says, that a robot emits radiation which is reflected back from its environment in such a way as to correspond to the structure of that environment, and that it moves about 'recording its "observations," enriching its tape with deductive and inductive "inferences" from its "observations" and guiding its "conduct" accordingly.' We might then allow ourselves to talk about the robot in human terms as finding out more and more about the world. What would be the analogue of our knowledge of, say, lightning, on the tape inside the robot? It would be 'the correspondence of the "place" of a certain pattern on the tape in the system of patterns on the tape to the "place" of the flash of lightning in the robot's spatio-temporal environment.' At that rate there is no need to postulate 'the absolute nature *lightning* existing immaterially in the robot's electronic system,' in the manner of Thomism. Only material entities are in question here; the relevant pattern on the tape means the same as our word 'lightning' due to its similarity of role in the robot's behaviour to that of the word 'lightning' in ours.[13]

Sellars draws from this what he regards as an important moral for our conception of the nature of our own inner states and, in particular, of our thoughts. Descartes, among many others, considered that we had non-inferential knowledge of these inner states of ours, including our thoughts and sensations. But the upshot of these reflections is that to know our inner states *as* thoughts and sensations *of* things in the world is to know them *in a role*, rather than *in themselves*. This leaves open the possibility, which is the only one really compatible with science but that the Cartesian conception would exclude, that in themselves they are states of the human organism as investigated by neurology. As to the intellect itself, 'I submit that as belonging to the real order it is the central nervous system ... There is no absurdity in the idea that what we know *directly* as *thoughts* in terms of *analogical* concepts may *in propria persona* be neurological states.'[14]

I believe this conception of human knowledge and its relation to the world, ingenious as it is, to be subject to the disadvantages of all consistently materialist accounts of knowledge. There is a conceptual crevasse, which Sellars has by no means managed to bridge, between an entity's

reaction to its environment at a particular place and time and its knowledge of a world vastly extended in space and time beyond that environment, and which exists and is as it is largely prior to and independently of
the entity and its reactions. Admittedly, we are stimulated to get to know
the world by the need to react adequately to our environment if we are to
survive and prosper, but this does not imply that the knowledge is ultimately reducible to the reaction. Consequently, Sellars's ingenious and
complex account of the building up of a pattern of reactions does not
begin to explain that acquisition of knowledge which he set out to
explain. Furthermore, Sellars will have it that the analogues in the robot's
tape, brought about by interaction with its environment, to elements in
that environment may fairly be compared to a picture of it. But, it may
fairly be asked, in virtue of what is a picture of something a picture of it?
It seems to me, only by virtue of a subject's intended use of it as such. The
simple fact is, I believe, that material object or complex *a* means material
object or complex *b* only by virtue of being or having been intended to do
so by some person or persons. Certainly, one can imagine limiting cases
where one such object or complex can mean another, when not specifically made or formed to do so. Thus a chimpanzee might scrawl random
pencil marks on a sheet of paper, which turned out to be usable as a map
of Medicine Hat, Alberta. But it would not *be* in any sense a map of that
town, nor would its lines represent its streets or its blobs its buildings,
until *someone* had hit on the idea of using them as such. When one attends
to these facts, Sellars's learned talk of 'projection' and 'isomorphism' and
allusions to recent developments in the science of cybernetics,[15] are like
so much whistling in the dark. The sequence of marks '$713,' appearing
directly after you have pressed a series of buttons outside your bank,
means that you have a balance of $713, by virtue of the fact that *someone*
has programmed a computer in such a way that it should mean this. In
fine, as I argued in chapter 2, meaning presupposes persons, and cannot
be explained exhaustively in terms of structural analogies between sets of
physical objects and events.

If the mental cannot be explained in terms of what is material, is it possible to explain the material in terms of what is mental, or do we simply
have to put up with dualism? In the relevant sense, I believe that the
material can be explained in terms of the mental, and that Thomism, at
least when expanded to take into account the transcendental considerations which have tended to preoccupy philosophers since Kant, is able
thus to explain it. As I have already said, reality, for the Thomist, consists
of potency, form, and act, which are the analogues in reality of the expe-

rience, the envisagement of possibilities, and the verification of some of these possibilities as so, by which the human mind comes to know reality. We spontaneously believe, and tend to confirm by rational investigation, that there are two overall types of being, that which is thus to be known as not itself knowing, and that which is to be known as itself knowing; these constitute the material and spiritual aspects of the world. Thus, briefly, matter and the material can be accounted for as an aspect of that which is to be known by mind or the spiritual, whereas mind cannot be accounted for as exhaustively constituted by matter, for all the ingenuity of Sellars and others who have tried to show that it can.

Sellars clearly thinks that his own account of the manner in which thought and speech reflect the world is to be commended as a means of laying the ghost of idealism.[16] This raises the questions: for what reason and in what sense of the term does Sellars object to idealism, and in what sense he is right in objecting to it. The reasons for which he is right to object to idealism, I believe, regard precisely those aspects of it in which it is opposed to Thomism. However, I think it can also be shown that his own account of knowledge and reality is defective so far as it fails to bring out the way in which the mind, as it were, constructs the reality which it comes to know, as emphasized in their different ways by both Thomists and idealists, who are at one in stressing the active role of the intellect in coming to know. In what sense, if at all, is Thomism, as I have described it, an 'idealist' doctrine? It is so, in the sense that it gives an account of what is real, including that which is material, as what is to be known by the human mind. But it is not so, in that it by no means denies, or implies the denial, that what is thus to be known exists largely prior to and independently of the human mind which thus comes to know it. Indeed, we have excellent reasons, as the result of the operations of our minds, to suppose that a world of things existed billions of years prior to the existence of human minds which could gain knowledge of it. Sellars is quite correct to object to any form of idealism which implies denial of this fact. However, it remains a question whether and how far such a world, which can be adequately characterized in general terms only as what a mind might discover, could exist prior to and independently of mind as such.[17] And, of course, it has been characteristic of Thomists to assert that at least one spiritual being exists prior to the material world, accounting for its existence and its overall nature and structure.[18] Let us distinguish between idealism (a) and idealism (b), between the view that the material universe has no existence apart from the human mind and the view that the universe has no existence apart from mind as such. Sellars would repudiate both idealism (a) and idealism (b), and is quite correct in see-ing Thomists as united with himself in opposing idealism (a). But his own repudiation of idealism (b), which would be maintained by Thomists, seems to depend on an account of how mind might be exhaustively expli-cable in terms of matter in a certain state of complexity, which I have already argued to be inadequate.

That the Thomist account of knowledge is 'oversimplified' may well be true, in so far as it was originally formulated by a thinker innocent of our modern information on the actual complexities of the process of acquir-ing knowledge. But the important question is whether it is correct, and an improvement on rival theories, so far as it goes; no Thomist worth her salt would deny that it is subject to supplementation in the light of investi-gations which have occurred since the thirteenth century. The facts seem to be these: (1) By means of scientific investigation we come to know of an intelligible world, existing prior to and independently of ourselves, which explains what we observe in the 'world' of common experience; (2) The former seems to be the 'world' which is ultimately real; (3) This 'world' is to be known by active inquiry into the data of experience, in which inquiry grasps 'quiddities' or 'essences' (examples would be 'phlo-giston,' 'oxygen,' 'ether,' and 'electron'), some of which tend to be veri-fied in experience as 'existent'; (4) This process through which by means of the 'active intellect' we come to grasp the real 'essences' of things is progressive and cumulative, and is not to be achieved all at once. (1) and (2) are propositions in support of which Thomism, Sellars, and the scien-tific world-view all concur, though, as I argued earlier, Sellars's aspersions on 'the given' make it impossible to show why these propositions are true. The cumulative and progressive character of science, alluded to in (4), was certainly not fully grasped by Aquinas or by classical Thomism; in this sense and to this degree, Sellars is quite right in calling the Thomist the-ory of knowledge oversimplified. But this is by no means to impugn the central and essential Thomist insight expressed by (3), especially when the failure of Sellars and others to set out an adequate alternative is taken into account.

Many of Sellars's arguments are developed further by Richard Rorty, in a direction of which one feels Sellars himself would not at all approve. Rorty's principal concern throughout his influential book, *Philosophy and the Mirror of Nature*, is to contest that claim, that mind is the mirror of nature, which he takes to be characteristic of traditional philosophy. What is implied by this claim? Evidently the assertion that 'mind is the mirror of nature' is metaphorical, since no one takes the mind to be literally a mirror; but what literal sense is conveyed by the metaphor? There are two obvious possibilities: (1) that just by contemplating nature, without using our minds in any active way, we may come to 'reflect' nature in the sense of making true judgments about it; (2) that our minds may come to 'reflect' nature, in the sense of coming to make true judgments about it, by following a certain set or sets of procedures. I will take for granted here that it is quite wrong to suppose that mind is the mirror of nature in the former sense. We do not come to find out the chemical processes within goats' kidneys, or the domestic habits of the people of ancient Ugarit, by passive contemplation of what lies about us. But I believe that mind is a mirror of nature in the latter sense, and that Rorty is wrong in denying this. I shall try to argue the point in two ways: first, by showing that the position leads to consequences which are paradoxical to an intolerable degree; second, by defending against Rorty's attacks some accounts given by philosophers of how we actually can come to make true judgments about the world.

It seems essential to Rorty's position that the 'correspondence' theory of truth is erroneous, and that the notion of 'truth' is simply internal to particular types of discourse.[19] It is not the case for him, apparently, that truth is a matter of a relation between what is stated within types of human discourse and facts which largely are and are as they are prior to and independently of human discourse. On the other hand, Rorty wishes, very properly in my view, to dissociate himself from the opinion that we really bring the world into existence in the process of 'getting to know about' it. However, it seems to me that, with the addition of a premiss which few would deny, the position which he maintains leads inexorably to the one which he repudiates. This premiss has been brought to the attention of recent philosophers by Alfred Tarski, who has made famous the principle that 'p' is true if and only if p.[20] From what Rorty says, it looks as though whether 'p' is true depends on nothing over and above the rules and methods of procedure governing human discourse about p. So, assuming Tarski's principle, whether it is the case that p also depends on nothing over and above these rules and methods. For example, whether there really was such a person as Moses, and whether there really are such things as black holes, depends on the savants within the relevant disciplines. If one follows through Rorty's principles, in other words, granted one additional and not very controversial assumption, it would seem that astronomers and historians, rather than finding out what is the case prior to and independently of their own inquiries, bring into being the states of affairs they are supposed to be investigating in the course of 'investigating' them. The states of affairs in the universe depend on the say-so of savants, rather than what savants say being true or false, as nearly everyone else would suppose, according to whether the relevant states of affairs are the case or not. The existence of ichthyosauri at an earlier era in the oceans of the earth and the presence of red giant stars in our galaxy depend on what palaeontologists and astronomers say, rather than the truth of what palaeontologists say on the matter depending on whether there were or were not ichthyosauri, and the truth of what astronomers say depending on whether there are or are not red giant stars in our galaxy. I submit that this is a little hard to swallow.

Rorty's views may not require any 'idealist metaphysical underpinnings,'[21] but if the essence of idealism is that there is no material world prior to and independent of our discourse about the world, they lead straight to idealism.[22]

Epistemology is concerned with the question of how, by the use of our minds, we are able to come to knowledge of states of affairs like the ones mentioned earlier, which, except on idealist assumptions, largely obtain and are as they are independently of our minds. According to Rorty, epistemology is not a proper area of inquiry at all; its very existence is based on a mistake. What is the truth on any topic, in Rorty's view, is simply to be established by the experts on that topic; there is no method which they all follow or all ought to follow, which it might be the business of the epistemological branch of philosophy to clarify. Knowledge consists of statements which are generally agreed upon, at least by those members of the community who are officially recognized as experts on the relevant topics; and the question of how and why they come to make the statements they do is one to be answered by the empirical psychologist.[23]

Rorty is quite right, I believe, in holding that it is of the essence of epistemology to maintain that there are two components of human knowing, that, on the one hand, there is a 'given' and, on the other hand, there is a set of mental procedures which one is supposed to apply to this 'given' in order to establish what is the case.[24] In Part I of this book, I argued at length that this view was not only of the essence of epistemology, but quite correct. But according to Rorty, all such arguments have been failures, and investigation of the issue shows that such failure is inevitable. I shall try in what follows to contest this claim. But first it is necessary to present Rorty's argument in sufficient detail to do it adequate justice.

What is it (asks Rorty) to conceive the mind as a 'mirror of nature'? It is to think of knowledge as 'accurate representation, made possible by special mental processes, and intelligible through a general theory of representation.' For all the notorious differences between the types of philosophy which derive from Frege and Russell, on the one hand, and from Husserl, on the other, they do have one crucial feature in common. In Kantian fashion, they try to put philosophy in the position of judging science and other areas of culture on the basis of alleged special knowledge of their 'foundations.' To be sure, analytical philosophy differs from its Kantian prototype in conceiving representation in linguistic rather than mental terms, and thus attempts to exhibit the representation through philosophy of language rather than quasi-psychologically in a 'transcendal critique'; but the basic conception is the same. Traditional philosophy, from Descartes through Kant to the analysts, is dominated by the picture of the mind as a great mirror, containing representations of reality some of which are accurate, some not, and susceptible to elucidation by 'pure, non-empirical methods.' Short of this picture, the idea that knowledge consists in accurate representation would never have occurred to any one. One reason for the persistence of this conception is that it seems to promise some future to philosophy since, if empirical psychology is recognized as being capable of telling us all we wish to know about knowledge, philosophers may well seem to be out of a job. This was an issue at the end of the nineteenth century, when analytical philosophy and phenomenology were both inaugurated as a way out of the apparent impasse. However, the protests against the assumption that culture needed 'grounding,' and against the pretensions of the theory of knowledge to be able to perform this task, made, for example, by Friedrich Nietzsche and William James, went largely unheard. But the issue is still more inescapable now.[25]

The very possibility of a philosophical, as distinct from a psychological, 'theory of knowledge' depends on the assumption that knowledge is a matter of adding something by the mind to what is given to the senses. But this distinction, between an empirical given and what is imposed upon it by our mental faculties, has been criticized on a number of occasions during the history of the analytical movement, and the criticisms came to a head in the early 1950s. Notably, Wilfred Sellars has attacked the 'myth of the given'; Willard Quine, the distinction between necessary and contingent propositions. Both criticisms are at bottom behaviouristic, and derive from the thesis that 'justification is not a matter of a special relation between ideas (or words) and objects, but of conversation, of social practice.' Sellars and Quine both attack logical empiricism by, in effect, raising questions about the privilege it claims for certain assertions, as direct reports of what is supposed to be 'given' to sensation.

Quine asks how an anthropologist could ever discriminate sentences, which natives confidently and constantly assert, 'into contingent empirical platitudes on the one hand and necessary conceptual truths on the other.' Sellars for his part demands 'how the authority of first-person reports of, for example, how things appear to us, the pains from which we suffer, and the thoughts that drift before our minds differs from the authority of expert reports on, for example, metal stress, the mating behaviour of birds, or the colours of physical objects.' Crucial to his argument are the premises that 'there is no such thing as a justified belief which is non-propositional, and no such thing as a justification which is not a relation between propositions.' So to speak of our (non-propositional) acquaintance with redness as 'grounding' our knowledge of the proposition that something is a red object is always wrong. So far as Sellars is concerned, the certainty of a subject's reports of her own pain derives from the fact that other persons are not disposed to question it, not the other way about. In Quine's view, private events in the mind are an idle hypothesis which explains nothing. 'In fine, if assertions are justified by society rather than by the nature of the inner episodes they express, there is no point in trying to isolate privileged episodes.'[26]

But, it may be asked, why *should* we suppose that fundamental epistemic notions should be accounted for in behavioural terms? What grounds are there for supposing that 'Smith knows that *p*' is a matter of the status of Smith's statements among his fellows, rather than of a relation between some subject and some object, between nature and its mirror? The answer is that the only alternative seems to be to take knowledge of inner states as premises from which our knowledge of other things is normally inferred, and without which knowledge would be ungrounded. But it is not really coherent, and does not in the last analysis make sense, to suggest that human knowledge has foundations or grounds. It should be remembered that to say that truth and knowledge 'can only be judged by the standards of our own day' is not to say that it is the less important, or 'more "cut off from the world,"' than we had supposed. It is just to say 'that nothing counts as justification, unless by reference to what we already accept, and that there is no way to get outside our beliefs and our language so as to find some test other than coherence.' The fact is that justification has always been as described here in behaviourist terms; only the professional philosophers have thought it might be otherwise, since only they are haunted by the bogey of epistemological scepticism.[27]

What Sellars and Quine oppose as 'residual Platonism' is not so much the hypostatizing of non-physical entities as the notion of 'correspondence' with such things as the final court of appeal for evaluating present practices. Unfortunately both of them, for all that it is incompatible with their basic insights, substitute for this correspondence to physical entities, and specifically to the basic entities, whatever they turn out to be, of physical science. But when their doctrines are purified, they converge on a single claim – that no account of knowledge can depend on the assumption of some privileged relation to reality. Their work brings out why an account of knowledge can amount only to a description of human behaviour.[28]

What, then, is to be said of these 'inner states,' and of the direct reports of them which have played so important a role in traditional epistemology? For a person to feel is nothing else than for him to have an ability to make a certain type of non-inferential report; to attribute feelings to babies is to acknowledge in them latent abilities of this kind. Nonconceptual, non-linguistic 'knowledge' of what feelings or sensations are like is attributed to beings on the basis of potential membership of our community. Babies and the more attractive animals are credited with having feelings on the basis of that spontaneous sympathy which we extend to anything humanoid, in contrast with the mere 'response to stimuli' attributed to photoelectric cells and to animals which no one feels sentimental about. It is consequently wrong to suppose that moral prohibitions against hurting babies and the better-looking animals are 'ontologically grounded' in their possession of feelings; the relation of dependence is really the other way round. Similarly, we could not be mistaken in supposing that a four-year-old child has knowledge but no one-year-old does, any more than we could be mistaken in taking the word of a statute that eighteen-year-olds can marry freely but seventeen-year-olds cannot. (There is no more 'ontological ground' for the distinction which it may suit us to make in the former case than in the latter.) Again, such a question as 'Are robots conscious?' calls for a decision on our part whether or not to treat robots as members of our linguistic community. All this is of a piece with the insight brought into philosophy by Hegel, that the individual apart from his society is just another animal.[29]

If philosophers give up their vain ambition to find 'solutions' to the so-called problem of knowledge, what is there left for them to do? Seventy years after Russell's and Husserl's attempt at a salvage operation, we are back with the problem which faced them: 'If philosophy becomes too naturalistic, hard-nosed positive disciplines will nudge it aside; if it becomes too historicist, then intellectual history, literary criticism, and similar soft spots in the "humanities" will swallow it up.' Quine seems disposed to take the first way out. After arguing that there is no hard boundary line between science and philosophy, he appears to draw the moral that science can replace philosophy. But it is not at all clear why science, rather than art, politics, or religion, should take over the vacated area. Quine admires the natural sciences, and evinces a fastidious distaste for the apparently ineliminable fuzziness of the humanities; but it is difficult to see his preferences in the matter as in the last analysis any more than aesthetic.[30]

The other option looks more promising; and the way forward in this direction has been shown especially by three philosophers, Wittgenstein, Heidegger, and Dewey. Each of these first tried to find a means of making philosophy 'foundational,' and each of them broke free of the presuppositions underlying such an attempt in their later work. This later work was 'therapeutic rather than constructive, edifying rather than systematic.' That is to say, it was aimed to help their readers, and society at large, to pass beyond outworn vocabularies and attitudes, and no longer to 'ground' intuitions and customs which prevail at present. On such a view, while knowledge does consist after all in what we are justified in believing, justification is 'a social phenomenon rather than a transaction between "the knowing subject" and "reality."'[31]

I agree with Rorty that, if the mind is to be the 'mirror of nature,' 'the given' must be no myth, that there must be some basis in experience on which supposition is to be erected and in relation to which it is to be justified, if any hypothesis is to be true of a world which exists independently of our suppositions. Science is taken by Sellars to be the measure of truth,[32] but the reason why it is the measure of truth, if it is, cannot be provided without what amounts to an appeal to epistemological foundations. Short of these, as Rorty says, one may properly ask why science and not rather politics or religion? But the most obvious route to the articulation of such foundations is blocked off by talk about 'the myth of the given.' Of course, if all that is at issue here is that the most widely admired scientists say what they say, and that one had better defer to them if one wants to get on in the world, there arises no problem of foundations. The problem only arises if one claims, as I think the vast majority of people would, that what the most widely admired scientists say is liable to be true of a world which largely existed prior to and independently of them and their sayings. Is it not very odd at once to make this claim and to deny that there is any basis (or foundation) for it?

Sellars has offered an argument, which is accepted by Rorty, to the effect that the kind of 'foundations' proposed for knowledge by traditional epistemologists cannot in fact be provided. Sellars's fundamental point in this connection is that statements can be justified only by other statements, and not by supposed data of experience.[33] It appears to me, as I argued at length in chapter 3, that there is a sense in which this is true, and a sense in which it is not, and that the distinction between these senses is fundamental to this whole issue. Suppose I am asked by someone outside the room I am occupying whether there is a black cat in it. I look up, observe, or seem to observe, a black cat a few feet away from my eyes, and report that there is. It seems clear to me that my experiences *as of* a black cat, whether I state that I have enjoyed them or not, do in a sense provide grounds for my report that there is a black cat with me in the room. No doubt I could have had just such experiences *as of* a black cat if quite other things were suitably disposed in my visual field (as might be the case in a psychology laboratory), or if my cerebral cortex were electrically stimulated in the appropriate way. But, given that I have no reason to suspect such special circumstances, I have excellent grounds *in* my experience for supposing that there would have been a black cat in the room whether I had attended to the matter – soliciting the relevant experiences by properly disposing my sense organs – or not. I could well report the experiences which are the ground of my claim, but Sellars provides no good reason that I can see for denying that the experiences are the grounds of my claim, whether I report them or not. The statement that I am enjoying sense-experiences as of a black cat is grounds for the statement that there really is a black cat where there seems to me to be, in a slightly different sense from that in which my sense-experiences as such are so, but that by no means shows that the sense-experiences as such are not grounds at all.

I have already, in chapter 3, dealt with the difficulty raised by recent philosophers against the notion that we can report experiences as such, as distinct from publicly observable states of affairs, in the world, and the manner in which 'private' experiences may be the basis for judgments about things in the 'public' world, without strict logical entailment being involved between the one and the other. Logic, in the strict sense of the word at least, while it does facilitate the business of finding out about the real world on the basis of our experiences, is incapable in principle of exhausting what is involved in it, as has been quite evident since Hume's remarks on induction, and has been re-emphasized in our own time by Sir Karl Popper and others. To concoct a hypothesis is not a matter of logic, at least in anything but a misleadingly broad sense of the term, nor is the matching of logical deductions from a hypothesis with items of experience. But both of these steps are essential aspects of finding out, on the basis of experience, about a world which exists (according to all but strict philosophical idealists) largely prior to and independently of our experience.

I am by no means trying to argue for empiricism, but I am trying to defend against Sellars and Rorty one cardinal thesis of empiricism, that there is a sense in which knowledge depends on, has 'foundations' in, experience. I have contested the view that the thesis that it is so dependent is incoherent, and I have admitted, but dismissed as irrelevant, the claim that the dependence of knowledge of the real world on experience cannot be reduced to logic in the strict sense. It appears to follow from this that it is incorrect to hold, in the matter of Rorty, that what makes one's opinions knowledge is nothing more or less than their acceptance by other members of one's community. According to nearly everyone else's account of the matter, knowledge is true and well-founded belief about a world which exists and is very largely as it is whether anyone holds true beliefs about it or not. Such true belief is apt to be arrived at (to cut a long story short) by attention to experience, by envisagement of hypotheses, and by acceptance as probably or certainly so in each case of the hypothesis best corroborated by the experience. As I argue in chapters 5 and 10, so far as pressures towards social agreement promote such mental activities, they are apt to increase knowledge, and so far as they inhibit them, they are apt to hinder it; but social agreement is at this rate certainly not *constitutive* of knowledge.

In this connection, it is worth considering the following valid argument:

If there were no experiential given, we could attain no knowledge of any world of things and events existing largely prior to, and independently of, ourselves.
But there is no experiential given.
Therefore we can attain no knowledge of any world of things and events existing largely prior to, and independently of, ourselves.

The conclusion is what is generally known as idealism, to which Rorty seems committed all but explicitly. The tradition which Rorty attacks affirms the first premiss, and denies the conclusion by dint of denying the second. Sellars appears to assert the second premiss, and to avoid idealism by denying the first. But I believe that Rorty is quite right in affirming the first premiss. Is it not rather odd, after all, to claim that we do, or might, gain knowledge of a real world independent of ourselves without such knowledge being grounded in experience? If there were grounds which did not at least include experience, what could these be? And in what non-Pickwickian sense can knowledge without grounds count as knowledge at all?

The argument taken from Sellars is, I think, Rorty's most serious warrant for his conclusion that knowledge cannot be grounded in experience. That derived from Quine seems based on a misunderstanding. Suppose one concedes to Quine his famous contention that no hard-and-fast distinction can be drawn between analytic statements and empirical truisms. This does not begin to imply that there is not a profound distinction, in degree if not in kind, between analytic statements and empirical truisms, on the one hand, and immediate reports of sensations and observed states of affairs, on the other, and, thus, between statements less or more subject to modification in the light of experience. There would not be the least difficulty in an anthropologist finding out the difference, in the case of a tribe she was studying, simply by distinguishing between those indicative statements which were used and agreed to by members of the tribe only within a restricted range of circumstances and those which were still used and agreed to in totally different circumstances.

I have tried to show that it is possible to defend an account of empirical foundations of knowledge against Rorty's objections. Is it possible to show that such an account is positively preferable to the one supplied by Rorty? It seems to me that it is, and this basically for two reasons: that Rorty's position, unlike its rival, gives rise to paradoxes which are an affront to common sense, and that it is actually self-destructive. I have already remarked that, with the addition of a premiss which nearly everyone would accept, his position leads to idealism, to the view that human beings by their thought or language make up the 'real world' in the process of coming to 'know about it.' Rorty maintains that we have no way of getting outside our beliefs and our language to find any test for truth other than coherence.[34] This is plausible by dint of being true in one sense, false in another. It is indeed true that we can never believe what is outside the range of our beliefs, or talk about what is beyond the scope of our talk. And yet it is also true that we can extend the range of our thought, and of our discourse, by the kind of attention to experience and envisagement and testing of hypotheses which I have described in Part I. Someone sees a tiny disc through a telescope, and postulates the existence of a planet of which no one before, perhaps, had any conception. In this kind of way, the scope of our discourse and of our true belief has come to extend vastly further than it did, say, five centuries ago; although pulsars and white-dwarf stars and radio galaxies apparently existed then, we know of their existence now, though our ancestors at that time had no conception of them. And of course the same process of observation, hypothesis, and testing, which has led from their view of the world to ours, is almost certain, if indeed it is allowed to continue, to lead from our view of the world to something different in the future, which will be 'truer,' in virtue of closer correspondence to the word as it really is. We can, in an indirect way, transcend the beliefs and the ways of speaking of our own place and time by understanding how observation, hypothesis, and testing gave rise to them, and are liable to modify them in the future. It is only with this crucial qualification that it is possible to accept Rorty's claim that truth and knowledge can only be judged by the standards of our own day. We do not simply accept the say-so of our most prestigious contemporaries about what is true and what is to count as knowledge; we can have some inkling at least of the mental processes by which the allegedly true propositions constitutive of knowledge were arrived at and by which they may be shown in future to be false.

I agree that appeal to 'inner processes' as the final arbiters of truth is the only alternative to behaviourism, but I believe that this alternative can be justified. The fact is that each of us learns in her own experience what it is to observe, to inquire, and so to discern what is probably or certainly so from what is probably or certainly not so. Admittedly, our capacity for doing so would be at best greatly impaired, at worst totally non-existent, if such mental capacities were not described in our public language; but of course they are so, as I illustrated in the last sentence. It appears to be false as a matter of common experience, though one would infer it from what Rorty says, that we learn the word 'true' simply in the context of deference to the opinion of the majority, or of the socially approved 'experts' in any field. On the contrary, we learn its meaning and use at least partly in the context of the use each of us makes of her own powers of observation and inquiry.

Rorty labels his own account of knowledge as 'behaviouristic,' but I think it can be shown actually in the last analysis to be incompatible with behaviourism. As I understand it, a strictly behaviourist analysis of the proposition 'Smith knows that p' would be a matter of Smith's disposition to assent to the statement that p and to act in a manner which was otherwise appropriate, and of the disposition of those in Smith's environment to evince approval of his expression of the belief that p. But what about Jones's knowledge that Smith knows p? On Rorty's account, it would apparently have no bearing on anything to do with Smith, but only with the behaviour of Jones, and the reaction to this by persons in Jones's environment. The upshot is that behaviourism, which is invoked by Rorty as an alternative to the correspondence theory of truth, is in fact indissolubly wedded to it, since on behaviourist assumptions Jones's knowledge about Smith's knowledge must *correspond* to that behaviour of Smith's which is an expression of his knowledge, if it is to count as 'knowledge' at all. Rorty protests that knowledge is by no means 'cut off from the world' on his account; but if what is actually the case about *x*, quite apart from what I and others in my environment believe about *x*, has no bearing on my knowledge of *x*, as would seem to follow from what Rorty says, then it is difficult to see how knowledge could be more 'cut off from the world' than that.

But quite apart from these antinomies with regard to behaviourism, Rorty's position can be shown to be self-destructive. Either he is advancing his position as justifiable on general principles against contradictory ones or he is not. If he is not, there is no point in listening to him. If he is, he is implicitly committing himself to the proposition that one tends to get at the truth about things by justifying one's position on such general principles. But it is just the existence of such principles which is asserted by that classical epistemology which Rorty attacks.

It is perhaps worth pointing out that behaviourism of the type advocated by Rorty has consequences which are horrifying as well as ones which are absurd. (As I suggested in chapter 5, one might speak in this connection of *reductio ad horrendum* arguments, and urge that a philosopher to whom it was demonstrated that his opinions entailed, for example, that all Caucasians ought to be shot at birth, or all Mongoloids might as well be consigned to slave labour, should feel somewhat uncomfortable with these opinions, even if he were under no immediate obligation to admit them as false.) Whether organisms feel pain depends, according to Rorty, on whether the linguistic community deems them to do so; so far from its being the case, as it is on the assumption of the correspondence theory of truth, that whether we truly believe an organism to be in pain depends on whether it is in pain or not, and would be so or not independently of our belief. On Rorty's view, an organism on a newly discovered planet would be 'capable of feeling pain' just as soon as it suited the human visitors to that planet to say that it did. The mangled and screaming hare, on our own planet, 'feels pain,' if at all, only in virtue of our attributions. It may be noted that this is a very convenient doctrine, especially as applied to human beings with whom we happen not to feel sympathetic. Whether the question, 'Do lonely old women who own cats feel pain when burned alive?' has an affirmative answer is a matter which we decide, on Rorty's account; for them to feel pain in the circumstances is for us to include them in the range of our sympathies, for them not to feel pain is for us to fail to do so. I submit that this is at once a consequence of Rorty's position, and both morally horrifying and grossly implausible.

Rorty maintains that only those who are haunted by the bogey of philosophical scepticism are concerned to raise epistemological questions, to seek for 'justification' of knowledge-claims which are not a matter of social concensus. But there is at least one other source of epistemological concern: the need to distinguish in non-arbitrary fashion between knowledge, on the one hand, and what merely purports to be knowledge, on the other. Granted the assumption that there is a real world prior to and independent of human society, at first sight at least one may have a legitimate concern to distinguish between those beliefs, whether widely and confidently maintained or not, which are likely to be *true of* it and those which are not. Even the most mutually consistent beliefs of the most prestigious group of natural scientists could not make it to be the case that the moon consists of green cheese, if the moon does not consist of green cheese. On the contrary, we believe what scientists tell us about the matter on the assumption that their methods are the right ones for getting at the truth about the constitution of the moon, and (except on an extreme idealist view) the constitution of the moon as it would have been even if mankind had never been in a position to inquire fruitfully about it. What differentiates methods liable to achieve the purpose from those not so liable is the proper concern of that aspect of philosophy known as epistemology. In spite of the claims of Quine and Rorty, epistemology as thus conceived cannot be taken over without remainder by empirical psychology. This is because psychology is the science concerned with why people actually behave, think, and speak as they do, whereas epistemology deals with how they ought to speak and think if they are to find out what is the case about the world.

Rorty maintains that knowledge does not need foundations any more than does culture in general. I would answer that knowledge and culture are both equally in need of foundations, and that to search for and articulate them is probably the most important task of the philosopher. Just as it is a good idea for us to be able to distinguish at least in principle between legitimate and spurious claimants to the status of knowledge, so it is useful and indeed increasingly urgent, given the magnitude of the dangers confronting us, to attend to the difference between what tends to enhance culture and what tends to destroy it. Rorty commends the 'therapeutic' function of philosophy and its use in dissolving 'outworn' conventions of speech and behaviour. But what can 'therapy' amount to when one has no articulate notion of what constitutes health, what sickness, and why? And what could it be, on Rorty's view, for a convention of speech or of behaviour to be 'outworn,' except for it no longer to be the fashion for people to conform to it?

I believe that it is Rorty's great merit to have drawn out the consequences of the principles underlying much contemporary philosophy. Yet I do not think he has drawn them out quite to the bitter end; had he done so, he would have revived idealism in an extreme form.

The human mind is, after all, the mirror of nature, or at least it can become so, in precisely the sense that this is denied by Rorty. That is to say, by the proper use of our minds, we can find out what is the case about a world which exists largely prior to and independently of our minds. It is, and will remain, a central task of philosophy to set out what it is for the human mind to be the 'mirror' of nature in this sense, to show how it can be so, and to work out the implications of the fact that it is so. However, I believe that Rorty is quite correct in maintaining that the mind cannot be the mirror of nature in the sense at issue unless there are 'foundations' of knowledge at least roughly of the kind sought by Descartes, and again by Russell and Husserl at the beginning of the present century. Furthermore (and perhaps this is the hardest saying of all), I think that Rorty is also right that the attempt of recent philosophers to find the mirror of nature in language as opposed to in mind is mistaken. The reason for this can be stated briefly as follows. Language may be understood either merely as an ordered series of noises or marks or as such a series as expressive of mental acts. In the former case, the problem of how language relates to an extra-linguistic reality is insoluble; in the latter case, it remains exactly where it was before it became fashionable to couch epistemological problems in linguistic as opposed to 'mentalistic' terms. The moral is that to search for the foundations of knowledge in language rather than in mind is to make half-hearted concessions to a behaviourism which cannot but be destructive of knowledge when consistently carried through.[35]

PART III: CONTINENTAL DRIFT

9

Consciousness and Existence: Husserl and Heidegger

How are we to justify our claims to knowledge of the real world and distinguish actual knowledge from knowledge falsely so called? This has been a recurrent problem for philosophers from the Greeks onwards, but has been especially pressing, as it seems, since the time of Descartes. Edmund Husserl developed the 'phenomenological' style of philosophy largely as an attempt to answer this question; as he saw it, such a philosophy would have to be free from any *a priori* metaphysical commitment, and indeed from any presuppositions whatever, being based on a thorough examination of experience. For so far as a philosophy retains any starting point or method of proceeding which is not clarified and justified, it may reasonably be objected to as uncritical and dogmatic.[1] Husserl complains of the 'unscientific' character of all philosophy previous to his own; he sees the continuing divergence of philosophical opinions and points of view as symptomatic of this.[2]

Phenomenologists are apt to be at one with positivists in the aversion they feel to traditional metaphysics. However, while all positivists aim at the abolition of metaphysics, some phenomenologists wish rather to provide foundations for the erection of a new metaphysics.[3] Again, while the phenomenologist as such would not be inclined to dispute the existence of an external world, she would insist that the doctrine that such a world existed should be justified on a phenomenological basis, through an analysis of actual experience. To say that the external world exists, with the objects and events which make it up, without such justification is to be no less dogmatic than the idealist metaphysician in his insistence that what pass for external things are really products of mind. We may well conclude that we may make meaningful and true statements about such an external world; all that the phenomenologist insists is that we should be able to explain and provide grounds for such a claim.

Basic to phenomenology is the notion of 'phenomenological constitution.' The phenomenologist aims to show how, starting from basic and indisputable phenomenological facts, 'we advance from subjective experiences where our analysis must begin to an objective world which we share with other people.'[4] Cognitive experiences (here the phenomenologist differs from the positivist)[5] are of object-constituting events which are to be explained in reflective consciousness. But how are we to determine and to justify our starting assumptions, and the principles according to which we build upon them, in this 'phenomenological constitution'? Husserl insists that knowledge has not only 'objective-logical' conditions, but also 'noetic' ones. This is as much as to say that, while one has to bear in mind that the facts that we know must be objective, independent of human subjects, it is also to be emphasized that they are able to be known by subjects who employ their minds in an appropriate way. He would agree with such sticklers for objectivity as Gottlob Frege and Bertrand Russell that truth is not merely a matter of what one person or even many persons may believe, but he vigorously contests the kind of 'objectivism' that would fail to take into account the subjective aspect of knowledge.[6] This last is the burden of Husserl's attack on 'naturalism.' It is an inevitable reaction to 'naturalism,' as he sees it, that a 'historicism' has grown up which sees all ideas and conceptions as equally historical creations, 'true for' the persons and groups who evolved them.[7] 'How are we to understand the fact that the "in-itself" of objectivity can be thought of by us and moreover "apprehended" in cognition and thus in the end yet become "subjective"; what does it mean that the object exists "in itself" and is at the same time "given" in knowledge ...?'[8]

What we have to come to grips with is our 'object-constituting subjectivity,' the activity underlying, for example, the formation of scientific theories, which activity the theorist herself generally fails to advert to because she takes it for granted.[9] 'We must rise above the self-obliviousness of the theoretician who while preoccupied with things, theories and methods is quite unaware of the interiority of his productive thought and who while living in these things, theories, methods, never focuses his attention on his own productive activity.'[10]

There is an important distinction to be made between those mental acts which presuppose the real extra-mental existence of their objects and those which do not. For example, I can *think about* or *desire* something which is unreal (like a bank account upon which I can draw indefinitely without putting any money in, or a lap dog which never urinates or defecates). On the other hand, I can only *know* or *perceive* states of affairs which are real. (Thus it is to be concluded that I did not actually perceive, but only seemed to perceive, the oasis in the desert which turned out to be a mirage. Similarly, however confidently you assert that there is a highest prime number or a hereditary monarch of the United States, you cannot properly be said to know either proposition, given that neither is in fact true.) But if objects are given us, as they appear to be, only in or through mental acts, how do we establish whether any object is real or merely imaginary? Furthermore, of what nature is the self-unity which stamps my mental acts as mine, as opposed to those of some other person? In attempting to solve problems such as these, Husserl eventually came to speak of 'transcendental subjectivity' and the 'transcendental ego' in order to avoid the 'psychologism' which seems inevitably to result from making everything dependent on the empirical ego and the thoroughgoing relativism which is its inevitable consequence.[11]

Those mental acts by which we mean 'general objects' or 'essences,' such as species and attributes, are fundamentally different, in Husserl's view, from those by which we mean individual objects or particulars.[12] However, we can apprehend such general objects no less directly than we can particular objects.[13] We cannot, as he sees it, get very far in our account of meaning unless we acknowledge this fact. The history of classical empiricism is full of unsuccessful attempts to show how our ideas of general objects are derived from our experience of particular objects (for example, our conceptions of 'horse' or 'green' from particular experiences of horses or green things). Berkeley, for instance, argued that we can form a mental image of a triangle from our particular experience of some triangle, and that this image may then be employed by our thought to stand for all triangles. But the trouble here is that the image of a triangle must be of an equilateral or right-angled or some other particular kind of triangle, yet the meaning of 'triangle' remains the same whatever sort of image we may happen to have conjured up in our minds. The fact is that we cannot account for our apprehension of the meaning of such general terms as 'red' and 'triangle' without postulating what Husserl calls an act of 'ideating abstraction' or 'ideation,' as a result of which the existence of any perceived object falls into the background and we are able to reach its 'essence.' 'We apprehend the species red directly, in itself as it were, on the basis of a single perception of something red. We look at the red colour of an object as given to us in a perception, but we do this in a special kind of act; an act which aims at the "ideal," the "universal.""[14] Empiricists are apt to attempt to wriggle out of these difficulties by trying to account for the meanings of terms as a matter of their extensions (for example, the meaning of 'horse' is somehow just a matter of reference to actual horses). But evidently this will not do for meanings of terms which are not instantiated in the real world, and hence have no extension. (And it would be ridiculous to maintain, for all that it would follow from an account of meaning in terms of extension, that the terms 'dragon' and 'unicorn' are meaningless merely by virtue of the fact that there are no dragons or unicorns.)

Descartes tried to discover the foundations of knowledge by doubting everything that could be doubted and building on the basic certainties which seemed to survive the purge.[15] What Husserl called the 'transcendental *epoché*' is a rather similar performance intended to achieve the same end.[16] In carrying it out, I suspend the 'natural attitude,' and all judgments about the existence of things which I normally assume to be out there and independent of myself; this is an arduous task.[17] The philosopher's business is to discover how that world of facts is possible of which the natural scientist, like the person of common sense, assumes the existence – science being a development of 'the natural attitude.' What the philosopher must do is to 'try to explain what is basically involved in our relationship with the world, how the world comes into being, *as it were.*'[18]

Since we may not assume uncritically the existence of a reality independent of ourselves, such an assumption cannot any longer form the basis of our understanding of the concept of truth. (It is natural to say that the judgment made by someone that 'House martins are summer residents in Europe' is true if and only if it is a fact, independent of all conscious judgments, that house martins are summer residents in Europe. But it is the very existence of such facts which, on Husserl's view, ought to be problematic to the philosopher.) If conformity with outer reality cannot be the criterion of truth, this would at first sight seem to have as a consequence that each individual person is the arbiter of truth. We find here a principal reason which appears to justify Husserl in postulating a transcendental ego or consciousness; truth can then be correlative with transcendental though not with empirical consciousness, and 'psychologism' is avoided. But there remain problems, quite apart from the obvious metaphysical extravagance of postulating a transcendental consciousness over and above the ordinary empirical consciousness clearly characteristic of human beings, and attributing to it remarkable world-constituting capacities. Perhaps the greatest of these problems is how we are to regain the real world once its existence is rendered problematic by the *epoché* and thus is no longer treated as a basic fact to be taken for granted. It is quite largely a conviction that Husserl has dug an unbridgeable chasm before his own feet at this point, which has made so many of his followers protest that philosophers must indeed take for granted the existence of the world, and confine themselves to an account of the vicissitudes of human existence within that world.[10]

How is one to make the leap from descriptive psychology to transcendental philosophy?[20] (And how is it that the latter enterprise is not fatally infected with the relativistic implications of the former, when it is taken as providing the foundations of knowledge in general?) As Husserl sees it, Kant was moving in the right direction with his doctrine of the *a priori*,[21] but did not take far enough the implications of his own apprehension of 'the intimate connection between the structure of subjectivity and the structure of "the world."' This defect is illustrated by Kant's doctrine of the 'thing in itself,' which is supposed to exist independently of the cognitive subject, and to be inaccessible to it. But Husserl is far more critical of those opponents of Kant who would deny altogether the possibility or usefulness of a transcendental and *a priori* analysis of human cognition such as Kant attempted to provide. In contrast to that of Kant, Husserl's transcendental analysis has a bearing not only on the structure of knowledge, but also on that of the world; it has implications such as Kant's did not have.[22]

Of Husserl's greatness as a philosopher there should, in my opinion at least, be no question. From the point of view represented by this book, he has a number of outstanding virtues: (1) he takes further Descartes's account of consciousness and Kant's of the *a priori*; (2) he realizes that there is more to experience than would be admitted by most of those who have called themselves empiricists; (3) he sees that the nature and structure of consciousness has a bearing on the nature and structure of the world; (4) he understands that an account of subjectivity is needed before the nature and rationale of scientific objectivity can be provided. Still, there remain difficulties with his thought which have militated against its wider acceptance. The ultimate effect of the phenomenological reduction – here once again Husserl is very reminiscent of Descartes – is to set up the 'transcendental consciousness' as something which cannot be 'put in brackets,' or be subject to the *epoché*; in fact, it turns out to be that on which everything else depends for its existence. 'The whole *spatio-temporal world* in which man and the human Ego view themselves as subordinate realities is *such that it has merely intentional existence*; in other words, it exists in a secondary, relative sense of the word ..., *for* a consciousness.'[23] But if it is thus 'merely intentional,' in what sense and by what token, one might ask, is it real rather than a fiction? Why should not the so-called natural world be just a dream or a mirage? Furthermore, once one has 'bracketed' the external world, and changed one's particular stream-of-conscious experiences into transcendental consciousness by the process of phenomenological reduction, it becomes difficult if not impossible to see how there could be different streams of consciousness, different consciousnesses, or different egos. Is it possible to carry out the *epoché* in a thoroughgoing manner without being committed to a transcendental solipsism, where one's own ego is the only one that exists? Such problems, apparently, could never be satisfactorily resolved by Husserl.[24]

The apparent failure of Husserl's program, and of the analogous program of the empiricists, has led many contemporary philosophers, as described in our earlier chapters, to conclude that the very attempt was mistaken, that knowledge has no foundations, and consequently philosophers should not waste their time looking for them. I have pointed out a number of difficulties in the carrying out of Husserl's program, yet it remains, I believe, that what he wanted to do, to provide foundations for knowledge, is of the utmost importance. Is it possible to point a way to the resolution of these difficulties? It seems to me that it is. I have already argued at length, first, that it is self-destructive to deny that knowledge, or true belief founded on good reasons, is possible, and second, that the real world, as opposed to the merely apparent world or the world *of* or *for* a particular conscious subject or group of conscious subjects, can be nothing other than what true beliefs *are* or *would be* about, and beliefs founded on good reasons *tend to be* about.

Where other persons are concerned, the evidence is just as overwhelming that each of them thinks, wishes, fears, undergoes sensations and feelings, and so on, much as I do myself. That I cannot directly experience these is beside the point, given that the ultimate criterion of the real is judgment based on the evidence provided by experience, rather than experience itself.[25] That people seldom if ever share streams of consciousness is again confirmed by a vast weight of evidence. When Henry is hacked on the shin, it is Henry and not George who winces or complains; and however sympathetic Mildred may be about Euphemia's headache, the headache belongs ineluctably within Euphemia's consciousness. Indeed, excellent evidence for Henry's sharp pain or the throbbing sensation inside Euphemia's head may be a part of George's or Mildred's experience; and this is quite enough, on the conception of knowledge and its grounds just outlined, for us to have knowledge of the contents of one another's consciousness.

In what sense, if at all, can one say that everything is *for* consciousness on this view? It would seem that there is a great deal which is not known to any human being; but it does seem incoherent in the last analysis to suppose that something could be such that it was unknowable to any consciousness whatever on the basis of any evidence whatever. It is notorious that this is the trouble with Kant's 'things in themselves,' which at once are supposed to be real and systematically elude all clearly conceivable criteria of 'reality' and 'thing-hood.' For *x* to be real is for *x* actually or potentially to be judged for good reason to be other than unreal, to exist rather than to fail to exist; for *y* to be a thing is for *y* actually or potentially to be judged for good reason to be identical within itself and distinct from other things, as the Duke of Wellington is identical with the victor of Waterloo and distinct from the captive of St Helena.[26]

The distinction just drawn between actual and potential knowledge is of the greatest importance for epistemology and metaphysics, since there is an obvious *prima facie* absurdity in denying that a great deal existed and does exist without actually being known. It also enables one to dispense with the troublesome Husserlian dichotomy between the 'transcendental ego' and 'empirical egos.' Sure enough, as I have briefly argued, a fundamental clue to the ultimate nature and structure of the universe is that it is potentially knowable; it is indeed nothing other than what is in principle knowable to human persons so far as they apply their minds appropriately to the data of experience. (Whether this provides any ground for asserting that there exists at the basis of the universe something analogous to the human ego is a separate and not immediately relevant question.)[27] The human person is cognitively 'transcendent' as in principle potential knower of the whole universe, but much less than 'transcendent' in her empirical nature as very limited by education and environment with respect to actual knowledge.

I can inquire about the world in the usual manner, both in matters of common sense and in the sciences. However, I may also inquire about myself as an inquirer, and about the overall nature and structure that the world cannot but have in virtue of the fact that I can fruitfully inquire into it and obtain knowledge. If the 'transcendental *epoché*' is conceived in this kind of way, as the movement of thought from the former kind of inquiry to the latter, there seems to be no difficulty about the return to 'the natural attitude,' given that the existence of things and of persons with minds other than myself, once one has come to conceive the 'transcendental *epoché*' rightly, is vindicated rather than put in jeopardy. And substantial gains for the 'natural attitude' may be achieved by resort to the *epoché*; a world to which we are intimately and as it were internally related by our thought may seem a far more spiritually attractive environment for us than a merely 'external' world with which we have no intimate connection, and which for that reason we may be disposed not so much to understand as to dominate and subdue.

But there is, after all, a world of things and facts which exists prior to and independently of human conscious inquiry; this comes to be known, fundamentally (from the point of view of what may be called 'generalized empirical method'),[28] by the threefold process of attending to evidence, envisaging hypotheses, and accepting in each case the hypothesis which best fits the evidence. The upshot of this is that the traditional correspondence theory of truth, once suitable qualifications have been made, turns out to be correct after all, as I argued at some length in the second chapter. Phenomenology indeed subverts crude versions of the correspondence theory of truth; but the generalized empirical method, in which I am arguing that phenomenology issues when fully and consistently worked through, vindicates after all what is essential to the theory.

Why is the phrase 'generalized empirical method' appropriate to the kind of approach to philosophy which I have set forward as resolving various *aporiae* of phenomenology? The main point of the phrase is that not only the data of sensation and feeling are matters of experience, but so are the operations of our minds upon these data, and they ought to be taken seriously as such. I am aware after all of the questioning, the hypothesizing, the marshalling of evidence, and the judgment, which I carry out on the basis of and with reference to sensations and feelings, as well as of the sensations and feelings themselves.[29]

It is often assumed that phenomenology, for better or worse, is essentially indifferent to science or even anti-scientific, whereas positivism is the properly scientific philosophy. That many phenomenologists have been hostile to science may well be true.[30] But the assumption seems quite wrong as applied to Husserl, and it is even more so in relation to the generalized empirical method of Lonergan. Husserl rightly emphasized the crucial role of conscious activity, largely neglected or repressed by positivists, in scientific discovery and progress. For Lonergan, science comes about simply by a thoroughgoing application and refinement of conscious processes universal among humankind.[31] A hunter in a primitive society notices a flicker or rustle among the leaves of the jungle, hypothesizes that there may be a poisonous snake in the vicinity, and judges that this is indeed so (and so is able to save his life by taking evasive action). Similarly, a contemporary scientist in her laboratory notices a streak on a photographic plate, hypothesizes that this may be due to the presence of a previously unknown type of fundamental particle, and judges that this is actually the case (and so is able very considerably to advance her career, perhaps winning a Nobel prize). However, neither the primitive hunter nor the contemporary scientist is liable to attend to the conscious processes involved; this is what the phenomenologist and the practitioner of generalized empirical method set themselves to do. But whatever may be true of phenomenology *de jure* or *de facto*, the generalized empirical method both accounts for science and vindicates it as tending to inform us of the real truth about those aspects of the world with which it deals; all the same, unlike the 'scientism' closely associated with positivism, it does not immediately or dogmatically foreclose the question of whether truth about some aspects of the world or the human condition is not available by some method which is not 'scientific' at least in any narrow sense. Indeed, by providing and vindicating norms for rational inquiry in general, it supplies means by which answers to this question may be found.[32]

Heidegger thought of himself as continuing and developing basic features of Husserl's work, though Husserl regarded the supposed continuation and development as something of a betrayal. I believe that there are a number of important insights to be gained from Heidegger's work, together with a few very perilous oversights. To my mind, Heidegger shows, with more conviction and power than any other thinker, how our anxieties and our trivial everyday concerns are apt to shut us out from apprehension of the deep mystery of things, and how great art and poetry, together with a sustained thinking-through of the nature of consciousness and of the world which it reveals, have the power of opening this up to us again. It is also to be acknowledged, in agreement with what Heidegger says, that the technical languages of the sciences, and of traditional metaphysics as well, are to a considerable extent means to the domination and control of things by human beings, and in consequence a standing pretext for self-deception about the real nature of the world and of ourselves within it.

But I will argue that Heidegger overlooks the fact that the specialized languages of science and traditional metaphysics have other roles and other possibilities. They may be an expression and result of contemplative wonder, and convey a grasp of a real intelligible world to be known by inquiry into the everyday world available to common sense and described by ordinary language. What appears to be Heidegger's view of scientific and metaphysical language, as more or less exclusively a means to control and domination, presents us in effect with a terrible dilemma; we must either abandon the scientific world-view along with the enormous benefits which it has conferred on humankind or we must resign ourselves to existence in a world conceived in a way which is utterly hostile to the life of the human spirit. I believe that this dilemma does not exhaust the possibilities; science and traditional metaphysics, on the one hand, and the life of the spirit, on the other, may greatly enhance one another when both are properly related to their basis in human consciousness. In what follows, I shall outline what I take to be Heidegger's views on human beings and their consciousness, the nature of truth, the world of 'things' which is given to consciousness, and the role of great art in restoring our vision of how 'things' really are when this has been obfuscated or corrupted.

It is specifically human nature, as concerned with the world and capable of raising questions about it, which Heidegger refers to as *Dasein*. 'In which being is the meaning of Being to be found; from which being is the disclosure of Being to get its start?'[33] The answer to the question can only be: 'this being which we ourselves in each case are and which includes inquiry among the possibilities of its Being.'[34] What has most strenuously to be avoided is any attempt to deal with *Dasein* in terms used to interpret other parts or aspects of the world, like material objects and processes. All metaphysical questions must be approached explicitly on the basis of *Dasein* which is the subject of questioning, which questions. From this point of view, one has to proceed to a dismantling of the conceptual apparatus which we take for granted, where answers are given or presupposed, but the questions are never experienced any more – least of all those about our own nature, destiny, and state in the world. In asking these questions, we must be constantly aware of the limitations which accrue from our particular historical situation. These were not sufficiently taken account of in the classical phenomenology of Husserl, with its 'transcendental subjectivity' based on an allegedly 'disinterested observer.' For all its determination to return to 'the things themselves,' this phenomenology did not attend sufficiently to the manner in which its own aims and procedures were determined historically.[35] Husserl, as he himself acknowledged, was very much in the tradition of Descartes, who was trying to find an unshakable basis for the practice of philosophy. But it is just this basis which Heidegger seeks to put in question.[36] We have to ask what is the decisive matter for thinking; 'is it consciousness and its objectivity or is it the Being of beings in its unconcealedness and concealment?'[37] Access to the things themselves is best thought of in true Greek fashion as '*alētheia*, the unconcealedness of what is present, its being revealed, its showing itself.'[38] (As he quite often does, Heidegger is here making capital out of an etymological point; *alētheia*, the Greek word for 'truth,' is equivalent to *a-lētheia*, non-concealment.)

So what is basic to truth, it must be inferred, is not the correctness of assertions, or their correspondence with states of affairs, or the agreement of subject and object expressed by them; it is the *self-showing* which is necessary for things if they are to become objects of assertions at all.[39] The fact is that all correspondence, 'adequation'[40] or whatever, between judgment and state of affairs presupposes a discovery or revealing of beings such as allows them to be seen.[41] The usual account of truth, as accordance between a statement or proposition, on the one hand, and a thing or state of affairs, on the other, is not at bottom intelligible. Suppose I say of a five-mark coin that it is round. How are statement and thing supposed to be in accordance, given that what are alleged to be related to one another are so diverse in their appearance and constitution? The five-mark piece is round and metallic, whereas the statement is neither spatial nor material. What relation there is depends on a certain bearing or comportment on the part of the one who makes the statement, which is 'invested with its correctness by the openness of comportment; for only through the latter can what is opened up really become the standard for the presentative correspondence.' (What this amounts to, I think, is that the correspondence of statements with things in which truth is supposed to reside depends ineluctably on openness of conscious subjectivity towards things; it is that in which truth fundamentally consists.) So the traditional assumption that truth belongs at bottom to statements or propositions turns out to be fallacious. The openness of comportment which is essential to truth is in turn grounded in freedom, freedom being a matter of 'the resolutely open bearing that does not close in on itself,' and thus of letting things be. So it was at the beginning of the Western tradition, in Greek thought. 'If we translate "*alētheia*" as "unconcealment" rather than "truth," this translation is not merely more literal; it contains the directive to rethink the ordinary concept of truth in the sense of the correctness of statements and to think it back to that still uncomprehended disclosedness and disclosure of being.'[42]

Unfortunately, we are too prone to trade this free openness for the security of agreeing with 'them' (that is, the thoughtless majority of people), with accepting without question whatever 'they' say is true. There are so many things besides to seduce and distract us from attending to the presuppositions of all this secure 'knowledge,' whether it takes the guise of science or of religious faith; what are called 'eternal truths' are apt to be nothing more than the most deeply ingrained prejudices. The temptation becomes all the greater when science has made such a wide range of things apparently familiar and well known, and when technical domination of the world may well appear virtually limitless. More authentic ways of knowing things tend ultimately to be no longer even a matter of indifference; they are simply forgotten. Everything becomes subjected to 'the levelling and planning of this omniscience, this mere knowing.' We distract ourselves further by proposing and planning on the basis of our latest needs and aims, thus fleeing from the basic mystery of things to what is readily available, 'onward from one current thing to the next.' Eventually a whole system of interlocking errors, with a long history of development, is built up, and any thoughtful questioning of the system is dismissed as 'an attack on, an unfortunate irritation of, common sense.'[43]

Obsession with manipulation and control is at the very bottom of our modern conception of what a 'thing' is. Things are envisaged in modern Western thought as subjects of accidents or predicates, as mentally grasped unities of sense-impressions or as parcels of matter invested with form; all these conceptions reflect their origin in a special kind of human activity, the use of tools or equipment.[44] The original Greek experience of things was expressed (notably by Aristotle) in terms whose meanings were subtly but definitely affected in their translation by medieval scholars into Latin; this translation is by no means as innocent as it is usually taken to be.[45] 'Roman thought takes over the Greek words without a corresponding, equally original experience of what they say.' Such is the origin of the rootlessness of thought in the modern West.[46] It seems rash indeed to question the relation which is now so taken for granted between statements and things, and between the structure of statements and the structure of things. Yet we have to ask whether the subject-predicate statement is really the mirror image of the structure of the thing (as substance characterized by accidents), or rather whether the structure of the thing as thus envisaged is not merely a projection of the structure of the subject-predicate statement, as opposed to existing in reality. And reflection on the matter does indeed indicate that the usual concept of the thing 'does not lay hold of the thing as it is in its own being, but makes an assault upon it.'

It is true that people are occasionally struck by the suspicion that thought has done violence to things, but they react to this by disavowing thought rather than being more thoughtful. Yet this reaction in favour of feeling or mood may in the last analysis be more reasonable, in the important sense of more intelligently perceptive and open to things than the insensitive and domineering 'rationality' against which it is a reaction. According to one influential conception of the thing, what we perceive in the first instance is a mass of sensations on which we impose a unity rather than something like a storm in a chimney, an airplane with three motors, or a Mercedes as opposed to a Volkswagen. But the fact is that the things themselves are closer to us, more immediately related to our consciousness, than the sensations; to get at mere sounds, at aural impressions, for example, 'we have to listen away from things, divert our ear from them i.e. listen abstractly.'[47] The matter-form structure on which this conception of a thing is based is in its turn ultimately grounded in assumptions about usefulness, where the 'matter' is imposed on the 'form' for a specific purpose. 'A being that falls under usefulness is always the product of a process of making. It is made as a piece of equipment for something.' Our current and allegedly self-evident assumptions about 'things' are based on this form-matter structure deriving from the medieval period, with the essentially pragmatic presuppositions which underlie it; to these assumptions, Kantian and transcendental qualifications have made no fundamental difference.[48]

How can we avoid such distorting preconceptions? Only by deliberately distancing ourselves from them, and leaving each thing 'to rest in its own self.' Or we may aspire simply 'to describe some equipment without any philosophical theory,' in order to see what it is to envisage it precisely as equipment. In this attempt great works of art will be of the utmost assistance to us. An excellent example of how they may be so is to be found in Van Gogh's well-known painting of a peasant's pair of shoes. This brings before us the peasant's weary tread, over furrows and through a biting wind, as she worries uncomplainingly about food for the future, and trembles at the imminent and deadly danger of bearing a child. So the 'equipmental quality' of this pair of shoes is brought home to us, not by actual observation of the thing itself, or of its manufacture or use, but by looking at Van Gogh's masterpiece. The painting does not merely evoke an emotion about or attitude to its subject; it 'is the disclosure of what the equipment, the pair of peasant shoes, is in truth.' We may generalize the point by saying that the essence of art is 'the truth of things setting itself to work.' What should concern us 'is a first opening of our vision to the fact that what is workly in the work, equipmental in equipment, and thingly in the thing comes closer to us only when we think the Being of beings.'[49]

The same principles apply to art that is non-representational, to a Greek temple, for example. This 'fits together and at the same time gathers around itself the unity of those paths and relations in which birth and death, disaster and blessing, victory and disgrace, endurance and decline acquire the shape of destiny for human being.' The temple stands against the violence of the storm, and by doing so manifests that violence; its repose and steadfastness bring out by contrast the surging of the surf and the tumult of the sea. Again, 'the lustre and gleam of the stone ... first brings to radiance the light of the day, the breadth of the sky, the darkness of the night.' In fact, 'to be a work means to set up a world.' This insight into things, and the place of human beings among them, which is afforded by the temple, remains open so long as the god of the temple has not left it. A similar conception of divine presence may be applied to Greek sculpture and Greek tragedy. The sculpture of a god is not a device for showing people how the god is supposed to look; 'it is a work that lets the god himself be present and thus *is* the god himself.' In the performance of a tragedy, the battle of new gods against old is being not merely represented, but actually fought.[50]

Thus far Heidegger; what is one to make of what he has to say? I believe that his attempt to found knowledge in *Dasein* or human consciousness is right in principle. For Husserl, as Heidegger puts it, 'the transcendental reduction to absolute subjectivity gives and secures the possibility of grounding the objectivity of all objects (the Being of these beings) in their valid structure and consistency, that is, in their constitution in and through subjectivity.'[51] This is as much as to say, I think, that only by being clear about the nature of conscious subjects, and the way in which they can come to know objects, can we properly ground our knowledge of objects, of things as they really are prior to and independently of the mental projections which we may impose upon them. But Heidegger raises against Husserl the question of whether we should be fundamentally concerned with consciousness and its objectivity or with the Being of beings in its unconcealment.[52] I believe that this is a false dilemma, due primarily to the fact that a misleading ambiguity lurks in the concepts of 'object' and 'objectivity.' It is one thing to impose our purposes on our environment in such a way as to envisage it all exclusively as 'gear' or 'tools'; it is another to set ourselves to find out how things really are. It is to do the latter, not merely the former, as Heidegger seems to assume, that one must have a clear doctrine of how the conscious subject is, or at least may become, sufficiently 'transcendent' of its particular situation to attain such knowledge.

However firmly each of us is embedded in our own historical situation, and conditioned by the needs and aims stemming from our past and driving us towards our future, we do have a certain degree of 'cognitive transcendence,' as it may be called, of this situation. This is to be asserted not because it is convenient or reassuring, but because denial of it leads quickly to absurdity. When we come to know that two plus two equals four, that William the Conqueror fought and won the Battle of Hastings in 1066, or that there is a giant planet in our solar system which is outside the orbit of Uranus, we know what absolutely is so, not just what is so for persons in our particular historical milieu. Even to say that each human being is too embedded in her own historical situation to state what absolutely is so, presupposes some degree of cognitive transcendence by the speaker of her historical situation. What is being said is about human beings in general, and supposed to be true of them; it is not about them as they are merely for the speaker or from her particular point of view. Any statement of cognitive relativism, supposed to derive from the embeddedness of each knower within her own historical situation, in fact presupposes the falsity of such relativism. Does all this imply that Heidegger's thought, which seems to make this concern of Husserl's to be based either on a mistake or on a matter of indifference, is thereby so fatally flawed that nothing useful is to be learned from it? I do not see why this should be so. Assertion of the cognitive transcendence of human subjects to know what is really so, and not merely so from a particular historical perspective (whatever this would amount to), can perfectly well be combined fruitfully with Heidegger's concern to make consciousness more sensitive, pliable, receptive, and reflective. Yet only from the Archimedean point afforded by the cognitively self-transcending subject can one in principle proceed to dismantle those aspects of the metaphysical tradition that ought to be dismantled, and to rehabilitate those that ought to be rehabilitated.

It is one important consequence of the conception of philosophy argued for at the beginning of this book that the traditional view of truth, that it is primarily a matter of judgments or propositions, is to be reaffirmed, in spite of Heidegger's authority. Heidegger is perfectly right, I believe, that attention to conscious subjects, and to the way in which they may be relatively 'open' or 'closed' to the world, is necessary if one is to understand much about the nature of truth; but it does not follow from this that truth is not after all primarily a matter of the relation between judgments or propositions and states of affairs. Still, while truth is to be found primarily in judgments, such judgments are an achievement of conscious subjects, who have to exert themselves to secure and maintain a certain openness towards the world in order to reach it. And Heidegger's work is extraordinarily instructive as to the nature of this openness.

I have argued that the actual world, or reality, is nothing other than what true judgments are about, and what properly justified judgments tend to be about. Attention to this point, I think, brings out the solution to Heidegger's puzzle about how there an be 'agreement' or 'correspondence' between entities so heterogeneous as propositions or judgments, on the one hand, and material objects, on the other. If the real world, including all the material objects which it may contain, is nothing other than what judgments would be about if all the relevant evidence in experience were attended to, and all the relevant possibilities envisaged, then the problem of how statements can agree with things disappears.

Heidegger stresses the manner in which what is called 'knowledge,' especially in an era which particularly prides itself on its technology, may represent an assault on things rather than an allowing of them to be as they are. Here, I believe, he is alluding to a distinction which is of the utmost importance; but the manner in which he makes it is unfortunate, and seems to obscure some vital issues. What is the proper role of mental 'activity' and 'passivity' in our coming to know things? It seems to be true and very important that there are two aims in science, that of contemplating the world as it really is and that of controlling it for our uses; and that however worthy the second aim, something deadly happens to the human spirit if the second aim altogether usurps the place of the first. And in fact first-rate natural scientists, from astronomers to zoologists, appear from their writings to be activated more by a love for and wonder at the object of their study than by a desire to control it.[53] (It seems that the 'disenchantment' with nature due to science, of which so many have complained, is actually due to the assumption that science is really about control rather than contemplative wonder.) But in order to know things as they really are, even when one is motivated by love and wonder rather than the urge to control, the use of active powers of the mind is necessary. These are clearly and distinctly described by the generalized empirical method, in a way that does not seem to be possible in terms of Heidegger's thought. In order to come to know white dwarf stars or peregrine falcons for what they are, I have to be sufficiently passive to attend to observations which go against the assumptions I bring to the subject. But I must also actively propound hypotheses and envisage possibilities, and actively employ my faculty of judgment to determine which of these possibilities is best supported by the observations I have made. It is in fact failure to be mentally active in these ways – as opposed to getting to know them as they really are – that is responsible for our imposing alien categories on things. As Heidegger rightly insists, things do not reveal themselves to me unless I open myself to them; but he is suggestive rather than precise, and in some ways positively misleading, about the nature of this openness. Generalized empirical method precisely articulates the three basic types of mental operation in which this openness consists. What is to be avoided is by no means the actively attending, hypothesizing, and judging mind, but rather the mind which is so obsessed with its pet theories that it is blind to other possibilities, and brushes aside any conflicting evidence.

On this account of the basic mental operations involved in coming to know, it is unfair to attribute the medieval account of 'substance' as 'matter' and 'form' exclusively, in Heidegger's manner, to the human tendency to dominate things rather than allowing them to be as they are. For the different realms of existence do in fact seem to form a hierarchy in which 'matter' is progressively 'informed'; chemical substances are a matter of the imposition of sets of 'forms' or structures on fundamental particles, organic life imposes another such set of 'forms' on chemical substances, sensitive animal life on organic life, and human existence in turn on sensitive animal life. Each such 'form' is to be grasped by hypothesis and verified in the data of experience; so the structure of what is to be known, which is nothing other than the real world, is analogous to the structure of knowing. Each level of existence has its own special set of intelligible properties, its 'forms' in the Aristotelian and medieval metaphysical sense, which distinguish it from the levels below it, while sharing the properties of all these levels. (A human being is to some extent characterized by the special human properties of intelligence and reason; but she is also subject to the organic laws of growth and decay, and to all the laws of chemistry and physics.) Thus the result of the application of the generalized empirical method is to bring out this basic Aristotelian and medieval insight into the nature of things as correct, and to show that there is no need to attribute it exclusively or even primarily to the human obsession with making and controlling. I believe that Heidegger is profoundly correct that Kantian and transcendentalist qualifications in the long run make no essential difference to the metaphysical analysis of the 'thing' which we have inherited from the medievals. But he infers from this that both are to be rejected, whereas the considerations which I have adduced seem to lead to the contrary and transcendental Thomist view that both should be accepted.

But even if it is wrong to envisage Scholastic categories too exclusively as means to use and control, there is no doubt that the urge excessively to use and control exists, and that it may poison and deaden our apprehension of the beauty and terror of the world. And Heidegger is surely right that it is one of the main functions of great art to reawaken us to this. We become so used to the uses of an old pair of shoes that we no longer see it for what it is. What was originally the rapture of scientific discovery becomes part of the stale and taken-for-granted furniture of the mind; a limited viewpoint adopted with a specific purpose is taken as universal and unquestionable, long after the specific purpose has been lost to sight.

Heidegger associates the traditional 'form-matter' schema with the belief that we mentally construct things out of data, rather than directly apprehending things as such. This association seems to me to be correct, but so, in the relevant sense, does the belief. It is true that, in the usual senses of 'see' and 'hear,' we see and hear soldiers marching by and oboists playing their instruments. But this is no more than to say that, when using the terms 'see' and 'hear' in these senses, we assume not only that we have visual and aural impressions as though of soldiers marching by and oboists playing, but that there are actually soldiers marching and oboists playing where there appear to be. In normal cases we leap spontaneously from a set of sensations to judgment, from a series of experiences *as though of* our most garrulous colleague walking towards us down the passage, to the judgment *that* he is doing so. Alternative possibilities do not occur to us, let alone commend themselves as likely. It is only special circumstances, like deception or psychological experiment, which induce us to draw out the distinction between the types of mental act involved. The fact that I do not usually attend to the distinction between the various mental acts involved by no means applies that no such distinction exists. I may engage in a number of types of mental activity without attending to the fact that I am doing so; and it seems clear that it is one thing to enjoy a pattern of sensation, another to judge that the state of affairs which would normally explain that pattern actually obtains.

I have tried in this chapter to show how, on the basis of the philosophical position set out in Part I of this book, one may derive very great enlightenment from the writings of Husserl and Heidegger, without getting entangled in Husserl's *aporiai* about our knowledge of the objective world and of other minds, and without accepting at face value Heidegger's aspersions on traditional metaphysics as a whole.

10

Deconstruction and the Ubiquity of Power: Derrida and Foucault

On a superficial overview, the upshot of Jacques Derrida's work seems to be to make nonsense of all human discourse and communication. When one looks at it more carefully, this impression is abundantly confirmed. Still, there are lessons of great importance to be learned from it, and I shall try in what follows to show what they are.

With regard to his well-known dispute with Derrida, John Searle has been taken to task for the crudity of his contrast between 'serious' and 'nonserious' discourse, as throwing light on the distinction between fictional talk and talk which is in the business of stating facts.[1] H. Staten suggests that, as a background to one's assessment of this dispute, one should keep in mind Derrida's 'dazzling reading' of some of the most difficult modern authors.[2] Yet those who are sensitive to the most refined distinctions may still overlook the more obvious ones, and I believe that Searle had a point. A description of a meeting of aldermen in Derby at some date in 1987 is obviously, in most senses of 'serious' at least, a less 'serious' document than *King Lear*. But it makes certain kinds of commitment which *King Lear* does not. It is not relevant to the criticism of *King Lear* that there was no king of Britain of that name whose later life was anything like what is narrated in Shakespeare's play. But if the author of the description of the meeting of aldermen states that alderman X was present at the meeting when he was not, or that alderman Y was absent from the meeting when actually she was present, or that a certain item of business was not discussed at the meeting when in fact it was, then we regard these things as defects in that kind of document. Derrida's undoubted skill in shedding light on various types of fictive discourse does not directly imply that he articulates, or even that on his principles he is capable of articulating, the difference between the sort of talk which commits itself to telling the truth about particular states of affairs and the sort that does not.

Fundamental to Derrida's enterprise is his criticism of those assumptions which he calls 'metaphysical,' and which he complains have dominated the European philosophical tradition from Plato to Husserl. A crucial feature of such 'metaphysics' is a series of contrasts that it sets up between pairs of terms, in each of which the former is supposed to mark something superior, the latter to mark a falling away from this – good as opposed to evil, truth as opposed to falsity, essential as opposed to accidental, and so on.[3] It is worth noting that there is a characteristic coyness, as one might put it, about Derrida, which makes is hard to say whether he is implying, on the one hand, that we might somehow conceivably do without such distinctions or whether he is reminding us that we should constantly make ourselves aware of what we are doing when we are employing them.[4] If the former, it appears to me that what he is saying is at once absurd and dangerous. It is false, as opposed to true, that the moon is made of green cheese; it is bad, as opposed to good, to torture children for fun; and it is both absurd and dangerous to entertain serious doubts on these matters. One notices that Derrida's polemic is directed mainly against philosophers and other savants; he is curiously quiet about the judgments of science or of common sense. Is he really saying that here as well we have no use for distinctions like those between true and false, good and bad? If so, to take him seriously is to imply that one might just as well say that the moon is made of green cheese as that it is not, that one might as well torture children for fun as not. It is indeed the case that a certain kind of moralism, or a certain sort of obsession with truth, may inhibit the free play of imagination. It is also the case that an unduly restricted or dogmatic view of what is true or false, or of what is good or bad, may distort both our view of how things are in the world and our moral sensitivity and perceptiveness. So far as Derrida's writing acts against such tendencies, it has a very useful function. (To say so, it is worth reminding oneself, is to commit oneself to another distinction which has the hallmark of 'metaphysics' in Derrida's sense, between the useful and the useless.) But so far as it seems to subvert the very standards that we apply to knowing what is true and what is good, it is quite another matter.

For Derrida does appear to be impugning in much of what he writes the assumption of common sense, and of science as generally understood, that by means of our conceptual apparatus when this is rightly applied we can come to think and speak truly about a world which exists prior to and independent of our conceptual apparatus. For if we are to do so, we have to follow certain norms, of good rather than bad reasoning, of pure reasoning applied to evidence rather than contaminated by the impurity of emotional attachment to our prejudices, as a means of getting at the truth rather than coming or continuing to believe falsely. But all of these contrasts seem to be impugned by Derrida as aspects of what he calls 'metaphysics.'

Someone might say, 'But isn't it very courageous to face the anxiety which confronts or ought to confront us all, that objective truth may be unobtainable, that the world may not be knowable by us at all?'[5] But I do not think that the supposition which evokes such anxiety is after all a coherent one. As I have already argued at length, it is self-destructive to deny that we can make true judgments, or that we can make judgments which are better grounded than their contradictories, and the world or reality is nothing other than what true judgments are about, and what judgments which are better founded than their contradictories tend to be about. It seems that these principles are central to what Derrida castigates as 'logocentrism,' which he significantly admits that he cannot ultimately escape.[6] What 'logocentrism' amounts to in the long run, I believe, is the thesis that the world is knowable by means of the concepts expressible through our language, that it has a nature and structure which makes this possible. Derrida is of course by no means unaware of the theological implications of 'logocentrism'; is not the permeability of the world to 'logos,' to reason as expressed in words, a strong hint that at least something analogous to human reason is at the basis of it?[7]

I believe that a great deal of Derrida's appeal is due to the assumption that the sort of search for truth about things which is exemplified in science, and the sort of striving for the good as opposed to the bad which is shown in serious ethical concern, is inimical to the 'free play of signifiers' and the feast of imagination and intellectual creativity which can result from this. I judge this to be a very great mistake. That true statements about what is so and what is good are one very important aim of language by no means implies that it is the only aim. What is and ought to be conceived or imagined goes far beyond what is or ought to be stated. And not only is the free play of conception and imagination of intrinsic value, quite apart from any use they may have as means to knowledge of what is true and what is good, but their employment is vitally necessary if we are to be alive to the distinction between what is really true and what only seems to be true, between what is good and what merely appears to be good. What is true and what is good are after all not known once and for all; their apprehension requires a constant liveliness of senses, mind, and heart.

Oddly enough, there is an assumption which appears to be shared by Derrida and Plato, that there is an ineluctable conflict between the proper use of the mind to find out the truth about things and to conform itself to virtue, and the sort of exercise of imagination and indulgence of feeling which is encouraged by much literature and art. I have argued at some length to the contrary elsewhere;[8] I can only sketch my case here. It seems that we advance in knowledge of things by attending to the evidence of our senses, by envisaging a range of possibilities which might account for it, and by judging to be true the possibility which is best supported by the evidence. The arts give us the satisfaction that they do by enhancing in us the capacities to experience and to imagine, and to envisage possibilities; they are not apt directly to involve us in judgment about what is so. However, the more we exercise these capacities for conception and imagination, the more likely we are to be in a position to judge truly, both about what is so in the world of common sense or science and about what is of positive value. Hence there is no conflict whatever in principle between science and morality, on the one hand, and the practice of the arts, on the other; on the contrary, the latter enhances the former.

I have already said what I think to be crucial to what Derrida calls 'logocentrism.' The contrast between speech and writing, on which he himself lays such stress,[9] I take to be a side issue. I concede to him that one might just as well say that speech is a debased form of writing as vice versa. Through both speech and writing, we may express judgments which are true or false, or comparatively well- or ill-grounded. Speech seems more appropriate than writing in some contexts, for example, in a teaching situation where one has to react quickly to the responses of pupils, or in conversation; writing is certainly better when one wants a relatively permanent record of what is stated, as in a scientific treatise or the record of an important event. Derrida seems correct in suggesting that any general tendency to devalue writing in relation to speech, for all that is exemplified by many influential thinkers such as Plato and Rousseau, is misconceived.[10]

One is inclined to say that well-grounded judgment depends upon certain 'givens'; I apply my given reason to given experience. That water consists of hydrogen and oxygen, rather than being itself a chemical element or a compound of other elements, is a hypothesis confirmed by reason in experience countless times. Again, there is massive evidence available in experience to support what is surely the reasonable judgment, that the first name of the president of the United States of America in 1987 was Ronald, as opposed to Raquel or Rabadash. The 'givens' on which adequately based judgments may be said to depend, it is plausible to claim in each case, are a certain range of experience, and the capacity to reason about it. Furthermore, it is plausible to maintain that my experience is in some sense directly 'present' to me, and that I am 'present' to myself, as Descartes notoriously argued, as a being applying reason to my experience. Short of these 'givens' which are 'present' to me, it is not unreasonable to ask, how can I have any foundation for what I claim to know?

As I have said in chapter 8, it is usual in contemporary analytical philosophy to attack such a 'myth of the given,' and as has been pointed out by Richard Rorty and others, this is closely parallel to Derrida's 'deconstruction' of the 'metaphysics of presence.'[11] But short of 'foundations' in what is thus 'given' or 'present,' it is not easy to see how a total relativism is to be avoided – such that 'the moon is made of green cheese' and 'the torturing of children for fun is right' are just as 'true' from some point of view as their contradictories are from our own. Views of the world differ widely from one another; unless there is some 'given' to which to appeal in adjudicating between them, how is one to be determined as better than another by anything other than individual or social fiat? And is not the view that views of the world have no intrinsic privilege over one another the very essence of relativism? But unfortunately, of course, even to propound relativism is to presuppose that such a privilege is to be had, and to take advantage of it; could one be a relativist, and admit that the position contradictory to relativism was equally true from another viewpoint which was intrinsically just as good as one's own?

But the arguments which I have already sketched are a means of establishing foundations of knowledge after all, and so turning the flank of relativism. If reality is what is known to us by means of true judgment, and tends to be known by us so far as we ensure that our judgments are properly grounded, it may be conceded to deconstructionists that our knowledge of reality is mediated, that reality is on the whole not directly 'present' to us in experience. On the other hand, there is every reason to revive the classical empiricist and foundationalist conviction that experience, both of the data of sensation and of the conscious self as operating upon these data, does provide the basis for our knowledge of reality.

Deconstructionists are right to draw attention to the manner in which philosophers and others are apt to use a sort of rhetoric to urge that their own work is structured by logic and aimed at truth, as opposed to being dominated by rhetoric.[12] But given the incoherence of the views that truth is unobtainable, or that people have no reliable way of arriving at it, the distinction has then to be made between the kind of rhetoric which tends to promote the discovery of truth and that which tends to hinder it. (One is reminded of the remark made about Macaulay's style, that it was one in which it was impossible to speak the truth.) My speaking or writing on, say, a religious or political topic may be infested by a 'rhetoric' which serves to whip up emotion and to militate against the use of reason and attention to evidence; on the other hand, my manner of using words may have exactly the opposite tendency. One may, of course, as is often done, persuasively define 'rhetoric' in such a way that 'rhetoric' is by its very nature opposed to rationality and the honest search for truth; in this case, one simply needs to coin another term for that element of 'rhetoric' which is inevitable in any use of language. I believe that one positive use of deconstruction is to draw attention to elements of 'rhetoric' (in the pejorative sense) which may lurk beneath the surface of professedly non-rhetorical uses of language. As Aristotle remarked, there is an element of ostentation in the exaggerated plainness of Spartan attire.[13]

It is a curious feature of deconstruction that what is at first sight an extremely radical critical thrust turns out on the last analysis to be quite half-hearted. The 'logocentrism' which it purports to attack appears, on its own admission, to be inevitable: its assaults on logocentrism being themselves conceded to be implicated in logocentrism. It looks as though everything after all is left just as it is; what is implicitly critical of every conceivable thesis is effectively critical of none. No wonder Derrida is coy about the practical effects of his ideas on politics and university teaching.[14] The critical principles which I have sketched as an alternative to deconstruction are by no means so broken-backed. Some ancient opinions on metaphysics, epistemology, ethics, and so on turn out to be deeply incoherent and based on error; others to be well founded after all. One of these is what I have argued to be essential to 'logocentrism.' It is self-destructive to deny that we are capable of coming to true or well-founded judgments; reality is nothing other than what true judgments are about and well-founded judgments tend to be about. So the language, and for that matter the writing, in which we express our judgments is after all in principle capable of describing reality.

In fact, one can readily conceive of a kind of deconstruction which was founded on these principles, but which was much clearer than its prototype on the issue of which opinions are to be rejected, which to be provisionally or definitively accepted, and why. Following a terminological hint in Derrida himself[15] (and not being too discouraged by the somewhat Trollopian suggestions), let us call this 'archdeconstruction.' Archdeconstruction would be fundamentally directed against those theses in epistemology, metaphysics, and ethics which contradicted, at least when their implications were fully worked out, the proposition that we can come to judge truly and for good reason, and that the world is nothing other than what true judgments are about and judgments for good reason tend to be about. So-called eliminative materialism would be a good example of a position liable to attack by archdeconstruction, since it can be inferred from it that we never really come to judge truly or for good reason, as talk in such terms is mere 'mentalism' destined to disappear in favour of a scientific psychology. Unfortunately, of course, it also can be inferred that no one could ever accept such a scientific psychology on the grounds that she had good reason to do so.

Archdeconstruction would concede to deconstruction that human thought and speech are strongly influenced by hierarchies of mutually opposed concepts such as those of truth and falsity, good and bad, pure and impure. It would also concede that the application of these opposed concepts constantly needs the most stringent attention; we should always be on the look-out for evidence that what we have previously assumed to be true may be false, what we have previously assumed to be good may be bad, and vice versa. But it asserts clearly and distinctly what deconstructionists seem, as it were, only regretfully and in spite of themselves to concede, that concepts – like true, false, good, bad – really do have an application. I have already said something about the way in which the 'hierarchical opposition' between truth and falsity may be vindicated. Much the same kind of thing applies to that between the good and the bad. To take Derrida's work seriously is to presuppose that its production and publication were responsible (good) acts intended to advance knowledge rather than, say, just to make fools of everybody. I do not care for peaceful co-existence between good and evil, true and false; and if I did, it would follow that I would have to admit the pointlessness of Derrida's polemics against the many authors at whom he has focused his criticisms.

It has been said that to deconstruct a discourse is 'to show how it undermines the philosophy it asserts, or the hierarchical oppositions on which it relies.'[16] Either this process can be applied equally to all discourses or it cannot. In the former case, if all discourse which purports to say what is the case can equally be deconstructed, one is left in the position ascribed to Cratylus, of being able to say nothing. Since no one can really remain long in this position, one merely resorts once more to one's initial prejudices – so the effect of what is at first sight utterly sceptical and destructive, as I have said, is ultimately to leave everything just as it was. If every position, including that of the deconstructionist herself, results equally in *aporiai*,[17] any position on matters of fact or of value is as good as any other – one might as well be a flat-earther as believe what is alleged in the last issue of *Science Today*, or commit oneself to genocide as well as to the advancement of science or the relief of hunger in the Third World. But if deconstruction can be applied negatively only to some positions, or to all positions only in some respects, it may then amount to a critical practice which will tend, by subjecting every judgment to examination and preventing it from being taken for granted, to confirm some judgments of fact as much as it falsifies others. And this could be effectively done by archdeconstruction. If in some cases it would subvert an argument by (in Jonathan Culler's words) 'identifying in the text the rhetorical operations that produce the supposed grounds of argument,'[18] in other cases it would corroborate it by vindicating the 'supposed grounds' as real.

A case in point is Nietzsche's allegedly 'deconstructive' account of causality in *The Will to Power*. We are apt, Nietzsche points out, to take it for granted that effects are dependent on causes; yet if we reflect upon our knowledge of causal relations, we find that there is a sense in which just the opposite is the case. 'In the phenomenalism of the "inner world" we invert the chronology of cause and effect. The basic fact of our experience is that the cause gets imagined after the effect has occurred.'[19] Thus deconstruction reverses the hierarchical scheme which seems so obvious a characteristic of causality; it seems after all that it is the effect which 'causes the cause to become a cause.'[20] Archdeconstruction would indicate rather quickly that though the effect is likely to be prior to the cause in the order of knowledge, the cause is prior to the effect in the order of reality. Human beings discover the measles germ by studying the disease called measles and inquiring how it comes about (thus measles is before the measles germ in the order of knowledge); yet the measles germ really causes measles in that, once knowledge has progressed beyond a certain point, it is known that, unless the measles germ is present and active there cannot exist the human illness of measles. In so far as Nietzsche's argument is supposed to show that there is some deep incoherence or confusion implicit in causal reasoning as such, it is shown up by archdeconstruction as a mere sophism.

Deconstructionists say that one should not infer from the fact that a concept has been deconstructed that it ought to be abandoned; on the contrary, the deconstructionist is liable to be depending on the deconstructed concept in the very act of deconstructing it. The use of the very conceptions she is undermining in the process of undermining them commits the critic to a stance, as it has been expressed, 'not of sceptical detachment but of unwarrantable involvement.' It has been lamented that many find this feature of deconstruction unappealing, difficult to either understand or accept.[21] From the point of view of archdeconstruction, there is every reason to find such a stance unpalatable. If to be committed to a concept or a conceptual scheme is 'unwarrantable,' then one ought not to be committed to it. If to believe that positrons or quasars exist is just as 'unwarrantable' as to believe that the earth is flat, then one should believe neither. The fact is, as I have said, that a procedure which is in principle critical of every conceivable position is effectively critical of none; and the complacent acceptance of *aporiai* to which it leads is the beginning of the end of the effective use of reason. If deconstruction is to be an effective instrument of criticism, it must be backed by an account, itself not liable to deconstruction, of what it would be for a judgment to be well- as opposed to ill-founded.

The notion of the meaning of being as presence, as Derrida sees it, brings most of traditional metaphysics in its train – including 'presence of the object to sight as *eidos*, presence as substance/essence/existence (*ousia*), ... self-presence of the cogito, consciousness, subjectivity ... Logocentrism would thus be bound up in the determination of the being of the existent as present.'[22] It seems almost tactlessly elementary to point out that *eidos*, as a technical term in Platonic philosophy, precisely does not mean what is 'present to sight'; it is what may be grasped by understanding, of which the 'sight' suggested by the etymology of the term is merely a metaphor. That this metaphorical basis infects the technical use of the term to such a degree as to invalidate it is not shown by Derrida. The traditional metaphysics which derives from Plato spells out what is presupposed by our common use of language, and even more by science, that by means of the concepts forged by our understanding we are capable, in principle at least, of grasping the real world. The world as so grasped and to be grasped consists of things (substances) characterized by properties, of which it can be known both *what* they are (their essence) and *that* they are (their existence). These are to be known by subjects who are in some sense directly aware of (present to) both their experience and themselves as reasoning about their experience (as in the Cartesian *cogito*).

However, as Derrida sees it, the metaphysics of presence always encounters an intractable problem; instances of the present offered as grounds invariably prove to be complex constructions. 'What is proposed as a given, an elementary constituent, proves to be a product, dependent or derived in ways that deprive it of the authority of simple or pure presence.' For example, the word 'dog' means something in the way that it does only by contrast with 'dig,' 'cod,' 'bog,' and so on. The sound that is 'present' when one utters it 'is inhabited by traces of the forms one is not uttering, and it can function as signifier only insofar as it consists of such traces.' What applies to the spoken applies of course equally to the written; to quote Derrida, 'each "element" – phoneme or grapheme – is constituted with reference to the trace in it of the forms one is not uttering, and it can be a signifier only insofar as it consists of such traces of other elements of the sequence or system ... Nothing, either in the elements or in the system, is anywhere simply present or absent. There are only, everywhere, differences and traces of traces.'[23] Certainly, it is true and significant that the elementary signs out of which we construct words and sentences, whether spoken or written, can only signify by virtue of their relation to and contrast with other such signs. But in such relation and by means of such contrast, there is no reason why they should not do so; and they clearly can do so, at least in some instances, by virtue of the fact that denial that they can do so is self-destructive. If the corresponding assertion has meaning, the terms in which it is expressed must in turn have meaning; this fact is not in the least affected by the fact that they have meaning only by virtue of the sort of mutual relations which have been pointed out by linguists since the time of Saussure.

There is an awkwardness about how we are to make sense of a 'given' on which knowledge is supposed to depend; the pointing-out of this awkwardness is a very interesting feature which is common to contemporary philosophers in the analytical (Anglo-Saxon) and continental (phenomenological) tradition. If we depend on 'givens' to speak truly or with good reason about the world, how is the difficulty to be resolved? I tried to deal with this issue at some length in chapter 3. To repeat summarily what I argued there: the primary reference of our language certainly is not to private 'givens,' but to things and events in the public world. It is only secondarily and derivatively that we can speak of the 'private' worlds constituted by the experience of each of us. Only by virtue of the fact that we can talk about red physical objects can we talk about visual data as of red. But this by no means implies that we cannot speak about visual data as of red at all, or even that it may not be useful for us to do so in some contexts, for example, when attempting to describe the basis for our knowledge. The same applies to our awareness of ourselves as subjects operating on data, asking questions, being puzzled, propounding hypotheses, making judgments, and so on. We do not learn the meanings of such phrases by somehow sticking labels on private episodes of our mental lives. But having learned them in discourse about others as well as ourselves, we can then use them to get clear the inner processes of our own mental lives.[24]

There is a sense in which I am directly aware of myself and my experience, but, as is shown by the efforts of philosophers of the phenomenological school, it takes strenuous efforts to spell out just what my awareness amounts to. (It is significant that Derrida's work takes its rise from a criticism of Husserl.)[25] And, as Derrida is quite correct to imply, simple awareness does not amount to knowledge; knowledge, properly speaking, of things and of the subject who knows them and the experience through which she knows them is only to be had in judgments mediated through concepts – it is not a matter of a direct apprehension which somehow bypasses concepts.

Since my assessment of Derrida's work has on the whole been somewhat negative, I would like to emphasize that his writing at its best is full of justified outrage against oppression and injustice; this ought to be acknowledged however much one deplores the frightening nihilism, both cognitive and evaluative, which seems to many of us such an inevitable consequence of many aspects of his thought.[26] I myself have stressed the inevitability and the usefulness, when rightly employed, of the 'hierarchical oppositions' decried by Derrida. But I admit that, at least as often as not, they are devices by which the more powerful can inflict suffering on the less powerful, and can deny their rights and restrict their liberty, when this is by no means in the public interest. The treatment of non-whites by whites, homosexuals by heterosexuals, and women by men[27] provide notorious instances (though, for my part, I am quite glad that compulsive rapists and axe-wielding maniacs are put under some form of restraint, and that cheats are reckoned to be, at least with respect to their cheating, inferior to honest folk). And Derrida's 'deconstructive' rhetorical techniques, if only they were backed by a coherent and articulate epistemology and axiology, could be of tremendous value in exposing the many hypocritical, vicious, or merely stupid pretensions to virtue, fairness, veracity, or intellectual merit which infest human affairs. There is a splendid example in his devastating account of the manner in which the French authorities sought to justify an act of extradition that was thought by many to be at best of dubious legality. '(O)ne can multiply signs of busyness round the very thing one wants to circumvent ... One can ... compulsively publish voluminous dossiers, juridico-constabulary organization charts, formal and allegedly exhaustive correspondences, all in order to turn around that which is in question ... to turn away that which ... one has always avoided.' Thus the 'finally published official dossier perpetuates' the avoidance, of which it is at once 'archive and consolidation.'[28] Granted only that an inexorably rational investigation would reveal the activities referred to be in bad faith, this is as fine an example of archdeconstruction as could possibly be wished.

In a curious way, Derrida's writing may be considered as a vindication of Platonism. What may be regarded as essential to Platonism is belief that the concepts forged by human understanding are capable, at least in principle, of representing the world as it really is. (Platonic 'forms' are that in the real world which corresponds to our acts of understanding.)[29] The real upshot of Derrida's attack on this 'logocentrism' is to demonstrate its inevitability, given that we are able to talk sense about things at all. In the long run, I suggest, Derrida's significance will be seen to have been that he has set forward in a very startling way the bleak alternative, either incoherent babble or 'logocentrism' with all its unpalatable metaphysical and, indeed, theological consequences. As Derrida says, 'It is a question of posing expressly and systematically the problem of the status of a discourse which borrows from a heritage the resources necessary for the deconstruction of that heritage itself.'[30] My complaint is that he does not pose the problem expressly and systematically enough. If he did so, he would come to see the self-destructive nature of the claim that we cannot make well-grounded judgments of fact or value. If he had done this, he would then have been able to apprehend the basic grounds for such judgments, and so have been in a position to distinguish between those aspects of a heritage which tend to be corroborated by a comprehensively critical analysis and those which tend to be impugned by it. Yet such a powerful apologetic for traditional metaphysics seems latent in his whole procedure that it is sometimes almost irresistible to attribute this as a motive to Derrida himself.

If any recent author excels Derrida in the enthusiasm with which he appears to saw off the branch on which he is sitting, it is Michel Foucault. If reading Foucault is an unsettling experience, if one seems in doing so to be confronted by a unique blend of brilliant insight and criminal lunacy, I think it is largely for the following reason. The reader appears for a while to be standing on the ground of certain basic cognitive and moral assumptions only to have them abruptly whisked from under her feet. She apparently learns, through copiously documented case studies, of how power may be abused in a manner which is morally wrong, or where alleged advances in knowledge may really not have been such, but have been instead mere pretexts for the extension of power by some persons over others. All this seems to presuppose a contrast with other actual or at least conceivable examples where knowledge is advanced or promulgated without the use of power, or where power is properly used for the advancement or promulgation of knowledge, and so on. But on further reading, it seems to transpire either that there is no justified use of power, in the advancement of knowledge or elsewhere, or that the questions of when and why power is abused, and when it is properly used, are pointless or meaningless. Power is ubiquitous and inevitable, we seem to be told; the question of its right or wrong use cannot arise. Thus what appears at first sight to be in the nature of a moral tract, expertly backed with facts and full of practical implications, becomes in the final analysis a counsel of despair or a pretext for total complacency.

'In a society such as ours,' Foucault writes, 'but basically in any society, there are manifold relations of power which permeate, characterize and constitute the social body, and these relations of power cannot themselves be established, consolidated nor implemented without the production, accumulation, circulation and functioning of a discourse.' The question then inevitably arises: how far is the power exerted within any society legitimate, how far is it unduly oppressive, how far does the discourse of the society encapsulate true judgments, and how far is it prevented from doing so by its involvement in the maintenance and extension of power? Undoubtedly, it is inconvenient for the powerful that certain evidence should be attended to, certain possibilities envisaged, certain judgments maintained. And so far as the exercise of such mental capacities favours the attainment of truth and of knowledge, which presumably it does, the power exerted to inhibit their exercise will hinder the attainment of truth and knowledge. One is inclined to say that such a use of power, to restrict knowledge in favour of privilege, is unjust; but this does not seem to be Foucault's view. To call something 'unjust' or 'wrong' is to presuppose a contrast with an actual or at least conceivable right. However, as Foucault sees it, 'Right should be viewed not in terms of a legitimacy to be established, but in terms of the methods of subjugation that it instigates.'[31]

It is true and important that the conception of right which actually operates within any society is largely, when all is said and done, a matter of maintaining the status quo of power and authority, or even of extending their hegemony. But, to say the least, it is not obvious that child rapists and compulsive killers might just as well be left at large. The legitimacy of the confinement or restraint of such persons, in other words, is at least something that is worth arguing about; we have to establish how far it is right in a sense which does not appear to be countenanced by Foucault. Furthermore, according to him, fear of the criminal in society has the function of making people put up with the presence of the police, with the control and constraint which this inevitably entails.[32] But is not a certain fear of criminals justified, and does this not give the average member of society good reason for accepting the existence and operation of a police force, along with the incidental infringements of her liberty which this inevitably entails? It might be objected, to be sure, that the institutional suppression of deviancy leads to more problems that it solves. But how seriously is one to take the conclusions inevitably to be inferred from this, that greatly increased carnage on the roads is preferable to a few rather tiresome traffic regulations, and that compulsive killers and violent robbers would be better left to act without restraint? Or is one being asked to believe that, if there were no laws to break or sanctions attached to the breaking of them, killing and violent robbery would cease forthwith?

It is to be noted that Foucault's view of right and wrong seems to have rather paradoxical consequences when one applies it to his presumed attitude to his own work. To take him seriously as a writer is to assume that he believed that it was right for him to compose and publish the material that he did, and that it would have been correspondingly wrong to censor his publications or to persecute him on their account. Yet this is not compatible with Foucault's own stated view that all talk of 'right' is simply a matter of instigating methods of subjugation. To take his writing, say, as intended by him merely to promote his own academic advancement would certainly be to rob it of its very considerable moral force.

The fact is, I believe, that Foucault's writings could be of very great political and moral usefulness if only certain issues were clarified. Is the use of power in human affairs necessary, and if so why? If it is necessary, how are the proper uses to be distinguished from the abuses? In particular, how is power rightly to be applied in relation to that aspect of the good which consists in the extension, maintenance, and promulgation of knowledge? To distinguish between a proper use and an abuse is to presuppose a further distinction between the good and the bad, and a means by which such a distinction can be made. And to know how power may be exerted in such a way that knowledge may flourish, one must know how knowledge properly speaking is to be distinguished from knowledge falsely so called. Only then is one in a position usefully to put the question: What is required to turn a merely factual into a normative archaeology of knowledge? That is to say, what is required for turning an account of the origin of knowledge-claims which happen to have established themselves into an account which tends to vindicate some of these knowledge-claims as worthy claimants to the title of knowledge, and to impugn others as not so?

A good example of the manner in which power is exercised in society, in Foucault's view, is the judicial apparatus. This, in societies like our own, has always been an important aspect of the state, but its history has constantly been obscured. At one time in the past its function was essentially fiscal, but as time went on it became 'organized round the effort to stamp out rebellion.' 'Dangerous' persons had to be isolated, in prisons, mental asylums, and colonies, so that they would not provide a focus for popular resistance. Another important role of the penal system was 'to make the proletariat see non-proletarianized people as marginal, dangerous, immoral ... trash, the "mob."' Fear of the criminal has the function (as we have already noted) of making people put up with the presence of the police and with control by them. The three prime means of distancing proletarianized from non-proletarianized people have been the army, prisons, and colonies, while within colonies a 'rigid racialist ideology' has been maintained in order to head off dangerous alliances. Elsewhere in society we find 'the gradual imposition of a whole system of values disguised as the teaching of literacy, reading and writing covering up the imposition of values.' Here one should attend to what might be called the 'capillary form' of the existence of power, where it 'reaches into the very grain of individuals, touches their bodies and inserts itself into their actions and attitudes, their discourses, learning processes and everyday lives.'[33]

Such institutions as courts presuppose that there are penal and moral categories common to the parties represented in them – theft, fraud, honesty, dishonesty, and so on. A really revolutionary movement would unconditionally eschew such a judicial apparatus and the bureaucracy which inevitably goes with it. The very existence of a court presupposes that it is tacitly accepted by all parties that the case of each party is neither just nor unjust until the court has pronounced it to be so, after consulting the law or some eternal principles of justice. But a truly popular justice would be in flat contradiction to all that. It is equally inimical to the notion of popular justice that for justice to be done detached intellectuals, experts in the realm of ideas, have to preside over the proceedings, persons, forsooth, who are supposed to be impartial with respect to the case presented by the workers on the one side, and the bosses on the other. 'Is not the setting up of a neutral institution standing between the people and its enemies, capable of establishing the dividing line between the true and the false, the guilty and the innocent, the just and the unjust, is this not a way of resisting popular justice?'[34]

As to the relation between truth and power, 'the important thing ... is that truth isn't outside power, or lacking in power: contrary to a myth whose history and functions would repay further study, truth isn't the reward of free spirits, the child of protracted solitude, nor the privilege of those who have succeeded in liberating themselves. Truth is a thing of this world: it is produced only by virtue of multiple forms of power.' When people ask about a form of knowledge, 'Is it a science?' one should ask in one's turn which types of knowledge they are trying to disqualify, which speaking and acting subjects they are striving to diminish. Thus it is no part of Foucault's intention to sanctify his scattered genealogies of knowledge by imposing a single theory upon them to unite them.[35] Similarly, he would by no means commend 'the nostalgia of some for the great "universal" intellectuals' or 'the desire for a new philosophy, a new world-view.'

Experience shows that institutions, practices, and discourses prove vulnerable to 'discontinuous, particular criticism'; one discovers along with this 'the inhibiting effect of global, totalitarian theories.' While Marxism and psychoanalysis, for example, have provided useful tools for the relevant research, this seems to have been the case only 'on the condition that the theoretical unity of these discourses was in some sense put in abeyance, or at least curtailed, divided, overthrown, caricatured, theatricalized, or what you will.' What Foucault aims at is 'an autonomous, non-centralized kind of theoretical production ... whose validity is not dependent on the approval of the established regimes of thought.' The object of the exercise is 'an insurrection of subjugated knowledges,' knowledges which are low-ranking, unqualified, or actually disqualified – like that of the psychiatric patient or the delinquent. Such a knowledge 'owes its force only to the harshness with which it is opposed by everything surrounding it,' but it is through its reappearance that criticism does its work. Foucault's genealogical project entertains the claims to attention of such 'illegitimate' types of knowledge 'against the claims of a unitary body of theory which would filter, hierarchize and order them in the name of some *arbitrary* idea of what constitutes a science and its object.'[36]

Genealogies do not aspire to a more accurate or careful or accurate form of science; 'they are precisely anti-sciences.'[37]

The following propositions seem worth considering in relation to Foucault's work:

1. There is no such thing as a just or rightful exercise of power.
2. The exercise of power contaminates all knowledge-claims, and consequently invalidates them.
3. The exercise of power, depending on its manner, tends to invalidate some knowledge-claims, though not others.
4. Knowledge-claims which are unsoundly based are often made on the basis of an unjust exercise of power.
5. True knowledge-claims can be abused in the exercise of unjust power, and can on occasion be made due to the exercise of such power.

In accordance with the account of knowledge and the good given in Part I of this book, propositions 1 and 2 may be regarded as absurd; 3, 4, and 5 as true. It does not immediately follow from the absurdity of 1 and 2 that they are not worth discussing. In fact, I believe that a good deal is to be learned by setting out clearly and distinctly why they are absurd.

With regard to 1, I do not see much reason to suppose that any society could exist in which no human being was able to exert power over any other human being. At least, such a state of affairs could not exist in societies at all like those that we know, or that are likely to exist in the foreseeable future. For the good of society at large, a brain surgeon should be able to give orders to her assistants, and should be able to apply sanctions against disobedience to these orders. Similarly, the tax authorities should be able to demand that a certain proportion of my income is to be surrendered to the state, and I should be liable to punishment if I refuse to pay up. (Someone of extreme libertarian views might deny this. But she would be likely to approve of the availability of other forms of coercion, applied, for example, against those who injure other persons or steal their property.) Again, a professor of engineering should be able to grade the performances of his students, and the grades given should have some potential effect on the students' subsequent careers; it is not desirable to have too many railway bridges collapsing unexpectedly. All of these examples are a matter of the exercise of power by some human beings over others.

But if the possession and exercise of power is absolutely necessary in any human society, it is impossible to doubt that such power is very liable to abuse. The brain surgeon may take advantage of her privileged position to become tetchy and tyrannical far beyond the limits of what is necessary to carry out her work effectively. The professor may grade his students according to how they reinforce his prejudices rather than on the basis of their qualities as assessable by more objective standards. The tax authorities may make unfair demands on one group of taxpayers as opposed to others, or be indiscriminately severe on different types of defaulters; the fool or incompetent, for instance, should not be treated with the same rigour as the knave.

Why does proposition 1 seem at all plausible to anyone? To put the question slightly differently: Why is any intelligent person an anarchist? One reason is a proper abhorrence of the abuse of power, and a by no means groundless fear that it is impossible for anyone to exercise power for very long without abusing it. Another reason is that it does seem intuitively correct to maintain that the more coercion (in the sense of exercise of power by one human being to restrain the will of another) is necessary within a social system, the less good that social system is. This is why most of us take for granted that 'police state' is a term of abuse. But it by no means follows from this that the best-run possible human social system would altogether be able to dispense with coercion. The existence of power, as the ability to impose coercion within society, seems to be at worst a necessary evil; and perhaps the most crucial of all questions in politics is how it may be exercised as far as possible for the best. In particular, to bring the discussion closer to Foucault's own specific interests, we do not seem to be able to do without prisons, or without places for restraining the mentally ill; and it should be a primary concern of conscientious persons that such institutions should be as beneficial and as little conducive to harm as possible. It is his systematic failure to attend to this point which is probably the most disturbing of all the special characteristics of Foucault's writing.

In reading *Madness and Civilization*,[38] one is appalled by what one learns about the manner in which many societies in earlier times treated those judged to be insane; such people were subjected to restraints, deprivations, and violence far beyond what was necessary to prevent them from doing harm to themselves or to others, and dealt with in a manner which certainly had no tendency to make them viable members of society. But as one reads on, one finds Foucault apparently attaching just as much blame to the humane Quaker founders of the York Retreat as to the authorities in the most brutal type of asylum (or, rather, should one put it that the latter are to Foucault as little deplorable as the former?). The reader of *Madness and Civilization* is disposed to wonder: Is it being implied that if no restraint whatever were imposed by society on any of those judged to be 'insane' no harm would be done? Or that a great deal of good would be done, which would more than counterbalance the harm? Or are no recommendations about the matter being made, or even implied? Or is the reader rather being teased or provoked into rethinking for herself the basis of the distinction which society makes between the 'sane' and the 'insane,' and making her recommendations accordingly?

Proposition 2 self-destructs. If it is to be taken seriously, it makes a knowledge-claim, yet it claims that all knowledge-claims are invalidated. Given its falsity, we seem to be in some position both to confirm proposition 3 and to sketch the crucial difference to which it alludes, between the kind of power that tends when exercised to invalidate knowledge-claims and the kind that does not. If cognitive authenticity (attentiveness, intelligence, and reasonableness) is, as I have suggested, the royal road to knowledge, then to encourage cognitive authenticity is by and large to promote knowledge. It seems clear that in some instances the exercise of power does promote cognitive authenticity, while in others it discourages it. The most obvious examples of this, I suppose, are to be drawn from the activities of the teaching profession. Teachers at their worst, from the level of the elementary school right up to that of doctoral supervision, proceed by dinning the received opinions into the heads of their students, while treating sarcastically or punitively any tendency within them to observe, raise questions, hypothesize, or judge for themselves. On the other hand, a good teacher will make it her primary aim to encourage these dispositions within her pupils, and will be at pains to show how the received opinions, so far as they are to be adopted, have been arrived at precisely due to the exercise of cognitive authenticity.

It is the essence of 'ideology' in its usual pejorative sense that knowledge-claims are not really made on the basis of cognitive authenticity, but are due to people's wishes and desires, and particularly the need of powerful groups within society to maintain and extend their hegemony – hence the truth of proposition 4. For example, it is in the interests of the rich man in his castle to believe that God has made him and the poor man at his gate, respectively, high and lowly, and has ordered their estate. But it must be remembered that while ideological motivation in its proponents gives rise to justifiable doubt whether a statement is true, it does not of itself establish its falsity. I may be sure that a man is a thief when all the evidence available to me is against it simply because I dislike the expression on his face, but all the same he may really be a thief. Again, a corrupt and oppressive political regime, which encourages the stronger to drive the weaker to the wall, is liable to have a strong ideological motive for promulgating Darwinism, with its corollary that breeding stock in all species is to be improved by fierce competition leading to elimination of the unfit. But this does not of itself show that Darwinism is false. On the other hand, if cognitive authenticity tends to confirm any belief here and now, this does not of itself prove that that belief is true; there may be evidence not yet attended to, and possibilities not yet envisaged, which would yield a theory incompatible with it such as would account more satisfactorily for the relevant data. This, of course, is to reinforce rather than to impugn the conviction that the only proper way to assess whether a belief is true or false is to be as cognitively authentic as possible with regard to it.

All this is by way of support of propositions 3, 4, and 5. Unsoundly based claims, which may all the same be true but tend not to be, are apt to reinforce and be reinforced by the unjust exercise of power. A male- or white-dominated society might well be inclined to put about the view that males or whites had innate mental or moral capacities which justified their position. Insuring that knowledge-claims are soundly based tends to act against the unjust exercise of power, which thrives on ignorance among all parties concerned of its true nature. If women and non-whites have no less of the requisite intellectual and moral qualities than males and whites, this will tend to be confirmed by the exercise of cognitive authenticity; and, accordingly, domination of society by males and whites, since it is now recognized to be arbitrary and unjust, will be the less likely to continue.

It would be a great mistake to infer, from the facts that cognitive authenticity tends to lead to knowledge and that power is often exercised in such a way as to discourage cognitive authenticity, that there is no place for the exercise of power in the acquisition and promulgation of knowledge. Most of what anyone can reasonably claim to know is derived from authority; very little has been found out at first hand by herself. However, one of the most significant areas for the exercise of cognitive authenticity is precisely in one's choice of authorities; with regard to authority for belief, just as in the case of belief itself, there is the constant danger of improperly following one's needs and desires. If I have, say, an instinctive or unconsciously acquired antipathy to certain human racial groups, I may be liable to join political organizations which put about ill-founded tales of the bad influence of these groups on our society, and work to get them expelled from it, or at least from positions of dignity and influence within it. On the question of whether very different types of organism descend from a common ancestor, again, I may properly exert my cognitive authenticity to determine that one set of authorities is more worthy of credence than another, on the ground that members of the former group, now or in the past, seem to have been motivated more by cognitive authenticity, and less by ideological factors, than the latter, in acquiring and putting about the opinions they do on the matter.

Armed with these somewhat rough and ready considerations on the bases of cognition and moral evaluation, it is time to address ourselves more closely to the details of Foucault's text.

In the course of Foucault's treatment of 'popular justice,' the reader will note, surely to her amazement and horror, that the question of whether alleged 'enemies of the people' are its actual enemies, whether they have committed the crimes with which they are charged, never arises for him at all. In discussion with Foucault, the case was cited of the French women who were subjected to public degradation for consorting with the Nazis at the end of the Second World War.[39] A series which appeared about the subject a few years ago on British television portrayed a woman who had acted with great heroism as an undercover agent for the Resistance, whose 'cover' was to appear to consort with Nazis as a bar-maid in a tavern frequented by them; she was all but subjected to public humiliation on the grounds of this 'cover.' Does Foucault really think that 'popular justice' would never make mistakes of this kind? Or that, if they were made, they would not matter? If he supposes that spontaneous outbursts of aggression by crowds of people would always be directed at genuinely guilty parties, he is obviously and outrageously wrong. But, of course, to make such objections to what he says is to make implicit appeal to those very 'eternal principles of justice' which Foucault purports to repudiate. Either 'popular justice' conforms to unchanging norms of right and wrong (that one is not to 'punish' the innocent, or bring about intense suffering or large-scale loss of life for one's own amusement, and so on) or it is deplorable and ought to be resisted.

So long as it is possible that mistakes of the kind that I have described might be made, it seems clear that institutions such as the courts which Foucault decries are necessary. That power is liable to corrupt the opera-tion of such institutions is of course true and important. But the moral is not that one should do away with courts, or that 'eternal principles' of right and wrong should be denied, but rather that courts should con-stantly be scrutinized lest they fail to apply these very 'eternal principles,' and defer to the interests of some powerful group. And given that there are principles of justice which transcend the special interests and concerns of litigants, and that courts exist to apply them, one would suppose that they should be staffed by persons with a training in these matters. To do such things well needs clerical work in the keeping of records and so on. 'Bureaucracy' is a dirty word; one has to distinguish between office work and related routines which are treated as ends in themselves and those which are means to the securing of real goods and the averting of real evils. Without a considerable measure of 'bureaucracy' in the second sense, life in a civilized society would be completely impossible. One important task of writers like Foucault is, it must be granted, to prevent the latter sort of bureaucracy from turning into the former. But Foucault fails to make the distinction at all; and his principles, or rather his lack of them, render it impossible for such a distinction to be made.

Just as there are, in spite of what Foucault says and implies, principles of right and wrong which transcend the apparent short-term interests (let alone the immediate impulses of cupidity or aggression) of individuals and groups, so there are ways of thinking and observing by means of which one tends to get at the truth and avoid falsehood about things. In the light of them, the merits in what Foucault has to say seem to amount to this: less powerful, or marginalized, or oppressed groups tend to be able and willing to attend to evidence, and to envisage possibilities, which are neglected or actively brushed aside by more powerful groups. Obvious examples of this are provided by certain kinds of racism. If all or most members of race *A* in a community have a lower social status and standard of living then the members of race *B*, it will suit members of race *B* to believe and to put it about that members of race *A* are congenitally unable to bear the responsibilities, or appreciate the refined pleasures, that they themselves enjoy. Race *B* will consequently discourage attention to evidence, and envisagement of possibilities, which might lead to the judgment that things are really otherwise. In the interests of truth, however, one has to attend with particular care to such evidence and such possibilities, especially when they go against one's own interests as an individual or member of a group. (The probable effect of a well-known beverage on the health of its consumers is one thing; what it suits its purveyors to state publicly, or even to believe privately, about it may be quite another.)

Power tends to corrupt the search for inconvenient truth, and therefore to preserve convenient falsehood; consequently, to pursue the truth is very often to resist established power. On the other hand, as in the ideal chemistry or history department within a university, power may be deliberately and effectively exercised in order to encourage the cognitive authenticity – the attentiveness, intelligence, and reasonableness – which tends to lead to truth. Contrariwise, the (probable) truth can sometimes be abused for the maintenance of unjust power, as I tried to illustrate earlier in the case of Darwinism; but there tends at least, for the reasons that I have just given, to be a correlation between the maintenance of unjust power and belief in falsehoods. But in order to see how this can be, and to work out what ought to be done about it, one has to be much clearer about the nature of the good and the true, and about the means by which they are in general to be attained, than Foucault ever is. Even to approve his work, after all, is to assume that it was good for him to write and publish it, and that his 'archaeologies' or 'genealogies' help us to get at the truth about the developments of the forms of actual or alleged knowledge which they describe.

A related point is to be made about Foucault's attitude to 'science.' Sure enough, the claim to scientific status can be used more or less consciously as a ruse to gain or maintain power, as Foucault tellingly shows in many of his writings. But it can amount to more than this. To put briefly once again what has already been argued at length, an account of things tends to be true if it is consistent within itself and with other accounts, and if it is corroborated by the relevant data.[40] Science at its best, in fact one might say science properly so called, strenuously aims for such consistency and corroboration. Claims to consistency are indeed subject to ideological abuse, as when they are unsound in themselves, or when they are not accompanied by corroboration; but they need not be so. On the contrary, consistency wedded to corroboration in experience would appear to be the most effective of all weapons against ideological avoidance and suppression of truth. On the particular issues of Marxism and psychoanalysis, I would agree with Foucault that each provides a fund of useful insights, but arguably a defective overall account of the matters with which it deals. Yet I would go on to maintain that, so far as they fail in this respect, this is by no means because of their overall consistency, let alone their scientific status properly speaking; rather, it is due to their mere appearance of consistency, and to their lack of comprehensive corroboration by the relevant data. In other words, if Marxism or psychoanalysis have defects as overall accounts of the matters with which they deal – and I do not commit myself in this context to the judgment that either of them is thus defective – it is due to mere pretension to scientific status, in conjunction with actual lack of it. And I hope I have persuaded the reader that the ideas of 'science' and of the 'scientific' involved here are the very opposite of 'arbitrary.' It may be added that the proper target of satire is not scientific theory as such, but the sententious and obfuscating jargon which so often parodies it.

The account of the true and the good which I have sketched enables one to put on a more satisfactory basis Foucault's efforts to rehabilitate suppressed, rejected, and outlawed ways of speaking and of understanding.[41] Indeed one should constantly attend sympathetically to these in the manner encouraged by Foucault.[42] This is because it is only too likely to happen, for reasons which I have already given, that a reigning discourse will be more dominated by ideological motives than a means of expressing and enhancing cognitive authenticity. The history of the proper applications, in contrast to the abuses, of the ideals of truth and of science would be well worth writing, and would consist very largely of the kinds of critical 'archaeologies' pioneered by Foucault. But his own epistemological principles, or rather his lack of them, leave him in a position from which it is impossible to make such a contrast, for all that it is clearly needed in the vindication of his own claims. For to take Foucault's writing seriously is precisely not to treat it as merely one more move in the game of power, but to accept it as aimed at, and more or less approximating to, expression of the truth about the matters with which it deals.

A person's environment, for reasons mentioned several times in this chapter, may be such as to encourage cognitive authenticity only to a limited extent, and it may not encourage it at all, or may even actively discourage it. This is why, contrary to what Foucault says, truth may well be 'the reward of free spirits, the child of protracted solitude,' or 'the privilege of those who have succeeded in liberating themselves.' How else, indeed, can one make sense of Foucault's own capacity to criticize the established myths against which he inveighs? I believe that it is the principal justification of literacy, that it is a prime means to the promotion of cognitive authenticity. This is because the reader's own judgments and assumptions are called into question by being confronted in what she reads by judgments and assumptions very different from her own; this is liable to evoke in her the rational examination of her own opinions and prejudices. It must of course be admitted that the teaching of literacy may incidentally serve as a way of putting over docile attitudes, and the beliefs which go with them, on underprivileged sections of the population. But with the abuse comes the remedy. If one teaches literacy through examples which inhibit cognitive authenticity, one does at least thereby give one's pupils access to literature of other and more worthwhile kinds.

I have tried to argue that there are certain defects in Foucault's writings which make them less effective and beneficial a force in morals, politics, and the critique of institutions than they would otherwise be. Chief among these defects is lack of a coherent idea of the good, and of the human mental capacities which favour the attainment of truth and the avoidance of error. Foucault also apparently fails to grasp the implications of the fact, which he himself admits, that the existence and implementation of power within human society is inevitable. If anyone were to remedy these deficiencies in Foucault's writings, she would indeed be able to use them to mount an effective critique of the abuses of power, and to show how it might be harnessed rather to the acquisition of genuine knowledge, and the securing of real benefit for the greatest number of people.

11

An Unstable Compromise: Habermas

What I want to argue in this chapter amounts, briefly, to this: Habermas's basic epistemological principles, as set out in *Theory of Communicative Action*,[1] are quite largely correct; but they commit him, when followed through, to something much closer to the traditional metaphysics and 'first philosophy' than he is prepared to countenance. In fact, his thinking appears to exhibit a curious oscillation between what is in effect the proposing of a 'first philosophy' and a denial that such a 'first philosophy' is possible.

The kind of totalizing view (says Habermas) which would purport to survey the whole of nature, history, and society is no longer possible. A realization of this fact has led philosophy to retreat to a critical position, and to be concerned with the conditions of rationality in knowledge, in action, and in the reaching of understanding; in its 'post-metaphysical, post Hegelian currents' it 'is converging towards the point of a theory of rationality.' How can sociology claim a competence in this matter, then? Philosophy, in surrendering its claims to totality, has abandoned at the same time its self-sufficiency; *a priori* reconstructions of consciousness in general have gone the way of traditional metaphysics. 'All attempts at discovering ultimate foundations, in which the intuitions of First Philosophy live on, have broken down.' Now any general account of communicative reason, such as we have to offer, may be thought to have fallen into the snares of a discredited foundationalism. However, such an assumption would be mistaken.

Of the social sciences, sociology is best equipped to approach the problem of reason as such; it was unable to brush aside the questions that politics and economics did on their way to becoming special sciences. But sociology has its own limitations, having arisen as the theory of bourgeois societies, attempting to explain the modernization of traditional societies by capitalism and the anomic side-effects of this. Thus, for all his great merits, Max Weber had the limitation that he identified the capitalist form of the application of reason to society, which overemphasizes technical mastery at the expense of communicative understanding, with the application of reason to society as such. This led him to believe that a moral consciousness which was guided by principles could not endure except in a religious environment. Now there is no doubt that religions played a significant role in the emergence of this kind of moral consciousness, but it by no means follows from this that they are needed for its survival. That they are so needed is nowhere demonstrated by Weber; and indeed such a view is supported neither by empirical evidence nor by strong theoretical arguments. And in fact we find in modern times that a secular sphere of reasoning about moral values, distinct from the spheres either of description or of self-expression, has developed quite independently of religion. The kind of reasoning involved is built partly on the Kantian principle that one should be able to universalize the maxims underlying one's actions (I should not do to anyone else what I would not wish her, in like circumstances, to do to me), partly on the utilitarian assumption that one ought to maximize happiness. Weber was hobbled by the positivism fashionable in his day, in accordance with which moral judgments merely expressed subjective attitudes – a doctrine to which he gives explicit assent. But his own arguments for the superiority of some moral stances to others are incompatible with it.[2]

It may be taken for granted that there is a close connection between the notions of 'rationality' and 'knowledge,' though rationality is less a matter of actual possession of knowledge than of how speakers and agents acquire and use it. One may note that two sorts of entity may be legitimately spoken of as more or less rational – persons who possess knowledge and symbolic expressions, whether spoken or written, which embody it. There is an important connection too between truth in judgment and effectiveness in action. As truth is related to states of affairs in the world, so effectiveness is related to interventions which can bring such states of affairs about. Claims as to truth and effectiveness can both be criticized and argued for, provided with grounds. These considerations suggest that one may look for an account of the rationality of expressions on the basis of their susceptibility to criticism and grounding. It may be added that what can be criticized is also fallible, and that such fallibility may well be regarded as a condition of relation to an objective world, and that criticism is essentially trans-subjective, in principle able to be offered by others than the person immediately concerned. One may conclude that assertions and actions are the more rational the more they can be defended against criticism. A rational person may be regarded as one who is in the habit of making such assertions and performing such actions, particularly in circumstances which are difficult. It may be seen that there is a close connection between intersubjectivity and rationality; unconstrained argumentative speech tends to bring about consensus, breaking down merely subjective opinions. Participants in such communication, 'owing to the mutuality of rationally motivated conviction, assure themselves of both the unity of the objective world and the intersubjectivity of their lifeworld.' There is an important corollary to this bond between objectivity and intersubjectivity: that while from one point of view rationality seems aimed at technical mastery, from another its goal is communicative understanding.[3]

There are also consequences to be drawn for ethics. Claims to normative rightness have something at least in common with the claims to truth and efficiency which we have already briefly considered – they are able to be criticized and defended against criticism. They may thus conform to the basic criteria of rationality. Whatever problems may arise in philosophical ethics, at least norms of action are apt to reflect common interest as it bears on matters requiring regulation, that the interest is common is what makes it deserve general recognition. At this rate one may assume a cognitivist position in ethics, since the availability of such criteria implies that moral questions can in principle be dealt with by argument. One more general use of argument is worth distinguishing, that which clarifies consciousness and works against self-deception; this may be called therapeutic critique.[4] The deformation of life under capitalism, so far as Habermas is concerned, is largely due to the development of one form of rationality, that of technical mastery, at the expense of the others – he writes of 'the jagged profile of rationality potentials that have been unevenly exploited.'[5]

It is to be regretted that, for all that it has a tradition which goes back to Aristotle, the theory of argument is still at rather an elementary stage. Deductive logic, which has of course been developed with enormous thoroughness and refinement, does not by itself take us very far; and there are notoriously intractable problems about the nature and justification of induction, that mental procedure by which we move from knowledge of particular instances to that of general principles and laws. In his *Introduction to Reasoning*, Stephen Toulmin has distinguished a number of fields of argument, but he doubts whether we have access to 'a fundamental and unchangeable framework of rationality.' While he does not wish to pay the price of relativism, it is not clear how he can avoid it once he has made this concession. Where Toulmin fails, in Habermas's view, is that he does not distinguish clearly enough between merely conventional claims which are indeed dependent on context and validity claims which are of universal import. What a theory of argument has to do is 'to specify a *system* of validity claims'; it does not have to derive it by something in the nature of a transcendental deduction. 'A *validity claim* is equivalent to the assertion that the *conditions for the validity* of an utterance are fulfilled.' Once it is made by a speaker, a hearer can only accept it, reject it, or leave it undecided for the present. As distinct from reactions to claims to power, which are a matter of arbitrary choice ('Shall I defer or shall I rebel?'), to say yes or no to such claims is done for reasons and on grounds, and expresses insight into, or understanding of, what is meant, and how it is supposed to be justified at the bar of those reasons or grounds.[6]

It is to be emphasized that, while claims about states of affairs, on the one hand, and normative or evaluative statements (which are concerned with the acceptability of actions), on the other, can both be grounded, the manners in which they are to be grounded are different. From the point of view of enlightened thought, the primitive mind appears to confuse these ways of grounding, and accordingly to be the victim of a twofold illusion about the world and about itself. Mere mental constructions are endowed with an existence independent of human beings, and the world is filled with beings analogous to humans who can understand their needs, and respond to them in a friendly or hostile way. To 'demythologize' is, by contrast, to de-socialize nature and to de-naturalize society. It is easy for us in our state of society to have access to this process at an intuitive level, but to analyse it adequately is by no means so simple. To articulate properly the advance which has to be made from the primitive state of mind, we have to differentiate sharply between two basic attitudes: that to be directed towards the objective world of what is the case, and that to be directed towards 'the social world of what can be legitimately expected, what can be commanded or ought to be.' It is one thing to observe or to manipulate, another to conform to or violate legitimate expectation; we have to be conscious of the change of perspective involved in moving from the one kind of activity to the other. In mythical thought, the different sorts of validity claims at issue in regard to factual truth, normative rightness, and expressive sincerity (where one makes clear to oneself and others the nature of one's feelings and attitudes) have not been effectively distinguished from one another.[7]

Mythical world-views mix up nature and culture, the objective and the social worlds. They reify the projections of language, and their conceptions have a dogmatic content which is insulated from rational discussion and consequently from criticism. At a more sophisticated level, one may have relatively rationalized world-views which refer in a theological manner to creation, or in a metaphysical manner to the totality of what exists. These are anchored in ultimate principles such as 'God,' 'Being,' or 'Nature,' which provide premises for arguments, but are not themselves subject to rational critique. The retention of such principles ensures that descriptive, normative, and expressive attitudes are still fused together, and 'the tradition-securing modes of pious belief or reverential contemplation' are not endangered. However, modern ways of thought do not recognize any exemptions from the activity of criticism, either in the realm of fact or in that of value. Validity claims on the modern view are all in principle open to criticism; they presuppose a world which is intersubjectively shared, 'identical for all possible observers,' and 'in an abstract form free of any specific content.' Only by contrast with clear conceptions of 'an objective world of states of affairs and ... a social world of norms' can the complementary conceptions of an internal world and subjectivity arise.[8]

Now what is counted as a good reason at any time and place clearly depends on criteria which are subject to a great deal of change in the course of history. But this does not imply that the conceptions of truth and rightness which intuitively underlie the choice of criteria are dependent on context to the same extent. And however plausibly some writers have sought to deny it, differing world-views can be compared with one another, and not only, say, from an aesthetic point of view, but also with regard to their cognitive adequacy. World-views, to use Karl Popper's distinction, may be evaluated as relatively 'open' or 'closed' to 'the degree to which they hinder or promote cognitive-instrumental learning processes.' This is by no means to deny that precious things may be lost by an 'open' mentality which are preserved by a 'closed.' Robin Horton speaks of 'an intensely poetic quality in everyday life and thought, and a vivid enjoyment of the passing moment,' as characteristic of some traditional African cultures in marked contrast to Western culture. What has to be learned from the contemporary debate on rationality is 'that the modern understanding of the world is indeed based on general structures of rationality but that modern Western societies promote a distorted understanding of rationality that is based too exclusively on its cognitive-instrumental aspects.' Societies modernized through capitalism seem specially subject to deformation of this kind, and also to that due to 'devaluation of their traditional substance.'[9]

When it comes to the social sciences, a lot of harm has been done by a misunderstanding of a grasp of what someone else means 'as empathy, as a mysterious act of transposing oneself into the mental states of another subject.' What is it, one may ask, to understand the meaning of, say, a text? 'The interpreter understands the meaning of a text only to the extent that he sees why the author felt himself entitled to put forward (as true) certain assertions, to recognize (as right) certain values and norms, to express (as sincere) certain experiences.' (But to understand these things is by no means necessarily to agree with the author concerned.) It is to be noted that, if the process of reaching understanding of another's meaning is to claim objectivity, the structures which it employs will have to be shown to be of universal validity. This is a strong requirement indeed for one who renounces the support of a metaphysics, or the transcendental ambition of providing ultimate grounds; 'we are taking on a sizeable burden of proof.'[10]

Thus far Habermas. In the light of the principles developed so far in this book, I am in agreement with him on many points. In particular, I am quite certain that he is right, against the deconstructionists and postmodernists, that we need a general theory of rationality; short of this, we have no non-arbitrary defence against any cognitive absurdity or moral atrocity. And I believe that he has gone a considerable way towards providing what is needed, in his articulation of general principles of criticism, to be applied in somewhat different ways to knowledge of facts, to morality,[11] and to self-knowledge. But it seems to me that such general principles inevitably lead to something like a metaphysics – if *this* is the way to knowledge, *that*, at least in very general outline, is the nature of what is to be known. It is of course true that it is impossible to specialize in the whole *of* knowledge. But, to employ a distinction of Hegel's, it does not immediately follow from this that some persons ought not to attend to the whole *in* knowledge. Does phenomenalism, or some form of idealism, or mechanical or dialectical materialism represent the truth about the world? Or is the truth about things something different from all of these? Unless one approaches these questions critically, uncriticized dogmas are bound to take over in one's thinking. And it is surely a part of Habermas's aim to argue that at least some of these positions are mistaken. But to claim or to argue that some of these very general accounts of reality are more or less correct than others is to be committed to a sort of metaphysics.

Habermas is quite right, I believe, against his relativist opponents, to insist that a theory of argument has to specify a system of validity claims which are universal in scope, rather than being simply the favoured methods of argument of a particular group. But such a theory also has to provide justification of such claims as liable to yield knowledge of a world which exists, and is very largely as it is, prior to and independently of anyone's getting to know about it by means of such a system of validity claims. If I want to find out the nature of thermonuclear processes in red giant stars, or of the breeding habits of the hooded merganser, I want to find out about things as they are quite independent of my activities as an inquirer. Either one can provide and justify an account of how, by means of our thought and language, we can come to think and speak of a world which is independent of our thought and language (which might have existed and been largely as it is if we had never evolved as thinkers and speakers) or we cannot. If we cannot, we remain inevitably enmeshed in the morass of relativism, where there is no objective world, but only a plurality of 'worlds for' different human groups. (When one presses the question of which world the different human groups themselves exist in, the mind-dissolving nonsense which is the inevitable consequence of this view becomes plain enough.) But if we can, we have performed the equivalent of a 'transcendental deduction,' and have involved ourselves in 'first philosophy' whether or not we care to call it by that name. That the rationality of our speech and action tends to promote in us real knowledge of the objective world shows us something about the nature of that world – briefly and summarily, that it is permeable to rational inquiry. Habermas is committed to implicit belief in this last proposition, just by virtue of the confidence and in my view the thoroughly justified confidence, which he has in critical rationality for putting us in touch with the real world. But to spell out the proposition, to justify it, and to work out its implications for the overall nature and structure of the world is the essence of that very 'transcendental' or 'first philosophy' which he says that he wishes to repudiate.

The invocation of sociology to supply an account of rationality, where philosophy is deemed to have failed, provides the misleading appearance of bringing things up to date, and of distancing any solutions which might be proposed from the abandoned 'first philosophy.' However, the problems of how thought and language are to represent a world which exists independently of them remain the old ones; and it is difficult to see how they are significantly advanced, as opposed to obfuscated, by the suggestion that the sociologist rather than the philosopher should solve them. It must of course be conceded that sociologists have had a great deal that is of value to say about how the social process may support or inhibit good reasoning, how it is itself to be submitted to reasoning, and about the gains and the losses which have so far accrued from this.

What is the 'abstract form freed of all specific content' which, on Habermas's view, all validity-claims presuppose? The world must be no more and no less than what we tend to get to know so far as we rigorously subject our beliefs to criticism very much in the manner that Habermas describes. But this assumption, when attended to and followed through, commits one to much more of the traditional metaphysics than Habermas seems willing to concede. We know *a priori* that the world will conform to some set of hypotheses, instantiate some range of possibilities, for all that what these are in detail could only be known at the ideal term of inquiry. (To those who doubt whether 'the world' or 'reality' has this overall nature and structure, one can only ask what else, in the final analysis, knowledge could consist in other than well-founded true judgments based on a range of understandings of experience, and what 'the world' or 'reality' could be other than what is thus to be known.) [12] And a world which instantiates some self-consistent set of possibilities is an intelligible world. That the real world is intelligible is what is central to Plato's 'theory of forms'; Aristotle hinted in passing, [13] and Aquinas set down more clearly, [14] that this real intelligible world is to be known by a twofold inquiry into things as they appear to our senses – one aspect seeking a hypothesis as to what some sensible thing or state of affairs may be or why it may be as it is, and the other aspect trying to determine whether this or some other hypothesis actually is so. Whatever the prodigious changes in the sciences, and so in our conception of the world, which have come about since ancient times, the basic scheme of classical metaphysics has always been presupposed; one is seeking out the intelligible reality which is the best explanation for the phenomena of the world as we all perceive it. [15] As a result of a reiterated process of perceiving, questioning, hypothesizing, marshalling evidence, and judging by many specialists over many generations, scientists have come to the conclusion, itself liable to be modified at least in detail by further applications of the same procedures, that the 'forms' of ordinary matter are what are represented by the periodic table of the elements, the 'forms' of life, what are articulated in terms of the theory of evolution, and so on. It is in these terms that we have come to know 'things in their causes,' as Aristotle would say, in terms that inform us not just *that* things are as they are, but *why* they are as they are.

Habermas will have it that the theory of argument is still at an elementary stage. But I think that he holds this largely because that theory, as it has actually developed, is too closely tied up with the traditional metaphysics for his comfort. There is still a great deal to be learned about the nature of good argument from the for:n of the *quaestio* used in the medieval *Summae*,[17] for all its incidental defects in actual practice. (It may plausibly be claimed, for example, that its practitioners were apt to misrepresent opposing positions by tearing quotations and fragments of argument out of their original context.) One set out the thesis which one intended to establish; one then set out the objections to it, in a manner which would so far as possible satisfy the objector himself (shorn of the kind of rhetorical devices which would prevent the unwary reader or listener from taking them seriously); one gave one's reasons for accepting the thesis; and finally one answered the objections previously set out. One important defect in the method was pointed out at the time of the Renaissance, particularly by Francis Bacon, who stressed the role of observation as a corrective to the emphasis on 'agitation of wit' characteristic of medieval scholasticism.[17] Observation is certainly of the utmost importance in suggesting to the mind more possibilities than had previously been envisaged as to what may be so, and in corroborating or falsifying such possibilities once they have been envisaged. This aspect of the matter was certainly underestimated by the medievals.[18] But to say so much is to indicate how the medieval scheme should be supplemented rather than supplanted; not only authorities and one's own sheer reasoning powers, but observed phenomena and experimental results, are relevant to the establishing of one's own position on any matter, and to the setting-out and refutation of positions incompatible with it. The medieval scheme certainly conforms to Habermas's ideal of 'communicative reason,' in that each hypothesis which has been advanced, whether consistent with the one which the investigator herself wishes to advance or not, is treated with full seriousness.

Habermas's association between objectivity and intersubjectivity is certainly thoroughly in accord with the scheme, as well as being profound and important in itself. To be objective is to be prepared to take into account another's viewpoint, as providing an account of things which is in principle as liable to be true of them as is one's own. But I think that there is a corollary of this which he does not attend to, or at least sufficiently emphasize. As we can have, and ought to aspire to, a knowledge of the thoughts and feelings of other people, which is not directed towards domination of them, so we can have and ought to aspire to such a knowledge of the rest of the world. Habermas seems content with a mere knowledge-for-domination of the non-human world. But this appears to me a conception of such knowledge which, at least when understood in an exclusive manner, is at once debilitating to the human spirit and at variance with the reported experience of great scientists. As I suggested in connection with Heidegger's work, many cosmologists, physicists, and students of animal behaviour – to take a fairly wide sample of types of scientist – seem to evince a delighted wonder in the matter which they study, rather than merely a desire to subdue and control it. Technological mastery is sure enough one proper aim of science – we should always be grateful for the achievements of modern medicine in lowering infant mortality and delivering us from the scourge of smallpox, for example – but something has gone badly wrong if it becomes its exclusive or even its dominant aim.[19]

Habermas is right to distinguish between certain basic aims to be pursued in the use of reason and to harp on the bad effects which ensue from confusion between them. But I am not perfectly happy with the way in which he allocates them to the natural world, on the one hand, and to the human or cultural world, on the other. If we are to regard nature as an object – to employ an unfortunate, ambiguous, but virtually inevitable word – of contemplation, as well as of control, our horizon seems open to the religious question, which in this context might be put in the following way: Does thoroughly 'objective' inquiry, in the sense of inquiry which relentlessly pursues all relevant questions, tend to show that there is something analogous to human thought and purpose in the world that exists prior to and independently of human society, or to show that there is not? The word 'objective' is advisedly to be put in inverted commas, as on one understanding even to use the term is to beg the question. If an 'objective' inquiry is as such aimed at manipulation and control, then the religious question is either ruled out from the start or given a negative answer by 'objective' inquiry. But if what is meant by it is inquiry concerned to find out what is the case, without any presupposition about manipulation or control, then a positive answer to the religious question is not necessarily put out of court; human beings may ask, using the utmost resources of their intelligence and reason over the widest possible range of experience, whether there is something analogous to intelligent will underlying the universe – whether, to put it briefly and crudely, there is a God or whether there is not. It is one thing to say that the concept of 'God,' along with other general metaphysical notions like 'being' or 'nature,' must be subjected to the most intensive possible rational scrutiny; it is another thing to say that they will have to be abandoned as a result of it.

One ought not, if one takes seriously Habermas's claim as to the merely abstract nature of the world as conceived by the fully modern critical attitude, to rule out the possibility that the proposition that God exists might reasonably be judged to be true after all, and certain traditional 'modes of pious belief or reverential contemplation,' to use Habermas's phrase, justified as a consequence. And this is just what is maintained by the rational theist – by the person who thinks one can, without assuming what one has to prove, show that there is better reason for thinking that God exists than that God does not exist. Habermas's scheme is in general remarkable for its range and generosity; but there seems to me an unfortunate tendency implicit in it to pre-empt, rather than carefully and objectively to ask and to answer, the question of whether there is (or are) some being (or beings) analogous to the human mind that underlie nature and history. Perhaps one of the disadvantages of 'first philosophy' for Habermas is that it makes it somewhat difficult for this question not to be clearly formulated and asked.

As for the moral consequences of religion or theism, Habermas says that there are neither empirical nor theoretical grounds for supposing that lack of such belief is liable to have a generally bad effect on human behaviour. That religion, as he says, has plainly had a great deal to do with the origin of morality does not necessarily imply that it is required for its survival. That there is so little hard evidence for the thesis that religious faith is on the whole morally beneficial ought indeed, I think, to be of constant concern to believers. The theoretical grounds for asserting a positive connection between religion and moral virtue seem to me rather stronger. Habermas does seem to me quite correct in asserting that the modern world-view does provide resources for constructing a morality which is conceptually quite independent of religion, in spite of the difficulties which have been alleged by so many modern philosophers. (It is worth remarking that similar resources were to be found in ancient and medieval times, for example, in the philosophies of Plato, Aristotle, and the Stoics, and that the 'ages of faith' seemed to evince remarkably little concern about the matter.) But the formal independence of morality and religion by no means entails their mutual irrelevance.

The fact is that society, as it is, always has been, and almost certainly will be for the foreseeable future, provides us with any number of inducements for self-preservation and self-indulgence as opposed to moral goodness, and for telling the powerful what they want to hear without regard for the small matter of whether it is true. The relevance of religion to morality which follows from this fact has been well expressed by Richard Purtill: 'Without the motivation of faith, doing good in the world at considerable personal sacrifice is not something most people can sustain.'[20] In the world as it is, people suffer not only *although* they put themselves out to do good, but very often *because* they put themselves out to do good. Faith provides a counterweight to this situation, as Kant plainly saw;[21] to the eye of faith, this pattern of the punishment of the good and the rewarding of the evil is not what will prevail in the long run. I conclude, against Habermas, that there are some theoretical grounds for supposing that consistent moral virtue does after all flourish best against the background of faith, even though the empirical evidence on the matter may be at best ambiguous and at worst positively damaging to religious faith. The real issue about the relation of religion to morality is not whether it is possible to work out a rational morality without explicit appeal to religion, which it plainly is, but about how people can be motivated to follow such a morality when the going gets tough – which it usually does sooner rather than later if one is honest about the nature of its demands. (Some few persons are of such moral heroism that they can remain virtuous however discouraging the circumstances, without religious faith or hope; but this is not to the point.) It would be very convenient if, as Marx and Engels proposed,[22] human society could be reformed in such a way that individual and general interest always coincided; but it is not at all obvious that such a state of affairs could ever come about, given the conditions of human life on earth. It should be noted, of course, that religious faith ought to provide an enhancement of the natural moral conscience and other critical faculties, rather than, as has happened much too often in history, being used as a pretext for setting them aside. Religions along with their moral claims are at least as much in need of comprehensive criticism and evaluation as anything else.

Though Habermas has tended, as he himself says, to avoid discussion of theological topics, theologians have shown considerable interest in his ideas, and their interest has provoked a thoughtful response from him.[23] Habermas admits that religious leaders and theologians have sometimes provided excellent moral and political guidance, as in Germany in the aftermath of the Second World War. But, in spite of the anti-metaphysical stance of some recent theologians such as Karl Barth, he is of the opinion that metaphysics and allegedly revealed religion are natural allies, and that consequently the modern collapse of metaphysics has made assent to religious truth-claims more problematic than ever. According to several of Habermas's theological interlocutors, religious belief is imperatively required if human beings are to have the heart to engage enthusiastically enough in the struggle for greater justice within human society. But even if it were conceded that religious belief, when properly understood and applied, had or could have this salutary effect, this would do nothing, as Habermas points out (and as I argued earlier in connection with Kant), to support religious truth-claims. Hegel's titanic effort to fuse philosophical reflection with religious content was generally repudiated by his successors, both from the philosophical and from the religious side; attempts to restore his synthesis have not been impressive. A merely moral or literary interpretation of religious language and symbols strips them of their specifically religious content,[24] and the very methodology of a properly modern philosophical inquiry must be atheistic. In the minds of believers, it is true, liturgical practice acts to keep religious beliefs and assumptions from erosion, but it is difficult to see how they can be preserved in a milieu of absolutely open and unprejudiced inquiry, where the various forms of validity, the ontic, the normative, and the expressive, are clearly distinguished one from another.[25] Habermas suggests that we may hope, without great confidence, that his own ideals of human emancipation, unrestricted conversation, and untrammelled inquiry may supply what is needful for the bringing into being of a better future for humankind, without any appeal to religion. Our moral intuitions are fragile and fitful, but that does not imply that they either can be or need to be backed by something other than themselves, and they do make some difference to our actions, or at least leave us with a bad conscience so far as they do not.[26]

Our very brief discussion of matters relating to religion, at the end of chapter 4, provides grounds for strongly agreeing with Habermas on many of these issues. The desirability of religion as a spur to moral virtue, even if granted, does not of itself entail that any of the truth-claims of religion are to be believed. And I think that Habermas, in common with the broad and persistent tradition of natural theology exemplified by Thomas Aquinas, Christian Wolff, and Richard Swinburne, is correct in seeing metaphysics as the area of inquiry within which some crucial religious truth-claims have to be critically examined, and justified if they are to be justified at all. The claim that God speaks to humankind in a definitive manner through the Torah, through Jesus Christ, or through the Koran invites the prior questions of whether there is a God, and whether there are grounds for supposing that God might have communicated the divine nature and purposes to humankind in these kinds of ways. The first question seems clearly metaphysical on the usual understanding of the term; given that the world or reality as a whole is of such-and-such an overall nature and structure, is there any reason to suppose that it is due to an intelligent and benevolent will such as has traditionally been called 'God'? If reality is as metaphysical materialists conceive it to be, the answer is definitely no; but there is some question whether metaphysical materialism is true. As I have argued elsewhere, if God exists, the question whether any particular putative revelation, say the Christian one, is true is partly socio-psychological and party historical in nature. Would the revelation, supposing it had been given, fit the human plight; and if it would, is there in addition ground for thinking that it actually has been given?[27] I do not wish to embark here on a consideration of what the answers are to these questions, but simply to point out the nature and import of the questions themselves.

The most important difference between my own view on this matter and that of Habermas is that I do not think he has given good enough reasons for supposing that metaphysics has actually collapsed. And the fact, if it is a fact, that Hegel's particular attempt at vindicating religion by means of reason has failed does not immediately entail that no other such attempt can be successful. As I see it, the fact that rational inquiry has a certain overall nature and structure, exemplified by the methods of science, presupposes that reality, or what is to be inquired into, has a nature and structure which is such as to make this possible. And the outline of this nature and structure is the basic aim of metaphysics. Habermas hints that materialism in the sense in which he would subscribe to it has got to be tentative and hypothetical,[28] and hence that the solid grounds for atheism imagined by some old-fashioned atheists are no more solid than the alleged grounds for theism. But what he apparently fails to see is that the usefulness of the methods of science for discovering what is true about the world presupposes some very general facts about the nature and structure of the world which are not held tentatively.[29] Any particular scientific conclusion must be less than absolutely certain, so far as it is possible that more evidence will have to be attended to, more possibilities envisaged, on the matter in question. But that intelligent and reasonable inquiry into the evidence of experience is in general the right way of finding out about the universe is not something which can be held tentatively. It has to be believed or assumed with certainty, if it is to be believed or assumed at all. For what evidence in experience could possibly turn up to corroborate or falsify the view that we tend to get at the truth about the world so far as we are as attentive as possible to experience, and as intelligent and reasonable as possible in questioning it? I have already argued at length that the position in question can be established with a kind of certainty, on the grounds that its contradictory is self-destructive.

It should be noted that the fact that metaphysics is a possible enterprise does not of itself imply conclusions which are favourable to any religion. As Habermas points out, in effect it was metaphysics which led some to confidence in their atheism, just as it led others to confidence in their theistic beliefs.[30] His remark about the role of liturgy in defending religious belief from fundamental questioning on the part of its adherents is of some interest. Certainly, from the point of view of this book, any sort of self-hypnosis which tends to confine or control human rationality is thorougly to be deplored. On the other hand, it will not do to beg the question of whether a comprehensive rationality might not tend to vindicate rather than impugn at least some sorts of religious belief. The fact that the term 'rationalism' is often used as it is, to imply a *parti pris* against religion as well as a reliance on reason, should not deceive any judicious or unprejudiced person. It may indeed be the case that reason tends to lead people away from religion, once its full implications are realized, but it will not do to use language in such a way as to conceal the unconscious assumption that it does.

It was the role of 'natural theology,' as conceived by traditional Catholics, as well as by many Protestants, Jews, and Muslims, to justify the assent to religious beliefs on the basis of reason alone and outside the liturgical or devotional context. C.S. Lewis took it as a main task of his life to weave an imaginative spell in favour of theism and Christianity, but he was neither so immoral nor so confused as to think that this was or ought to be a substitute for rigorous argument. He believed that reason, when honestly and rigorously followed for its own sake, actually led to theism and indeed to Christianity, and it appeared to him that much of contemporary life had the effect of casting a spell that was woven in such a way as to discourage people from following their reason to this conclusion.[31] And it is surely true that atheism and irreligion have their own hypnotic devices as well, arguably more insidious than those of religion beause they tend to be less obvious – the slant of the eyes, the shrug of the shoulders, the use of formulae like 'Well, you won't be believing *that* stuff for long.'[32]

Liturgy is one means by which believers preserve and enjoy the life that they suppose themselves to have with God. If it inhibits some people from using their powers of reasoning to the full, then it ought not to do so. But while there are occasions when it is proper for believers to express their love of, and submission to, God in the liturgy, there are other occasions when they may remind themselves of why this is not thorougly irrational; and these occasions should probably not be mixed up with one another.[33] A wife and a husband, when they express their love for one another, are not constantly having to justify to themselves the trust which that love implies, but it is good that they should sometimes remind themselves of the reasons that they have to believe that this trust is not misplaced, though probably not on the same occasions.

I conclude by putting a dilemma to Habermas. Either his critical theory can show how we have cognitive access to a world which exists largely prior to and independently of ourselves or it cannot. If it cannot, it collapses into the postmodernist scepticism and relativism which Habermas is rightly concerned to contest.[34] If it can, it must inevitably issue in that kind of 'totalizing' view of reality which Habermas insists that modernism has outgrown, and indeed one that yields a 'metaphysics' or 'first philosophy' of a very traditional cast.

PART IV: RECOVERING THE TRADITION

12

How Right Plato Was

It is characteristic of the 'forms' of Plato (1) that they correspond to universal terms; (2) that they are realities as opposed to appearances; (3) that they are intelligible as opposed to sensible; (4) that they make knowledge possible; (5) that they are permanent as opposed to changeable, 'being' rather than 'becoming'; (6) that mathematics as well as ethics and aesthetics have a great deal to do with their apprehension.

I think the 'forms' constitute just about the most important discovery ever made in philosophy.[1] I shall try, in what follows, to show why.

Aristotle says that the identification of forms with that to which universal terms refer is due to Socrates; he also maintains that the Pythagoreans and Plato were inferior to Socrates in that, unlike him, they divided (echōrisan) forms from things.[2] The latter charge will have to be touched on later. Certainly, the notion that there is a form corresponding to each universal term is characteristic of many of Plato's earlier dialogues, which have the best claim to be historical reminiscences of Socrates' conversations. In discussing the nature of 'virtue' in the *Meno*, Meno insists, in a manner we have come to associate with the later Wittgenstein, that there are a variety of virtues, related to one another in a number of ways perhaps, but with nothing common to all. Thus the virtue of a man is to be capable of public affairs, to be a valuable ally and a dangerous enemy, and to know how to defend his own. The virtue of a woman is quite different from this; it is to look after the home and to obey her husband. There are yet other kinds of virtue appropriate to a child, an old man, a slave, and so on. It would seem that every age and every station in life has a kind of virtue peculiar to itself.[3]

But Socrates insists that we still want to know what the essence (*ousia*) of virtue is; there must be just one pattern (*hen eidos*) due to which the term 'virtue' (*aretē*) is appropriately bestowed in particular cases. This 'objective reality indicated by the employment of a common predicate of many subjects' is denoted by various terms: *ousia*, or what the thing is, *eidos*, or pattern, that which is through all the instances (*dia pantōn estin*), and that which is the same over them all (*epi pasi tauton*). (In the *Euthyphro*, the common character of everything 'holy' or religiously right is spoken of as a single *idea*, and later as an *eidos* and an *ousia*.) Meno's objection is countered by Socrates with the argument that what he considers man's and woman's different work are alike done well only if done with temperance (*sōphrosunē*) and justice, and that wilfulness and unfairness are faults in children and in elderly men. One may compare the case of health: there isn't one kind of health for a man and another for a woman, but the same for both.[4]

The view that there is or must be any 'objective reality indicated by the employment of a common predicate of many subjects' is now pretty generally, and in my view with justice, regarded as wrong; Peter Geach has labelled it 'the Socratic fallacy.' The most famous argument against the view is that mounted by Ludwig Wittgenstein in *Philosophical Investigations*. Wittgenstein asks his readers to consider whether there is anything that all games – 'board-games, card-games, ball-games, Olympic games, and so on' – have in common. 'Don't say: "There *must* be something common, or they would not be called 'games'" – but *look and see* whether there is anything common to all. For if you look at them you will not see something that is common to *all*, but similarities, relationships, and a whole series of them at that.'[5] But I am inclined to say that, though Wittgenstein is right as far as he goes, a determined Platonist might have some kind of a comeback, even on the ground chosen by Wittgenstein. Paradigm cases of games, she might urge, have in common that they are activities carried on according to rules, engaged in for their own sake, rather than as a means to ends, unless 'pleasure' or 'satisfaction' is to count as such. Bridge 'played' for a living or tennis 'played' to reduce one's weight have precious little in common, for all that they are both, in a sense, games. But they are so, surely, only by virtue of the fact that bridge and tennis as usually played are paradigm cases of games in the sense just given; the aberrant cases are 'games' only by courtesy or in an extended sense. One could pointedly say of them, 'Well, I would hardly call *that* a proper game.'

It is important to note that terms in common use, like 'game,' 'love,' 'democracy,' and so on, are apt to have a kind of penumbra of meaning; there are cases where we want to say, 'Isabella is in love with Theobald in a way, but in a way not,' or, 'Whether Ruritania is a democracy or not depends on what one is going to count as a democracy.' In this, they differ rather sharply from terms current in the mature sciences. Of a pure sample of a gas, it would never be right to say, 'That's hydrogen in a way, but in a way not,' or, 'You *might* say this was oxygen.' Strictly speaking, sure enough, there is a 'Socratic fallacy' involved in the expectation that all universal terms in ordinary langauge are susceptible to exact definition. But the same does not apply to the terms of mathematics or of any mature science. And these are apt to have another feature characteristic of Platonic forms, that their meaning is grasped by means of an intellectual act which does not consist simply in the apprehension of sameness and difference in sensible properties.

Of course, even in everyday contexts, to grasp an individual as belonging to a type involves at least a rudimentary intellectual act. Each individual raven can be an object of sense-perception, but we do not strictly speaking see or otherwise sense the raven-hood which they have in common. However, the forms, at least as envisaged by Plato's more mature philosophy, are grasped by an intellectual act in a manner more radical than that. In the critique of the sciences attributed to Socrates in *The Republic*, 'the main thought,' as A.E. Taylor says, is that 'in all the sciences the objects we are studying are objects which we have to think but cannot perceive by any of our senses. Yet the sciences throughout direct attention to these objects, which are, in fact, forms, by appealing in the first instance to sense.'[6] The geometry teacher or pupil may draw a visible figure which she calls a square and a straight line across it from corner to corner which she calls its diagonal. However, what she proceeds to demonstrate concerns *the* square and *the* diagonal; and these are not to be seen except with 'the mind's eye'.[7]

How are the forms supposed to be related to sensible particulars – for instance, 'the square' or 'the diagonal' as such to any particular square or diagonal drawn in the sand or on a blackboard? This question seems to have caused a good deal of difficulty in the Academy, as it is canvassed in several of the dialogues. In the *Phaedo* the relation is asserted, but not explained; and Socrates' hesitation about the proper name for the relation[8] has been noted as suggesting that there was felt to be a problem about its nature.[9] In the *Parmenides*, it is not so much the theory of forms as such that is subjected to criticism as the assumption that the objects of sense have any degree of reality at all; the *Phaedo* and *The Republic* assume that sensible things have a kind of secondary reality, 'partaking' in the forms as they do.[10] Pressed by Parmenides on the question of whether there are forms corresponding to every universal term, Socrates replies that he is sure that there are forms corresponding to the fundamental notions of ethics, such as right and good, but doubtful whether there are forms equivalent to species of organisms and physical substances such as fire and water. Where such things as mud and dirt are concerned, he tentatively suggests that there are no forms, and that what we see is all that there is. However, he has a feeling that consistency might demand of him forms for these things too, though he fears that such a step might lead to the most abysmal nonsense. Parmenides ironically suggests that he will get over this prejudice against forms of mud and dirt once he gets older and becomes more of a philosopher.[11]

One might perhaps hope to shed some light on 'participation,' on the relation of sensible things to the forms, by considering how it is that, as a matter of historical fact, human beings have progressed from description of things in terms derived from ordinary experience to explanation of them in terms of exact science – the conceptions of which we have already noted as having rather a striking analogy with Plato's forms. The details of this process are hotly disputed by historians and philosophers of science, yet surely one can sketch the wood with sufficient accuracy for our purposes here without getting inextricably entangled in controversies as to the shape of individual trees. Confronted by a puzzling world of experience, human beings wonder of what nature things are and why they come to pass as they do. In doing this, they get hunches, and try whether or how far they work out – if x were so, you would be liable to get experimental result y, and make set of observations z. Many of the hunches turn out, immediately or after a period of trial, to be mistaken (the phlogiston theory of combustion, the Lamarckian theory of evolution), while others emerge as satisfactory enough (the oxygen theory of combustion, the theory of evolution by mutation and natural selection) to be worth retaining only with minor modifications (oxygen as conceived by Lavoisier is somewhat different from the element as conceived by a contemporary theoretical chemist, but the two conceptions are sufficiently alike for one to say appropriately that it is one and the same element which is differently conceived by various authorities over the course of time). Idealists, rationalists, and empiricists might squabble over subsequent details, but I do not think that the rightness of this sketch as far as it goes would be at issue between them.

How does this bear on the theory of forms? As I maintained in Part I, by asking questions about things and events as experienced, by excogitating theories, and by subjecting these theories to testing at the bar of experience, the scientific community has arrived at a peculiar conception of things in various fields. What is characteristic of this conception? (1) It is in terms of entities and properties which, while they are (at least provisionally) verified[12] in experience, are not themselves direct objects of experience. Newtonian mass is not exactly the weight you feel when you lift an object, but it is logically related to a 'force' and an 'acceleration' which similarly are not directly perceptible; and no sensation, or imaginative picture based on sensation, could really be *of* a photon with its paradoxical part-wave part-particle nature. And even the child's conception of an elephant as a large animal with trunk and huge ears is hardly the same as the zoologist's conception of it, as member of a species related more or less closely with other mammalian species, and having evolved in morphology and habits to survive within a certain range of environments. The elephant of the zoologist, scarcely less than the photon of the physicist, is not so much a direct object of experience as an intellectual construction rather comprehensively verified in experience; one might in both cases, with only a little poetic licence, say that the entities and properties concerned can be grasped only 'with the eyes of the mind.' (2) It is plausible (here a subjective idealist would disagree) to say that the aspects of the world so envisaged constitute the real world, or at least tend to constitute it (since scientific theory is in a constant state of revision), in contrast to the merely sense-related world of ordinary experience. We may say that by means of scientific inquiry we come increasingly to know things as they really are, as really related to one another, 'in their causes' as Aristotle would say, as opposed to merely as related to ourselves. (3) It seems to follow from this last point that the existence of such things and properties makes knowledge properly speaking possible, if by 'knowledge' one means well-grounded apprehension of the truth about what really is so.[13] (4) Mathematics (at least in the case of physics, chemistry, or astronomy) is *par excellence* the discipline by way of which these entities and properties may be grasped. It is by now a cliché, of course, that 'mathematics is the language of science.' In each of these four respects, it seems evident that the whole development of science constitutes a massive vindication of Platonism.

It is certainly not surprising that the advances in physics made in the seventeenth century, which involved the stringent application of mathematics to the world, were associated with a revival of Platonism and a repudiation of Aristotelianism. In this context, Aristotle's criticism of Plato's doctrine of forms is of special interest. Aristotle commended the thesis, which he ascribed to Socrates, that forms are universals, but censured the tendency of Plato and the Pythagoreans to associate forms with numbers.[14] In the light of history, this criticism seems to have been curiously unfortunate, though it was perhaps natural to a biologist. As to universals, the suspicion ascribed by Plato to Socrates in the *Parmenides*, that not all universals have forms corresponding to them, seems in effect to have been proved correct by science. 'Silver' and 'elephant' survive within a scientific conception of reality, albeit in a form slightly different from the common-sense conceptions of them, in a way that 'mud' (to take one of the examples Plato attributes to Socrates) does not. From a scientific point of view, a sample of mud would presumably be a very amorphous and unstructured conglomeration of chemical elements and compounds; as Taylor suggests, the lack of a corresponding 'form' to a universal term has something to do with lack of structure in what is designated, at least at the level of our ordinary apprehension of it.[15]

What of Aristotle's charge that Plato and his followers inappropriately 'divided' the forms from sensible things? This could be taken as a salutary reminder that science, at least when mathematics is excepted, has an ineluctably empirical component. In other ways, too, scientific developments seem to bring out the mixture of justice and injustice in the charge. Sir Arthur Eddington made a famous distinction between two tables, one that of common experience, hard, coloured, and stable, the other that of the nuclear physicist, consisting largely of empty space interspersed with perpetually mobile particles. Aristotle is surely in the right so far as he is insisting that it is after all one and the same table which is to be described in one way in terms relevant to common sense and experience, to be explained in another in terms of the science of physics. Yet in another sense the 'division' between the two is palpable; what could be more different than a hard solid coloured object, on the one hand, and a largely empty space inhabited by the occasional wave particle, on the other? One can only conclude rather lamely that in a sense the 'division' between the forms and ordinary sensible things is right in the light of science and, in a sense, not. The same may be said of another error with which Plato has been charged, of assuming that where the manner of belief is different, the object of belief must also be so.[16] The table is after all the same object, but the two sets of properties in which it is described do diverge greatly from one another.

In *The Republic*, Socrates is made to point out that each science makes postulates which are taken for granted while one is pursuing that science itself. But he argues that these postulates themselves are in need of justification; this is the role of what he calls 'dialectic.' Until rather recently, among nearly all schools of philosophy, it has been taken for granted that something like Plato's 'dialectic' was an intellectual necessity, and that it was the role of philosophy to provide it. But it is quite usual among contemporary philosophers roundly to deny both propositions. Was it not the great advance of Wittgenstein over Russell, of Heidegger over Husserl, to declare once and for all that no 'foundations' of knowledge can or ought to be provided, and that in any case philosophy, so far as it has a right to survive at all, ought to content itself with less grandiose tasks?[17] I have already, in chapter 8, argued at length against this position. Short of subjective idealism, in accordance with which subjects simply mentally construct the world (including each other – I invent you; you, if indeed you exist, invent me), there is a real world, which exists prior to and independently of ourselves; and presumably some ways of applying our minds to experience are more liable to issue in the truth about it than others. The role of what Plato calls 'dialectic' would simply be to articulate these, to justify them, and to show how they tend to issue in some sets of propositions rather than others in each field of inquiry – so that history may be distinguished from legend, chemistry from alchemy, and the Einsteinian cosmology may be vindicated as against the Aristotelian. Dialectic would also aspire, if conceived in the manner of Plato, to present an overall view of the universe thus to be known, in such a way, for instance, as to determine what kind of answer ought to be given to the burning questions of religion and of human destiny.[18]

'Dialectic' is thus appropriately divided into epistemology (how one is to go about getting to know) and metaphysics (the general outline of what is thus to be known). The general answer constitutive of metaphysics is provided by the theory of forms; the real universe is a vast array of intelligibles, to be known by inquiry into the sensible. Sensible things do have a secondary reality, relative to ourselves, neither existing in themselves nor (in spite of Eleatic polemics) absolutely non-existent. The epistemological component of 'dialectic' is to be found by combining one suggestion (apparently rejected by Plato himself) in the *Theaetetus* with the practice implicit in all the earlier dialogues. Knowledge is true belief backed up by discourse;[19] one tends to come by it through a series of questions, attempted answers to the questions, and a critical testing of these answers – the kind of process which is exemplified by serious conversation.[20] The 'knowledge' thus arrived at is stable and reliable in a way that mere 'opinion' is not;[21] in a lawcourt, or in a historical inquiry, we are less apt to have to alter a belief which has already been subjected to such a process than we are one which has been adopted merely out of habit, caprice, or deference to authority.

What of the 'discourse' with which true belief is to be supported if it is to count as knowledge? In one passage in *The Republic*,[22] Socrates maintains that a complete account of things would dispense with appeal to sensation, and would advance 'from forms by means of forms to forms and terminate upon them.' It is as well to bear in mind that the only science which was at all well developed in Plato's time was that of mathematics. In the case of geometry or arithmetic, once it is grasped, say, that two times three is six, or that the square on the hypotenuse of a right-angled triangle is equal in area to the sum of the squares on the other two sides, appeal to the sensible diagram or collection of objects (one might have inferred the conclusion from counting twice three pebbles or cows or triremes), which was incidentally of assistance in arriving at the knowledge in question, is no longer of the essence of it. Whatever the world happens to be like, twice three is six, and Pythagoras' theorem is true. But this is just where mathematics differs from empirical science. In not merely asserting the law of free fall discovered by Galileo, but in justifying it as liable to be true in opposition to other possible laws, one has to appeal to sensible data, to the results of observations and perceived experiments – thus trespassing outside the realm of forms.

The role of the empirical in mathematics is merely to provide a springboard for knowledge which does not of itself depend on anything empirical; but physics, chemistry, biology, and so on ineluctably depend on an empirical component, as indicating that the facts to which their constitutive propositions refer are so and not otherwise, as they might have been for aught we can possibly know *a priori*. Plato seems right in his suggestion that a complete account of the world, which gave the *what* and the *why* of everything in fully explanatory terms, could dispense with reference to the merely sensible properties of things, which strictly speaking are a matter only of their relations with ourselves. But the fact remains that in justifying this account, in showing why it was more likely to be true than some alternative possibility, reference would have to be made to sensation. It is worth noting that Plato stressed the merely provisional nature of all accounts of the world that human beings were likely to obtain – as is evident from many passages in the *Timaeus*.[23] Here is another respect in which his influence on empirical science is healthier than that of Aristotle, who is rather inclined to write as though one could reach a definitively correct account of the world at short notice.[24]

In the *Phaedo*, the forms appear to be a vast multitude, but no hint is given as to their arrangement among themselves. In the *Symposium* and *The Republic*, on the other hand, they are set within a hierarchy, culminating in the one case in the form of the Beautiful, in the other in that of the Good.[25] According to *The Republic*, the form of the Good is the source at once of the being of the rest of the forms and of their capacity to be known, enabling them to be known just as the sun enables them to be seen.[26]

Assuming, as I think it is reasonable to do, that the forms of the Good and of the Beautiful are to be identified with one another as far as Plato is concerned,[27] one may ask what, if anything, is of permanent value in these conceptions? Also, what relation do they have to the Jewish, Christian, and Islamic conception of God, with which they are evidently allied? From the discussion of God in the *Timaeus* and the *Laws*,[28] it is clear that God is a soul and not a form. Indeed, God could not possibly be a form, since God's agency is needed to explain how our changeable and becoming universe could exist at all, over against the eternal and changeless universe of the forms.[29]

Thus for Plato, so far as one can recover his actual views from the dialogues, God as creator and the form of the Good are distinct beings, and the universe is dependent on both. Yet Christians and other theists have tended in a manner to identify the two, with God as somehow both an active soul and having properties which Plato attributes to the form of the Good.[30] I think it is easy to understand how this could have come about. Roughly, the God of theism is the intelligent will on which the nature and existence of all else, both *how* it is and *that* it is, are supposed to depend. The realm of 'forms' reduces to possibilities within the divine mind, some of which are actualized by the divine will in the real universe; science is a matter of finite minds approaching, by means of inquiry into empirical phenomena, towards the actual intelligibility that God has willed for the universe. God, as the source of the harmony which constitutes the universe, and as the giver of every gift, is indeed the supreme beauty and goodness of which earthly beauty and goodness are only a reflection.

I have remarked that it is in the matter of ethics and aesthetics, as well as that of mathematics, that Plato regards us as most directly approaching the forms. It is easy to see why this is so. Just as the perfect circle or straight line is never the direct object of our senses, so we never perceive any thing or person which is perfectly good or wholly beautiful. Yet somehow, from examples presented to our senses of the imperfectly straight and circular and good and beautiful, we acquire conceptions of these qualities which can be used to assess as imperfect in those respects the things and persons which come within the range of our experience. In the case of values as well as of mathematics, we are consciously or unconsciously using 'the eyes of the mind' to discern qualities apparently belonging to real things which are not given to our senses. But it might well be protested that, in the very measure that science has corroborated Plato's conception of the forms as associated with mathematics, it has tended to impugn his postulation of objective norms of goodness and beauty. Is it not an inescapable, if unpalatable, consequence of the scientific world-view that goodness is simply a matter of favourable subjective assessment, and beauty in the eye of the beholder?

However, it must be insisted that the doctrine that science is the only measure or criterion of 'objective' reality, of what exists independently of the opinions or feelings of subjects, is itself a doctrine not of science, but of philosophy, and of highly questionable philosophy at that. It is a corollary, sure enough, of empiricism and materialism. But both of these philosophies may be objected to as making nonsense of that very relation of the human mind, on the one hand, to what exists prior to and independently of that mind, on the other, on which Plato laid so much stress. The empiricist, so far as she is consistent in her reduction of reality to the data of the senses, ends up by reducing what usually passes as knowledge of the world, including most of science, to a subjective construction. The materialist fails to advert to the fact that the whole of 'material' reality is nothing but what is potentially to be conceived and affirmed by mind, and that all attempts to define mind and the mental in terms of matter have failed and must necessarily fail. Thus both the usual metaphysical bases – and they are metaphysical, for all their usual pose of being anti-metaphysical[31] – for asserting the mere subjectivity or relativity of goodness and beauty can be shown to be mistaken. There is a real goodness and beauty to be apprehended in the intelligible harmony which is the universe, and this leads us on to look for the transcendent goodness and beauty of the intelligent will which is its source. The good of our own actions, as individual and social beings, confirms, fosters and enhances this harmony; it is thus no wonder that political leaders in *The Republic* are supposed to spend so much time contemplating it, in order that they may the more effectively fulfil their charge. Short of some conception of an objective good to be realized for society, after all, what can an effective politician be but an adroit and cynical manipulator of popular sentiments and opinions?

Are the 'forms' eternal, as distinct from the transitory nature of the objects of our senses, as Plato supposed? One is inclined to say that in a sense they are and, in a sense, not. It is true, but to a large extent trivial, to say that oxygen-ness and elephant-hood are for ever what they are; it is not so much, though, that oxygen-ness and elephant-hood have the remarkable property of existing from eternity to eternity, as that it makes no sense to say that such abstractions come into being and pass away. But oxygen as defined by present-day physicists and chemists and the elephant as conceived in terms of modern evolutionary theory certainly exist within certain limits in space and time. Contemporary cosmologists speculate that, for the first period of the existence of our universe, none of the chemical elements as we know them existed, but only fundamental particles, and elephants have existed only on the surface of the earth in recent geological epochs. As to our knowledge of 'forms,' it has often been pointed out, and I think rightly, that the knowledge that the scientist aspires to of reality is in a sense timeless, in opposition to the merely temporary conception of things afforded by the senses – what Plato would call mere 'opinion.' But if it is true at all, it is true for ever, that oxygen and elephants have the nature they have, and exist in the universe within certain bounds of time and space.[32]

13

On Being an Aristotelian

Plato may be regarded as having made the great discovery, of which modern science is a colossal vindication, that the real is intelligible. But as a result of this he made what is on the whole too radical a dichotomy between the true and unchanging world of intelligible 'forms,' on the one hand, and the fleeting and merely apparent world of our ordinary experience, on the other. Aristotle pulled the two worlds firmly together again, and stressed the role of experience in knowing, while by no means neglecting the role of intelligence and reason (to use the terminology we introduced in the first chapter). For him, it was after all the same world which is known in an elementary way by the ordinary human being, and understood[1] by the scientist and the philosopher. What linked the two worlds was our subjective capacity for asking what and why and the objective causal nexus in things which corresponded to it. An Aristotelian, in the most fundamental terms, is one who attends to this link and takes it into account in all her thought about the ultimate nature and structure of things.[2]

How right was Aristotle in the overall principles of his thought, and what, if anything, does the modern world stand to learn from him? His reputation has been greatly tarnished by incidental defects in his thinking which proved to be obstructions to the advancement of science in the seventeenth century, but probably rather more by the antics of his self-styled followers at that time.

I shall begin by making a list (A) of Aristotle's main errors; this is followed by another list (B) of what I take to be his enduring virtues, and of matters about which I think he was largely or wholly right.

(A) 1. His laws of motion.

2. His dichotomy between 'superlunary' and 'sublunary' science.
3. His assumption that final causes operated in nature more generally than has turned out to be the case.
4. His reaction against the Platonic stress on mathematics as key *par excellence* to the understanding of the world.
5. His assumption that reality could be known immediately as a result of inquiry into experience, rather than only at the end of an indefinitely reiterated process.[3]
6. His notion that science in a strict sense is a matter of deduction from self-evident axioms, rather than from theories invented, corrected, and corroborated over an indefinite period through appeal to experience.
7. His belief that science in a strict sense is deterministic. (With respect to these last two points, Aristotle's practice is an improvement upon his precept.)
8. His views on slavery and the natural inferiority of women to men.

(B) 1. His blend of 'rationalism' and 'empiricism.'
2. His conception of reality as what we get to know by asking what and why, and the account of causality deriving from this.
3. His account of the relation of knowledge of 'things in their causes' to ordinary common-sense knowledge.
4. His view of reality as characterized by a hierarchy of 'forms,' with the 'forms' restored to the world in which we live.
5. His (very fleeting) distinction of two fundamental types of questions to be asked in the course of acquiring knowledge.
6. His conviction that the universe is intelligible, and of the need for a transcendent intelligence to account for this.
7. His distinction in psychology between a passive and an active component of the mind.
8. The snug mesh of his theory of reality (science and 'metaphysics' – what Aristotle calls 'first philosophy') with his theory of value (ethics, aesthetics, politics.)[4]

I shall in the course of this chapter devote a brief discussion to each point.

Aristotle's underplaying of the role of mathematics in the investigation of real things is, as has often been remarked, what one would expect of a biologist; the behaviour of the great crested grebe is at best less obviously subject to mathematical analysis than the observable motions of the planets (A4). It is worth pointing out that it was his very respect for observation which was largely responsible for this and those other mistakes of his which precipitated the reaction against Aristotelianism at the time of the Renaissance. At least so far as our immediate observation of our surroundings goes, things tend to stop when you do not go on pushing them, as Aristotle said they should; they do not go on for ever unless prevented from doing so as on the account which has superseded Aristotle's (A1). Again, while plants, animals, human persons, societies, and even rocks may be observed to come into existence, to go through a series of changes, and at last to perish and disintegrate, the sun, moon, and stars appear changeless and incorruptible, and subject only to local motion (A2). Yet again, function and purpose are obviously characteristic of life, both human and non-human; it is not at all evident on the face of it that explanation in such terms should not be extended to the cosmos as a whole (A3).

One Aristotelian mistake might be picked out as especially absurd and arbitrary: that the stars are embedded in a solid crystal sphere. But this again makes clear observational sense. The stars seem to retain their positions in relation to one another as they move in relation to us. It seems to follow directly from this either that the earth itself is spinning round or that the stars collectively are moving round the earth while rigidly fixed in their relations one to another. The first possibility seems at first sight to be eliminated by many observed facts, for example, that the surface of the earth is not subject to a constant hurricane blowing in one direction, and the oceans are not incontinently pouring over the continents. We are thus left with the second possibility, which is obviously best explained by the notorious crystal sphere. It is largely an empiricist myth, fostered by Baconian polemics, that Aristotle's system relies too much on the 'agitation of wit,' and not enough on observation;[5] Galileo was surely nearer the mark when he insisted that, to get beyond Aristotle, one had to defy the evidence of one's senses.

To get the best out of Aristotle, it is better to attend to his methods than to his scientific conclusions (his 'metaphysical' conclusions may be a different matter, as I shall hope to show). Of the three kinds of reasoning distinguished by Aristotle in the *Organon*, two are of special significance in shedding light on the methods of science: the dialectical and the demonstrative. He conceives dialectic as applicable not so much to thinking by ourselves as to talking with others and trying to convince them; one works out the consequences of 'opinions that are generally accepted, accepted by all, or the majority, or by the most notable and illustrious of them.'[6] (What the third or 'eristic' kind of reasoning does is simply to clear away preliminary confusions or sophistries, where one only seems to reason from generally accepted opinions, or where the opinions only appear to be generally accepted, but in fact are not so.)[7] It is the demonstrative kind of reasoning which produces genuine knowledge or *epistēmē*. Here, according to Aristotle, the *archai* or premises of one's demonstration, as well as the particular facts which are demonstrated, have to be true; that they have to be true rather than merely probably or widely accepted is what for him distinguishes science and demonstration from mere dialectic. Furthermore, as Aristotle will have it, the principles must themselves be 'better known' and 'more certain' than the facts to be demonstrated, and thus must themselves be 'undemonstrated' and 'immediate.' However, in our actual inquiries, Aristotle admits that the principles or *archai* are not the starting point; in fact, establishing what the real principles of demonstration are is apt to be the very last step in our investigations.[8]

That the ultimate principles from which the explanations in any science derive have to be 'better known' than the observed facts to be explained by them is, at least taken in the sense in which it is most natural to interpret it, a mere error. It seems furthermore correct to allege, as is often done, that Aristotle was persuaded into this error by taking as his model geometry, the science which was most fully developed in his own time and, in addition, by taking geometry in the way in which it was understood at that time, with its 'axioms' as certain truths rather than mere postulates. In other respects his methodological proposals are largely right, particularly if one does not confine 'dialectic' to argument with others, but allows it a role in one's own investigations. At this rate 'dialectic' would provide the investigator with a range of hypotheses, whether thought up by herself or by others, from which she can work out the consequences for the observed facts, for 'what we see' as Aristotle puts it,[9] thus reaching a position from which she can reject those hypotheses that are inconsistent with observation. What Aristotle does not seem quite to have grasped is that the *archē* from which demonstration proceeds in any particular case is a mere survivor of the dialectical process, to be rejected or revised in its turn when we have adduced more observed facts against which to test deductions from it. But it is remarkable and very important that his ideal of science remains in most of its essentials perfectly right; what we are after in the case of each science is a set of principles which will explain 'what we see.' The arcana of quantum theory, the periodic table of the elements, and the evolutionary scheme for the ordering of living beings are so many *archai* by means of which the particular collocations of observable facts which are the concern respectively of physics (in the modern sense), chemistry, and biology can be reduced to true science or *epistēmē*. The conception of a hierarchy of different sciences, all characterized by certain basic methods and assumptions, but each having *archai* peculiar to itself, was an advance made by Aristotle from Platonism, and is set out by him in the *Posterior Analytics.*[10]

That science involves explanation from principles as well as mere description, as Aristotle rightly saw, does not directly entail his view that science strictly speaking must be deterministic in its assumptions and aims (A7). Against the background of science in our own time, we can see how a theory, while it explains in a sense why events of a certain kind occur, need not by virtue of that very fact explain why they cannot but occur. For example, in the case of any sample of radon of more than a very small size, it is known that in 3.7 days half of its atoms will have changed into atoms of polonium by emission of an alpha particle, but it is not known of any one atom whether it will undergo this change in the next millionth of a second or after a million years. And in the case of the evolution of the giraffe, no sane biologist would hope to explain why such a species of animal was bound to come into existence exactly when and how it did, but only why it was liable to do so given the environment and the nature of the species which was its immediate ancestor. This is not to prejudge the issue of whether nature will ultimately turn out to be deterministic (though to my mind we have more or less decisive evidence that it will not), but only to make the point that, in spite of Aristotle's authority and its deterministic legacy to classical physics and to Kant, it is not a consequence of the very applicability of scientific method to nature that determinism must be true.[11]

But, it may be urged, even if the real laws of nature and the initial conditions on which they operate are only to be known at the end of an indefinite process, what of the process itself? From what self-evident axioms is it to be deduced? And if it is not to be deduced from such axioms, is it not arbitrary? It is the elusiveness of such axioms, and the apparent non-viability of any alternative to them in the justification of scientific knowledge, which have largely brought about the scepticism, relativism, and sociologism which are so conspicuous a feature of contemporary thought. Does Aristotle provide any solution to this problem? It seems to me that he gives at least a number of vital hints as to its solution, which I believe is to be found by attention to those basic mental operations of the conscious subject by means of which he or she progressively discovers nature and its laws. As Aristotle rather fleetingly notes,[12] and has been strongly emphasized in their different ways by Thomistic philosophers and by natural scientists,[13] the truth about things in themselves, things as they are in real relation to one another rather than merely to our human senses and interests, is to be known as the result of two sorts of questions put to experience. The first asks what or why of an observed phenomenon or sequence of phenomena; the second asks 'Is that so?' of each of the possibilities yielded by the first sort of question.[14] (It is one thing to provide a hypothesis or a range of hypotheses to explain some puzzling phenomenon; it is another to have adequate grounds for supposing that a hypothesis is true.)

But, it may be asked, is this not just another opinion that some societies may sanction, others not? Why should what is suggested be more adequate as foundation than anything else which might be proposed? As I have argued at length in this book, the adequacy of this foundation is due simply to the fact that its removal removes the foundation of any opinion whatever, even of the opinion that no opinion has foundations. The point was grasped at least implicitly by Aristotle himself, as well as by Thomas Aquinas, that most perceptive of Aristotelians.[15] In the *Metaphysics*,[16] Aristotle remarks that one who denies the principle of contradiction is no better than a vegetable, and is not worth arguing with; if he says anything at all, and agrees at the same time to the truth of its contradictory, he is refuted out of his own mouth. In his commentary on Aristotle's *De Anima*,[17] Aquinas points out that it is a consequence of the Averroist position that no particular man thinks, and that this applies to the Averroist himself. But if the Averroist on his own admission does not think, it follows that he is not to be listened to. This point is, of course, the same as the one that I argued at length in the first chapter; it is self-defeating to deny that one tends to get at the truth by attending to phenomena, producing hypotheses which may account for them, and judging to be so that hypothesis which does best account for them.

Thus, by application of principles at least adumbrated by Aristotle himself, we can articulate the principles of scientific method, and justify them, without resort to the view that science as such must involve deduction from self-evident axioms. One might, I suppose, regard the transcendental argument just sketched as a matter of 'deduction' from 'axioms' which are 'self-evident.' But the 'self-evidence' is a matter not of what plainly lies open to view; but rather of what appears inevitable once one has thought clearly about what is essentially involved in human thinking about anything real. (Aristotle calls his mode of argument on this matter 'negative proof,' and clearly distinguishes it from 'demonstration.')[18]

That Aristotle, for all his greatness as a scientist (particularly in the field of biology), is so flagrantly out of date as such ought surely, it may be said, to have repercussions on one's estimate of him as a metaphysician, a moralist, and a political philosopher. The point has additional force if we admit, as I think we must, that science has a vitally important bearing on metaphysics.[19] But it is important to attend to the nature of this bearing. What is really at issue, I believe, is the method of science rather than the results of the application of this method at any one time. Given that knowledge is to be had, as Aristotle was at least intermittently aware, by the putting of two kinds of question to the world given in experience, we can distinguish between the details of this knowledge, on the one hand, and the overall nature of the world which follows from the fact that we can get to know it in this way, on the other. That Aristotle is superseded with respect to the former matter does not in the least imply that he must be so with respect to the latter. Plato had made the great discovery that reality was characterized by 'forms,' intelligible entities, types, and structures which somehow transcend the realm of the merely sensible. Aristotle added to this that these 'forms' were to be discovered by inquiry into our experience, and by verification of the putative results of our inquiry through appeal to experience. It is as well founded and timely a contention now as it was when Aristotle taught that we do live in such an intelligible world; and it is important now as it was then to work out and live by the ethical, political, and (if any) theological consequences of the fact that we do so.

As J.H. Randall rightly remarks, 'The real question' for Aristotle 'is: In what kind of a world is knowing possible?' What does the fact of knowing imply about our world?' And he adds, very justly, 'Modern philosophy, since the coming of the science of mechanics in the seventeenth century, has not been able to find any intelligible place for mind, for science itself, in the world that science describes.'[20] Nor, it may be added – and this is if possible a still more serious defect – does it leave any place for objective value, one collocation of mechanically acting particles being no better or worse as such than any other. So morality is driven into being a matter of merely arbitrary decision, politics into a more or less consciously cynical manipulation of people.

It is largely the work of Kant that has given rise to the nightmarish and typically modern suspicion that the world which we progressively get to know by the use of our minds might somehow be quite different from the real world of 'things in themselves,' as it exists and has existed prior to, and independently of, the use of our minds upon it. If Aristotle ever entertained this suspicion, he suppressed it; and careful reflection on the nature of our knowledge, and of the implications of this for the nature of the real world which can be nothing other than what there is to be known, shows that he was right to do so.[21] In the long run, it may be seen that it makes nonsense of any effective distinction between reality and appearance to suppose that the real might somehow lie beyond not only what we actually know, but anything that could conceivably be known. It is of course to be emphasized that the real 'forms' constitutive of the world are only to be known at the end of an indefinite period of inquiry, through reiteration of the process of attending to experience, formulating possibilities, testing these possibilities, accepting provisionally the possibilities which seem to fit the experience, attending to a wider range of experience which falsifies these possibilities, and so on. Aristotle certainly underestimated both the arduousness of this task and the length of time and amount of collaboration that would be needed to achieve it.

Aristotle's psychology is by no means the least controversial aspect of his writings; here as much as anywhere commentators have seen an unsuccessful attempt by Aristotle's editors to blend his allegedly thoroughgoing late functionalism and behaviourism with his earlier Platonism. This applies especially, perhaps, to his notion of the 'active intellect.'[22] In Randall's view, the mature Aristotle saw *nous* or mind as being receptive to the intelligible aspect of things, just as our senses are to the sensible.[23] This I believe to be a true account, not only of Aristotle's opinion, but of how things really are; but it is not the whole truth, and both common experience and the text of Aristotle clearly show that it is not. It is quite usual for commentators to dispose of this fact, as of others which go against preconceived ideas of the viewpoint of the mature Aristotle, by claiming that the relevant section of Aristotle's text is early, and so redolent of the Platonism which he outgrew.[24] But even if Aristotle did reject the view there expressed, and there is no evidence that he did, it remains that it is at once correct and profound. That there is an 'active' as well as a 'passive' part or aspect of the human intellect may be known by the practice of a little introspective psychology, as well as by attention to the nature of scientific method. The fact is that for the passive aspect of one's mind to be receptive of knowledge of real things another aspect of it has to be active first. We have not got to know about argon and xenon, or the relationships between the orders of mammals as they have evolved, just by letting things soak into our senses and minds. We have actively hypothesized and actively tested our hypotheses. This kind of activity is a fact of our mental life, and, on the evidence of a short and notoriously fragmentary and obscure paragraph in the *De Anima*, Aristotle knew that it was. What is more, the expression of this view is by no means a sort of erratic block in Aristotle's scheme; it fits in very well with the emphasis on the role of questioning in the acquisition of knowledge which we find in both the *Posterior Analytics* and the *Metaphysics*.[25]

The 'form' of things is their intelligible essence and structure which we may grasp (as we know by experience in modern times, only cumulatively and progressively) with our 'active' intellects and retain in our 'passive.' Exactly what Aristotle meant by relating soul to body as form to matter[26] is a well-known puzzle. But approached on the basis just outlined, it seems clear enough. If we want to understand specifically human behaviour, as opposed to that of animals or merely physical events and processes, we have to assume that here is an intelligent and reasonable agent, as well as something that feels, grows, and has the properties of any physical object. The intelligibility of minerals or of plants and animals does not at all consist in intelligence; the intelligibility (or 'form') of human beings, who are not in this sense merely material, does consist (partly) in it. To understand human beings, that is to say, we have to take their intelligence into account, and this cannot be reduced, in empiricist or Democritean atomist fashion, to anything else. Any attempt thus to reduce intelligence, for Aristotle, would be destructive of the very basis of science. And to my mind it is quite clear that Aristotle was right about this, whatever the reductionist ambitions of some modern psychologists. If there is in the last analysis no such thing as human understanding, what becomes of science, which is nothing but an effort by human beings to understand the world?[27]

So much, very briefly, for Aristotle's psychology. What of his theology? Following Werner Jaeger, the view has become quite widely current that Aristotle's thinking developed from a religiously inspired Platonic theism to a naturalism of which the logical issue would have been atheism and repudiation of religion. (This was 'the secret of Aristotle' as Santayana saw it.)[28] Let us grant Jaeger the truth of the hypothesis, for which there is no historical evidence whatever, that Aristotle not only entirely gave up his earlier religious interests, but privately believed in his maturity that the principles of his thought were incompatible with belief in a God. A traditional Aristotelian of the Thomist type could still protest that he was wrong to do so, and might add that the dogma that there is a necessary conflict between the urge to religious contemplation and a strong interest in scientific research is a typically modern error which goes against the whole tenor of Aristotle's thought. The corpus of his writings as we have it is on the whole intellectually coherent, as the Arabic, Jewish, and Christian commentators of the Middle Ages saw, with the scientific and religious aspects arising from, and giving support to, one another. The intelligibility of the universe, which science at once presupposes and confirms, gives rise to the well-founded supposition that there is something of the nature of intelligence behind the universe, to gain some knowledge of which is the highest human vocation. One aspect of this vocation is the use of scientific method to get to know the world. Book XII (Lambda) of the *Metaphysics*, with its account of God, even if it is an early writing of Aristotle, is thus quite consistent with his later work.

It is frequently and rightly remarked that Aristotle's 'unmoving cause of motion, ... transcendent and without knowledge of the world he moves'[29] is hardly to be identified with the Creator God of Judaism and Christianity. As I mentioned earlier, the whole development of science tends to show that the ultimate *archai* – the basic laws and initial conditions – underlying the things of our world do not have to be as they are, but are to be progressively established by inquiry into experience. In other words, there is an ineradicable element of brute fact within the universe. This may be, in a sense, accounted for all the same, if Aristotle's transcendent *nous* or intelligence is also a will which determines that the basic laws and initial conditions of the universe shall be just as they are. In fact, the turning of Aristotle's God into a Creator, and the alteration of his method in accordance with the exigences of empirical science, dovetail very neatly together.[30]

Much has been made, and I believe rightly so, of the influence of biology on Aristotle's overall view of things.[31] Two effects of this may be noted. The Platonic doctrine, that true knowledge is knowledge of what is changeless, would seem especially paradoxical to a biologist. If there is one thing that is obvious about living organisms, it is that they come into being, perish, and undergo a great deal of change in between; so, unless all apparent knowledge of living things is to be discounted as such, knowledge of the changeable is possible. Another consequence is the importance for Aristotle of grasp of the end or function in understanding the nature of anything, and why it has the particular features that it has. However misleading application of this principle turned out to be for the understanding of non-living nature, it seems to be pretty well indispensable in the understanding of life, and is very helpful (as I shall briefly argue) in making sense of human beings and their communities, and in determining what is good or bad for them.[32]

Aristotle's technical distinction between 'potency' and 'act' has its most obvious applications in biology; to understand a chicken or sunflower seed is to understand it as a potential fowl or sunflower. Given the right conditions, then 'always or for the most part' (as Aristotle would say) the fowl will result from the chicken, the sunflower from the seed. When it does not do so, natural process has been interfered with by violence (*bia*); there is deprivation (*sterēsis*) of what there might have been, of what there was a possibility of there being. The potency-act schema does seem applicable to the whole world-process, as we tend to regard it at present, in evolutionary terms; the coming into being of chemical elements actualizes potentialities in fundamental particles, the emergence of life actualizes potentialities in the chemical elements which constitute it, and so on.[33]

The human being, as Aristotle noted, has a 'form' which is rational as well as vegetative and sensitive; thus a fully realized human being will be one who lives in accord with her rational nature. But this by no means implies, as one might gather from some of Plato's writings, that the emotional and sensitive nature which we share with the other animals is to be suppressed; on the contrary, it is a main function of reason to direct emotion and sensation to their highest potential. It is from this viewpoint that Aristotle's conception of the moral virtues is to be understood. The intellectual virtue of prudence or practical wisdom[34] – it is 'intellectual' because it is a matter of knowledge, in this case of how to secure the ends of human life[35] – enables one to know what will contribute to long-term happiness or fulfilment.[36] But such knowledge will not be useful to a person who is apt to be deflected from long-term goals by short-term impulses of desire or fear; that is why we need the virtues of temperance and courage. One's individual needs and goals have to take into account those of others; this is the province of the virtue of justice.

It is easy to misunderstand Aristotle's account of virtue as a 'mean'[37] by taking him to be saying that to live virtuously is the opposite of living intensely and to the full. Thus, while the doctrine is rightly taken as a monument to the philosopher's sanity and good sense, it has given him a certain reputation for dreariness. (One has only to think of the modern connotations of the word 'prudence,' briskly summed up by William Blake: 'Prudence is a rich ugly old maid courted by incapacity.')[38] But the fact remains that, in the interest of her long-term happiness or the good of the community, it is important for the individual to avoid extremes of rashness and cowardice, of self-restraint and self-indulgence, of demanding less than her share and demanding more than her share, and so on. Aristotle remarks that the virtuous mean between the extremes of vice is not, as it were, geometrically exact; courage is, after all, closer to rashness than it is to cowardice. And the mean that is appropriate to one person in one situation will be very different from that which is appropriate to another.[39] Temperance for a young bride on her honeymoon will not be the same as for a Mother Superior of a convent, or courage for a policeman on his beat as for a hospital nurse or a mother of young children, and so on. The virtues are unequivocally desirable, but the details of their expression depend on immediate circumstances and on the particular manner in which the individual, due to innate temperament or background or whatever, is able to achieve happiness for herself and contribute to the general well-being. What is more, they seem to be relevant to all actual or conceivable human cultures; there are no circumstances in human life in which the restraint of immediate impulse for long-term advantage and the tempering of one's own interests by consideration of those of others are not worth while.

What applies to the human individual applies very largely, so far as Aristotle is concerned, to the human community as well. To need a community in which to flourish, according to him, is a part of being human; someone who can get on just as well without is either a beast or a god.[40] In making sense of Aristotle's conception of politics, the fact that his father was a doctor is worth bearing in mind; he is preoccupied with the question of how human communities may achieve and maintain health. A healthy community is at once stable, and such that its members are encouraged to lead a virtuous, fulfilling, and excellent life; indeed, to promote the one end is on the whole to promote the other. A fundamental cause of instability is gross inequality of wealth and power between citizens, since the wealthy will be inclined to abuse their power and the poor to be moved to resentment, resistance, and the undermining of the social fabric.[41] The ensuing conflict will soon lead to radical social upheaval (stasis), a state of affairs by no means compatible with the good life.[42]

Though he has an eye on the social ideal, like Plato in The Republic, Aristotle is more concerned than was his teacher with research into the working of actual societies.[43] Some modern scholars have seen a trend on Aristotle's part away from the Platonic political ideals of his youth to preoccupation with 'value-free' empirical studies, and have been able to use as a pretext for this view the undoubted dislocations in the text of the Politics as we have it.[44] However, this is an unnecessary hypothesis if ever there was one; Aristotle, sane man that he was, believed that one has to have an accurate conception of things as they are, and of the potentialities really latent in them, before one is able to make useful proposals for their maintenance, alteration, or improvement. The 'fact-value dichotomy' is not to be imposed on Aristotle; indeed, it is a main virtue of his philosophy that it shows that alleged 'dichotomy' up for the baseless and calamitous superstition that it is.[45]

One unfortunate result of Aristotle's disposition to attend to things as they were is a certain complacency. It is notorious that he did not question the institution of slavery, or (as Plato did) the classical Greek view of the inferior nature and status of women. But many still have to learn from him that proposals for the improvement of human society in general, or of any particular society, have to take into account the human material as it actually is both in general and in the particular instance. On this basis, indeed, we now have excellent reasons for believing that societies on the whole flourish better without slaves and with women on terms of equality with men. Other possible consequences of taking human nature into account are less convenient or fashionable. For example, Plato's *Republic*, in common with many other ambitious programs for the reform of society, proposes to break down the special relations between parents (or parent-substitutes) and children which are so striking and determining a feature of most human communities.[46] But this proposal overlooks what appears to be a universal need by the young human being for one or more adults with whom relations of love and trust can be built up and maintained over a considerable span of time.[47] To what extent this and other social needs of ours are 'natural,' and to what extent they are imposed by particular historical circumstances, is an urgent question; social arrangements which pre-empt the answer to it on ideological grounds could ruin the emotional lives of multitudes of human beings, and as a consequence wreck any capacity they may have to achieve happiness for themselves or to promote, or even to allow, happiness in others.

What is to be concluded from this discussion? A number of important mistakes in Aristotle's work had to be repudiated if modern science was to come into its own; yet I have been urging that science has remained after all a very Aristotelian business. And I believe that it would have been much better if this had been borne in mind more by those concerned with the metaphysical, theological, ethical, and political bearings of the scientific world-view. The mechanistic materialism which was the legacy of one side of Descartes's thought was very useful for the development of physics over the next few centuries; but its ubiquitous application has led to a divorce of the 'objective,' on the one side, from the 'subjective' and 'evaluative,' on the other, which would never have occurred if people had kept their minds on what was of permanent validity in the Aristotelian system. One collocation of mechanically interacting particles is of no more or less value than another; if reducibility to such interaction is in the last analysis the only criterion of the 'real' or 'objective,' then value inevitably becomes reduced to a matter of mere 'subjective' preference. At this rate morality becomes a basically arbitrary business, and politics is apt to be dominated by mere opportunism. But Aristotelianism is at bottom a systematic realization of the insight that 'genuine objectivity is the fruit of authentic subjectivity,' as a great modern Aristotelian has expressed it,[48] that good morality and good politics are a matter of intelligent and reasonable action in an environment to be intelligently and reasonably apprehended, and that there are objective norms to be articulated and followed which lead to fulfilment in the lives of human individuals and societies.

14

Two Methods: Descartes and Lonergan

In the last two chapters, I have argued that claims central to the philosophies of Plato and Aristotle are true and of permanent significance and relevance for a proper understanding of the world and of human life. What difference is made to them by that 'turn to the subject' which has been so striking a feature of philosophy since the seventeenth century? In this chapter, I shall compare two accounts of how 'subjects' may be so 'objective' as to come to know the real world, those of Descartes and Lonergan. I shall argue that Descartes was largely right in the respects in which his work anticipated that 'generalized empirical method' of Lonergan which I have been commending throughout this book; and that Descartes's notorious errors were mostly due to the ways in which his method differed from it.

About two decades ago, R.G.A. Dolby described Bernard Lonergan as a 'Cartesian.'[1] At the time, the epithet seemed to me to be absurd, but on maturer reflection I have concluded that, whatever the differences between them, there is a deep affinity between Descartes's method, together with the conclusions which he draws from it, and the practice and upshot of Lonergan's 'generalized empirical method.' I shall set out immediately in summary form what seem to me the similarities (A1, A2, etc.) and the differences (B1, B2, etc.; in the case of each difference I shall state Descartes's view first), and then discuss the similarities and differences at rather greater length.

A1 There is a general method of inquiry, which is applicable to all subjects within the scope of potential human knowledge.
A2 Things as they really are, as opposed to merely related to our senses, are to be known in terms of intelligible concepts (Descartes's 'clear

and distinct ideas') rather than concepts more immediately related to sensation.

A3 The ground of knowledge and the existence and nature of the self in its role as subject of knowledge are to be determined by a transcendental argument – to the effect that one cannot coherently doubt that one is a doubter.

A4 A kind of certainty is available on questions of epistemology; the availability in principle of such certainty is a necessary condition of ordinary empirical knowledge.

A5 Truth is apprehended in judgment, not in sensation.

A6 The nature of God accounts for the nature of the world as knowable to us *a priori* (in very general terms for Lonergan, in more particular terms for Descartes [cf. B3]).

A7 Being methodical in the gaining of knowledge is a special case of being morally virtuous; sincerely to seek the truth is an aspect of being good.

B1 That knowledge of any reality over and above that of the self is possible can only be established by way of demonstrating the existence and veracity of God; that knowledge of reality other than the self is possible may be established by an argument which makes no reference to God.

B2 Experience has only a marginal role in establishing which sets of and 'clear and distinct ideas' characterize the real world; experience has an essential role not only in determining which sets of 'clear and distinct ideas' characterize the real world, but in giving rise to the questions which are the source of 'clear and distinct ideas' in the first place.

B3 Mechanistic determinism is an essential postulate of scientific explanation, and intrinsic to the intelligibility of material objects in general; the intelligibility of things demanded *a priori* by science may in principle be satisfied by statistical as well as by deterministic laws, and in fact statistical laws appear to form an essential component of our universe.

B4 There is a radical dualism between mind and matter, such that any interaction between them, or knowledge of the latter by the former, must remain highly problematic without appeal to the special providence of God; there is certainly an essential difference between what is intelligible as intelligence and what is intelligible not as intelligence ('spirit,' 'matter'), but both are to be known by the same basic method of inquiry into experience, and 'spirit' acts on 'matter' by determining and systematizing what remains undetermined and unsystematic in suitable material processes.

The problem which Descartes confronts at the beginning of the *Meditations* is surely one which, in some form or other, must concern any thoughtful person at some stage in her education. How much of the supposed 'knowledge' which I have absorbed from my environment, whether automatically or through conscious learning, is well founded? How much of it really puts me in touch with things as they actually are, rather than with things as my society or my teachers suppose them to be, or perhaps merely would like me to suppose them to be? Some of it appears to me a good deal more well founded, and so deserving of my belief, than the rest; but how am I to be sure even about that?

The way in which Descartes goes about revising his opinions, and putting those which remain on what seems to him to be a sound basis, is too familiar for it to be worth giving anything but the briefest summary here. Descartes notes that he has been deceived in the past not only about abstruse matters, but about states of affairs which one would have thought were immediately evident to his senses – that he is at present sitting where he seems to himself to be, dressed in the manner that he seems to himself to be. Might he not feel just as assured of these supposed facts as he is now, if he were in fact lying in his bed and dreaming that they were the case? It thus makes perfectly good sense for him to doubt that he is now where he has experience of himself as being, dressed as he has experience of himself as being, and so on. Geometry seems uniquely impressive to him among the subjects that he has been taught, both in the clarity and self-evidence of its axioms, and in the rigour of the deductions derived from them. But how can he be quite sure of the truth or well-foundedness of his beliefs, even in geometry? If he is to reach the security in knowledge which he desires, he will have to doubt everything which can be doubted. To make sure that the conditions are as rigorous as possible, he will suppose the existence of an almighty and malevolent demon, exerting itself so far as possible to ensure that Descartes is deceived on every matter on which he can possibly be deceived. But even to be deceived, Descartes must exist and be the kind of being who is capable of being deceived, in other words, a thinking being. So Descartes has now found what he was looking for, an indubitable certainty, that of his own existence and his own existence as a thinking being.[2]

Descartes is now assured that he exists and is a thinking being, and also that he has various experiences, thoughts, and beliefs as a thinking being.

On what basis can he gain knowledge of the nature of anything else, or indeed even that there is anything else? Descartes finds that he has a number of conceptions in his mind, including those of ordinary material objects, those of spiritual and immaterial beings like angels, and those of beings both spiritual and material like he seems to himself to be. He also has the conception of a being, known as God, who is the sum of all perfections. Descartes considers that he might himself be unwittingly responsible for his conceptions of all other beings, but, as an imperfect being subject to doubts, he could not possibly have given rise to the conception of a perfect being. Such an inadequate cause could not possibly have given rise to so mighty an effect – and the fact that causes must be adequate to account for their effects is something that we know by the light of nature. The only thing which could be a sufficient cause of the conception of a perfect being which Descartes has in his mind is a real perfect being. Thus a real perfect being must exist to account for the conception which Descartes has in his mind of such a perfect being. Also, it occurs to him that, since God is essentially a being who possesses all perfections and existence is a perfection, then, for God to be God, it is necessary that he should exist. It is of the essence of God that God exists, just as it is of the essence of a triangle that its angles add up to two right angles.[3]

How, having reached this point, can Descartes be assured of the existence or nature of anything other than himself and God? His basic strategy is to argue that, if God exists and is perfect, God will not be such a cad as to allow Descartes to be so totally deceived about things that he cannot extricate himself from his errors by the proper use of his mental faculties. Descartes thinks that he has a clue to what is the proper use of his mind in the method by which he has progressed up to now from apparent error or ignorance to apparent truth, especially in geometry. He has been apt to be deceived when he is precipitate in judgment on any matter, rather than refraining from judgment till he has obtained 'clear and distinct ideas' about it.[4] For example, I might precipitately judge, on the basis of what appears to my senses, that the sun is much smaller than the earth, or that it is in motion while the earth is stable, but once I have formed clear and distinct ideas about the subject, I realize that the sun is much larger than the earth, and that it is the earth which is in motion in relation to the sun rather than the other way about.[5] Again, I am apt spontaneously to suppose that a pain or other sensation that seems to be in some part of my body, say my foot, really is in my foot, but reflection teaches me that this is not in fact the case. I would have just the same sensation if the nerve were suitably stimulated between my foot and my brain. It is to be concluded that the pain 'in my foot' is a purely mental event which occurs when my brain is stimulated in the appropriate way, as normally happens only when my foot is physically affected.[6] Further reflection of the kind assures me that, while the physical objects which I seem to perceive are (usually) real, the properties which I am apt to attribute to them on the basis of my sense-perceptions are not. The real properties they have are ones which are subject to analysis in mathematical terms[7] – extension, weight, motion, and so on – and which cause sensations in my mind by their influence on my brain through my sense-organs. For example, a vase which appears to me as blue is not blue, at least in the sense in which it appears to me to be so; rather, it has properties which affect me in such a way that my mind has the impression of blue. But it should be noted that our ordinary experience, of seeing, hearing, feeling, and so on, for all that it is apt to lead to the confused and erroneous judgments which have just been diagnosed, is well adapted for practical purposes and the preservation of our lives and health; we therefore have no reason to reproach divine providence about the matter.[8]

By the grace of God, then, according to Descartes, I can be sure that there is a world other than myself, and I can know the truth about what it contains so far as I form 'clear and distinct ideas' about it. It thus seems essential, in coming to grips with Descartes's thought, to understand what he means by clarity and distinctness in ideas. We learn from the *Principles* that 'clear' conceptions[9] are ones that appear to the mind that studiously attends to them, just as clearly seen physical objects are clear to a good and attentive eye which sees them in a good light. 'I term that clear which is present and apparent to an attentive mind, in the same way as we assert that we see objects clearly when, being present to the regarding eye, they operate upon it with sufficient strength.'[10] While all distinct ideas are clear, not all clear ideas are distinct. Descartes uses the example of bodily pain to articulate the difference. 'When ... a severe pain is felt,' the conception one had of the pain 'may be very clear, and yet for all that not distinct, because it is usually confused by the sufferers with the obscure[11] judgment that they form upon its nature, assuming as they do that something exists in the part affected, similar to the sensation of pain of which they are alone clearly conscious.' My idea of the itch that I have in my scalp, for example, may be bound up with the erroneous assumption, whether explicitly formulated by me or not, that the itch as I feel it really is in my scalp, as opposed to in my mind. Similarly, my idea of the yellowness of the typing paper before me might be ever so clear, but fail to be distinct so far as I assumed that the sensation of yellow in my mind was actually in the paper, rather than being caused by properties of other kinds in the paper which impinged on my brain by way of my optic nerve.

It appears to me that the notion of 'clear and distinct ideas' is crucially ambiguous. On one obvious interpretation, we can have ever so 'clear and distinct an idea' of something, say, of a plesiosaurus living in the twentieth century or an aegithognathous bird with webbed feet, without being any the wiser as to whether such a thing actually exists. Here the example of geometry, as well as the limitations which happened to be characteristic of the geometry of Descartes's own times, appear to have misled him. Granted the axioms of Euclidean geometry, to see that any of its theorems is so is to see that it must be so; thus one might say that to get a 'clear and distinct idea' of one of the theorems is of itself to see that it is true. But in the case of most other judgments, however 'clearly and distinctly' we conceive what is involved in them, to see whether it or its contradictory are so, we have to appeal to experience. Furthermore, it is of course notorious that Euclid's axioms themselves are regarded by modern geometers not as self-evident truths but as postulates; Euclidean geometry as they interpret it merely shows you what follows from the axioms, and neither establishes nor depends on the truth of the axioms themselves.

But on another conception of what it would be to have a 'clear and distinct idea' of something, which appears sometimes to be at least adumbrated by Descartes, there is built into it not only the having of a lucid notion of *what* is conceived, but also the grasp of *why* such a conception is deemed to be instantiated in reality. (Descartes's example, of our knowledge of the sun's being larger than the earth,[12] is of something that is not only clearly conceivable, however repugnant to uninstructed common sense, but also the best explanation of the evidence when one takes a sufficient range of observable phenomena into account.) On this view, to have clear and distinct ideas about anything seems at least to approximate to what is required by Lonergan's generalized empirical method, if propositions are to be well founded and so liable to be true.[13]

Have we any sure basis for our knowledge of the real world? There is something approaching a consensus among contemporary philosophers that we do not, that the task which Descartes set himself, of finding such a basis, is an impossible one.[14] However, as will be evident from the argument of this book so far, I myself maintain that such a foundation may after all be found, and that it can be set out most adequately in terms of the generalized empirical method, which in this respect was in some ways anticipated by Descartes.[15]

We can come to make true and well-founded judgments, and we know in principle how to do so; reality is nothing other than what true judgments are about, and well-founded judgments tend to be about. Of so much, at least, we can be said to be certain. But according to one of Descartes's *Principles*, 'we cannot err if we give our assent only to things that we know clearly and distinctly.'[16] In accordance with generalized empirical method, together with what is now virtually the universal consensus of philosophers, this is not so even if we interpret Descartes's recommendations in the charitable sense suggested in the last paragraph but one. On Lonergan's view, while we can attain certainty of a kind on the questions of epistemology and metaphysics (on the nature and conditions of knowledge, and the overall nature and structure that the world must have by virtue of the fact that we can get to know it), we cannot obtain such certainty on ordinary matters of fact, whether these pertain to the world of common sense or to that of science. We can know for sure that we as conscious subjects are capable of experience, understanding, and judgment, and that there is a real world to be known so far as we exert these three capacities to the uttermost. But our knowledge of ordinary matters of empirical fact is bound to be fallible, since there may on any particular issue be evidence in experience to which we have not yet attended, possible explanations which our intelligence has not envisaged.

If Descartes exaggerated the scope of potential certainty, contemporary philosophers have tended to minimize it. It is often claimed nowadays that the only real certainties are trivial, either 'analytic' and true by the definition of their terms or to the effect that one is undergoing the experience that one is in fact undergoing. Otherwise we have to be content with merely probable and intrinsically fallible knowledge, and have no need of any non-trivial certainties to undergird it. These claims seem to me to be false. It does seem to be the case that most ordinary empirical judgments are merely probable,[17] that they cannot aspire to certainty strictly speaking, since they are always in principle vulnerable to further experience and further envisagement of possibilities. But what about the judgment itself, that we tend in general to get to know what is the case so far as we test our statements by experience, so far as we persistently regard them as fallible in this respect? The fallibility criterion cannot itself be fallible, if it is to operate at all; and there can be no empirical test for the correctness of the criterion of empirical testability. How then are these criteria to be established, as they apparently must be if we are to have solid grounds for our knowledge? They can be established as corollaries of the principle that one tends to know the truth about things by having good reasons for one's judgments, which is certain by virtue of the fact that its contradictory is self-destructive, for reasons already given. What is it to have good reason for our empirical judgments, whether pertaining to ordinary knowledge or to science? It is for them to have been corroborated by experience when they might in principle have been falsified by it – which is, of course, the essence of the criteria of fallibilism and empirical testability.

With God relieved of the epistemological role assigned by Descartes, there disappears the notorious problem of the 'Cartesian circle,' first pointed out by Antoine Arnauld.[18] It seems that Descartes presupposes his method of 'clear and distinct ideas' in establishing the existence of God, but that he uses belief in the existence and veracity of God to support the conclusion that one can establish the existence and nature of any being apart from God and oneself. But if what I have already argued is correct, we can in general by the appropriate use of our thoughts establish the reality of things which exist apart from ourselves and our thoughts, and then go on further to apply the principles to the special case of the existence of God. I will not take up space here to argue what is agreed by almost all contemporary philosophers, that Descartes's arguments for the existence of God as they stand are unsound. But there is no contradiction in maintaining that Descartes fails to prove the existence of God, and that he is wrong in his insistence that one has to be sure of God's existence before one can be sure of the existence of any other being apart from oneself, and yet that he was on to something in suggesting that there is some kind of connection between belief that there is a God and our general confidence that our cognitive powers are capable of apprehending what exists prior to, and independently of, ourselves. It may be asked: Is the amenability of the world to our intellectual powers not best explained if one supposes that there is something like intelligence at the base of the world?[19]

When it comes to cosmology, Descartes maintains that physical nature is a vast deterministic system, virtually every aspect of which is to be deduced from the nature of God.[20] By obvious analogy with geometry as conceived at the time, the ultimate principles constitutive of our knowledge of the world are to be grasped by 'intuition' that they must be as they are, and every other state of affairs is to be known by 'deduction' from these principles.[21] On occasion, indeed, observation or experiment may determine what laws God has actually instilled in nature, when *a priori* two or more options would have been equally possible.[22] This view of things must of course inevitably lead to difficulties about how human beings can operate in a more or less rational manner when they are so intimately associated with bodies which are completely determined by laws of quite a different kind. While Descartes himself may be said to have ducked the problem by proposing that the soul acted upon the body through the pineal gland,[23] his 'Occasionalist' successors confronted it head-on, and could only extricate themselves from its implications by proposing that divine Providence had ordained the world from the beginning with such wonderful foresight, that entities of two utterly disparate kinds, namely souls and bodies, would always exactly coincide in their operations, though they never really interacted with one another.[24] (As I write this sentence, I, who am essentially a soul, am trying to make a point about seventeenth-century philosophies of mind; while this has no effect whatever on my body, according to Occasionalist theory, God in God's goodness has arranged physical nature from the very beginning in such a way that my body will necessarily behave in the appropriate fashion.)

The universe as conceived in terms of generalized empirical method is not deterministic; as well as the 'classical' laws which tell you what must happen if and so long as certain states of affairs obtain (as one can predict indefinitely into the future where the planet Venus will be in relation to the earth unless the general disposition of the solar system is disturbed, perhaps by the arrival from outside of a sufficiently large body), there are 'statistical' laws from which events non-systematically diverge (as the number of sixes in a sufficiently long series of throws of fair dice will approximate to a sixth of the total, even if the outcome of no particular throw can be predicted). In a sample of a radioactive element, it may be known for certain that half the atoms will have changed into atoms of another element after a certain length of time, but there is no good reason to suppose that we could ever know for certain how soon any atom is going to make the change. The intrinsically statistical talk of the 'half-life' of such elements is not a mere cloak for ignorance. Similarly, a social scientist may make very reliable predictions about the behaviour of large groups of people without being any the wiser as to how any particular person will behave.[25] The principles underlying physical reality as a whole, and those specially characterizing each level in the hierarchy of beings in which it consists (the physical, the chemical, the biological, the sensitive-psychological, and so on), are to be grasped not by 'intuitions' of what cannot but be the case, but by acts of understanding awaiting confirmation in experience, and indefinitely to be improved and revised in the light of such experience.[26]

As to minds and bodies, the conscious human subject can impose laws of rational thought more or less on what remains unsystematic and indeterminate at the sensitive psychological level, just as the laws of neurology are imposed on the underlying cytological material, and the laws of chemistry, on the underlying physical material. Thus the laws of 'mind' can supervene quite snugly upon the laws of suitably organized 'matter.' Yet some element of dualism may be said to remain, in that there is no question of any 'reduction' of the mental to the physical. Some observable phenomena can be best explained in terms of intelligible states of affairs which do not themselves involve the operations of intelligence and others, in terms of states of affairs which do. The writing of Albert Einstein, or for that matter of the most assiduous and ingenious of psychological reductionists, cannot be explained in terms of the mere operation of physical and chemical laws, but some measure at least of intelligence and reason have to be invoked. In the matter of natural theology, for Lonergan as for Descartes, the overall intelligibility of the world is ultimately to be attributed to the divine nature as intellect; but Lonergan insists against Descartes that which particular set of classical and statistical laws is realized in the universe is up to the divine will, and can be established by humans not *a priori*, but only at the term of prolonged exercise of intelligence and reason on experience over many generations.

Generalized empirical method issues in overall agreement with Descartes, as with the *prima facie* implications of the whole scientific worldview, on the nature of physical things as they are in themselves, as opposed to how they appear to us to be. As a result of prolonged inquiry, qualities are discovered to belong to things such that, while they are not directly identical with what we may experience, they are verifiable by reference to such experience.[27] (One may consider the 'mass' of a cannon ball in relation to the 'weight' we feel as we try to lift it, or measurable waves of light in relation to seen colour.)

C.S. Peirce argued that logic is properly speaking a part of ethics.[28] The point he was making becomes clear when one reflects that to exert one's mind appropriately for discovering the truth is one aspect of acting well. In this matter, he agrees in principle with both Descartes and Lonergan. For Descartes, abstaining from judgment on something until I have a 'clear and distinct perception' of it is a matter of the proper use of my will, and so of moral virtue. In accordance with the findings of generalized empirical method, one ought to exert oneself to make responsible decisions; and among the most important of these are to try to be as attentive, intelligent, and reasonable as possible in the making of judgments.

The attitude to Descartes of the leading thinkers of the Enlightenment was ambivalent. Most of the *philosophes*, for example, as Peter Schouls has pointed out, accepted Descartes's ideals of progress and of mastery of the circumstances of human life, and his method as the most effective way of implementing them. This made them all the more resentful of what they regarded as his failures; and their resentment was increased by the fact that some of their opponents actually appealed to Descartes's metaphysics.[29] They themselves considered that his metaphysics, for all his protestations to the contrary, was more influenced by imagination than by reason; in illustration of this, they cited his urge to build systems and the dualism with its attendant psycho-physical parallelism which resulted from this.[30] One may surely retort, on Descartes's behalf, that not to think systematically may well be to lay oneself open to the danger of being dominated by a system which is unconsciously and therefore uncritically accepted. Simply to adopt materialism in the place of dualism seems to be an abandonment of, rather than a solution to, the problem which Descartes faced. How can it be that the same human organism can at the same time direct itself by thoughts which are to some extent intelligent and reasonable and also be totally subject to the laws of physics and chemistry? Descartes's resort to the pineal gland and the thoroughgoing psycho-physical parallelism of the Occasionalists, for all their *prima facie* absurdity, do have the merit of taking the measure of the problem.

The common Enlightenment claim, that to practise metaphysics at all is to take reason beyond its proper limits, ought to lead to total agnosticism about the typical issues of metaphysics, such as the existence of God and the relation of the mental to the physical aspects of reality. But of course those who make the claim are apt to use it to justify the assumption that there is no God, and that materialism is true. However, it is one thing to say that reason is incompetent in some sphere of human concern and quite another to hold that reason shows that this sphere of concern should be abandoned, or that the assumptions on which the concern is based are probably or certainly false. Indeed, a moment's reflection will show that the two propositions are actually inconsistent with one another. The thinkers of the Enlightenment who were opposed to religion, whether their beliefs about the subject were actually true or false, seem largely to have overlooked this crucial distinction, and hence to have failed to think as clearly as Descartes about the implications of his method, rather than, as they claimed, to have taken those implications further than he did himself.[31]

One effect of Descartes's influence on the Enlightenment was certainly to encourage the wholesale repudiation of tradition. Opinions about the world, humankind, and God were to be retained only so far as they could be vindicated at the bar of the method, and rejected so far as they could not. It is one thing, of course, to say that such a stance was in fact justified by appeal to Descartes's method and quite another to say that it is a necessary consequence of its application. Descartes himself was notably scrupulous in regard to tradition with respect to Catholic belief and practice;[32] the possibility that he was sincere or even consistent in this matter cannot be dismissed out of hand. It is conceivable after all that the most rigorous possible application of our reasoning powers might confirm the belief that there is a God, and that the divine nature and purposes for humankind have been specially revealed in the way that Catholics have supposed. And, quite apart from Descartes's attitude to Catholicism, a hint at least of the basis of a more favourable attitude to tradition than was usual in the Enlightenment may be found in his suggestion that persons of the past, so far as they reached well-founded or true beliefs on any matter, must themselves have had some knowledge of his method.[33] Could not much or most of what has been handed down to us by tradition have been attained by means liable to ensure that it was good or true, even if those responsible were not able to spell out with any precision that or why this was so in the manner attempted by Descartes himself? People have often argued quite logically, though in total ignorance of the rules formulated by Aristotle and others, which they were following in doing so; and many speak grammatically by instinct without any acquaintance with the rules of grammar.

But at all events, whatever may be the case *de jure* or *de facto* about the application of the Cartesian method to the beliefs and the values constitutive of tradition, the generalized empirical method is as apt to confirm as to repudiate them. Notoriously, Lonergan was at least as committed to Catholicism as was Descartes, and regarded the application of his method not only as consistent with this, but as actually tending to support it.[34] And on many matters other than religious faith, it seems plausible to suppose that our predecessors have thought and spoken attentively, intelligently, and reasonably; it would thus be folly rather than wisdom to reject their beliefs and values root and branch. And in any case, every person in every culture but the most primitive takes on trust the vast majority of the beliefs and values on the basis of which she lives her life; abruptly to stop doing so would be the road to barbarism rather than to an enhancement of civilization.[35] But this is by no means to imply that the methodical critique of tradition is impossible, or that it is superfluous. A thorough investigation of relevant evidence, and a vigorous canvassing of alternative possibilities, is likely to reveal that much traditional belief is mistaken, and that many revered customs and institutions would be better abandoned or revised.[36] Contemporary defenders of tradition have a lively sense of the outrages committed against it by one kind of self-styled 'rationalism,' which does indeed owe something to Descartes's method,[37] but they do not seem to me to offer us any very clear conception as to how we are to discriminate between the good and the bad, the well-founded and the ill-founded, in what our predecessors have handed down to us.

What is to be concluded about what may be called 'the Cartesian nightmare' of a universe of dead, mechanical, pointless, and ultimately unintelligible 'matter,' utterly indifferent to the human spirit? How did it come about, how is it to be counteracted, and what virtues, if any, does it have or has it ever had? To take the last question first, it ought to be acknowledged that Cartesian assumptions proved invaluable for the development of the sciences over several centuries. And it will not do to submit uncritically to the present fashion of undervaluing the Cartesian ambition of directing and controlling the physical environment for the enhancement of human life; it is easy to forget, in a mood of sentimental and one-sided nostalgia for the past, that we are the better off for the majority of our children not dying in infancy, and for being without the periodic scourges of typhus, bubonic plague, and smallpox. Technology is a proper aim of science, however wrong-headed it is to assume that it is its only aim or even its essence. What does seem essential to science is the Platonic vision of a universe which is intelligible, and so radiant with intellectual light; this was modified and refined, but not intrinsically altered, by Aristotle's more empirical emphasis.[38] Such a conception of the universe makes it connatural to the human mind, and fitted to encourage the expansion of the human spirit; but it has been succeeded in modern times, quite largely due to the influence of Descartes himself, by that of a dead and intrinsically unintelligible waste awaiting human manipulation and control. The crucial false step made by Descartes, I believe, is in conceiving the material world no longer as essentially related to minds as that which they can know, but rather as artificially linked to minds which have nothing essentially to do with it by special divine dispensation. When God drops out of the picture, one is left with a material universe which essentially has no place for mind. Fortunately, the errors in this view are being made ever clearer by developments in modern science (especially physics) itself,[39] as well as being able to be clearly diagnosed and rejected by a sufficiently sophisticated philosophy.[40]

15

Conclusion

A common view of where we are at present in philosophy could be expressed in some such way as this: the attempt to articulate general criteria of knowledge and value, which has characterized philosophy since the seventeenth century, has ended in failure. This is not in the least to be regretted. The sciences can and do establish their own criteria, and are not and should not be dictated to by philosophy, and the same goes for morality, politics, and other aspects of culture. Philosophy, if it has a future, must thus give up its pretensions to be a sort of universal arbiter. It can retain perhaps the humbler function of promoting conversation between groups which differ from one another in factual beliefs or in general aims of life and, as a consequence, tend to be mutually estranged.[1]

The truth about the matter, if what I have been arguing in this book is on the right lines, is more or less the reverse of this. The old questions about the basic criteria of fact and value, of how we are to know what is really true about the world and ourselves and what is truly good, remain as pressing as ever. Short of the existence of general criteria, which at least in principle can be articulated, the distinctions between science and pseudoscience, and between human acts which are excellent and those which are abominable, must remain wholly arbitrary in the last analysis. The fact that erroneous views on these matters, such as those advanced (with respect to our knowledge of fact) by the positivists, have led many to scepticism does not imply that we cannot attain the correct view. In fact Plato, Aristotle, and the pioneers of scientific method in the seventeenth century were all on the right track, and we can find the way forward from our present parlous position by respectful attention to what they had to say. The promoting of conversation is unquestionably a worthwhile aim, but it becomes far more so when one realizes that sympathetic attention to the beliefs and arguments of others is among the best means of enhancing our own attentiveness, intelligence, and reasonableness, and so of coming closer to knowing what is really true and good.

To the 'generalized empirical method' which I have been commending in this book, which has been most comprehensively developed and applied in the writings of Bernard Lonergan, the empiricism of the first phase of twentieth-century analytic philosophy may be seen as some kind of approximation. All knowledge is certainly based on experience, but it is essential to get clear about how it is based on it, and not to understand 'experience' in too narrow a sense. John Locke was right to claim, in effect, that we have experience of a kind not only of our feelings and sensations, but also of the mental activities – of wondering, questioning, coming to understand, judging, deciding, and so on – which we perform with respect to them. The denial that one can attain true belief, or that one can believe for good reasons, is self-destructive. The same applies, as Descartes pointed out, to the giving of reasons in support of the conclusion that one is not a reasoner. To the notorious question, which led Descartes to invoke special divine aid, of how our thoughts can be of a world which exists independently of them, the short answer is that the real world can in the last analysis be nothing other than what true judgments are about and what well-founded judgments tend to be about. Our judgments are well founded to the degree that they are attentively, intelligently, and reasonably arrived at, in the manner exhaustively discussed in the previous pages; thus empiricism and rationalism are both partial truths about the nature of human knowledge. Some of the phenomena to which we may attend seem after sustained inquiry to be explicable without reference to intelligence, but some do not; this gives us the basic distinction between natural and human science, a distinction which cannot be erased short of a generalized animism, at one extreme (whereby planets and plants and atoms are credited with thoughts like those of human persons), and a self-destructive materialism, on the other (such that no one, even the materialist, can really believe what she does because there is good reason for her to do so). Psychologists in particular should heed the warning that one must not confuse the legitimate demand that everything be explained with the absurd requirement that a fully 'scientific' explanation of human behaviour must be able to get by without any reference to human thought at all.

The human good is a matter of happiness and fairness, and is as subject to investigation by empirical and rational means as every other matter of fact. This provides the basis for a normative political, as well as moral, theory, since a society is good so far as happiness is maximized among its members without undue sacrifice of fairness either to them or to others. Some human artifacts contribute signally to human happiness by extending and clarifying human capacities to have experiences, to imagine, and to grasp intelligible structure; the discussion of how they do so, and why this is valuable for human life, is the subject matter of aesthetics. When it comes to the questions of religion, one may usefully ask whether it is more reasonable than not, or less reasonable than not, to believe that something like what all have called God is responsible for the existence of the world; and if it is more reasonable than not, whether one ought to believe that the nature and purposes of this being are specially revealed through some particular historical community, set of writings, or whatever.[2] It must be reiterated that, if the principles outlined in the first paragraph of this chapter are consistently maintained and seriously applied, these questions, which one would have thought were of some importance, can be settled by nothing other than fashion, prejudice, or caprice.

In answer to those who consider that in future we would be as well or better off without philosophy, one can only say that those who cannot or will not think critically about the basic problems of knowledge, reality, and value are not really innocent of theories about these matters; they are inevitably dominated by uncriticized ones. And to think about them not only remains the central task of philosophy as it has been at least since the time of Plato, but is at least as urgent now as it ever was.

Notes

Chapter 1: Scepticism

1 For Hume's views on the topic, see especially his *Enquiry Concerning Human Understanding* (Oxford: Clarendon Press), section V, part 1, and section XII, part 1. For those of Nagarjuna, see K. Satchinanda Murty, *Nagarjuna* (New Delhi: National Book Trust, 1971).

2 For an excellent defence of the anti-foundationalist position, see M.E. Williams, *Groundless Belief* (Oxford: Blackwell, 1977).

3 Williams, *Groundless Belief,* 23 and chapter 4.

4 Cf. J. Kekes, 'The Case for Scepticism,' in *Philosophical Quarterly* 25, no. 98 (1975): 38.

5 Of course, there is a sense, as Karl Popper has emphasized, in which one should do the very opposite of attempting to 'justify' one's beliefs and assumptions if one aspires to come closer to the truth; see *Objective Knowledge* (Oxford: Clarendon Press, 1972), 29–30. But I believe that what I am arguing here is in merely verbal disagreement with Popper on this point.

6 Kekes, 'Case for Scepticism,' 35.

7 Ibid., 36. Cf. A.J. Ayer, *The Problem of Knowledge* (Harmondsworth: Penguin Books, 1956), 78–83.

8 Barry Stroud, 'Transcendental Arguments,' in *The Journal of Philosophy* 65, no. 9 (1968), apropos of P.F. Strawson, *Individuals* (London: Methuen, 1958), 36.

9 J. Kekes, *A Justification of Rationality* (Albany: State University of New York Press, 1976); cited in Corbin Fowler, 'Kekes and Johnson on Rationality,' in *Philosophical Quarterly* 28, no. 112 (1978): 259.

10 Fowler, 'Kekes and Johnson,' 259–60.

11 Ibid., 264.

12 See R.M. Chisholm, *Theory of Knowledge* (Englewood Cliffs, NJ: Prentice-Hall, 1966), 6–7. For more on 'the given,' see chapter 3 below.

13 For a useful account of Russell's theory of knowledge, see A.J. Ayer, *Russell* (London: Collins, 1972), chapter 3.

14 See Wittgenstein, *Philosophical Investigations* (Oxford: Blackwell, 1958), II, xi.

15 This paragraph is, it need hardly be said, only a sketch of the manner in which I think the problem of foundations ought to be handled. For the infinite regress argument, see Williams, *Groundless Belief.* On foundations in general, see chapter 3 below.

16 For the importance of such propositions for the theory of knowledge, see G. Grisez, *Beyond the New Theism* (Notre Dame, IN: Notre Dame University Press, 1975). But their most thorough and ingenious exploitation is to be found in B.J.F. Lonergan, *Insight: A Study of Human Understanding* (London: Longmans, Green, 1957), especially chapter 11.

17 Hume, *Enquiry*, section IV, part 1.

18 See Kant, *Critique of Pure Reason*, B ix–x, xvi–xix.

19 For an extensive discussion, see Lonergan, *Insight*, xxvi, 252, 272–8, 282–3.

20 Hume, *Enquiry*, section IV, part 2.

21 See especially T.S. Kuhn, *The Structure of Scientific Revolutions* (Chicago: University of Chicago Press, 1962); and P.K. Feyerabend, *Against Method* (London: New Left Books, 1975). Also chapters 6 and 7 below.

22 The fact that the process of coming to know involves such 'leaps,' which cannot be reduced to logic or experience, seems to account for a great deal of contemporary scepticism and anti-foundationalism.

23 Stroud, 'Transcendental Arguments,' 253–5.

24 For an example of this pattern of argument, see Lonergan, *Method in Theology* (London: Darton, Longman, and Todd, 1972), 16–17.

25 Kekes, 'Case for Scepticism,' 38.

26 Hume, *Enquiry*, section V, part 2.

27 Sextus Empiricus, *Outlines of Scepticism*, trans. Julia Annas and Jonathan Barnes (Cambridge: Cambridge University Press, 1994), I ix, 8. (The Arabic numeral refers to the page of the Annas and Barnes edition.)

28 As Sextus says, sceptics 'say what is apparent to themselves and report their own feelings without holding opinions, affirming nothing about external objects' (I vii, 7; I x, 8).

29 Sextus, *Outlines of Scepticism*, I vii, 7; iv, 4–5; xiii, 12.

30 Ibid. 'Those who make no determination about what is good and bad by nature neither avoid nor pursue anything with intensity; and hence they are tranquil' (I x, 10).

31 Ibid., III xxiii, 200.

32 This was argued in ancient times by Aristocles, an opponent of the Sceptics.

33 In all fairness, I ought to record that the motto he assigned to me was: 'Give me the job, and I will finish the tools.'

34 Cf. the abominable suggestion of Foucault mentioned below.

35 Cf. the deep incoherence of the notorious Kantian view, that our knowledge can extend only to 'appearances,' and 'things in themselves' are for ever hidden from us.

36 C.S. Peirce had a similar opinion of Cartesian doubt. See *Values in a Universe of Chance*, ed. P.P. Wiener (Stanford: Stanford University Press, 1958), 40, 99; also *The Collected Papers of C.S. Peirce*, ed. C. Hartshorne and P. Weiss (Cambridge: Harvard University Press, 1931–5), 5.265; cited by W.B. Gallie, *Peirce and Pragmatism* (Harmondsworth: Penguin Books, 1952), 74–5.

37 *Summa Theologica*, I, ii.

38 Antony Flew, *The Presumption of Atheism* (Buffalo: Prometheus Books, 1984), 29.

39 For the parallel with Derrida, see the introduction to *Outlines of Scepticism*, xii: 'Sceptics do not start from a position of their own – they do not have a set of beliefs, or even a view as to how philosophy ought to be done. Rather, they follow the going practice of philosophy, and work from within it to undermine it.'

Chapter 2: Truth

1 The problem of the nature of 'data' will be dealt with in the next chapter.

2 H.B. Acton, 'Idealism,' in *Encyclopaedia of Philosophy*, ed. Paul Edwards (New York: Macmillan, 1967).

3 Michael Dummett, *Truth and Other Enigmas* (London: Duckworth, 1978), 14.

4 For brevity and convenience, I will simply use the phrase 'the threefold process' in what follows.

5 Dummett, *Truth and Other Enigmas*, xl.

6 Plato, *Euthydemus*, 276e–277c.

7 D. Davidson, 'A Coherence Theory of Truth and Knowledge' (*Kant oder Hegel?*) (Klett-Cotta, 1983), 425. I am indebted for this reference to an unpublished paper by C.B. Martin, 'The New Cartesianism.'

8 Ibid.

9 G. Pitcher, ed., Introduction to *Truth* (Englewood Cliffs, NJ: Prentice-Hall, 1964), 19.

10 Ibid., 10.

11 N. Chomsky, *Syntactic Structures* (Gravenhage: Mouton, 1957).

12 Pitcher, *Truth*, 19.

13 This is, of course, the point of the joke about the engineer, who when asked

'What is 3 times 4?' fishes a contraption known as a slide-rule out of his pocket, fiddles with it for a moment, and then says, 'Oh, about 12.' See W.W. Sawyer, *Mathematician's Delight* (Harmondsworth: Penguin Books, 1943), 69.

14 A. Adjukiewicz, *Problems and Theories of Philosophy* (Cambridge: Cambridge University Press, 1975).

15 G.E. Moore, *Some Main Problems of Philosophy* (New York: Macmillan, 1953), 261.

16 H. Putnam, *Realism and Reason* (Cambridge: Cambridge University Press, 1983), xvii. I owe this and the following two citations to an unpublished thesis by A. Wickings.

17 Putnam, *Reason, Truth and History* (Cambridge: Cambridge University Press, 1981), 49–50.

18 Ibid.

19 R. Rorty, *Philosophy and the Mirror of Nature* (Princeton: Princeton University Press, 1979), 280–1.

20 A. Tarski, *Logic, Semantics, Metamathematics* (Oxford: Clarendon Press, 1956), 152–278.

21 On this, Sir Karl Popper seems worth quoting: 'To me, idealism appears absurd, for it ... implies something like this: that it is my mind which creates this beautiful world. But I know I am not its creator.' See *Objective Knowledge* (Oxford: Clarendon Press, 1972), 41.

22 Bernice Goldmark, *Social Studies: A Method of Inquiry* (Belmont: Wadsworth, 1968); cited by J.A. Banks and A.A. Clegg, *Teaching Strategies for the Social Studies: Inquiry, Valuing, and Decision Making* (Reading, MA: Addison Wesley, 1977), 16.

23 Dummett, *Truth and Other Enigmas*, xxxviii–ix.

24 I believe that it is misleading of Strawson to say that 'if you prize the statements off the world you prize the facts off it too; but the world would be none the poorer' (quoted by Pitcher, *Truth*, 39). Strawson's basic point seems to be that there is no more to statements corresponding with facts than referring expressions referring, and descriptions correctly describing (36–7). I would concede this; but would regard it as an analysis of what it is for a statement to correspond with a fact or a state of affairs, rather than as a refutation of the claim that it did so. It seems to accord better with ordinary usage to regard facts as belonging to the real as opposed to the linguistic order. Is it not natural to say that Sirius' distance of between five and ten light-years from the earth would have been a fact, even if no human beings had evolved to talk about it?

25   'Two added to one, if it could but be done'
        It said, 'on one's fingers and thumbs!'
        Recollecting with tears how, in earlier years,
        It had taken no pains with its sums.

26 Cf. G.E. Moore, 'Proof of an External World,' in *Proceedings of the British Academy*, vol. 25 (1939).

27 I have tried to develop this distinction elsewhere: cf. Meynell, *The Intelligible Universe* (London: Macmillan, 1982), 43.

28 This will depend on whether the evidence for beliefs is taken to consist, in the last analysis, in the observation of events in the world about one, or the undergoing of sense-impressions. See the next chapter.

29 L. BonJour, *The Structure of Empirical Knowledge* (Cambridge: Harvard University Press, 1985); Jonathan Dancy, *An Introduction to Contemporary Epistemology* (Oxford: Oxford University Press, 1985). For a useful if somewhat hostile survey, which does not take very recent work into account, see Alan White, 'Coherence Theory of Truth,' in *Encyclopedia of Philosophy*, vol. 2: 229.

30 White, 'Coherence Theory of Truth,' 229.

31 Michael D. Lemoniak and J. Madeleine Nash, 'Unravelling Universe,' *Time*, 6 March 1995, 37.

32 Though one should bear in mind the warning of the Chicago astrophysicist David Schramm: 'Whenever you are at the forefront of science, one-third of the observations always turn out to be wrong,' in Lemoniak and Nash, 'Unravelling Universe,' 37.

33 Ralph C.S. Walker, 'Spinoza and the Coherence Theory of Truth,' in *Mind* 84, no. 1 (January 1975): 4.

34 BonJour's coherentist stance has been attacked convincingly by Paul K. Moser in 'Internalism and Coherentism: A Dilemma,' and 'How Not to Be a Coherentist,' *Analysis* (October 1988).

35 BonJour, *Structure of Empirical Knowledge*, xi, 33, 69, 72, 75, 78, 77, 75, 79.

36 Ibid., 58.

37 One needs in addition some justification of the assumption that our experiences can provide us with evidence for states of affairs which obtain prior to and independently of those experiences. I have tried to provide such justification in chapter 1. For discussion of Lewis and Quinton, cf. BonJour, *Structure of Empirical Knowledge*, 65–79.

38 BonJour, *Structure of Empirical Knowledge*, 73–4.

39 Ibid., 32. BonJour's italics; but it would have suited my book to add them had they not been in the original.

40 'Follows' in the sense that, in the example which I discussed, it 'followed' from my visual experiences *as though of* my grey overcoat hanging on the wall of my room in a certain position, that it probably really *was* hanging there.

41 The point of the qualification is to anticipate Kuhn-type objections culled from the history of scientific development (e.g., 'No scientific theory was ever confirmed more thoroughly than Newton's. But it turned out to be wrong.'). But from an Einsteinian point of view, as Popper has pointed out, Newtonian

science is an excellent approximation. Cf. chapters 6 and 7 below.

42 Cf. J.L. Mackie, *Truth, Probability and Paradox* (Oxford: Clarendon Press, 1973), 17f. This book has the best treatment known to me of the topics dealt with in the rest of this chapter.

43 This is close to the account given at one time by Bertrand Russell, who distinguishes between propositions as 'factual occurrences' and as 'vehicles of truth and falsehood.' He regards the former as identical with sentences (A.N. Whitehead and B. Russell, *Principia Mathematica* [Cambridge: Cambridge University Press, 1925], 665; quoted by G.H. von Wright, *Truth, Knowledge and Modality* [Oxford: Blackwell, 1984], 15–16).

44 G.E. Moore carefully observed a distinction between sentences, on the one hand, and propositions as what sentences mean or express, on the other (*Some Main Problems of Philosophy* [London: Allen and Unwin, 1953], 57, 259; cited Mackie, *Truth, Probability and Paradox*, 17). At that rate, as he pointed out, talk of meaningless propositions would make no sense. But Russell was as a rule, as I have said, of the opinion that propositions were linguistic entities (ibid., 19).

45 This is von Wright's view. As he sees it, '[T]ruth and falsity are commonly and naturally predicated of beliefs and judgments. Also of statements, and, maybe, assertions,' though he finds this last problematic. To predicate truth and falsity of sentences seems to him 'definitely barbaric' (von Wright, *Truth, Knowledge and Modality*, 14).

46 The map analogy is much used by D.M. Armstrong in *A Materialist Theory of the Mind* (London: Routledge, 1968).

47 See Margaret A. Boden, et al., *Artificial Intelligence and the Mind* (London: Royal Society, 1994).

48 One might, of course, rescue this corollary of materialism by saying that God had programmed us as physical objects and complexes to *mean* (say) the Pole Star by 'the Pole Star'; just as the programmer enables the computer to *mean* by its output the state of my pension contributions. But I doubt if many materialists would thank me for this suggestion of a way out of their difficulties. For an argument along these lines for the existence of God, see R. Taylor, *Metaphysics* (Englewood Cliffs, NJ: Prentice-Hall, 1963), 96–101.

49 On the 'philosophical mist' that arises from the term 'proposition,' see von Wright, *Truth, Knowledge and Modality*, 15. In two publications of 1919, Russell expresses two different and incompatible views of their nature: on the one hand, he says that they are primarily forms of words expressing what is true or false and, on the other, he distinguishes between 'word-propositions' and 'image-propositions,' of which the former *refer to* the facts which render them true or false, and *mean* the corresponding examples of the latter (von Wright,

Truth, Knowledge and Modality, 16). For the second view, see Russell, *Logic and Knowledge*, ed. R.C. Marsh (London: Allen and Unwin, 1956) 308–9. The disagreement is an old one; for the Stoics, truth was to be attributed primarily to *axiomata* which exist independently of being expressed; for most medieval philosophers, truth was a property of spoken or written sentences. Cf. A.N. Prior, 'The Correspondence Theory of Truth,' in *Encyclopedia of Philosophy*, vol. 2: 224.

50 See Mackie, *Truth, Probability and Paradox*, 19, on a similar ambiguity in 'statement.'

51 Cf. Russell in 'The Philosophy of Logical Atomism': '[F]acts belong to the objective world. They are not created by our thoughts or beliefs except in special cases' (Russell, *Logic*, 183).

52 Though apparently Moore held at one stage that they did.

53 In order not to complicate the issue, we will suppose, for the purposes of the immediate argument, the non-existence of God, angels, or other conscious beings who might be in the know.

54 This seems to be a dominating preoccupation of the philosophy of Quine. See A. Orenstein, *Willard Van Orman Quine* (Boston: Twayne Publishers, 1977).

55 Mackie, *Truth, Probability and Paradox*, 28.

56 In the case of belief, in disposition to thought. I am probably not thinking about the Queen of Alaska, during most of the time when I can truly be said to believe that there is no Queen of Alaska.

57 Eubulides of Miletus expressed the paradox in the form, 'The statement I am now making is a lie,' whereas Epimenides the Cretan said, 'The Cretans are always liars.' The former statement is intrinsically paradoxical in a way that the latter is not; it only becomes so when uttered by a Cretan. See A. Gupta and N. Belknap, *The Revision Theory of Truth* (Cambridge: MIT Press, 1993), 6.

58 Gupta and Belknap, *Revision Theory of Truth*, 9. These authors provide a good example of the tangle one gets into if one thinks in terms of 'propositions' here.

59 This solution is proposed by Yehoshua Bar-Hillel, who distinguishes between sentences and statements and suggests that in the paradoxical instances, no statement is made ('Do natural languages contain paradoxes?'; cited Gupta and Belknap, *Revision Theory of Truth*, 7). In the same vein, William Kneale maintains that the Liar paradox holds no terror for those who distinguish between sentences and propositions. It was the Stoic Chrysippus who first proposed the solution, that the paradoxical sentences do not say anything (Gupta and Belknap, *Revision Theory of Truth*, 7).

60 Bertrand Russell solves the same problem in much the same way with his 'theory of types.' Cf. Russell, *Logic*, 59ff.

61 Cf. Prior, 'Correspondence Theory of Truth,' 230. In connection with the

thesis about self-destructive statements and their contradictories which is fundamental to the argument of this book, it should be noted that 'I am not lying,' so far as it is self-referential, has a kind of necessity about it. It cannot be that I am lying, so far as my doing so is deemed to have self-reference.

62 For alternatives to the approach by way of 'metalanguages,' see Saul Kripke, 'Outline of a Theory of Truth,' in Robert L. Martin, ed., *Recent Essays on Truth and the Liar Paradox* (Oxford: Clarendon Press, 1984).

63 *De Veritate*, q. 1, art. 1, reply. It will be seen that my conclusions are almost the polar opposite to those arrived at by Barry Allen in his *Truth in Philosophy* (Cambridge: Harvard University Press, 1993).

Chapter 3: Data

1 For very clear accounts, see Bertrand Russell, *Logic and Knowledge* (London: Allen and Unwin, 1956); A.J. Ayer, *Russell* (London: Collins, 1972).

2 The principal influence here is the later philosophy of Wittgenstein, especially *Philosophical Investigations* (Oxford: Blackwell, 1953), and *On Certainty* (Oxford: Blackwell 1969). A recent and influential attack on the idea that human knowledge has or needs foundations is Richard Rorty's *Philosophy and the Mirror of Nature* (Princeton: Princeton University Press, 1979).

3 Only 'probable' in that future experience may give reasons for overturning even a very well-established scientific theory.

4 See Wittgenstein's aspersions on 'private languages,' in *Philosophical Investigations*, I, paragraphs 243–315.

5 That 'basic statements' should be reports of observed physical states of affairs is the view of Karl Popper (see *Objective Knowledge* [London: Oxford University Press, 1972]) and Anthony Quinton (see *The Nature of Things* [London: Routledge and Kegan Paul, 1973]).

6 For a useful summary of such attitudes, see G.J. Warnock's Introduction to *The Philosophy of Perception* (London: Oxford University Press, 1967).

7 Michael Williams, *Groundless Belief* (Oxford: Blackwell, 1977), 14–15. Cf. A.J. Ayer, *The Problem of Knowledge* (Harmondsworth: Penguin Books, 1956), 76–8.

8 Williams, *Groundless Belief*, 15; Ayer, *Problem of Knowledge*, 79.

9 Williams, *Groundless Belief*, 16; Ayer, *Problem of Knowledge*, 79.

10 Bertrand Russell, *The Problems of Philosophy* (London: Oxford University Press, 1959), 21–4; Williams, *Groundless Belief*, 16.

11 Williams, *Groundless Belief*, 16–17; Ayer, *Problem of Knowledge*, 80. I am greatly indebted to Williams for these formulations of the attack on empiricist accounts of foundations.

12 Williams, *Groundless Belief*, 17; Ayer, *Problem of Knowledge*, 83.

13 Cf. Ayer's own famous aspersions on theism in chapter 6 of *Language, Truth and Logic* (London: Gollancz, 1946).

14 See W. Sellars, *Science, Perception and Reality* (London: Routledge and Kegan Paul, 1963), 140, 157, 160f., 169, 174, 177, 193.

15 See especially T.S. Kuhn, *The Structure of Scientific Revolutions* (Chicago: University of Chicago Press, 1962); P.K. Feyerabend, *Against Method* (London: New Left Books, 1975); and chapters 6 and 7 below.

16 On this and related topics, see Rorty, *Philosophy and the Mirror of Nature*, 295–305.

17 On the idea that knowledge has two components, see Rorty, *Philosophy and the Mirror of Nature*, 169.

18 Sellars has a similar point to make; see *Science, Perception and Reality*, 170.

19 Kuhn, *Structure of Scientific Revolutions*, 128.

20 Sellars's discussion of this matter in 'Empiricism and the Philosophy of Mind' seems at first sight to advance this view (*Science, Perception and Reality*, 144). But elsewhere (ibid., 47) he appears to take a position more consistent with the one I am defending.

21 See Hugo Meynell, *The Intelligible Universe* (Totowa, NJ: Barnes and Noble, 1982), chapter 3. Cf. also P.F. Strawson, Introduction to *Philosophy of Logic* (London: Oxford University Press, 1967), 3: 'If we are to be able to say how things are in the world, we must have at our disposal the means of doing two complementary things, of performing two complementary functions: we must be able to specify general types of situation, thing, event, etc., and we must be able to attach these general specifications to particular cases, to indicate their particular incidence in the world.' Evidently Strawson's 'two complementary functions' correspond closely to (2) and (3).

22 See Locke, *An Essay Concerning Human Understanding*, Book II, chapters 1, 6, 7.

23 Hume, *A Treatise of Human Nature*, Book I, part 4, section 6.

24 See note 4 above.

25 See note 10 above.

26 Sellars, *Science, Perception and Reality*, 170.

27 Cf. P.K. Feyerabend, *Against Method*.

28 See the many citations of Sellars's work in Rorty, *Philosophy and the Mirror of Nature*.

29 For some shrewd comments about this charge, see Stanley Rosen, *The Limits of Analysis* (New York: Basic Books, 1980), xiv, 11–12, 109, 176, 218, 253.

Chapter 4: Reality

1 T.S. Kuhn, *The Structure of Scientific Revolutions* (Chicago: University of Chicago

Press, 1962), 172. '[The] problem – What must the world be like in order that man may know it? – ... is as old as science itself, and it remains unanswered.'

2 W.C. Sellars, *Science, Perception and Reality* (London: Routledge and Kegan Paul, 1963), 173.

3 Cf. B.J.F. Lonergan, *Method in Theology* (London: Darton, Longman and Todd, 1972), 16–17.

4 Cf. J. Monod, *Chance and Necessity* (London: Collins, 1972), 154.

5 *An Enquiry Concerning Human Understanding*, section IV, part 2.

6 A. Orenstein, *Willard Van Orman Quine* (Boston: Twayne Publishers, 1977), 52–3.

7 I have tried to argue this at length in *The Intelligible Universe: A Cosmological Argument* (London: Macmillan, 1982). See also chapter 14 below.

8 B.J.F. Lonergan, *Insight: A Study of Human Understanding* (London: Longmans, Green, 1957), 416. The account of metaphysics given here is largely based on Lonergan's thought.

9 Aristotle, *Posterior Analytics*, II, 2.

10 B.J.F. Lonergan, 'Isomorphism of Thomist and Scientific Thought,' in his *Collection* (London: Darton, Longman and Todd, 1967), 151. Lonergan remarks shrewdly that the traditional attachment of scientists to a mechanistic view of reality is in fact due to a confused apprehension of the requirement that reality should be intelligible.

11 This paragraph is based on A.J. Ayer, *The Central Questions of Philosophy* (London: Weidenfeld and Nicholson, 1973), 1–5.

12 R. Carnap, *Meaning and Necessity* (Chicago: University of Chicago Press, 1956), 43, 205–21; Orenstein, *Quine*, 69.

13 The technical distinction made by Lonergan between 'things' and 'bodies' (*Insight*, 250–4) is not germane to this point.

14 *Enquiry*, section VII, part 2.

15 W.H. Walsh, 'Metaphysics (Nature of)' in *Encyclopaedia of Philosophy* (London: Collier-Macmillan, 1967), vol. 10: 5, 301.

16 K.R. Popper, *Objective Knowledge* (London: Oxford University Press, 1972), 28–9, 38, 40, 96, 196, 203–4, 323.

17 Ibid., 12–14, 20, 26, 38–9, 196–7.

18 For provocation of the argument of the next few pages, I am indebted to an anonymous critic of an earlier draft of this book.

19 I have this story from Professor Jack Granatstein, but cannot vouch for the details.

20 It is sometimes worth reminding oneself that Platonism, even if the set of ideas which it denotes is almost wholly wrong, is a label for the way of thinking of a very great human mind, and not merely a term of abuse.

21 This view appears to be espoused by Larry Laudan. See his brilliant and witty dialogue in *Science and Relativism: Some Key Controversies in the Philosophy of Science* (Chicago: University of Chicago Press, 1990).

22 This point has been mentioned by Peter Preuss.

23 See Hugo Meynell, *The Nature of Aesthetic Value* (Albany: State University of New York Press, 1986).

24 The classical statement of the former position is J.S. Mill's *Utilitarianism* (London: J.M. Dent, 1964); of the latter, Kant's *Groundwork of the Metaphysics of Morals*; trans. H.J. Paton as *The Moral Law* (New York: Harper and Row, 1964).

25 This seems to have been the crucial point overlooked by G.E. Moore, in his influential delineation of the so-called naturalistic fallacy. See *Principia Ethica* (Cambridge: Cambridge University Press, 1956), 10, 13–14, 18–20, 38–9.

26 The 'emotivist' position is well set out in chapter 6 of A.J. Ayer's *Language, Truth and Logic* (London: Gollancz, 1946); the 'prescriptivist' position in R.M. Hare's *The Language of Morals* (New York: Oxford University Press, 1964).

27 I have argued for this general position on ethics at some length in *Freud, Marx and Morals* (Totowa, NJ: Barnes and Noble, 1981), chapter 6.

28 See, for example, *The Intelligible Universe: A Cosmological Argument* (New York: Barnes and Noble, 1982).

29 See *An Enquiry Concerning Human Understanding*, section VIII.

30 Those who, like Hume, would reconcile determinism with a freedom sufficient for morality, are apt to say that 'She could have done otherwise' means 'She would have done otherwise, if she had reflected further,' or something of that kind. (I owe this point to U.T. Place.) But one may retort that if, given that she *did not* reflect further, she *could not have* reflected further, it is abusing words to say that she really could have done otherwise.

31 For a relatively clear and succinct statement about these matters by Kant himself, see the preface to the second edition of the *Critique of Pure Reason*, B xxiv–xxx (*Kant's Critique of Pure Reason*, trans. N. Kemp Smith [London: Macmillan, 1933], 26–9), and *The Moral Law* (translation by H.J. Paton of Kant's *Groundwork of the Metaphysics of Morals* [London: Hutchinson, 1958]), 67, 84, 90–1.

32 See Kant, *Critique of Practical Reason*, trans. L.W. Beck (New York: Liberal Arts Press, 1956), 126–39. Cf. S. Korner, *Kant* (Harmondsworth: Penguin Books, 1955), 136, 165–7. For Kant's view of religion in general, see *Religion Within the Limits of Reason Alone*, trans. T.M. Greene and H.H. Hudson (New York: Harper and Row, 1960).

33 Cf. Shadia Drury, *The Political Ideas of Leo Strauss* (New York: St Martin's Press, 1987). I am told by Professor David Jeffrey that the contemporary authorities in China want to have Christian morality instilled in young people without the

theology or eschatology which has traditionally been associated with it. But I wonder how far this is really a feasible project.

34 Matthew 5: 6.

35 Cf. Kai Nielsen, *Philosophy and Atheism* (Buffalo: Prometheus Books, 1985).

36 For arguments to the contrary, see A. Flew, *God, Freedom and Immortality* (Buffalo: Prometheus Books, 1984), chapters 1 to 5.

37 For the view that theism makes perfectly good sense, but is overwhelmingly likely to be false, see J.L. Mackie, *The Miracle of Theism* (Oxford: Clarendon Press, 1982). On the other side of the question, see Meynell, *Intelligible Universe*, also R. Swinburne, *The Existence of God* (Oxford: Clarendon Press, 1979).

38 Matthew 5: 4, 5, and 7.

39 This seems, in brief, to be Thomas Aquinas's argument for the immortality of the soul; cf. *Summa Contra Gentes*, 2, 49; F.C. Copleston, *Aquinas* (Harmondsworth: Penguin Books, 1955), 158–63.

40 Cf. Flew, *God, Freedom and Immorality*, chapters 8 to 11.

41 See Hugo Meynell, 'On Investigating the So-Called "Paranormal,"' in *Critical Reflections on the Paranormal*, ed. M. Stoeber and H. Meynell (Albany: State University of New York Press, 1995).

42 For a great deal to this effect, see Paul Kurtz, ed., *A Skeptic's Handbook of Parapsychology* (Buffalo: Prometheus Books, 1985).

43 In a brief account which is a model of succinct philosophical discussion, Roderick Chisholm argues (1) that we are responsible for many of our actions; (2) that our actions are caused; (3) that these convictions appear to be incompatible with one another. See 'Responsibility and Avoidability,' in Sidney Hook, ed., *Determinism and Freedom in the Age of Modern Science* (New York: Collier Books, 1961), 157–9. It is interesting that Flew seems to have changed quite recently from being a determinist-compatibilist (that is, maintaining that determinism is compatible with freedom in any sense that we should be seriously concerned about) to being an indeterminist-incompatibilist. Cf. Flew's *God, Freedom and Immortality*, chapter 7, and his 'The Legitimation of Factual Necessity,' in *Faith, Scepticism and Personal Identity*, ed. J.J. MacIntosh and H.A. Meynell (Calgary: University of Calgary Press, 1994), 113–15.

Chapter 5: Limits of Sociology

1 Cf. Wittgenstein, *On Certainty* (Oxford: Blackwell, 1969), 105, 410, 110, 204, 336, 63, 513, 517, 617. With regard to the title of Part II, it has occurred to me that many of the philosophers described are not Anglo-Saxon. But the fact remains that their sphere of influence is the Anglo-Saxon world. I prescind from the disputed question, as not directly relevant to my purposes here, of

whether Wittgenstein *really* meant what he *may* not wholly implausibly be taken to mean, and *has* been taken to mean.

2 Derek L. Phillips, *Wittgenstein and Scientific Knowledge: A Sociological Perspective* (London: Macmillan, 1977), 80, 200–1.

3 Ibid., 201–2. 'If there are indeed a variety of language-games, with different standards for truth and knowledge, does this not call into question *all* conceptions of truth and knowledge?'

4 D. Bloor, 'Wittgenstein and Mannheim on the Sociology of Mathematics,' *Studies in the History and Philosophy of Science* (1973), 173, 176, 184. Wittgenstein, *Remarks on the Foundations of Mathematics* (Oxford: Blackwell, 1956), I, 2.

5 Bloor, 'Wittgenstein and Mannheim,' 185, 177; D. Bloor, 'Popper's Mystification of Objective Knowledge,' in *Science Studies* (4) (1974), especially 75–6: 'To appraise an argument for validity is to apply the standards of a social group. It cannot be other, or more, than this because we have no access to other standards ... The objectivity of knowledge resides in its being the set of accepted beliefs of a social group ... The authority of truth is the authority of society.'

6 For example, *On Certainty*, 83, 204.

7 Cf. *On Certainty*, 110, 204.

8 Chapters 2 and 3 above.

9 R.M. White, 'Can Whether One Proposition Makes Sense Depend on the Truth of Another?,' in *Understanding Wittgenstein*, ed. G.N.A. Vesey (London: Macmillan, 1974), 25.

10 Wittgenstein, *Notebooks 1914–16* (Oxford: Blackwell, 1961), 53.

11 A. Kenny, 'The Ghost in the Tractatus,' in Vesey, ed., *Understanding Wittgenstein*, 12; citing Wittgenstein's *Philosophische Grammatik* (Oxford: Blackwell, 1969), 129; *The Blue and Brown Books* (Oxford: Blackwell, 1978), 54; *Philosophical Investigations* (Oxford: Blackwell, 1953), I, 251.

12 *Philosophische Grammatik*, 186; Kenny, 'Ghost in the Tractatus.'

13 Wittgenstein, *On Certainty*, 454, 114, 306, 369, 456, 486, 507, 125, 163, 337, 341; cf. Kenny, *Wittgenstein* (Harmondsworth: Penguin Books, 1973), 205–7.

14 Wittgenstein, *On Certainty*, 94. Cf. Kenny, *Wittgenstein*, 216–17. It is of crucial importance that, as Wittgenstein says, doubt and truth have a specifiable relation to grounds; what would *count*, he asks, as grounds for a grown man believing he lived in America when in fact he lived in Britain? (*On Certainty*, 71, 75; cf. Kenny, *Wittgenstein*, 218).

15 Cf. K. Marx and F. Engels, *On Religion* (Moscow: Foreign Language Publishing House, 1957), 25.

16 R.M. White, 'Can Whether One Proposition,' 28.

17 In this discussion of Wittgenstein, I have been greatly helped by talks with

Christopher Coope, Peter Geach, Ullin Place, George Ross, and Roger White; an unpublished essay by Br. Dunstan Jones, C.R., was also very suggestive.

18 The works referred to in the rest of this chapter are: S.B. Barnes, *Scientific Knowledge and Sociological Theory* (London: Routledge and Kegan Paul, 1974); D. Bloor, 'Wittgenstein and Mannheim on the Sociology of Mathematics,' in *Studies in the History and Philosophy of Science* 4 (1973): 173–91; D. Bloor, 'Popper's Mystification of Objective Knowledge,' in *Science Studies* 4 (1974): 65–76; D. Bloor, 'Rearguard Rationalism,' in *Isis*, 65 (1974): 249–53; and S.B. Barnes and D. Bloor, 'Is the Sociology of Knowledge Possible?,' a paper, unpublished when I had access to it, presented to a meeting of the British Society for the Philosophy of Science at Edinburgh in September 1973. At this point, see 'Is the Sociology of Knowledge Possible?' 2; 'Rearguard Rationalism,' 253; 'Wittgenstein and Manneheim,' 173–4.

19 Cf. below.

20 'Is the Sociology of Knowledge Possible?' 3–4, 8–9, 11; 'Popper's Mystification,' 66–7, 70, 75; 'Rearguard Rationalism,' 250; 'Wittgenstein and Mannheim,' 181–2, 184–5; *Scientific Knowledge*, 156. It should be noted that Barnes also assents to a view incompatible with this, which I believe to be correct, that justification in an unqualified sense may be approached asymptotically by justification according to social convention (*Scientific Knowledge*, 156).

21 'Is Sociology of Knowledge Possible?,' 12; *Scientific Knowledge*, 70, 154. Cf. Bloor's account of the 'materialist function' of the notion of truth in his *Knowledge and Social Imagery* (London: Routledge and Kegan Paul, 1976), 36–8. I do not think that the argument of this book modifies Bloor's position in a way relevant to my argument in this chapter.

22 It is *implied*, as I shall try to show, by those who claim that 'truth' and 'validity' are simply a function of social systems within which persons make statements and indulge in reasoning and argument, even when they insist that there is, all the same, a real world, independent of societies, characterized by some qualities and states of affairs rather than others.

23 For this term, cf. Bernard Lonergan, *Method in Theology* (London: Darton, Longman and Todd, 1971), 45, 114, 122, 233, 239, 243, 252, 289.

24 'Wittgenstein and Mannheim,' 175–6, 184.

25 For the conception of mutually irreducible 'forms of knowledge,' cf. P.H. Hirst, 'Liberal Education and the Nature of Knowledge,' in R.D. Archambault, ed., *Philosophical Analysis and Education* (London: Routledge and Kegan Paul, 1965), 113–38.

26 Cf. Lonergan, *Method in Theology*, chapter 1.

27 For these pitfalls on the way to knowledge, see Lonergan, *Insight: A Study of Human Understanding* (London: Longmans, Green, 1957), chapters 6 and 7.

28 Cf. below.

29 For a compulsively readable account of such behaviour among scientists, see A. de Grazia, ed., *The Velikovsky Affair* (London: Herbert Jenkins, 1966); also the first three papers in *Velikovsky Reconsidered* by the editors of *Pensee* (London: Herbert Jenkins, 1976).

30 See especially R. Crookall, *The Supreme Adventure* (Cambridge: James Clarke, 1975).

31 I have heard this view ascribed to Professor R.B. Braithwaite.

32 This is, in effect, the third suggestion made, and rejected, in Plato's *Theaetetus*; it appears to me essentially correct, as can be seen from the course of argument of this book.

33 On what it is to act well or badly, see above.

34 R. Bierstedt, introduction to Judith Willer's, *The Social Determinants of Knowledge* (Englewood Cliffs, NJ: Prentice-Hall, 1971); see also 4, 16, 141, 145.

35 *Scientific Knowledge*, 153–4. Barnes says that his position should not be taken as tending to impugn natural science ('Sociological Explanation and Natural Science,' in *European Journal of Sociology* 13 [1972]: 391). Certainly it does not impugn science just as an activity in which some members of some societies happen to engage, but it does impugn it as an enterprise concerned with finding out what is the case, and would have been the case even if there had been no scientists to investigate it.

Chapter 6: Primitives and Paradigms

1 D.Z. Phillips, 'Religion and Epistemology: Some Contemporary Confusions,' in *Australasian Journal of Philosophy* (1966): 322. I owe this citation to P.J. Sherry.

2 Winch, 'Understanding a Primitive Society,' in *American Philosophical Quarterly* (1964); reprinted in D.Z. Phillips, ed., *Religion and Understanding* (Oxford: Blackwell, 1967). My page references will be to the latter source.

3 The distinction between objective and subjective worlds is closely parallel to Anselm's distinction between what exists *in re* and what exists merely *in anima* (*Proslogion*, ii–iv; *Anselm of Canterbury*, ed. J. Hopkins and H.W. Richardson [New York: Edwin Mellen Press, 1974], 93–5).

4 Cf. Phillips's remark that some thinkers have created 'a false gap between the act of praying and the God to whom prayer is addressed' (*The Concept of Prayer* [London: Routledge and Kegan Paul, 1965], 189). Certainly there is no gap, if the only existence that God is deemed to have is in the subjective world of those who pray.

5 Winch explicitly disavows 'Protagorean relativism' ('Understanding a Primitive Society,' 12), but it is not clear to me how he can properly do so on his

own premises. If each culture has its own standards and criteria of truth, how does one consistently deny the same privilege to every group within a culture which according to the standards of that culture is deviant? Thus, on his own account, his treatment of European belief in witchcraft seems unduly hard (14). Surely this belief was and is less 'parasitic' on scientific and religious beliefs more characteristic of Europeans than were, for example, Galileo's theories in relation to the tradition within which he grew up.

6 This will, of course, be a matter of exercising the mental capacities distinguished in the first chapter. It is close to the 'comprehensively critical rationalism' advocated by W.W. Bartley on principles derived from the work of Karl Popper (cf. Bartley, *The Retreat to Commitment* [London: Chatto and Windus 1964]).

7 Cf. chapter 7 below.

8 Winch, 'Understanding a Primitive Society,' 30.

9 Ibid., 19.

10 Winch 'Understanding a Primitive Society,' 15.

11 Ibid., 22–4. That is, of course, from discourse claiming to describe what is actually so, as opposed to fairy stories, and so on.

12 Ibid., 34.

13 Ibid., 14.

14 Ibid., Cf. R.G. Collingwood, *The Principles of Art* (Oxford: Clarendon Press, 1963), 65–9.

15 Cf. *Religion and Understanding*, 1. I am grateful to Peter Preuss, for raising the point discussed in the next paragraph.

16 Thomas S. Kuhn, *The Structure of Scientific Revolutions* (Chicago: University of Chicago Press, 1962), 169.

17 Ibid., 7, 125–6.

18 Ibid., 13, 15; 4–5, chapter 3; 5–6, 24, 77; 5, 24; 39; 82, 145; 67–9; 70–1, chapters 6, 7; 12.

19 Kuhn does advert to this fact on pages 72 and 154, but does not appear to me to grasp its significance.

20 Kuhn, *Structure of Scientific Revolutions*, 57.

21 Ibid., 95.

22 Cf. Kuhn, *Structure of Scientific Revolutions*, 108–9.

23 I. Lakatos, 'Criticism and Methodology of Scientific Research Programmes,' in *Proceedings of the Aristotelian Society* (1968–9), 149–86. See especially 160–2.

24 For the scope and limits of Popper's account, see the following chapter.

25 Cf. Kuhn, *Structure of Scientific Revolutions*, 79.

26 Ibid., 161, 165.

27 Ibid., 4; cf. 93.

28 Ibid., 139.
29 B.J.F. Lonergan, *Insight: A Study of Human Understanding* (London: Longmans, Green, 1957), chapter 1; Wittgenstein, *The Blue and Brown Books* (Oxford: Blackwell, 1964), 44–5.
30 Ibid., 125–6.
31 Ibid., 166.
32 Ibid., 169.
33 Cf. A. Koestler, The *Case of the Midwife Toad* (London: Hutchinson, 1971); A. de Grazia, ed., *The Velikovsky Affair* (London: Sidgwick and Jackson, 1966).
34 Kuhn, *Structure of Scientific Revolutions*, 169–71.
35 For the argument of this paragraph, see Lonergan, op. cit., chapters 1–4, 12–14.
36 Kuhn, *Structure of Scientific Revolutions*, 172.

Chapter 7: Anarchy and Falsification

1 P.K. Feyerabend, *Against Method* (London: New Left Books, 1975), 11, 19, 38–9; cf. 41: 'Both the relevance and the refuting character of decisive facts can be established only with the help of other theories which ... are not in agreement with the law to be tested.'
2 Ibid., 19.
3 Feyerabend, 'Consolations for the Specialist,' in *Criticsm and the Growth of Knowledge*, ed. I. Lakatos and A. Musgrave (Cambridge: Cambridge University Press, 1970), 225. Cf. *Against Method*, 66, 76, 80.
4 'Consolations,' 215, 218; *Against Method*, 65–6, 143, 182ff; 153–5, 159; 14.
5 'Consolations,' 216. The reference is to the fourth edition of *The Logic of Scientific Discovery* (London: Hutchinson, 1961), 388.
6 *Against Method*, 14, 47, 18, 141, 171, 180, 189, 11, 35, 52, 175; 'Consolations,' 203, 209, 228, 224; cf. *Against Method*, 230: 'As regards the word "truth" we can at this stage only say that it certainly has people in a tizzy, but has not achieved much else.'
7 'Consolations,' 197, 198.
8 'Consolations,' 228; *Against Method*, 18, 14.
9 *Against Method*, 71, 81ff., 98, 112, 141, 143.
10 In fact, his view is that the search for truth may itself be a distraction from the scientific enterprise.
11 'Consolations,' 203.
12 'Virtually,' in that one might by chance, on some particular matter, come to state the truth without exercising any of these capacities. For example, in a

murder investigation, someone might correctly pick out the murderer after studying the pattern of tea leaves at the bottom of a cup, for all that detectives working with much assiduity and competence had failed to do so. But such possibilities by no means entail that the truth is not as a rule arrived at by exercise of the mental capacities alluded to.

13 'Consolations,' 203.

14 Cf. I. Lakatos, 'Criticism and the Methodology of Scientific Research Programmes,' in *Proceedings of the Aristotelian Society* (1968–9), 149–86.

15 Cf. Nigel Calder, *The Violent Universe* (New York: Penguin Books, 1975), 75, 79–80.

16 Chapter 3 above.

17 B. Lonergan, *Insight: A Study of Human Understanding* (London: Longmans, Green, 1957), 291.

18 Cf. Berkeley, *The Principles of Human Knowledge*, 105, in Berkeley, *A New Theory of Vision and Other Writings*, ed. A.D. Lindsay (London: E.J. Dent, 1910). Much the same view seems to be defended in our own time by Bas van Fraassen, who maintains that 'scientific activity is one of construction rather than discovery: construction of models that must be adequate to the phenomena, and not discovery of truth concerning the unobservable' (*The Scientific Image* [Oxford: Clarendon, 1980], 5).

19 Cf. 'Consolations,' 209.

20 Cf. chapter 1 above.

21 'The idea that the telescope shows the world as it really is leads to many difficulties. But the support it lends to, and received from, Copernicus is a hint that we might be moving in the right direction,' in that there may one day be found, in support of both, 'fully-fledged positive evidence' (*Against Method*, 158).

22 Cf. *Against Method*, 165–6.

23 I believe that this remains so, for all that Popper professes to be hostile to such 'foundations,' apparently as redolent of the kind of attempt to 'justify' one's position which is anathema to a conscientious falsificationist.

24 Cf. Bryan Magee, *Popper* (Glasgow: Collins, 1973), 43; Popper, *Objective Knowledge* (Oxford: Clarendon, 1972), 12.

25 Magee, *Popper*, 45–6. Cf. Popper, *Conjectures and Refutations* (London: Routledge, 1972), 37–8; *The Logic of Scientific Discovery* (London: Hutchinson, 1961), 278.

26 Popper, *Objective Knowledge*, 12, 14, 21.

27 Cf. note 23 above.

28 This has been suggested to me in conversation by Bryan Magee.

29 Popper, *Objective Knowledge*, 39–42.

30 Cf. P.F. Strawson, *The Bounds of Sense* (London: Methuen, 1966), 250.

31 *First Meditation.*

32 Of course, as Popper rightly points out, this is not 'probability' in the sense at issue in the 'probability calculus' (*Objective Knowledge*, 40). The same point was made by Bertrand Russell; see A.J. Ayer, *Russell* (London: Collins, 1972), 96.

33 Perhaps the whole business of attending to data, asking questions, coming to conclusions, and reflecting on this process might (at a pinch) be said to be a matter of 'experience' in a very extended sense, in which case one could be said to come to know such things by experience.

34 This is, of course, the usual, and in my opinion quite justified, objection to Kant's conception of the *Ding an sich.* For a modern work which repeats this error of Kant's, see Milton K. Munitz, *The Mystery of Existence* (New York: New York University Press, 1974).

35 Popper, *Objective Knowledge*, 28.

36 Ibid., 27–8.

37 Cf., for example, B xx of the *Critique of Pure Reason* (*Immanual Kant's Critique of Pure Reason*, trans. N. Kemp Smith [London and Basingstoke, Macmillan, 1978], 24).

38 David Hume, *Treatise of Human Nature*, I, III, xiv; *Enquiry Concering Human Understanding*, section V, part I.

39 Complete scepticism must ensue, if we do not judge it to be certain that whatever method we have determined upon at least tends to get at the truth to a degree that rival methods do not. This would not be inconsistent with the truth being arrived at by way of exception through arbitrary means (e.g., the contemplation of tea leaves or the entrails of birds) where the application of appropriate methods had failed.

40 Popper, *Objective Knowledge*, 29.

41 Cf. S. Haack, 'Two Fallibilists in Search of the Truth,' I, in *Proceedings of the Aristotelian Society*, supplementary vol. II (1977), 68.

42 K. Kolenda, 'Two Fallibilists,' II, 85.

43 Popper, *Objective Knowledge*, 86.

44 Haack, 'Two Fallibilists,' I, 86.

45 Kolenda, 'Two Fallibilists,' II, 85. Cf. p. 92: 'Percepts are visual data, perceptual judgments are thoughts. The former are "absolutely dumb" (Peirce), "lifeless" (Wittgenstein), the latter are interpreted, understood. To ponder these remarks, by both philosophers, is to be drawn away from the idea of a correspondence of thought to reality.'

46 A. Adjukiewicz, *Problems and Theories of Philosophy* (Cambridge: Cambridge University Press, 1975), 11.

47 S. Hampshire, *Thought and Action* (London: Chatto and Windus, 1965), 39.

48 Popper, *Objective Knowledge*, 47.

Chapter 8: The Self-Immolation of Scientism

1 W.C. Sellars, *Science, Perception and Reality* (London: Routledge and Kegan Paul, 1963), 173; 140, 161; 41ff; 1.
2 Cf. Ibid., 14, 142, 144–6.
3 Ibid., 143.
4 For ingenious discussion of examples of this kind, and convincing argument for the claim that there are sense-data, see J.R. Smythies, *The Analysis of Perception* (London: Routledge and Kegan Paul, 1956), 70ff.
5 Sellars, *Science, Perception and Reality*, 170.
6 See Aquinas, *Disputations*, X *de Veritate*, 6; *Summa Theologica*, I, lxxix, 4; lxxxvii, 1. Thomas Gilby, *St. Thomas Aquinas: Philosophical Texts* (London: Oxford University Press, 1951), 627, 645, 662.
7 See B. Lonergan, *Collection* (London: Darton, Longman and Todd, 1967), 142.
8 Ibid., 143–6.
9 See Anthony Kenny, *Aquinas* (Oxford: Oxford University Press, 1980), 79–81.
10 Sellars, *Science, Perception and Reality*, 170.
11 Ibid., 4–5.
12 Karl Popper would not like this way of talking, but I believe the disagreement between this position and his would be merely verbal. Instead of 'verification,' he would speak of 'corroboration.'
13 Sellars, *Science, Perception and Reality*, 41, 31, 53, 54, 57; cf. 199–200.
14 Ibid., 58–59.
15 Ibid., 52, 57, 59.
16 Cf. Ibid., 42.
17 For an account of idealism which makes these distinctions with admirable clarity, see H.B. Acton, 'Idealism,' in *Encyclopaedia of Philosophy*, vol. 4, 110f.
18 Cf. *Summa Theologica*, I, ii, 3.
19 Rorty, *Philosophy and the Mirror of Nature* (Princeton University Press, 1979), 280–1.
20 A. Tarski, 'The Semantic Conception of Truth,' in *Logic, Semantics, Metamathematics* [Oxford: Clarendon Press, 1956].
21 Rorty, *Philosophy and the Mirror of Nature*, 174.
22 Of course, none of the classical representatives of idealism (Berkeley, Schelling, or Hegel) was quite so extreme as this.
23 Rorty, *Philosophy and the Mirror of Nature*, 211, chapter 5.
24 Ibid., 168.
25 Ibid., 4, 6, 8, 12, 165.
26 Ibid., 168, 169, 170, 173, 174, 183.
27 Ibid., 175, 177, 178, 181.

28 Ibid., 179, 182.

29 Ibid., 184, 187, 189, 190, 192.

30 Ibid., 168, 171, 202.

31 Ibid., 5, 6, 9, 11–12.

32 See Sellars, *Science, Perception and Reality*, 173.

33 Cf. Rorty, *Philosophy and the Mirror of Nature*, 183.

34 Ibid., 178.

35 I have referred to the work of Quine on a number of occasions in this and earlier chapters; so it seems worthwhile to add a brief note here about the bearing of his philosophy on the questions discussed in this book. Quine's attempt to construct a 'naturalized' epistemology, which is simply a branch of empirical psychology, must founder for the following reasons. An empirical psychology can help explain to us how we do happen to think, not how we ought to think if we are to get to know the truth about things, which is the business of epistemology. If empirical psychology favours the thoughts and opinions of Einstein over those of a flat earther, it transgresses its proper bounds. To provide norms for thinking, on the other hand, is to get involved in that very 'first philosophy' which Quine repudiates. The point is nicely made by Jonathan Dancy: 'Traditional epistemology studied the relation between data and belief, between evidence and theory. It attempted to show how our beliefs (for instance, in an external world) are justified by the data from which they spring; how our scientific theories are justified by the evidence which supports them. Is this study to be abandoned and replaced or can it be continued within the new perspective? Quine seems to vacillate between these alternatives. Sometimes he suggests that the old questions smack of first philosophy, and that anyway the attempt to discover a relation between evidence and theory which would make the theory justified has proved to be unsuccessful. Why not then, he asks, simply study how we do go about moving from our data to the formulation of belief? This factual study, squarely within the bounds of psychology, is what he calls naturalized epistemology. It leaves aside justification and considers only the genetic, causal questions. We cease to worry about the gap between evidence and theory, and study instead the causal relations between the two.' (*Contemporary Epistemology* [Oxford: Blackwell, 1985], 235). The same general lesson is to be learned from Quine's efforts in this direction as from Sellars's; all attempts to deal with properly epistemological problems in physicalistic terms are inevitably doomed to failure.

Chapter 9: Consciousness and Existence: Husserl and Heidegger

1 See E. Pivcevic, *Husserl and Phenomenology* (London: Hutchinson, 1970), 12–13,

20. 'Generally speaking,' as Pivcevic says, 'the method of phenomenological reduction is a means of detecting what is constitutive and essential in our cognitive relationship with the world' (65). In extenuation of my frequent references to Pivcevic's book in what follows, I should say that I have found this author as admirable in conveying clearly and distinctly what seems to be implied by Husserl's 'labyrinthine prose' (74), as in stating the *prima facie* objections to it.

2 See Husserl, 'Philosophy as Rigorous Science,' in *Phenomenology and the Crisis of Philosophy* (New York: Harper and Row 1965), 74–5. *Cartesian Meditations* (The Hague: Nijhoff, 1960), 5.

3 The latter was true of Husserl himself, at least towards the end of his career: 'To bring latent reason to the understanding of its own possibilities and thus to bring to insight the possibility of metaphysics as a true possibility – this is the only way to put metaphysics or universal philosophy on the strenuous road to realization' (*The Crisis of European Science and Transcendental Phenomenology* [Evanston: Northwestern University Press, 1970], 15.)

4 Pivcevic, *Husserl*, 17.

5 According to Husserl, the positivist's preoccupation with sense-data makes her miss the essentially 'intentional' character of mental life, that is, the fact that sensations, concepts and so on are *of* and *about* things. 'Even Hume says (and how could be avoid it?): impressions *of*, perceptions *of*, trees, stones, etc.' (*Crisis*, 242). Cf. *Cartesian Meditations*, 33.

6 Pivcevic, *Husserl*, 19–20, 40–2. On Frege's charge against Husserl that the latter was guilty of 'psychologism' and the manner in which Husserl later took this to heart, see Pivcevic, *Husserl*, 30–5.

7 *Phenomenology*, 78–9.

8 Husserl, *Logische Untersuchungen*, vol. II; quoted in Pivcevic, *Husserl*, 42.

9 'What was lacking, and what is still lacking, is the actual self-evidence through which he who knows and accomplishes can give himself an account ... of the implications of meaning which are closed off through sedimentation or traditionalization – i.e., of the constant presuppositions of his (own) constructions, concepts, propositions, theories' (*Crisis*, 52).

10 Husserl, *Formale und Transzendentale Logik*; quoted in Pivcevic, *Husserl*, 43–4.

11 Pivcevic, *Husserl*, 46–7, 49, 51.

12 On 'essences,' see *Phenomenology*, 111.

13 Ibid., 115: 'The whole thing ... depends on one's seeing and making entirely one's own the truth that just as immediately as one can hear a sound, so one can intuit an "essence" – the essence "sound," the essence "appearance of thing," the essence "apparition," etc.' (*Phenomenology and the Crisis of Philosophy*, 115). In the first volume of the *Ideen*, Husserl writes of 'phenomenology,

whose only aim is to be a doctrine of essences in the framework of pure intuition' (*Phenomenology*, 93, note).

14 *Logische Untersuchungen*, vol. II, 1; Pivcevic, *Husserl*, 62.

15 Descartes is described by Husserl as 'the primal founder not only of the modern idea of objectivistic rationalism but also of the transcendental motif which explodes it' (*Crisis*, 73). He adds, 'Even today, and perhaps especially today, everyone who would think for himself ought, it seems to me, to study these first Meditations (of Descartes) in the utmost depth, not being frightened off by the appearance of primitiveness, by the well-known use of the new ideas for the paradoxical and basically wrong proofs of the existence of God, or by many other obscurities and ambiguities – and also not being too quickly comforted by one's own refutations' (*Crisis*, 74–5).

16 In *Crisis*, Husserl writes of 'a sort of *radical, skeptical epoché* which places in question all (one's) hitherto existing convictions, which forbids in advance any judgmental use of them, forbids taking any position as to their validity or invalidity. Once in his life every philosopher must proceed in this way ... Prior to the epoché "his philosophy" is to be treated like any other prejudice' (76).

17 'We do not easily overcome the inborn habit of living and thinking according to the naturalistic attitude, and thus of naturalistically adulterating the psychical' (*Phenomenology and the Crisis of Philosophy*, 109).

18 My italics. Pivcevic, *Husserl*, 70–2. Cf. *Cartesian Meditations*, 21, 24.

19 Pivcevic, *Husserl*, 69–70, 73, 82.

20 The trouble with descriptive psychology in its usual sense is that it must by its very nature overlook the norms essentially implicit in knowledge. How people happen to think, and why they happen to think as they do, is one thing; how they *ought* to think if they are to get to know the truth about things, and *why* they should think in this way if they are to do so, is another. See *Phenomenology*, 88, 92, 102, 119.

21 'In so far as phenomenological investigation is essence investigation and is thus a priori in the authentic sense, it takes into account all the justified motives of apriorism' (*Phenomenology*, 121).

22 This last is Pivcevic's judgment, which I shall assume to be broadly correct (*Husserl*, 76–7). 'If knowledge theory will ... investigate the problems of the relationship between consciousness and being, it can have before its eyes only being as the correlate of consciousness, as something 'intended' after the manner of consciousness; as perceived, remembered, expected, represented pictorially, imagined, identified, distinguished, believed, ... evaluated, etc.' (*Phenomenology*, 89). On the virtues and limitations of Kant, see *Crisis* 91–3, 97, 103.

23 *Ideen*, I; quoted in Pivcevic, *Husserl*, 77.

24 Pivcevic, *Husserl*, 74–8, 80.
25 It may thus reasonably, if unkindly, be said that the so-called problem of other minds is an artefact of empiricism.
26 Cf. *Insight*, chapter 8.
27 In chapter 19 of *Insight*, it is argued that the intelligibility of the universe is only fully to be explained if God exists. Husserl also sees a connection between the question of God and the intelligibility of the universe (*Crisis*, 288–9).
28 For 'generalized empirical method,' as Lonergan's term for his own basic philosophical procedure, see *Insight*, 243.
29 *Insight*, chapter 11. With Lonergan's phrase 'generalised empirical method,' one may compare Husserl's remark about phenomenologists, 'We are the true empiricists.'
30 Cf. Pivcevic, *Husserl*, 84.
31 *Insight*, chapters 2 to 4.
32 The present discussion may be regarded as complementary to that of William Ryan in his 'Intentionality in Edmund Husserl and Bernard Lonergan,' *International Philosophical Quarterly*, 13, no. 2 (June 1973): 173–90.
33 Martin Heidegger, *Being and Time*; cited by David F. Krell, *Martin Heidegger: Basic Writings* (New York: Harper and Row, 1977), 47.
34 Heidegger, *Being and Time*; Krell, *Heidegger*, 48. Cf. Heidegger, *Being and Time* (London: SCM Press, 1962), 36–40.
35 Cf. Krell, *Heidegger*, 'Introduction,' 19, 21, 13. Heidegger, 'What Is Metaphysics?'; Krell, *Heidegger*, 95–6.
36 Cf. Walter Biemel, *Martin Heidegger* (London: Routledge and Kegan Paul, 1977), 8–9; Krell, *Heidegger*, 31. On the alleged errors of Descartes, see *Being and Time*, 123–33.
37 Heidegger, *On Time and Being* (New York: Harper and Row, 1972), 79; Krell, *Heidegger*, 14.
38 Heidegger, *On Time and Being*, 79; Krell, *Heidegger*, 13–14.
39 Krell, *Heidegger*, 18; cf. Heidegger, 'On the Essence of Truth'; Krell, *Heidegger*, 117ff.; and Heidegger, 'The Origin of the Work of Art'; Krell, *Heidegger*, 173ff. See also *Being and Time*, 257–73.
40 Cf. the scholastic tag to the effect that truth is 'adaequatio rei et intellectus,' or 'adequation of thing and intellect.'
41 Heidegger, 'On the Essence of Truth'; Krell, *Heidegger*, 115.
42 Krell, *Heidegger*, 122, 124, 125, 134, 127–8.
43 Krell, *Heidegger*, 115; 20, 131; 134–6; 138. On the 'they,' cf. *Being and Time*, 163–8.
44 Krell, *Heidegger*, 145; cf. *Being and Time*, sections 15–18.
45 Heidegger, 'The Origin of the Work of Art'; Krell, *Heidegger*, 153. For a sketch

of the development and alleged distortion of Greek ontology through the history of European thought, see *Being and Time*, 43–4.

46 Krell, *Heidegger*, 154.

47 Ibid., 155–6. One may compare the aspersions of 'linguistic philosophers,' notably J.L. Austin, on the 'sense-data' postulated as direct objects of sensation by representatives of an earlier stage of analytical philosophy. Cf. Austin, *Sense and Sensibilia* (Oxford: Clarendon Press, 1962); and chapter 3 above.

48 Heidegger, 'The Origin of the Work of Art'; Krell, *Heidegger*, 158–60.

49 Krell, *Heidegger*, 161, 165, 166.

50 Krell, *Heidegger*, 169, 170.

51 Heidegger, 'The End of Philosophy and the Task of Thinking'; Krell, *Heidegger*, 382.

52 Cf. note 38 above.

53 For the physicists and cosmologists, one might refer to the writings collected in K. Wilber's *Quantum Questions* (Boulder: Shambala, 1984); and for the zoologists, to K. Lorenz's *Studies in Animal and Human Behaviour* (London: Methuen, 1971).

Chapter 10: Deconstruction and the Ubiquity of Power

1 See H. Staten, *Wittgenstein and Derrida* (Lincoln: University of Nebraska Press 1984), 124, 129.

2 Ibid., 129.

3 Cf. Derrida, *Limited Inc.* (Baltimore: Johns Hopkins University Press, 1977), 66; J. Culler, *On Deconstruction: Theory and Criticism after Structuralism* (Ithaca: Cornell University Press, 1982), 93.

4 With regard to the former interpretation, one can hardly wonder at Derrida's admission that the future glimpsed by deconstruction 'can only be proclaimed or presented as a sort of monstrosity' (*Of Grammatology* [Baltimore: John Hopkins University Press, 1976], 5; Culler, *On Deconstruction*, 158).

5 Derrida notes that the apparent 'effacement of the signifier' in speech, which is a prime target of deconstruction, is 'the condition of the very idea of truth' (*Of Grammatology*, 20).

6 As Culler puts it, exercises in deconstruction 'do not escape the logocentric premises they undermine; and there is no reason to believe that a theoretical enterprise could ever free itself from those premises' (*On Deconstruction*, 7). The critic is left 'in a position not of sceptical detachment but of unwarrantable involvement' (*On Deconstruction*, 88).

7 As well as Derrida's allusions to 'theologocentrism,' the following is notable. In elucidating texts, 'the motif of homogeneity, the theological motif par

excellence, is what must be destroyed' (*Positions* [Chicago: University of Chicago Press, 1981], 64; Culler, *On Deconstruction*, 135).

8 *The Nature of Aesthetic Value* (London: Macmillan, 1986), 39–45.

9 This, of course, is a recurrent theme of *Of Grammatology*. Cf. also Derrida, *Dissemination* (Chicago: University of Chicago Press, 1981), 158; and Culler, *On Deconstruction*, 89.

10 Though Plato's point in the *Phaedrus* seems to be the limited and reasonable one that a speaker can modify his discourse at short notice for the benefit of the listener, in a manner that is not possible with what is committed to writing. Cf. *Phaedrus*, 275d.

11 See R. Rorty, *Consequences of Pragmatism* (Minneapolis: University of Minnesota Press, 1982), chapter 6.

12 Cf. Culler, *On Deconstruction*, 91.

13 Aristotle, *Ethics*, IV, 7.

14 Cf. the quotation from Derrida's 'The Conflict of the Faculties,' in Culler, *On Deconstruction*, 156.

15 Derrida refers to 'arche-writing' in *Of Grammatology* (for example, 128).

16 Culler, *On Deconstruction*, 86.

17 Culler disarmingly remarks that sawing off the branch on which one is oneself sitting is a physically perfectly possible operation (*On Deconstruction*, 149). But perhaps a closer analogy is with the would-be mass murderer who inadvertently shoots himself before turning his machine gun on his intended victims.

18 Culler, *On Deconstruction*, 86.

19 Nietzsche, *The Will to Power*, cited Culler, *On Deconstruction*, 86.

20 Culler, *On Deconstruction*, 86, 88.

21 Culler, *On Deconstruction*, 88.

22 Derrida, *Of Grammatology*, 12; Culler, *On Deconstruction*, 92–3.

23 Derrida, *Positions*, 26. Cf. Culler, *On Deconstruction*, 100.

24 Cf. Wittgenstein's classical attack on the notion of a 'private language' in the *Philosophical Investigations* (Oxford: Blackwell, 1958).

25 Cf. Derrida, *Speech and Phenomena and Other Essays on Husserl's Theory of Signs* (Evanston: Northwestern University Press, 1973).

26 His own protest that he has been 'trying, explicitly and tirelessly ..., for thirty years,' to refute charges of nihilism, scepticism, or relativism, seems to me to carry no conviction. See J. Derrida, *Points ... Interviews, 1974–1994* (Stanford: Stanford University Press, 1995), 402.

27 Though it would be wrong to assume uncritically, as so many do, that this last form of oppression is entirely or even virtually a one-way street. See Warren Farrell, *The Myth of Male Power* (New York: Simon and Schuster, 1993).

28 Jacques Derrida, *The Post Card* (Chicago: University of Chicago Press, 1987), 506.

29 As John Raven puts it, forms are 'objects of knowledge, apprehended by thought, not senses' (*Plato's Thought in the Making* [Cambridge: Cambridge University Press, 1965], 251). See chapter 12 below.

30 Derrida, *Writing and Difference*; quoted by Culler in 'Jacques Derrida,' in *Structuralism and Since*, ed. J. Sturrock (Oxford: Oxford University Press, 1979), 175.

31 M. Foucault, *Power/Knowledge* (Brighton: Harvester Press, 1980), 93, 96.

32 Ibid., 47

33 Ibid., 14, 15, 47, 17, 20, 39.

34 Ibid., 27, 29–30, 2.

35 Ibid., 131, 83, 130.

36 My italics.

37 Foucault, *Power/Knowledge*, 80–3.

38 London: Tavistock Publications, 1967.

39 Foucault, *Power/Knowledge*, 9.

40 The term 'corroboration,' characteristic of the writing of Sir Karl Popper, seems among the best to characterize whatever relation it is that the relevant experience has to scientific theories. A theory is 'corroborated' to the extent that, while it might very well have been falsified by such experience, in fact, it is not so. Popper argues that the theories of Einstein, for example, meet this requirement, in a way that those of Freud and Marx do not. Cf. Popper, *Objective Knowledge* (Oxford: Clarendon Press, 1972), 17–20, and chapter 7 above.

41 I disapprove of the term 'knowledges,' favoured as it is by the translator of *Power/Knowledge* and by many English-speaking sociologists and anthropologists. The usage tends to obliterate what seems to me the all-important distinction between socially approved systems of belief as such, and socially approved systems of belief which enshrine cognitive authenticity to such an extent that they are likely to be true, or at least to approximate to the truth.

42 Cf. R.D. Laing's wonderful books, *The Divided Self* (Harmondsworth: Penguin Books, 1965) and (with A. Esterson) *The Families of Schizophrenics* (London: Tavistock Publications, 1964).

Chapter 11: An Unstable Compromise

1 Habermas, *Theory of Communicative Action* (Boston: Beacon Press, 1984), 1–2, xii.

2 Ibid., 4–5, 229–31.

3 Ibid., 8–11. Cf. also Habermas, *Knowledge and Human Interests* (London: Heinemann, 1972), 195–6.

4 Habermas, *Theory of Communicative Action*, 16, 19, 21. On the significance and limits of Freud for 'therapeutic critique,' see *Knowledge and Human Interests*, 214–85.

5 *The Philosophical Discourse of Modernity* (Cambridge: MIT Press, 1987), 338.

6 Habermas, *Theory of Communicative Action*, 23, 33–4, 36, 38.

7 Ibid., 39, 47–50.

8 Ibid., 50–1, 214.

9 Ibid., 55, 61, 65–6, 74.

10 Ibid., 109, 132, 137–8.

11 The usual objections by philosophers to this kind of grounding of moral judgments can be met by the consideration that the fact that goodness cannot be precisely defined in terms of happiness and universalizability does not entail that it is not largely a matter of them. Cf. H. Meynell, *Freud, Marx and Morals* (New York: Barnes and Noble, 1981), chapter 6; and chapter 4 above.

12 Obviously, this point needs arguing at much greater length, and I have no space to do this here. See my *The Intelligible Universe* (New York: Barnes and Noble, 1982), chapters 3 and 4.

13 *Posterior Analytics*, II, 2, 89b 36ff.

14 In *Posterior Analytics*, II, 1. Cf. B. Lonergan, *Verbum: Word and Idea in Aquinas* (London: Darton, Longman and Todd, 1968), 13.

15 Cf. Lonergan, 'Isomorphism of Thomist and Scientific Thought,' in *Collection* (London: Darton, Longman and Todd, 1967).

16 Cf. Thomas Aquinas, *Summa Theologica*, passim.

17 Francis Bacon, *Novum Organum*, I, 64.

18 Though not so much by Aristotle himself, whose practice, as evinced for example in the biological works, is an improvement on his precept as set out in the *Posterior Analytics*, where science strictly speaking is held to be a matter of deduction from self-evident first principles. See chapter 13 below.

19 I believe that it is not science as such, but science as thus misunderstood, which gives rise to that *Entzauberung*, that taking of the wonder and magic out of the world, which Max Weber thought was a necessary consequence of the progress of reason.

20 Richard L. Purtill, 'Chesterton, the Wards, the Sheeds, and the Catholic Revival,' in *G.K. Chesterton and C.S. Lewis: The Riddle of Joy*, ed. M.H. Macdonald and A.A. Tadie (Grand Rapids: Eerdmans, 1989), 30.

21 According to Kant, we should always act dutifully for the sake of duty. On the other hand, we ought to believe that ultimately happiness will be apportioned to virtue, which can only happen if the soul survives death and if there is a just and omnipotent God. See *Religion Within the Limits of Reason Alone* (New York:

Harper Torchbooks, 1960).

22 In *The Holy Family.* Cf. *On Religion: Writings by K. Marx and F. Engels* (Moscow: Foreign Languages Publishing House, 1957), 67.

23 See Habermas, 'Transcendence from Within, Transcendence in This World,' in *Habermas, Modernity, and Public Theology*, ed. D.S. Browning and Francis Schussler Fiorenza (New York: Crossroad, 1992), 226. I am grateful to Professor Leslie Armour for drawing my attention to this work.

24 Habermas, 'Transcendence,' 238, 231, 224, 233–5. Habermas politely but trenchantly criticizes some proposed reductions of this sort.

25 Ibid., 233. '[I]t could be said that faith is protected against a radical problematization by its being rooted in cult.' For the different forms of validation distinguished by Habermas, see above.

26 Ibid., 240, 239.

27 *Is Christianity True?* (Washington: Catholic University of America Press, 1994), especially chapters 3 and 4.

28 Habermas, 'Transendence,' 228.

29 Cf. the discussion of Popper's views in chapter 7 above.

30 Habermas, 'Transendence,' 228.

31 Cf. the powerful scene in Lewis's *The Silver Chair* (London: Geoffrey Bles, 1953), where a witch in the underworld weaves a spell to make her hearers believe there is no upper world.

32 See Basil Mitchell, 'Faith and the Limitations of Open-Mindedness,' in *Faith, Scepticism and Personal Identity*, ed. J. MacIntosh and H. Meynell (Calgary: University of Calgary Press, 1994).

33 Anselm in the *Proslogion* (2 to 4) more or less gets away with it, but I cannot think of another instance.

34 They are trenchantly attacked by Habermas in *The Philosophical Discourse of Modernity*, 336–8.

Chapter 12: How Right Plato Was

1 What is essential to 'forms' as I shall be concerned with them is well caught in John Raven's phrase: they are 'objects of knowledge, apprehended by thought, not senses' (*Plato's Thought in the Making* [Cambridge: Cambridge University Press, 1965], 251).

2 A.E. Taylor, *Plato: The Man and His Work* (London: Methuen, 1960), 508. Aristotle, *Metaphysics*, A 987b. Readers may be surprised at my dependence on Taylor's work in this chapter and Randall's in the next. As I am not a specialist in ancient philosophy, competent surveys of the work of Plato and Aristotle were very much to my purpose. Of course, neither book is up-to-date, but I was not

mainly interested in these authors as exegetes, and, in any case, I have yet to learn that older authorities are necessarily worse than newer ones.

3 *Meno*, 72a; Taylor, *Plato*, 132.

4 *Meno*, 72b–e, 74a, 73a–b; *Euthyphro*, 5d, 6d, 11a; Taylor, *Plato*, 132–3, 149.

5 Wittgenstein, *Philosophical Investigations* (Oxford: Blackwell, 1958), part I, para. 66. Cf. Aristotle, *Nicomachean Ethics*, A 1096a.

6 Taylor, *Plato*, 290.

7 *Republic*, vi, 510 d–e; Taylor, *Plato*, 290–1.

8 *Phaedo*, 100d.

9 Taylor, *Plato*, 202. Aristotle remarks, apropos of Plato and the Pythagoreans, 'what the participation or imitation of the Forms could be they left an open question' (*Metaphysics*, 987b).

10 Taylor, 350–1.

11 *Parmenides*, 130 b–e; Taylor, *Plato*, 354, 351.

12 There is a sense, of course, in which no hypothesis in science is ever 'verified.' The more fastidious might prefer 'corroborated through survival of attempts to falsify, and actual falsification of suggested alternatives.' Cf. chapter 7 above.

13 Aristotle says that Plato derived from Cratylus, and retained to his old age the view 'that all sensible things are ever in a state of flux, and that there is no knowledge about them' (*Metaphysics* A 987a).

14 *Metaphysics*, A 987b. How mistaken Aristotle turned out to be on the mathematical issue is illustrated by the dictum of the nineteenth-century chemist A.E.B. de Chancourtois that 'the properties of elements are the properties of numbers.' This has been remarked to be very prophetic in the light of still later developments in theoretical chemistry ('Periodic Law,' in *Encyclopaedia Britannica*, 15th ed.). For all the *prima facie* absurdity of the attempts by the Pythagorean Eurytus to assign numbers to man, horse, and other things (Taylor, *Plato*, 354), he was evidently on to something.

15 Taylor, *Plato*, 354.

16 R.M. Hare, *Plato* (Oxford: Oxford University Press, 1982), 36–7.

17 See especially Richard Rorty, *Philosophy and the Mirror of Nature* (Princeton: Princeton University Press, 1979). Either Rorty is presenting his views as the most reasonable available account of the relevant data or he is not. If he is, he is implicitly committed to the foundationalist view that one tends to get at the truth about things by giving the most reasonable account of the relevant data. If he is not, it seems pointless to pay any attention to him. Cf. chapter 8 above.

18 The *Phaedo* argues to the immortality of the soul largely from its relation to the forms, and consequent transcendence of mere sensible appearances.

19 *Theaetetus*, 202C.

20 The earlier Platonic dialogues apply this kind of inquiry to the problem of the nature of courage (*Laches*), friendship (*Lysis*), piety (*Euthyphro*), and so on.

21 *Meno*, 98a.

22 *Republic*, vi, 511b–c; Taylor, *Plato*, 292.

23 Taylor, *Plato*, 294. Cf. *Timaeus*, 29b–d.

24 Taylor, *Plato*, 294.

25 *Symposium*, 210d; *Republic*, vi, 508b–509b; vii, 532a. Taylor, *Plato*, 286.

26 *Republic*, vi, 508a–c.

27 Cf. Taylor, *Plato*, 287.

28 *Timaeus*, 28a–31b; *Laws*, x, 889a–907a.

29 This problem haunted Schelling through much of his career. See A. White, *Schelling: An Introduction to the System of Freedom* (New Haven: Yale University Press, 1983).

30 A.N. Whitehead is notable among modern philosophers who have put asunder those elements of the Platonic theology which Christians and others have joined toether. See *Process and Reality* (Cambridge: Cambridge University Press, 1929), part 5, chapter 2.

31 Any thesis or assumption about what exists in the last analysis – matter but not mind, mind but not matter, sense-data but neither mind nor matter, and so on – is 'metaphysical' in this sense. It has lately been the fashion too often to make unexamined and unjustified assumptions of this kind, on the basis of which one may attack or, even worse, sarcastically dismiss opposed positions on these matters as 'metaphysical.' See chapter 4 above.

32 I have to thank John Baker for much helpful conversation on the topic of this chapter.

Chapter 13: On Being an Aristotelian

1 J.H. Randall, in his *Aristotle* (New York: Columbia University Press, 1960) writes of the human being's 'nousing' of the universe on the Aristotelian view. I find the terminology attractive, but have finally decided not to use it. On my use of Randall's book, see note 2 of the last chapter.

2 Bernard Lonergan once suggested that, although all human beings understand and judge, only Aristotelians take philosophical advantage of the fact that they do so (*Verbum: Word and Idea in Aquinas* [London: Darton, Longman and Todd, 1968]).

3 On this matter, Plato seems to have come closer to the truth. Cf. Plato, *Timaeus*, 29b–d; cited in A.E. Taylor, *Plato: The Man and His Work* (London: Methuen, 1960), 294, 441. This is not to deny, of course, that the *Timaeus* contains outrageous evolutionary and astronomical theories.

4 B 2, 4, 6, and 8 are obvious points of continuity with Plato's teaching. In the
 light of them one can understand Aristotle's claim, in the dialogue *On Philosophy*, that he himself rather than Speusippus, in spite of the latter's role as
 Plato's official successor as head of the Academy, was Plato's true successor.
 Cf. Randall, *Aristotle*, 18.

5 See Francis Bacon, *Novum Organum*, I, 64; cited by Robin Attfield, *God and the
 Secular* (Cardiff: University College of Cardiff Press, 1978), 20.

6 *Topics*, I, 1; 100b 23–4; Randall, *Aristotle*, 38.

7 *Topics*, I, 24–6. Randall's book can be used as an excellent summary of
 Aristotle's thought, so far as one can shut out the sound of the grinding of
 axes. He is enamoured of the view of W. Jaeger that Aristotle developed from
 a thoroughgoing Platonist with a taste for religion and a *penchant* for system
 into an a-religious and non-systematic empirical scientist. Randall is inclined
 to date the elements of the corpus accordingly, yet he engagingly admits the
 very considerable, and to my mind, quite conclusive evidence against so
 doing.

8 Randall, *Aristotle*, 41. *Posterior Analytics*, I, 2, 71b 20–2; I, 4, 73a 20–4.

9 Randall, *Aristotle*, 42. On the manner in which a range of opinions may contribute to the truth, see *Metaphysics*, II, 1, 993b 1–4 (Randall, *Aristotle*, 53).

10 Randall, *Aristotle*, 33; *Posterior Analytics*, I, 28, 87a 38 – 87b 4.

11 Aristotle was not, of course, a determinist, as is made clear by his discussion of
 luck and chance in *Physics*, II 5–6; but his ideal of science strictly speaking is
 deterministic. It seems that he held that such science is not applicable to the
 whole of nature.

12 *Posterior Analytics*, II, 1. Aristotle first distinguishes four types of question (89b
 22–6), and then divides these into two pairs (31–40). See Lonergan, *Verbum*,
 12–13.

13 Cf. Lonergan, 'Isomorphism of Thomist and Scientific Thought,' in *Collection*
 (London: Darton, Longman and Todd 1967), 142–51.

14 Cf. Lonergan, *Verbum*, chapters 1 and 2.

15 Cf. Lonergan, *A Second Collection* (London: Darton, Longman and Todd,
 1974), 53.

16 *Metaphysics*, IV, 4, 1005b 35 – 1006a 28.

17 *In III de Anima*, lect. 7, 690. Cf. Lonergan, *Verbum*, 218. I prescind here from
 the question of whether this is a fair treatment of the views of Ibn Rushd
 (Averroes) himself.

18 *Metaphysics*, IV, 4, 1006a 15–18.

19 A 'metaphysician' in this sense is one who propounds or compares very general overall views of the nature of things – such 'metaphysical' accounts would
 include objective and subjective idealism, mechanistic and dialectical materi-

alism, phenomenalism, dualism, and so on. Most forms of alleged 'anti-metaphysics' show clear signs, in my opinion, of trying to impose without justification a set of views which are 'metaphysical' in the above sense. See chapter 4 above.

20 Randall, *Aristotle*, 6.

21 Cf. Lonergan, *Insight*, 339–41, 412–14.

22 The phrase '*nous poiētikos*' is not Aristotle's own, but it does seem to catch the drift of one notoriously controversial and obscure paragraph of the *De Anima* (III, 5, 430a 10–25).

23 Randall, *Aristotle*, 89.

24 Randall, *Aristotle*, 16.

25 *Posterior Analytics*, II, 1, 89b 22–37; *Metaphysics*, VII, 17, 1041a, 9–30.

26 *De Anima*, II, 1, 412a 20–1.

27 Averroists and Alexandrists in the Middle Ages and the Renaissance, followed by many moderns, have sought to drive a wedge between what they regard as the strictly 'mortalist' implications of Aristotle's mature doctrine that the human soul is related to the human body as 'form' to 'matter,' and the hints in Aristotle's text as it stands that he thought the 'active intellect' was in some sense immortal (*De Anima*, III, 5, 430a 17–19). Here especially the temptation seems strong to mark a firm division between Aristotle's mature views and relics of his early Platonism. In the case of a china dish, the dish-hood (its shape and function) is related to the china as form to matter. But few would be so bold as to claim that when the china is shattered the essential dish might continue to exist. Was not Professor John Wisdom right to call the soul's survival of death 'a logically unique expectation'? But looked at in the way that I have suggested, I think a case can be made for the 'Thomist' view that the immortality of one aspect of the soul is an authentically Aristotelian doctrine, in harmony with his mature thought. The intelligent will to be known through the sensible operations of the body might conceivably be knowable in some other way after the dissolution of the body. What was the 'form' of the body might thus conceivably continue to exist in some other mode.

28 G. Santayana, *Dialogues in Limbo*, cited in Randall, *Aristotle*, 103.

29 John Ferguson, *Aristotle* (New York: Twayne Publishers, 1972), 123–4.

30 I have tried to argue this point at length in *The Intelligible Universe* (Totowa, NJ: Barnes and Noble, 1982).

31 According to Harold D. Hartz, 'in the biological works the reader witnesses the emergence of "form," "matter," "end," "mover," "potentiality," and "actuality," the terms which carry Aristotle's system of thought, biological and otherwise ... On the evidence of the corpus, irrespective of the tradition, Aristotle's philosophy appears to be a system of knowledge which grows from inquiries,

conspicuously biological, into natural things, expanding into a problem like that of the *Metaphysica*, the problem of what it means to be. His philosophy seems to be this rather than a metaphysics imposed upon natural inquiries' (*The Biological Motivation in Aristotle*; quoted in Randall, *Aristotle*, 225).

32 The arguments for a general functional and teleological understanding of things are put forward in the *Physics* (II, 8, 198b 10 – 199b 33). Cf. Randall, *Aristotle*, 225.

33 'Motion (*kinēsis*) is a process in which something which has the power to become a definite something else, becomes that something else ... It is thus the continuous actualization of what is potential, taken as being potential' (*Physics*, III, 1, 201a 10–14). Cf. Randall, *Aristotle*, 178. On the relation of Aristotle's account to the evolutionary world-view, Ferguson is worth quoting. 'Aristotle's theory was not of course evolutionary; he believed in the fixity of species. But it is not wholly fanciful to say that all the evolutionists had to do was to transform his ladder of nature into an escalator' (*Aristotle*, 96).

34 *Nicomachean Ethics* VI, 5, 1140a 24 – 1140b 30.

35 This useful phrase is due to Richard McKeon, *The Basic Works of Aristotle* (New York: Random House, 1941), 931.

36 Cf. *De Anima*, III, 10, 433b 7–10; also Randall, *Aristotle*, 74 (where the quotation is incorrectly placed): '*Nous* bids one resist because of the future, while appetite has regard only for the immediate present. For the pleasure of the moment appears to be both pleasant and good without question, since one does not see the future.' On the nature of happiness and its role in morality, see *Nichomachean Ethics*, I, 4–13. It is typical of Aristotle that he gets at the definition of happiness by considering the characteristic function of the human being (I, 7, 1097b 23–5), which he sees as 'an activity of soul which follows or implies a rational principle' (1098a 6–8). Aristotle does not, in my view, sufficiently take into account cases where the long-term good of the individual and that of the community are seriously at odds with one another.

37 *Nicomachean Ethics*, III, 10–12, 6–9; V; II, 6. I have sketched what were later called the 'cardinal' virtues, not isolated as such by Aristotle.

38 William Blake, *The Marriage of Heaven and Hell*.

39 Cf. *Nicomachean Ethics*, II, 6, 1106b 1–5: 'If ten pounds are too much for a particular person to eat and two too little, it does not follow that the trainer will order six pounds; for this also is perhaps too much for the person who is to take it, or too little – too little for Milo, too much for the beginner in athletic exercises.' In seeing extreme self-abnegation as a vice, whether in respect to pleasure or in deference to others, Aristotle provides a much-needed corrective to some excesses of the Christian tradition.

40 *Politics*, I, 2; Cf. Randall, *Aristotle*, 254. That community is natural to humankind for Aristotle sets him in sharp opposition to thinkers like Augustine and

Hobbes, who see it wholly or largely as a means for the restraint of individual cupidity and violence.

41 *Politics*, IV, 9, 1295a 36 – 1296a 1: 'In the ownership of all gifts of fortune, a middle condition will be the best. Men who are in this condition are the most ready to listen to reason. Those who belong to either extreme ... find it hard to follow the lead of reason ... It is clear ... that the best form of political society is one where power is vested in the middle class, and ... that good government is attainable in those cities where there is a large middle class ... It is therefore the greatest of blessings for a city that its members should possess a moderate and adequate property.' Cf. Randall, *Aristotle*, 263–4.

42 Aristotle's aversion to 'stasis' or revolution is perhaps less contrary to the spirit of Karl Marx than would appear at first sight. You could say that the point of 'revolution' in the Marxist sense is to do away with the gross inequalities in riches and power complained of by Aristotle, and to set up a more equitable society. The leadership of the proletariat by the Party, who are presumably responsible to them as well as leading and directing them, may be seen as one way of implementing Aristotle's recommendation of a blend of democracy and oligarchy (Randall, *Aristotle*, 263), and the Western system of government, by delegates periodically subject to popular vote, as another.

43 Cf. *Politics*, IV, 1, 1288b 25–8; Randall, *Aristotle*, 259. Book V presents a pathology of different types of city, Book VI methods of setting up democracies and oligarchies with a special view to stability and avoidance of corruption and *stasis*. Cf. Randall, *Aristotle*, 265, 267.

44 Cf. Randall, *Aristotle*, 256–7. Sir Ernest Barker, introducing his edition of *The Politics of Aristotle*, complains that applications to it of the genetic method are vitiated by subjectivity, and that the results contradict one another (Cf. Randall, *Aristotle*, 258).

45 Basically, the point is that moral goodness may be largely a matter of contribution to happiness and of fairness, without being strictly definable in terms of them. See H. Meynell, *Freud, Marx and Morals* (Totowa, NJ: Barnes and Noble, 1981), chapter 6; and chapter 4 above.

46 Plato, *Republic*, V.

47 Cf. John Bowlby, *Child Care and the Growth of Love* (Baltimore: Penguin Books, 1965). For corroborating material from the study of non-human animals, see K. Lorenz, *On Aggression* (London: Methuen, 1966).

48 Lonergan, *Method in Theology*, 292.

Chapter 14: Two Methods

1 In conversation.

2 *Meditations on First Philosophy*, I and II. Cf. *The Philosophical Writings of Descartes*,

trans. Elizabeth S. Haldane and G.R.T. Ross (Cambridge: Cambridge University Press, 1969 [HR in subsequent references]), I, 144–53.

3 *Meditation* III (HR I, 157–71); *Meditation* V (HR I, 180–3).

4 *Meditation* IV (HR I, 176).

5 *Meditation* III (HR I, 161).

6 *Meditation* VI (HR I, 198).

7 Cf. *Meditation* VI (HR I, 191). Here the translation by Elizabeth Anscombe and Peter Geach seems more helpful: 'their (i.e. corporeal bodies') nature must comprise whatever I clearly and distinctly understand – that is, whatever, generally considered, falls within the subject-matter of pure mathematics.' (*Descartes: Philosophical Writings* [Edinburgh: Nelson, 1954], 116).

8 *Meditation* VI (HR I, 197–8).

9 Descartes actually says 'perceptions,' but I think the term as understood in contemporary English, whether ordinary or philosophical, only serves to generate confusion in this context.

10 *Principles of Philosophy*, part I, 45 (HR I, 237).

11 Or, according to the French version, 'false.' *Principles*, part I, 46.

12 *Meditation* III (HR I, 161). On the relation of 'clear and distinct' conceptions or ideas to truth, see also *Principles*, part I, 30 and 43 (HRT I, 231, 236); and Peter A. Schouls, *The Imposition of Method: A Study of Descartes and Locke* (Oxford: Clarendon Press, 1980), 31.

13 Cf. especially the remark in *Meditation* IV: 'For by the understanding alone I *neither assert nor deny anything, but* apprehend the ideas of things as to which I can form a judgment' (HR I, 174). Descartes omitted the equivalent of the italicized words, which of course are crucial for the point I am trying to make, in the French version.

14 Cf. the frequent contemporary polemics against 'foundationalism.' Unregenerate foundationalists may perhaps wonder how, if there are no 'foundations' for asserting any judgment rather than its contradictory, one is to avoid the conclusion that any judgment is as good as any other.

15 See B.J.F. Lonergan, *Insight: A Study of Human Understanding* (London: Longmans, Green, 1957), chapters 11, 12; *Method in Theology* (London: Darton, Longman and Todd, 1971), chapter 1. Lonergan would be in sympathy with John Locke's criticism of a philosopher like Descartes, who ventures to 'establish maxims ... about the operations of nature' without prior recourse to sensation, and thus only succeeds in constructing 'a world to himself, framed and governed by his own intelligence' (*De Arte Medica*, 1668; cf. Schouls, *Imposition of Method*, 22).

16 *Principles of Philosophy*, 43 (HR I, 236).

17 One should perhaps mention in passing the kind of certainty harped on by

G.E. Moore and the later Ludwig Wittgenstein, exemplified by my judgment that I am in an office at the University of Calgary as I write the first draft of this sentence. The certainty of this judgment consists in the fact that it happens to be supported by all the sensory evidence available to me. It is not quite the certainty to which Lonergan has drawn attention, which is implicit in what he calls 'positions,' where the contradictory of what is certain is incompatible with its being intelligently and reasonably stated. Cf. *Insight*, 387–90, 488–9, 495–6.

18 In the fourth set of Objections to Descartes's *Meditations* (HR II, 92). Cf. Schouls, *Imposition of Method*, 43.

19 Cf. Lonergan, *Insight*, chapter 19; *Method*, 101.

20 On how the basic characteristics of matter are to be inferred from the divine nature on Descartes's account, see Bernard Williams, *Descartes: The Project of Pure Enquiry* (Harmondsworth: Penguin Books, 1978), 268–70. Descartes's various treatments of this matter do not appear to be quite consistent with one another.

21 On 'intuition' and 'deduction' as together constituting the sole means of knowledge for Descartes, see *Rules for the Direction of the Mind*, 9 and 11 (HR I, 28, 33). On what can be directly 'intuited,' cf. Rules 2, 6, and 12 (HR I, 7, 15, 41; see Schouls, *Imposition of Method*, 33, 35–7); it seems to be rather a mixed bag, including that one exists, that one thinks, that a triangle is bounded by only three lines; the meanings of 'cause,' 'one' and 'straight'; and what knowing, doubt, ignorance, figure, extension, motion, and existence are (cf. Schouls, 36). In generalized empirical method, the equivalent of Descartes's 'intuition' is grasp of the principles of that method, and of how they justify themselves in the way already sketched; that of his 'deduction,' its application to the acquisition of knowledge in general.

22 See *Principles*, part III, 46; Williams, *Descartes*, 272.

23 See *Passions of the Soul*, I, 31 (HR I, 345–6); Williams, *Descartes*, 289.

24 See Bertrand Russell, *A History of Western Philosophy* (London: Allen and Unwin, 1946), 590.

25 On the necessary complementarity of classical and statistical law and the operation of both types of law within our universe, see *Insight*, chapter 4. From the point of view of generalized empirical method, Descartes confuses the correct requirement that matter be in a sense wholly intelligible (since a state of affairs which instantiates no coherent possibility is nothing), with the error that it must be subject to mechanistic determinism. A great many persons of science have, of course, followed him in this.

26 On the hierarchy of 'forms' in the universe, see *Insight*, 437–42.

27 On 'pure' or 'explanatory' as opposed to 'experiential' conjugates, see *Insight*, 79–82.

28 See Vincent G. Potter, *Charles S. Peirce on Norms and Ideals* (Worcester: University of Massachusetts Press, 1967), 3, 18–20. Cf. C. Hartshorne and P. Weiss, eds, *The Collected Papers of Charles Sanders Peirce* (Cambridge: Harvard University Press, 1931–5), 1.573–4. Ethics, Peirce claimed was in turn an aspect of what he called 'aesthetics'; to act well is an aspect of being an excellent person, and 'aesthetics' treats of this kind of excellence.

29 Cf. Peter A. Schouls, *Descartes and the Enlightenment* (Montreal: McGill-Queen's University Press, 1989), 176.

30 Ibid., 175.

31 An oversight like the one just pointed out may be said to lurk in Condillac's distinction between two sorts of metaphysics, of which 'the one, vain and ambitious, wants to search into every mystery,' while 'the other more reserved, proportions her researches to the weakness of the human understanding; and not concerning herself about what is above her sphere, but eager to know whatever is within her reach, she wisely keeps within the bounds prescribed by nature.' (E.B. de Condillac, *An Essay on the Origin of Human Knowledge*; cited by Schouls, *Descartes*, 9.) D'Alembert's complaint about the lack of 'taste' shown by those who pursued metaphysical questions (cf. Schouls, *Descartes*, 8–9) brings out what is really at issue; the *philosophes* disliked these kinds of questions, and therefore were inclined to dissuade others from pursuing them. But the sensibilities of the *philosophes* really have no bearing on the issue of whether the questions were actually worth pursuing.

32 Schouls, *Descartes*, 37. Schouls maintains that, for all that Descartes remained a devout Catholic, the essential thrust of his thought was against Catholicism, in that human beings are given the first and last word in determining what is truth. One might make the same objection surely to the thought of Augustine or Thomas Aquinas, on the grounds that they submit to human judgment reasons for believing in the existence of God and for accepting the Christian revelation.

33 Apropos of Rule 4 (HR I, 10); see Schouls, *Imposition of Method*, 57.

34 For Lonergan's arguments for the existence of God and for the truth of Christianity, see, respectively, chapters 19 and 20 of *Insight*.

35 On the role of 'belief' (the acceptance of a judgment as true on the authority of others) in human affairs, see *Insight*, 707–13. It should be noted that Lonergan's use of the term 'belief' is somewhat different from that generally found among contemporary philosophers.

36 On the methodical critique of 'belief,' see *Insight*, 713–18.

37 Cf. especially H.-G. Gadamer, *Truth and Method* (New York: Crossroad, 1982).

38 That Plato and Aristotle are complementary thinkers, and that one should

look for a synthesis between them, is argued by F.C. Copleston. See *A History of Philosophy*, vol. 2 (London: Burns, Oates and Washbourne, 1950), 561.

39 Cf. F. Capra, *Science, Society and the Rising Culture* (Toronto: Bantam Books, 1982).

40 I have been reminded, by an anonymous reviewer, that Lonergan makes a sharp distinction between the act of understanding, on the one hand, and that of setting up conceptions or formulations, on the other. I agree that he does, but the distinction has not seemed to me relevant to the special purposes of this book.

Chapter 15: Conclusion

1 This position is approximated to by a number of contemporary philosophers, but is probably most clearly set out in Richard Rorty's *Philosophy and the Mirror of Nature* (Princeton: Princeton University Press, 1979).

2 I have tried to tackle the questions mentioned in this paragraph in *Freud, Marx and Morals* (London: Macmillan, 1981), *The Nature of Aesthetic Value* (London: Macmillan, 1986), and *The Intelligible Universe* (London: Macmillan, 1982).

Index

Abelard, 19
Acton, H.B., 285, 302
Adjukiewicz, A., 286, 301
Alexandrists, 315
Allen, B., 290
Anscombe, G.E.M., 318
Anselm, 297, 311
Aquinas. *See* Thomas Aquinas
Aristocles, 285
Aristotle, xi, xii, 15, 23, 66, 67, 68, 71, 75, 190, 195, 202, 224, 229, 232, 245, 246, 247, 248, 252–65, 266, 277, 278, 279, 292, 308, 310, 312, 313, 314, 315, 316, 320
Armour, L., 310
Armstrong, D.M., 288
Arnauld, A., 273
Attfield, R., 314
Augustine, 316, 320
Austin, J.L., 306
Averroism, 257, 314, 315
Ayer, A.J., 48, 68, 284, 290, 291, 292, 293, 301

Bacon, F., 67, 230, 254, 310, 314
Baker, J.A., 313
Bar Hillel, Y., 289

Barker, E., 317
Barnes, B., 94, 95, 105, 106, 296, 297
Barth, K., 125, 233
Bartley, W.W., 298
Belknap, N., 289
Berkeley, G., 17, 181, 300, 302
Biemel, W., 306
Bierstedt, R., 105, 297
Blake, W., 262, 316
Bloor, D., 88, 89, 94, 95, 96, 105, 106, 295, 296
Boden, M.A., 288
Bode's Law, 137
BonJour, L., 34, 36, 287
Bowlby, J., 317
Braithwaite, R.B., 297

Calder, N., 300
Calvin, J., 83
Capra, F., 321
Carnap, R., 69, 70, 292
Chesterton, G.K., 310
Chisholm, R.M., 284, 294
Chomsky, N., 23, 285
Chrysippus, 289
Churchill, W., 144
Collingwood, R.G., 66, 116, 298

Columbus, C., 107
Condillac, E.B. de, 320
Coope, C., 296
Copleston, F.C., 321
Cratylus, 312
Crookall, R., 103, 297
Culler, J., 307, 308, 309

Dancy, J., 287, 303
Darwin, C., 67, 128
Davidson, D., 22, 285
De Grazia, A., 297, 299
Democritus, 260
Derrida, J., xi, 19, 197–208, 285, 307,
    308, 309
Descartes, Cartesian, xii, 64, 65, 91,
    144, 148, 149, 159, 165, 175, 179,
    182, 183, 188, 197, 264, 266–74, 276,
    277, 278, 280, 304, 306, 317, 318,
    319, 320
Dewey, J., 168
Disraeli, B., 134
Dolby, R.G.A., 266
Drury, S.B., 293
Dummett, M., 21, 27, 285, 286

Eddington, A.S., 246
Einstein, A., 23, 62, 112, 113, 122, 144,
    275, 288, 303, 309
Engels, F., 232, 295, 311
Epimenides, 289
Esterson, A., 309
Eubulides, 289
Eurytus, 312
Evans-Pritchard, E.E., 114

Farrell, W., 308
Ferguson, J., 315, 316
Feyerabend, P., x, 18, 57, 130–42, 284,
    291, 299

Flew, A.G.N., 285, 294
Foucault, M., xi, 19, 197, 208–21, 285,
    309
Fowler, C., 8, 283
Frege, G., 44, 165, 180, 304
Freud, S., 309, 310

Gadamer, H.-G., 320
Galileo, 74, 75, 133, 141, 248, 254, 298
Gallie, W.B., 285
Geach, P.T., 242, 296, 320
Gilby, T., 302
Goldmark, B., 286
Granatstein, J., 292
Grisez, G., 284
Gupta, A., 289

Haack, S., 301
Habermas, J., xi, 18, 78, 222–37, 309,
    310, 311
Hampshire, S., 150, 301
Hare, R.M., 293, 312
Hartz, H.D., 315
Hegel, G.W.F., 61, 167, 222, 227, 234,
    235, 302
Heidegger, M., xi, 168, 179, 187–95,
    231, 247, 306, 307
Hirst, P.H., 296
Hobbes, T., 317
Holmes, S., 134
Horton, R., 226
Hume, D., 4, 10, 14, 55, 58, 63, 71, 81,
    93, 147, 149, 157, 169, 283, 284, 291,
    293, 301
Husserl, E., xi, 64, 165, 167, 175,
    179–87, 304, 305, 306

Ibn Rushd, 314

Jack the Ripper, 134

James, W., 165
Jeffrey, D., 293

Kant, Kantian, 10, 39, 64, 69, 79, 80, 81,
    82, 146, 147, 149, 160, 165, 183, 185,
    191, 195, 223, 233, 234, 256, 258,
    284, 285, 293, 301, 305, 310
Kekes, J., 8, 13, 283
Kenny, A., 91, 295, 302
Kepler, J., 67
Kneale, W., 289
Kolenda, K., 301
Koestler, A., 299
Korner, S., 293
Krell, D.F., 306, 307
Kripke, S., 290
Kuhn, T.S., x, 51, 62, 107, 119–29, 130,
    132, 135, 136, 140, 142, 284, 287, 291,
    298, 299
Kurtz, P., 294

Laing, R.D., 309
Lakatos, I., 124–5, 131, 132, 140, 298,
    300
Lamarck, J.B., 244
Laudan, L., 293
Lavoisier, A.L., 108, 110
Leibniz, G.W., 61, 71
Lemoniak, M.D., 287
Lewis, C.I., 35, 37, 287
Lewis, C.S., 236, 310, 311
Locke, J., 54, 58, 65, 75, 280, 291,
    318
Lonergan, B., xi, xii, 66, 126, 157, 186,
    266, 271, 272, 275–7, 278, 280, 284,
    292, 296, 299, 300, 302, 306, 310,
    313, 314, 315, 317, 319, 321
Lorenz, K., 307, 317

Mackie, J.L., 41, 288, 294

Macaulay, T.B., 202
Magee, B., 300
Mannheim, K., 96, 295, 296
Marx, K., 212, 219, 233, 295, 309, 311,
    317
McKeon, R., 316
Michelson-Morley experiment, 113
Mill, J.S., 293
Mitchell, B.G., 311
Monod, J., 292
Moore, G.E., 24, 29, 56, 286, 288, 289,
    319
Moser, P.K., 287
Munitz, M.K., 301
Murty, K.S., 283

Nagarjuna, 4, 283
Nash, J.M., 287
Newton, I., 23, 58, 113, 245, 287, 288
Nielsen, K., 294
Nietzsche, F., 165, 204, 308

Occasionalism, 274, 276
Orenstein, A., 64, 289, 292

Peirce, C.S., 148, 149, 275, 285, 301,
    320
Phillips, Derek L., 88–9, 295
Phillips, Dewi Z., 107–9, 117, 297
Pitcher, G., 22, 23, 285, 286
Pivcevic, E., 303, 304, 305, 306
Place, U.T., 293, 296
Plato, Platonism, xi, xii, 61, 66, 67, 75,
    118, 166, 197, 200, 205, 208, 229,
    232, 241–51, 252, 256, 258, 259, 260,
    261, 262, 263, 264, 266, 278, 279,
    285, 292, 297, 308, 311, 312, 313, 314,
    320
Popper, K.R., x, 71, 95, 124, 125, 130–
    1, 132, 142–51, 157, 169, 226, 283,

288, 290, 292, 298, 300, 301, 302, 309, 311
Potter, V., 320
Pound, E., 60
Preuss, P., 293
Prior, A.N., 289
Protagoras, 109, 297
Proust, J.L., 124, 136, 137
Purtill, R., 232–3, 310
Putnam, H., 24, 25, 135, 136, 137, 286
Pyrrhonism, 14, 15, 17, 18
Pythagoreanism, 15, 245, 312

Quine, W.V.O., 64, 69, 70, 165–8, 171, 174, 289, 292, 303
Quinton, A., 36, 287, 290

Randall, J.H., 258, 259, 311, 313, 314, 315, 316, 317
Raven, J., 311
Röntgen, K., 122
Rorty, R., x, 25, 162–75, 197, 286, 290, 303, 308, 312, 321
Rosen, S., 291
Ross, G.M., 296
Rousseau, J.J., 200
Russell, B., 8, 55, 56, 94, 165, 167, 175, 180, 247, 284, 288, 289, 290, 301, 319
Rutherford, S., 98, 99, 153

Sallust, 77
Santayana, G., 260
Sawyer, W.W., 286
Schelling, F.W.J., 302, 313
Schouls, P.A., 318, 319
Schramm, D., 287
Searle, J., 197
Sellars, W., x, 49, 56, 57, 62, 152–62, 165, 166, 168, 169, 170, 171, 291, 292, 302, 303

Sextus Empiricus, 14–19, 284
Shakespeare, W., 197
Sherry, P.J., 297
Smythies, J.R., 302
Socrates, 241, 242, 243, 245, 246, 248
Speusippus, 314
Spinoza, B., 70
Staten, H., 197, 307
Stoics, 15, 232, 289
Strauss, L., 82
Strawson, P.F., 27, 41, 283, 286, 300
Stroud, B., 10, 11, 283, 284
Swinburne, R., 234, 294

Tarski, A., 25, 42, 286, 302
Taylor, A.E., 243, 246, 311, 312, 313
Taylor, R., 288
Thomas Aquinas, Thomism, 19, 42, 67, 68, 75, 152, 157–62, 195, 229, 234, 257, 260, 294, 302, 310, 315, 320
Thomson, J.J., 98, 107
Toulmin, S., 224–5
Trollope, A., 203

Van Fraassen, B., 300
Van Gogh, V., 191
Velikovsky, I., 297, 299
Victoria, 134

Walker, R.C.S., 33, 287
Walsh, W.H., 71, 292
Warnock, G.J., 290
Weber, M., 223, 310
White, A., 287, 313
White, R., 91, 94, 296
Whitehead, A.N., 288, 313
Wickings, A., 286
Wilber, K., 307
Willer, J., 105, 297
Williams, B.A.O., 319

Williams, M.E., 283, 284, 290
Winch, P., 107, 110, 112–17, 297, 298
Wisdom, J., 28
Wittgenstein, L., x, 9, 28, 39, 51, 55, 56, 87–92, 94, 95, 96, 126, 241, 247, 284, 290, 294, 295, 296, 299, 301, 308, 312, 319
Wolff, C., 234
Wright, G.H. von, 288